Managing Organizational Behavior

To Sue Lowry Tosi, by Henry Tosi
To Mariangela Turini Pilati, by Massimo Pilati

Managing Organizational Behavior

Individuals, Teams, Organization and Management

Henry Tosi

University of Florida, USA

Massimo Pilati

University of Modena and Reggio Emilia, Italy

Edward Elgar
Cheltenham, UK • Northampton, MA, USA

Published by
Edward Elgar Publishing Limited
The Lypiatts
15 Lansdown Road
Cheltenham
Glos GL50 2JA
UK

Edward Elgar Publishing, Inc.
William Pratt House
9 Dewey Court
Northampton
Massachusetts 01060
USA

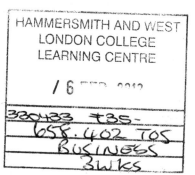

A catalogue record for this book
is available from the British Library

Library of Congress Control Number: 2010939262

MIX
Paper from
responsible sources
FSC
www.fsc.org   FSC® C018575

ISBN 978 1 84980 247 5 (cased)

Typeset by Servis Filmsetting Ltd, Stockport, Cheshire
Printed and bound by MPG Books Group, UK

Contents

Preface

We are very pleased to write this current edition of *Managing Organizational Behavior*. Some years ago we decided to work together on an adaptation of an earlier edition of the book from English to Italian. The book was well received in the Italian version and appeared on the publisher's bestseller list. Recently we decided to do a new English edition. Both of us were pleased when we were able to arrange this with Edward Elgar.

We both have profited greatly from the contribution of co-authors and scholars who worked on earlier editions. Steve Carroll, who was at the University of Maryland when the first edition was published, was immensely important. Later, John Rizzo became a co-author for an edition that appeared in 1986. Then Neal Mero became involved for the 2000 edition.

Because the book has a long history in print the reader will find several important references from the early years of the field of organizational behavior. The obvious reason for this is that the book has always been based on the best research that was available at the time of any revision. In later editions, outdated and irrelevant references were deleted so that the book contained the best theory and research available. We've done the same thing in this edition, but believe strongly that the earlier, seminal work in organizational behavior that we had cited is worth keeping. It not only will give the reader a sense of the constant evolvement of the field of organizational behavior, but that what constitutes the current state of the field is based upon some very key, early scholarship.

Our personal experience in the classroom with this book has always been very positive. The book has been used with undergraduates and masters students in both on-campus and external executive programs. There are even a few cases in which the book was used as a basic concept text at the doctoral level. At the same time, many of our colleagues who liked the book feared using it with undergraduates because they thought that the book is too theoretical. Our answer to that is straightforward; the theory of the book is accurately explained, but in a very reachable way that students can understand quite easily. Students at all levels have never had trouble with it. Our own bias about this criticism has been that we have attempted to present the book in a simple way, assuming a 'college level' of understanding on the part of both the students and the instructors.

Henry Tosi and Massimo Pilati

1. Personality and individual differences

PREPARING FOR CLASS

Since this chapter is about personality, make a list of three or four people that you know. Choose some on your list to be from the same family, but not all of them.

1. How are the people on your list different? How are they the same?
2. To what do you attribute the differences?
3. To what do you attribute their similarities?
4. How are these different people likely to react in their work situation?

Think about these questions (and your answers) as you read this chapter and when you discuss the material in class.

*　*

If you believe that people can 'make or break' an organization, then it is critical to know something about human behavior. Such knowledge will be useful to you when selecting and training employees, trying to increase motivation, improving decision making, reducing stress, and enhancing teamwork. Managers can't be professional psychologists, but they need to know enough to manage from sound principles rather than from myths and guesswork. Had this been the case, Jean Moore might have avoided a lot of problems when she hired a new writer for the sports section of the *Times Leader*, the most important newspaper in town. She was happy when she hired Dale Felton because she had been reading his articles for several years and he had exactly the investigative and reporting style that Jean thought would significantly increase the readership of the *Times*. In his first couple of months, everyone liked Dale. He was bright, literate, funny and always uplifted the humor of any group he was in.

But recently, Jean had been hearing rumors about Dale – and also rumors about other people from Dale himself. For example, Dale told

Jean, in confidence, that Pete O'Doul, who had been writing a sports column for ten years, was thinking about leaving for a rival paper. Dale assured Jean that all of this was secret, but he had a close friend who had told him how unhappy Pete was with the *Times* since Jean had hired Dale. This led Pete to start negotiating with another paper. Dale thought that if Pete left, it wouldn't be a problem. He told Jean how Pete was undercutting her reputation with everyone at the *Times*. Jean's next surprise came from Pete. Pete asked for a meeting with her. They talked and Pete told her how much respect he had for Dale and, surprisingly, that Dale had for him. Pete wanted to tell Jean, further, that both he and Dale were disappointed with the work of Luis Mendez, a Hispanic reporter whose work was always good, who had a wonderful reputation in the local sports community.

As time passed, Jean began to notice a pattern. Dale was at the center of these rumors, either coming directly to her or passing them to her through someone else. She noticed something else. Almost everyone with whom she talked seemed to be having the same experience with Dale. He was complimentary when he talked with them about themselves but negative, even mean-spirited, when he spoke about others. It seems that was his modus operandi. He was spreading gossip and rumor and, Jean concluded, he was benefiting from it more than anyone else. Morale at the *Times* was suddenly very low. People were upset, they were talking of leaving. And all of this began to happen after Dale arrived. Jean wondered to herself, 'What is the matter with Dale? He is competent and conscientious, but insecure. He seems very agreeable, but only when you're with him. Otherwise, he's political, malicious and neurotic. I don't understand him at all.'

The example of Dale Felton can help you understand something important about people at work. It isn't all about performance. Dale, after all, was a great writer. A lot of it is about the kind of person that Dale is, his personality. And in this case, it is a personality that is destructive for the *Times Leader*. When you finish this chapter, you will understand this sort of problem much better.

Personality is a useful concept for interpreting and managing in many organizational situations like the one that Jean Moore is facing. The attraction–selection–attrition cycle in organizations explains how personality and organizations affect each other (Schneider et al., 1995). People are attracted to and select the situations they prefer to enter. Once they are in the organization, they make the situation what it is. As similar people become attracted, and as dissimilar people leave, the organization becomes more homogeneous because the personalities are more alike.

Spotlight 1.1   Personality and labor market entry in Netherlands

How important is personality in obtaining a job in the Netherlands? A study of graduates in economics from Maastricht University showed that the most important things that employers wanted were grades and work experience. But the second most important factors were personality and the students' preference for the kind of work they wanted to do (Semeijn et al., 2005).

The people who make up the organization define it by establishing norms and maintaining the culture. So, while the situation may affect behavior, it is the people who define the situation. Homogeneity of personalities may become a threat to the organization's survival. If you want to change such a situation, it is necessary to change the mix of people and to select new people so as to add variability. Throughout this book, reference is made to personality in explaining a variety of topics.

- The personalities of managers in the dominant power coalition determine an organization's culture.
- Personality is a key factor in understanding adjustment to work and career, coping with stress, and problem-solving and decision-making behavior.
- Personality is central to the dynamics of motivation, and interpersonal conflict and politics.

There are a few things to keep in mind as you read about these different ways to characterize personality:

1. There are different ways to view people and you will see that some of the approaches are similar in some ways with others, while some are very distinct.
2. Each perspective represents a motivational force that is likely related to some important organizational behavior, attitude or perception.
3. Most of the characteristics we are describing represent just one way to describe behavior, and each of us can be described in terms of any one of the theories, and some may seem to be more accurate than others.

We have selected only some of the more important personality approaches to highlight in this chapter. As you read other parts of the book you will find other ways to characterize personality, but these are more strongly associated with a specific subject area in organizational behavior, such as stress, perception, leadership and motivation.

A GENERAL MODEL OF HUMAN BEHAVIOR

The complexity of subjects in the social sciences such as personality make the description and the interpretation of them difficult to reduce to 'models' with arrows connecting boxes, but Figure 1.1 is our attempt to set out a simple approach to illustrate how individual behavior in organizations is related to some other important and key elements:

1.   The environment.
2.   The person.
3.   Actual behavior.
4.   The consequences of behavior.

The environment contains the many elements that exist in the world outside the person that may trigger behavior. It interacts with the attributes of the person, which also explain and govern behavior. A few important attributes are shown in Figure 1.1, but there are many more. To discover these attributes, we must infer what goes on inside a person or rely on what he or she tells us.

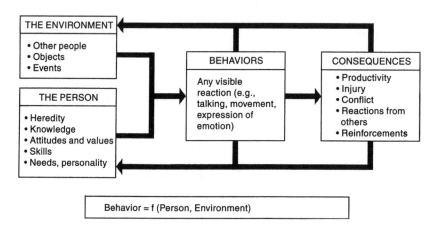

Figure 1.1   Basic model of individual behavior

Actual behavior refers to an overt act of the person that can be observed and measured, but tells us little about why it occurred. Observable behavior can never give a complete picture of what goes on inside people, but such behavior does serve as a window to it.

Behavior has consequences; it has intended and unintended effects. For example, behavior at work can produce products for sale, it can lead to conflict, or trigger positive or negative reactions in others. Behavior also has reinforcing consequences that affect the probability of its recurrence. Pleasurable consequences will have a different effect than painful ones.

Spotlight 1.2　*Faber est suae quisque fortunae*

The ancient Romans had an existential approach to happiness, fate and the meaning of life. The Roman saying that 'Everyone is the author of his own luck' is a view of their thoughts on happiness and, ultimately, on the meaning of life. The thought expresses a level of psychological maturity that implies that we decide what we want from life in a way that does not depend on others or on fate to determine what happens to us. This saying still has a modern feel to it. You can see it demonstrated by the enormous amount of time and money that organizations spend today training their members on empowerment, positive thinking, accountability, time management, and so forth. Nevertheless, today some people in everyday life and business depend on astrological forecasts, horoscopes and sometimes even fortune tellers for advice. Perhaps the basic reason for this is that if we think that we can control events and be architects of our own destiny, we might take a more positive attitude toward decisions and choices that seem difficult and complex. Perhaps we wish to feel responsible for our decisions and actions.

Finally, the feedback arrows in Figure 1.1 show how a person can learn from their behavior and its effects. Also, behavior can change the environment, such as when we turn down the volume on a loud stereo to make it less annoying to others.

PERSONALITY

The term 'personality' is used in many different ways. Sometimes we say that a person has a good personality or a bad personality, meaning that he or she is pleasant or unpleasant. Sometimes the word is used to indicate an important or famous person, like saying that the President of the USA is an important personality. In this book, we use the term 'personality' to mean the relatively stable organization of all a person's characteristics, an enduring pattern of attributes that define the uniqueness of a person. Because attitudes and values are part of the pattern, personality includes predispositions as well as patterns of actual behaviors. Personality plays an important role at work, as the example of Dale Felton illustrated. How else can you explain the reason why he was such a successful writer, but a serious problem for the rest of the organization? It is a wonderful example of the importance of understanding both the person and the environment in which he or she operates. In one environment, his personality was fine; in another, it caused problems.

Spotlight 1.3   Freud on personality

Freud's psychoanalytic theory is an example of a psychodynamic theory of personality. He believed a person's thoughts and feelings range from unconscious to those that are quite conscious. The personality has three parts: a set of basic impulses (the id); a mechanism to relate our impulses to the outside world (the ego); and a moral conscience (the superego) that evaluates our thoughts and actions. The id seeks pleasure, the ego attempts to satisfy impulses in the real world, and the superego attempts to govern behavior toward socially acceptable acts.

The key dynamics of Freud's theory describe how the ego defends and protects the person against danger, taboo ideas from the id, and negative sanctions from the superego. Some defense mechanisms are repression (of impulsive thoughts), projection (attributing our feelings to others), and sublimation (converting taboo impulses to productive and creative behavior). Freud believed that all human beings have deep urges that exert themselves. These have to be dealt with through the action of our ego and its defense mechanism; the superego is also involved. It expresses our values and ideals, and can create feelings of guilt. The manner in which we resolve impulses helps determine how our personality gets formed. This takes place very early in life, especially in relationships with our parents.

In this chapter, we present several different perspectives on personality because there is no single theory that integrates all we know about personality; each theory and approach has its own way of characterizing it. For example, some approaches emphasize predispositions, and the traits, attitudes and needs that drive behavior (Cattell, 1950; Allport, 1961; Murray, 1962; Maslow, 1970). There are learning theories of personality, such as social learning theory. Other approaches stress personality in terms of the perceptions, thoughts and judgments people engage in as they cope and mature in the world around them (Rogers, 1942). Finally, some theories look at the tensions that exist inside a person, and see personality as the consequence of internal conflicts and how they are resolved. You are probably familiar with the work of Freud who dramatized the struggle between our inner impulses and our moral conscience (Freud, 1933).

Personality: Nature or Nurture?

A very old debate about the source of personality revolves around whether it is innate or developed, or the result of 'nature' or 'nurture'. Those on the nature side of the question believed that personality is genetically determined, that is it is inherited from one's parents. We know that physical features, dispositions and other human tendencies are innate. While it is apparent that one's physical appearance may be very similar to that of a parent, it is not so clear that human personality and dispositions are totally a function of genetics. Those on the nurture side of the question argue that personality, dispositions and human tendencies are learned as a result of socialization experiences starting at birth and operating through one's life.

Spotlight 1.4   The big five: nature or nurture

An international study of almost 2000 sets of twins from Canada, Germany and Japan examined whether the big five personality characteristics, discussed later in this chapter, are a function of nature (genetics) or nurture (socialization). In the study, 1200 sets were identical twins while the other 700 were not. It appears that the Big Five model of personality has a strong biological base and may be a common heritage of human beings (Yamagata et al., 2006).

There is research support for the nature side of the argument. For example, studies of identical twins, orphaned at birth and raised in separate and very different environments, have shown that oral expressions and other expressive modalities are similar to those of the parents, even though that person did not have any contact with them. This would suggest that these have not been acquired through learning and socialization, they have rather been transmitted to the person genetically (Watson and Clark, 1984; Watson and Tellegen, 1985).

A more reasonable position is that both nature and nurture processes operate to form personality. Certainly some genetic properties are passed on from parents that may be a base of our personality, but also as we are exposed to different experiences as we are socialized in the world, our character, temperament and personality become formed. The evidence from the 'Twin Studies', done primarily at the University of Minnesota, addresses this. These are studies of identical, monozygotic twins who have been raised in different families, often in very different national cultures. They have shown that about 30 percent of the variance in job satisfaction and 40 percent of the variance in work values can be explained by heredity (Arvey et al., 1989; Keller et al., 1992). This still leaves a large part of the personality that is likely to develop as a result of socialization: how we actually learn to adapt to the world around us.

Socialization and Personality

Socialization is the process through which a person learns and acquires the values, attitudes, beliefs and accepted behaviors of a culture, society, organization or group. It can be understood through learning theory. We learn that some behaviors are more rewarding while others lead to negative consequences; we learn group norms and values from our parents, as well as by observing the behaviors of others. Over time, these experiences shape the way we adapt to the world in which we live. The result is our personality, the unique set of values, attitudes and behaviors in our adult lives that have been shaped around our genetic character. Learning and socialization are basic to understanding how people acquire knowledge, attitudes, skills and their unique personalities. They are also central to interpreting how people perceive events and make judgments about them.

Learning Theories and Personality

Theories of learning are very important to know because they can help you understand several critical topics that we cover in later chapters. For example, learning theories are a very basic approach to understanding

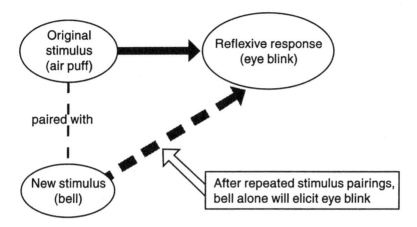

Figure 1.2   Classical model of learning

attitudes and perception (see Chapter 2), motivation (see Chapter 3) and leadership (see Chapter 10), to name just a few. But in this chapter, we discuss three approaches to learning that help us to understand socialization: classical conditioning, reinforcement theories and vicarious learning.

Classical conditioning
Some responses, for example, can be understood through the classical conditioning model based on the work of Pavlov (1927). In his most famous study, Pavlov conditioned a dog to salivate at the sound of a bell, just as it would if it were hungry and food were presented to it. He did this by first denying food to the dog, then showed it food, leading to the dog salivating. At the same time, he rang a bell. This continued until eventually the dog would salivate when the bell rung.

Classical conditioning requires the presence of an existing and reflexive stimulus–response pattern, such as withdrawing your hand from a hot object or blinking an eye in response to a puff of air. When such a reflexive pattern exists, it is possible to pair the original stimulus (for example, the puff of air) with a new, different stimulus by presenting the two close together in space or time. Eventually the new stimulus will elicit the same response as the original one. The new stimulus is called a conditioned stimulus. For example, suppose a bell is rung just as the air hits your eye. After repeated pairings, the bell alone will cause you to blink; see Figure 1.2.

Reinforcement theories
Reinforcement theories of learning are very useful in understanding how personality develops, and they are also central to many topics covered

---

Spotlight 1.5   Blindness of the instinct

In *Principles of Psychology*, one of the founding works of experimental psychology, William James (1890) considered the instincts as specialized neuronal circuits, common to each member of a species and produced from the evolutionary history of that species. Taken together, for our species these circuits are what we call and think of as 'human nature'. It was commonly thought that other animal species were governed by instinct, while the human species had lost instincts in favor of reason, because we had developed beyond animal intelligence. William James took the opposite path, arguing that human behaviour is more dynamically intelligent than other animals because we have more instincts. We often hide the existence of these instincts out of fear of them, because they work very well, processing information automatically and without effort.

In his work James argued that the our thoughts are so powerful that we begin to consider some behaviors as 'normal' without considering why this is the case. This kind of 'instinct blindness' makes the study of the personality and behavior complex (Wilshire, 1968).

---

in this book such as culture and socialization, attitude formation and perception, career choices, motivation and training. The reinforcement approach accounts for a wide range of learning, from the simplest to the most complex behaviors. It explains many aspects of our behavior and attitudes, not only in the workplace, but also in everyday life.

Reinforcement occurs in situations where behavior is affected by its consequences (Weiss and Adler, 1984). This approach is shown in Figure 1.3. It is also called instrumental learning. The basic idea is simple: when a behavior results in a positive consequence, it is likely to be repeated and, eventually, learned. This is different from classical conditioning because it is not necessary to have a reflexive stimulus–response pattern for learning to occur.

Social learning theory and vicarious learning
People can also learn by observing other people and imitating or modeling their behavior on what other people do (Bandura, 1977). This is called vicarious learning (Wood and Bandura, 1989); and it involves more than just reinforcing behavior. It is part of what is called social learning theory. This learning involves thinking, including

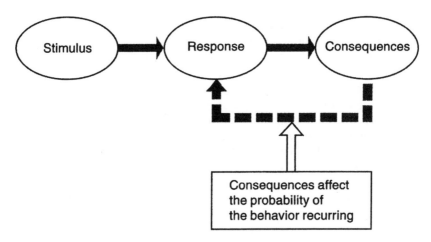

Figure 1.3   Reinforcement or instrumental model of learning

intentions, goal setting, reasoning and decision making, in addition
to reinforcements. Learning can take place by reading books, watching television or interacting with people. Social, or vicarious, learning
occurs quite naturally at home, at school and at work. For example,
one key to a manager's success is to have a mentor to emulate. One
stage of vicarious learning involves observing and thinking. Another
stage occurs when the individual actively engages in new behaviors, or
modeling. Several conditions are involved in vicarious learning (Weiss,
1977; Baron, 1983):

1. You must have a reason to pay attention to the model or stimulus.
   Anything that attracts attention, such as expertise or status, will contribute to attention.
2. You need to retain sufficient information to pattern your behavior on
   the model.
3. The person must have enough ability to engage in the model's behavior. Most of us cannot model ourselves after a great athlete or Nobel
   Prize winner in physics.
4. There must be a motivational or reinforcement element. The person
   must perceive the probability of rewards and eventually receive reinforcement for imitation. There must be some incentive and encourage-
   ment involved.

   All of these theories can help you understand how learning and socialization affect personality. For example, classical conditioning starts early

in one's life when the mother feeds the infant, which is crying as a result of hunger pangs. The infant learns that crying results in being fed, but also associates crying with the type and level of affection that the mother shows during the feeding. As time passes, the child learns to respond to the mother's requests in order to gain her affection. Another example of classical conditioning is the fear and anxiety that you once experienced as a child when you did something that angered your parents and they disciplined you in a harsh way. The same fear and anxiety, perhaps in a different form, may well recur later in life when you make a serious mistake in school or later at work, and fear what negative result there might be. You can imagine how, over time and in different circumstances, our personality is affected by classical conditioning.

During our early life, significant persons reinforce our behaviors, attitudes and beliefs. For example, rewards such as praise from a parent, a coach, teacher or supervisor can be instrumental in sustaining particular actions and feelings. Similarly, we are often punished for actions that we learn later to avoid, or feelings and sentiments that are not deemed 'appropriate' by parents and teachers. Again, over time, we learn what behaviors and attitudes are 'right' and what is 'wrong', and what works best for us in dealing with others.

During our formative years we also learn vicariously from observing others. We want to be like our father or mother, so we try to act as they do. Young children 'dress up' like Mom or Dad in 'adult' clothes. They play 'go to work', 'house', or have 'tea parties' like Mom and Dad do. When we see others (whether or not they are friends) rewarded or punished for an action, we learn that it is something that we should do or not do. And children also often have role models, other than parents or important relatives, such as some athlete, actor or politician that they try to emulate.

These learning experiences interact with genetic tendencies, and the result is the personality structure of the individual. For example, later in this chapter, we introduce the concept of organizational personality orientations, or how individuals adapt to work. The organizationalist orientation is a result of learning experiences in which the person develops an early respect for authority figures (Presthus, 1978; Tosi, 1992). Often this occurs in families in which the father controls the rewards and sanctions. These circumstances lead to a recognition of the importance and power of authority figures in general, in the distribution of rewards and/or sanctions. The 'professional' learns early in life that performing well at home and at school results in idiosyncratic credits that may be used to offset compliance with parents and, later, with organization requirements. The 'indifferent' learns in early life not to expect much from either the work they will do or the organization in which they will be doing it. These expectations are often reinforced after joining an organization. Some become alienated by the routine nature of their assigned tasks that minimize autonomy, leave little room for application of individual skills and knowledge, and seldom provide a challenge.

Personality Manifestations: A Contingency Approach

There is an old saying that you cannot know a person until the two of you argue, meaning that an argument is a good situation in which to get to know someone more authentically. For us, in this chapter, it means that there are some situations that favor the expression of personality.

Even though the environment affects behavior, personality-driven behavior can show a good deal of consistency across different situations (Epstein and O'Brien, 1985). This is especially true for a broad disposition such as one's need for social approval. A specific trait such as honesty may vary more with the situation, but even specific traits will affect behavior when conditions are appropriate (Funder, 1991). It is also likely that personality will help to determine the kinds of situations that people enter. Shy persons will avoid social situations. When in these situations, the trait may still emerge, such as when a shy person experiences tension at a party. In some settings, however, personality attributes may be squelched. For example, sociability may be impossible to express in a hostile or threatening environment.

When is personality more or less likely to operate, and to be the main cause of behavior? It seems that personality is less powerful in 'strong situations'. These are structured situations where constraints such as clear and precise cues, rules and task demands act to limit behavior (Weiss and Adler, 1984; Mischel, 1977). Rewards, tight standards and expectations can add to the limits, making personality differences between individuals less evident. Think, for example, about watching a military unit in a parade, where the constraints on behavior are very tight: all wear the same uniform, march at the same pace, move on command and salute when ordered. It is impossible to know anything about the personality differences of the soldiers from watching them march – this is the epitome of a strong situation.

However, the role of personality is much stronger in 'weak situations'. These are ambiguous situations that are loosely structured, so personality characteristics become a stronger explanation and cause of behavior. You would therefore expect personality characteristics to be more evident in loosely structured organizations with few rules and policies, as compared to bureaucratic settings. This is why you can see prima donna singers or musicians act very individualistically in rehearsals, expecting to be treated as special because of their unique skills. However, when the time comes to go on stage, a more controlled situation, usually they play their part and sing on cue. Therefore, if you want to understand behavior in personality terms, it is best to observe people when structure is loose or has broken down. Also, if you want personality to operate more fully in a situation so that you might capitalize on personality differences, you may have to loosen controls and expectations, and otherwise permit more situational freedom. This may be helpful when creativity or adaptation to a novel problem is needed. One example is an unstructured selection interview. When the interviewer is relatively silent, not posing the usual type of questions, the situation may not be easy for the candidate, whose reaction might furnish a better understanding of the emotions, feelings and personality of the job applicant.

PERSONALITY IN THE ORGANIZATIONAL SETTING

A trait is some particular relatively stable and enduring individual tendency to react emotionally or behaviorally in a specific way. For example, we might characterize a person as being agreeable, responsible or considerate. Over the years, hundreds of studies have identified many specific traits that were used to characterize personality, but there were so many different traits that this was not a very fruitful approach. However, these many trait studies have now been analyzed, and it was found that some of these personality traits are very similar. Similar traits that reflected similar specific characteristics were grouped into higher-level classifications that have resulted in the identification of the 'Big Five' dimensions of personality.

The 'Big Five' Personality Dimensions

This approach is extensively used in employee selection and in the evaluation of persons for promotions. It is simple to understand for the non-specialist because each personality characteristic is labeled with language used in daily conversation. The Big Five dimensions of personality are:

1. Extroversion. Some of the more specific traits of persons high in extroversion are that they tend to be sociable, like to be with others, and are energetic. Of course, introverts are the reverse. They tend to be less sociable, like to be alone and do not interact much with others.

Extroversion is related to job success for managers and salespeople, and success in training (Barrick and Mount, 1996), job satisfaction (Judge et al., 2002; Thorensen et al., 2003), organizational commitment and sense of personal accomplishment (Thorensen et al., 2003). It is negatively related to emotional exhaustion and turnover intentions (Thorensen et al., 2003).

2. Emotional stability. Emotional stability, viewed from the negative side, is called neuroticism. People low in emotional stability (or highly neurotic) tend to be emotional, tense, insecure, have high anxiety levels, are depressed, easily upset, suspicious and low in self-confidence (Barrick and Mount, 1996). Emotional stability is related to supervisory ratings of performance (Barrick and Mount, 1991) and the neuroticism dimension is negatively related to job satisfaction (Judge et al., 2002), organizational commitment, sense of personal accomplishment (Thorensen et al., 2003) and performance motivation (Judge and Ilies, 2002). Highly neurotic persons are also more likely to experience emotional exhaustion and have higher intentions to leave their place of work (Thorensen et al., 2003).

3. Agreeableness. Agreeable people are simply easier to get along with than others. They are likely to be more tolerant, trusting, generous, warm, kind and good-natured. They are less likely to be aggressive, rude and thoughtless, as well as being more satisfied with their work (Judge et al., 2002).

4. Conscientiousness. Conscientious persons are more responsible, dependable, persistent, punctual, hard-working and more strongly oriented toward work. Conscientiousness managers, professionals, salespeople, police and skilled or semi-skilled workers respond more favorably to training (Dunn et al., 1995; Barrick and Mount, 1996). They are also more likely to perform better (Hurtz and Donovan, 2000), be more motivated to perform at work (Judge and Ilies, 2002) and be more satisfied with their job (Judge et al., 2002).

5. Openness to experience. Persons more open to experience are imaginative, curious, cultured, broad-minded, have broad interests and tend to be self-sufficient. Those who are more open to experiences appear to react very positively to different kinds of training (Barrick and Mount, 1991).

Positive and Negative Affectivity: Being in a Good or Bad Mood

Two traits that have been related to how people are oriented toward their work are positive affectivity and negative affectivity (Thorensen et al., 2003). Positive affectivity, similar to extroversion, means that you have a strong, positive sense of your personal well-being, that you think of yourself as active and involved in activities that you like, and that you are, overall, a pleasant person in most situations. If you are high in positive affectivity, you are active, elated, enthusiastic, peppy and strong. If you are low in positive affectivity, you are drowsy, dull, sleepy and sluggish (Watson and Clark, 1984). The term that comes to mind for a person high in positive affectivity is 'an overall happy, nice human being'.

Negative affectivity, similar to neuroticism, means that you are not very happy, you feel under stress and strain, you tend to focus on failure and you tend to view yourself and others in negative ways, even when the conditions in which you are operating do not warrant these perceptions. The high negativity person is distressed, fearful, hostile, jittery, nervous and scornful. The low negativity person is at rest, calm, placid and relaxed. The term that comes to mind for a person high in negative affectivity is 'sourpuss'.

The research to date suggests that these two traits – positive affectivity and negative affectivity – are independent; they do not exist as separate ends of the same continuum. If they were on the same continuum, it would mean that if you are high on positive affectivity, you must be low on negative affectivity. Instead, being independent means that a person might be high on both positive affectivity and negative affectivity, low on both, or high on one and low on the other (Watson and Clark, 1984; George, 1992), as shown in Figure 1.4. There you can see what this trait independence means. It shows, for example, that the person with high positive affectivity is more active and enthusiastic while the low positive affectivity person is more dull, slow and sleepy. On the other hand, the person high in negative affectivity is more likely to be nervous and hostile, while the low negative affectivity person is more relaxed and laid back.

Having a strong positive or a strong negative disposition can affect your work life. If you are a high on positive affectivity, you are less likely to have accidents at work than if you are high on negative affectivity (Iverson and Erwin, 1997). Or, if you are positive at work, you are more likely to be rewarded by your boss for good performance (George, 1995). Also, effective managers tend to be highly positive (Staw and Basade, 1993). Highly positive people are seen as better leaders, having higher management potential, and are more satisfied with their work and their life; they have higher organizational commitment and a stronger sense of personal accomplishment (Thorensen et al., 2003). Persons with high negative affectivity have lower job satisfaction, lower organizational commitment, a lower sense of personal accomplishment, but tend to experience higher emotional exhaustion and have stronger turnover intentions (Thorensen et al., 2003).

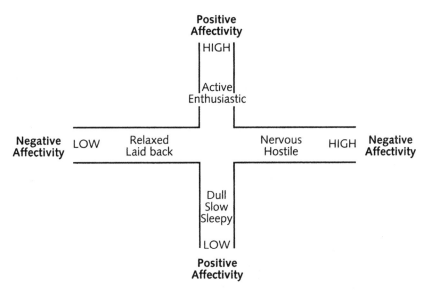

Figure 1.4   Positive and negative affectivity

Adjusting to Organizational Work Life

Earlier in this chapter we defined personality as the relatively stable organization of all a person's characteristics, an enduring pattern of attributes that define the uniqueness of a person, or how a person adapts to the world he or she lives in. We think that most approaches to personality in this chapter tend to be general, in the sense that the concepts, traits and predispositions were developed by studying persons in a wide range of situations. But thinking about it, a big part of the world we live in is at work, so it makes sense to think, in a more specific way, about how people might adapt to the work situation.

Anyone who remains in an organization for any period of time has to come to terms with working in it, and as we will discuss in the next chapter, people come to terms with it in different ways. An approach that we call 'organizational personality orientations' considers different ways that individuals accommodate to organizations (Presthus, 1978; Tosi, 1992). There are three organizational personality orientations in this approach, and each represents a particular focus: one on the organization itself, another on the work itself, and one away from either of these. These orientations will help you to understand more clearly the different ways that a person can be personally committed to, or linked to, where he or she works. The orientations are:

1. The organizationalist.
2. The professional.
3. The indifferent.

The 'organizationalist' is a person with a strong commitment to the place of work. A person with this orientation exhibits these tendencies:

1. A strong identification with the organization; seeking organization rewards and advancement, which are important measures of success and organizational status.
2. High morale and job satisfaction.
3. A low tolerance for ambiguity about work goals and assignments.
4. Identification with superiors, showing deference toward them, conforming and complying out of a desire to advance.
5. Maintains the chain of command and compliance, and views respect for authority as the way to succeed.
6. Emphasis on organizational goals of efficiency and effectiveness, avoiding controversy and showing concern for threats to organizational success.

Early in life organizationalists develop an early respect for authority figures, realizing that they have the power to dispense rewards and/or sanctions. They are success-oriented, and seek it in the organizational context. They learn how to avoid failure experiences that stem from being a troublemaker. Often, the organizationalist comes from a family in which rewards are controlled primarily by the father (Presthus, 1978).

'Professionals' are persons who are job-centered – not organization-centered – and see organization demands as a nuisance that they seek to avoid. However, that avoidance is impossible since the professional must have an organization in which to work. At work, professionals experience more role conflict and are more alienated (Greene, 1978). A professor who values teaching and research may not be very loyal to the university, but needs the university to teach and research, so this is a very conflicting role for the professional. A professional exhibits these four tendencies:

1. An experience of occupational socialization that instills high standards of performance in the chosen field; highly ideological about work values.
2. Sees organizational authority as non-rational when there is pressure to act in ways that are not professionally acceptable.
3. Tends to feel that organizations don't fully utilize their skills; self-esteem may be threatened when they do not have the opportunity to do those things for which they have been trained.

4. Seeks recognition from other professionals outside the organization, and refuses to play the internal organizational status game except as it reflects their worth relative to others in the organization. Professionals are very concerned with personal achievement and doing well in their chosen field. Organizational rewards are not without value, however, since they may reflect the professional's importance relative to others in the system. The recognition may be extremely fulfilling, especially when he or she is accorded higher status and pay than others.

In early socialization, the professionals learn that successful performance, not compliance with authority, is more rewarding. Many professionally oriented people come from the middle class and have become successful through a higher level of education or by other efforts to acquire competence (Presthus, 1978).

Indifferents are people who work for pay. For them, work is not a critical part of life. They may do their work well, but they are not highly committed to their job or the organization. These are some of the characteristics of the indifferent:

1. More oriented toward leisure, not the work ethic; separates work from more meaningful aspects of life, and seeks higher-order need satisfaction outside the work organization.
2. Tends to be alienated from work and not committed to the organization; more alienated than either organizationalists or professionals.
3. Rejects status symbols in organizations.
4. Withdraws psychologically from work and organizations when possible.

Indifferents often come from the lower middle class (Presthus, 1978). With a limited education, indifferents often work in routine jobs with few advancement opportunities. Research indicates that commitment is lower when jobs have narrow scope and more stress (Fukami and Larson, 1984). Do not assume, however, that only lower-level personnel are indifferents. Some may be organizationalists and others might have a distinctively professional orientation to their work. Also, it could come to be that higher-level employees, who once had an organizational orientation and were highly loyal, may no longer follow orders without question. For example, early in a working career, a manager may be extremely committed to the organization. He or she may seek its rewards and want to advance. However, in later career life, after having been passed over several times for promotion, the person seeks reinforcement elsewhere.

Thus, it is possible that through their promotion practices, organizations may turn highly committed organizationalists into indifferents.

The Machiavellians

Remember our reporter, Dale Felton, at the beginning of this chapter. One way to characterize him is as having a Machiavellian personality. Machiavellianism is another personality dimension that has interpersonal and leadership implications for the workplace (Christie and Geis, 1970). People who are 'high Machiavellians' (high Machs) have high self-esteem and self-confidence and behave in their own self-interest. They are seen as cool and calculating, attempt to take advantage of others, and seek to form alliances with people in power to serve their own goals. When they do form these alliances, high Machs are envied by their coworkers (Vecchio, 2005). High Machs are more likely to distrust others (Burks et al., 2003) and to lie, deceive or compromise morality, believing that ends justify means. Truly high-Mach people experience no guilt; they somehow detach themselves from the consequences of their actions. High Machs, not distracted by emotions, are able to exert control calmly in power vacuums or novel situations. They are able to select situations where their tactics will work: face-to-face, emotional, unstructured and ambiguous conditions. They also use false or exaggerated praise to manipulate others. For example, high Machs use impression management techniques indiscriminately (Bolino and Turnley, 2003) and they believe that using them when interviewing applicants is fair (Lopes and Fletcher, 2004). They take care not to be swayed by loyalty, friendship or trust. A high Mach might give lip service to such things, but when the chips are down, they will stand in the way of personal gain. This gives them a big advantage over those who value friendship and act on trust, something that is supported by a study that shows that high Mach stockbrokers are more successful than less Machiavellian brokers (Aziz et al., 2002).

Core Self-Evaluation: How Individuals See Themselves

The core self-evaluation is the fundamental, subconscious conclusion that you reach about yourself (Judge et al., 1997). Each of us arrives at a basic sense of who we are and what we are, and this is reflected as a broad personality trait that is a function of four more narrow traits which are self-evaluative, fundamental source traits that underlie surface traits, and are relatively broad in scope (Judge et al., 2004). The specific, narrow traits that form the core self-evaluation have been widely studied individually and have been related to a number of very important aspects of work and life in organizations, such as job satisfaction, performance, organizational commitment and the effects of stress (in fact, in later chapters we discuss many of them in detail as predictors of these outcomes). However, they are highly related to each other and can be thought of having a common underlying theme that reflects the person's core self-evaluation. These traits are:

1. Self-esteem. This is a trait that refers to the way that you perceive and evaluate yourself. Those who have a positive and a reasonably accurate concept of 'self' have high self-esteem. They tend to have confidence in themselves – not that they charge headlong into unknown situations with adventurous disregard, but that they know their capacities and potential and act accordingly.
2. Emotional stability (neuroticism). Emotional stability refers to the tendency of persons to be less emotional, experience lower tension, feel secure and have low anxiety. The traits of highly neurotic persons are that they tend to be emotional, tense, insecure, have high anxiety levels, are depressed, easily upset, suspicious and low in self-confidence.
3. Generalized self-efficacy. This is the degree to which an individual believes it is possible to achieve a particular performance level or behavioral standard (Bandura, 1982). Self-efficacy can stem from a variety of personal experiences. One source is someone's actual achievements. When a task is performed successfully, the person gains a sense of enactive mastery and will feel capable of performing that way again.
4. Internal locus of control. Locus of control refers to whether a person believes that what happens to them is externally controlled, or controlled internally by their own efforts (Rotter, 1966). Internal locus of control reflects self-control over one's outcomes. A person with an internal locus of control has a need for independence and a desire to participate in decisions that affect them. A person who believes that others control important outcomes has an external locus of control.

Thus, a person with a strong or high core self-evaluation would have high self-esteem, a strong sense of self-efficacy, an internal locus of control, be emotionally stable, be more satisfied with work and life and perform better at work (Judge and Bono, 2001).

Myers–Briggs Personality Dimensions and Work Style Preferences

The Myers–Briggs approach to personality classifies people according to the kinds of jobs and interactions they prefer, and the ways in which they approach problems (Jung, 1939; Myers and Briggs, 1962). Four Myers–Briggs dimensions are used to describe the personality underlying these preferences:

1. Sensing–intuition dimension.
2. Thinking–feeling dimension.
3. Introversion–extroversion dimension.
4. Perceptive–judgment dimension.

Each dimension forms a continuum that people fall along. Sensing-oriented people like structured situations, an established routine, realism, and precise and uncomplicated details. They enjoy using skills already learned. Intuitive people prefer new problems, they dislike repetition and are impatient with routine. They enjoy learning new skills; they follow their inspirations, and jump to conclusions.

Thinking individuals are unemotional and often, unknowingly, they hurt people's feelings. They like to analyze and put things in a logical order. They seem impersonal and hard-hearted. Feeling types are more aware of other people, and enjoy pleasing them. They like harmony and are influenced by other people's needs; they relate well to most people.

Introverts prefer quiet concentration and think a lot before acting. They work well alone and can stay with one project for a long time. Much thought precedes action, sometimes without action. Introverts dislike interruptions, they forget names, and can have problems communicating. Extroverts show impatience with long, slow jobs and like to work fast, uncomplicated by procedures. They prefer variety and action to contemplation. They are good with people and like them around; usually they communicate quite well.

Perceptive people adapt to change and welcome new ideas. They can leave things unsolved and delay decisions without grave concern. They may start too many new projects, postpone unpleasant ones and leave things unfinished. Judgment types prefer to plan work and follow the plan. They settle things on just the essentials and are satisfied with conclusions. They decide too quickly and dislike switching off a project in progress.

These four Myers–Briggs concepts can be used in a variety of ways, such as making employees appreciate the different styles of their co-workers, or in selecting people for different types of assignments. They can also be used to improve decision making. People can be taught when it is best to exert their sensing, intuition, thinking or feeling modes. They can also learn when it is best to pair with each other to improve decision making. This is referred to as the 'mutual usefulness of opposites' and it works as follows:

1. The sensing type needs an intuitive to generate possibilities, to supply ingenuity, to deal with complexity and to furnish new ideas. Intuitives add a long-range perspective and spark things that seem impossible.

2. The intuitive needs a sensing type to bring up facts to inspect, to attend to detail, to inject patience and to notice what needs attention.
3. The thinker needs a feeling type to persuade and conciliate feelings, to arouse enthusiasm and to sell or advertise, and to teach and forecast.
4. The feeling type needs a thinker to analyze and organize, to predict flaws in advance, to introduce fact and logic, to hold to a policy, and to stand firm against opposition.

Spotlight 1.6   Personality view of culture

Personality can be a way to view culture. For a country, its dominant values are called the national character, or the modal personality (Hofstede, 1980). The modal personality represents the degree of homogeneity and strength of the dominant personality orientations in the society. The modal personality of a culture can be profiled on five different personality dimensions that are the basis of attitudes and behaviors, organization practices and social practices such as marriages, funerals and religious ceremonies. These are as follows:

1. Uncertainty avoidance refers to whether a society tends to prefer rules and to operate in predictable situations as opposed to situations where the appropriate behaviors are not specified in advance.
2. Power distance is the degree to which differences in power and status are accepted in a culture. Some nations accept high differences in power and authority between members of different social classes or occupational levels; other nations do not.
3. Individualism–collectivism refers to whether individual or collective action is the preferred way to deal with issues.
4. The masculinity–femininity dimension of a culture refers to the degree to which values associated with stereotypes of masculinity (such as aggressiveness and dominance) and femininity (such as compassion, empathy and emotional openness) are emphasized.
5. Long- versus short-term patterns of thought reflects a culture's view about the future. The short-term orientation, a Western cultural characteristic, reflects values toward the present, perhaps even the past, and a concern for fulfilling social obligations.

We discuss how these dimensions are related to different concepts in this book in the spotlight items that focus on the role of culture on the specific chapter topic.

SUMMARY

Personality is a way to characterize people. Many theories and concepts of personality exist. It is a useful way to understand and predict success at work and accommodations to organizational life. Personality is central to understanding many aspects of work, ranging from culture to motivation. For example, the neurotic and Machiavellian personality types are of interest in interpreting interpersonal and hierarchical relationships, and a high core self-evaluation may be related to a person's leadership ability and promotability.

Managers should learn all they can about human behavior because people are critical to an organization's success. The knowledge and skills a manager uses in dealing with people should be based on sound behavioral science models and principles. A complete model would include what is known about the person, the environment of behavior, the behavior itself and its effects. Key principles are that much behavior is learned, and the behavior is both stable and changeable.

Learning is a lifelong process. It takes place in a number of ways, such as through classical conditioning, reinforcement and modeling. Learning theories explain how people acquire knowledge, attitudes and skills. They are also central to understanding socialization and personality development. Schedules of reinforcement are also important – the timing and frequency of reinforcements makes a difference in how quickly something is learned and how resistant it is to extinction.

GUIDE FOR MANAGERS: UNDERSTANDING WHY PEOPLE BEHAVE AS THEY DO

Trying to make judgments about people is one of the most frustrating aspects of managerial work. Too often, as amateur psychologists, we make mistakes about others as we try to judge whether they will work out well. Many times, this is because of attribution errors of the type that we will discuss in Chapter 3. Having good models about personality to work from is a good place to start, and that is what we have provided you with in this chapter. Here are some things that you can do with these models to help you make better judgments about the personality of others.

Don't Trust Explanations

People cannot always fully explain their own behavior (Maslow, 1970). The employee who refused an assignment might say, 'I don't feel very well today.' But this does not explain the cause of the resistance. Because of the difficulties in interpreting what people say, we need to seek other information to help understand the behavior.

Look for Causes

When interpreting employee behavior, look for causes in both the employee's characteristics and in the environment or situation that might have triggered the behavior. How a person behaves is determined by the person's characteristics interacting with the elements in his or her environment. You must understand this interaction between the person and the environment, and avoid overemphasizing one in favor of the other when interpreting human behavior. You might decide that an unproductive worker is lazy or inattentive (personal attributes) when actually the worker was behaving in response to pressure from peers or faulty equipment (environmental forces).

Look for Several Causes

Behavior may result from one or more causes. Suppose an employee gets very upset over a request to perform an assignment. If you believe that your request is the only cause of the employee's reaction, you might conclude that this is just another case of uncooperativeness. Suppose, however, that you think about other possible causes that might explain the employee's refusal. You might discover that the employee is not only worried about falling behind in his work, but also feels unfairly treated because co-workers are not carrying their share of the load.

Account for Individual Differences

Try to account for individual differences and don't overgeneralize about them when you deal with people. People are alike in many ways. Similarities allow us to generalize about people. Some generalizations are relatively safe (for example, people dislike being embarrassed). Others are more questionable or even dangerous (for example, punishment will eliminate behaviors that cause work accidents). On the other hand, knowing that people are different can complicate things because we might try to treat every person as unique. When dealing with others, it is probably best to err on the side of appreciating individual differences. This, at least, can help prevent poor generalizations.

Use Past Behavior as a Predictor of Future Behavior

Keep in mind that past behavior is a pretty good predictor of future behavior. In many ways people are stable and predictable. There is some truth to the statement that past behavior is the best predictor of a person's future behavior. It is fairly safe for a manager to assume that what a worker has done in the past is quite likely to be repeated unless something significant changes. Stability of behavior, however, does not mean that people do not change. Given the right circumstances, even personality and values may be changed.

Recognize Personality Differences

Consider important personality differences when selecting and assigning people to jobs. Try to make sure that personality is related to what the job requires for success. For example, don't assume that all people are equally dedicated to work or to your organization; know the difference between organizationalists, professionals and indifferents. Try to minimize authoritarian and Machiavellian influences: they create an overemphasis on hierarchy and political behaviors which all too often interfere with task accomplishment. Expect some of your employees to be much more internally motivated, self-controlling and independent. They will expect more freedom and responsibility. At the same time, however, avoid actions that fail to recognize that most all employees will exhibit frustration if they are treated as immature, rather than as people with adult personalities and needs.

CASE: LAURELLI BEDDING COMPANY

The Laurelli Bedding Company is a manufacturer of a well-known brand of mattresses. Because mattresses are bulky and are costly to ship, the manufacturing is franchised to various local bedding companies around the nation who produce for local department stores. The Laurelli Bedding Company employed 32 assemblers, carrying out the various specific operations required in the making of a mattress. The springs inside the mattress were purchased from another company. The mattress core of springs or foam had to be covered with cloth. Different assemblers performed different parts of this operation as the mattress was pushed along the assembly line on rollers. Each assembler had a specific task to perform. For each task there was a performance standard established, and a basic incentive was paid for reaching or surpassing the performance standard established by means of time study.

Recently, Professor Catherine Wulf asked the Laurelli Bedding Company if she could conduct a study of the performance of the assemblers. She wanted to administer a number of psychological tests to the workers and see if variations in their scores were predictive of the actual performance of the workers. One of her instruments measured locus of control – the degree to which individuals feel that their life is controlled by themselves or by events outside of themselves. The former are considered to be 'internals' and the latter 'externals', depending on the location of the perceived life control. Professor Wulf assumed that most of the workers would probably be 'externals', given the fact that they were production workers. Much to her surprise, almost all of the assemblers scored quite high as 'internals'. She wondered why this was so.

What is your judgment of her findings?

REFERENCES

Allport, G.W (1961), *Pattern and Growth in Personality*. New York: Holt, Rinehart & Winson.

Arvey, R.D., B.P. McCall, T.J. Bouchard, P. Taubman and M.A. Cavanaugh (1989), Job Satisfaction: Environmental and Genetic Components. *Journal of Applied Psychology*, **74**(2): 187–93.

Aziz, A., K. May and J.C. Crotts (2002), Relations of Machiavellian Behavior with Sales Performance of Stockbrokers. *Psychological Reports*, **90**(2): 451–60.

Bandura, A. (1977), *Social Learning Theory*. Englewood Cliffs, NJ: Prentice-Hall.

Bandura, A. (1982), Self-Efficacy Mechanism in Human Agency. *American Psychologist*, **37**: 122–47.

Baron, R.A. (1983), *Behavior in Organization: Understanding and Managing the Human Side of Work*. Boston, MA: Allyn & Bacon.

Barrick, M.R. and M.K. Mount (1991), The Big Five Personality Dimension and Job Performance: A Meta-Analysis. *Personnel Psychology*, **44**: 1–26.

Barrick, M.R. and M.K. Mount (1996), Effects of Impression Management and Self-Deception on the Predictive Validity of Personality Constructs. *Journal of Applied Psychology*, **81**(3): 261–73.

Bolino, M.C. and W.H. Turnley (2003), More than One Way to Make an Impression: Exploring Profiles of Impression Management. *Journal of Management*, **29**(2): 141–60.

Burks, S.V., J.P. Carpenter and E. Verhoogen (2003), Playing both Roles in the Trust Game. *Journal of Economic Behavior and Organization*, **51**(2): 195–216.

Cattell, R.B. (1950), *Personality: A Systematic, Theoretical and Factual Study*. New York: McGraw-Hill.

Christie, R. and F. Geis (eds) (1970), *Studies in Machiavellianism*. Academic Press: New York.

Dunn, W.S., M.K. Mount, M.R. Barrick and D.S. Ones (1995), Relative Importance of Personality and General Mental Ability in Managers' Judgements of Applicant Qualifications. *Journal of Applied Psychology*, **80**(4): 500–510.

Epstein, S. and E.J. O'Brien (1985), The Person–Situation Debate in Historical and Current Perspective. *Psychological Bulletin*, **98**(3): 513–37.

Freud, S. (1933), *New Introductory Lectures on Psychoanalysis*. New York: Norton.

Fukami, C.V. and E.W. Larson (1984), Commitment to Company and Union: Parallel Models. *Journal of Applied Psychology*, **69**: 367–71.

Funder, D.C. (1991), Global Traits: A Neo-Allportean Approach to Personality. *Psychological Science*, **2**(1): 31–9.

George, J.M. (1992), The Role of Personality in Organizational Life: Issues and Evidence. *Journal of Management*, **18**(2): 185–213.

George, J.M. (1995), Leader Positive Mood and Group Performance: The Case of Customer Service. *Journal of Applied Psychology*, **25**(9): 778–95.

Greene, C.N. (1978), Identification Modes of Professionals: Relationship with Formalization, Role Strain and Alienation. *Academy of Management Journal*, **21**: 486–92.

Hofstede, G. (1980), *Culture's Consequences: International Differences in Work-related Values*. Newbury Park, CA: Sage.

Hurtz, G.M. and J.J. Donovan (2000), Personality and Job Performance: The Big Five Revisited. *Journal of Applied Psychology*, **85**(6): 869–79.

Iverson, R. and P. Erwin (1997), Predicting Occupational Injury: The Role of Affectivity. *Journal of Occupational and Organizational Psychology*, **70**(2): 113–29.

James, W. (1890), *Principles of Psychology*, Vol. 1. New York: Henry Holt & Co.

Judge, T.A. and J.E. Bono (2001), Relationship of Core Self-evaluations Traits – Self-esteem, Generalized Self-efficacy, Locus of Control, and Emotional Stability – with Job Satisfaction and Job Performance: A Meta-analysis. *Journal of Applied Psychology*, **86**(1): 80–92.

Judge, T.A., J.E. Bono, R. Ilies and M.W. Gerhardt (2002), Personality and Leadership: A Qualitative and Quantitative Review. *Journal of Applied Psychology*, **87**(4): 765–80.

Judge, T.A., D. Heller and M.K. Mount (2002), Five-Factor Model of Personality and Job Satisfaction: A Meta-analysis. *Journal of Applied Psychology*, **87**(3): 530–41.

Judge, T.A. and R. Ilies (2002), Relationship of Personality to Performance Motivation: A Meta-analytic Review. *Journal of Applied Psychology*, **87**(4): 797–807.

Judge, T.A., E.A. Locke and C.C. Durham (1997), The Dispositional Causes of Job Satisfaction: A Core Evaluations Approach. *Research in Organizational Behavior*, **19**: 151–88.

Judge, T.A., A.E.M. Van Vianen and I.E. De Pater (2004), Emotional Stability, Core Self-Evaluations, and Job Outcomes: A Review of the Evidence and an Agenda for Future Research. *Human Performance*, **17**(3): 325–46.

Jung, C.G. (1939), *The Integration of the Personality*. New York: Farrow & Rinehart.

Keller, L.M., T.J. Bouchard, R.D. Arvey, N.L. Segal and R.V. Dawis (1992), Work Values: Genetic and Evironmental Influences. *Journal of Applied Psychology*, **77**(1): 79–89.

Lopes, J. and C. Fletcher (2004), Fairness of Impression Management in Employment Interviews: A Cross-Country Study of the Role of Equity and Machiavellianism. *Social Behavior and Personality*, **32**(8): 747–68.

Maslow, A.H. (1970), *Motivation and Personality*. New York: Harper & Row.

Mischel, W. (1977), The Interaction of Person and Situation. In *Personality at the Crossroads: Currents Issues in Interactional Psychology*, D. Magnusson and N.S. Enders (eds). Hillsdale, NJ: Erlbaum, pp. 333–52.

Murray, H.A. (1962), *Explorations in Personality*. New York: Science Editions.

Myers, I.B. and K.C. Briggs (1962), *Myers–Briggs Type Indicator*. Princeton, NJ: Educational Testing Service.

Pavlov, I.V. (1927), *Conditioned Reflexes*. New York: Oxford University Press.

Presthus, R. (1978), *The Organizational Society*. New York: St Martin's Press.

Rogers, C.R. (1942), *Counseling and Psychotherapy*. Boston: Houghton Mifflin.

Rotter, J. (1966), Generalized Expectancies for Internal vs. External Control of Reinforcement. *Psychological Monographs*, **80**(609): 397–404.

Schneider, B., H.W. Goldstein and D.B. Smith (1995), The ASA framework: An Update. *Personnel Psychology*, **48**(4): 747–73.

Semeijn, J., C. Boone, R. van der Velden and A. Van Witteloostuijn (2005), Graduates' Personality Characteristics and Labor Market Entry: An Empirical Study among Dutch Economics Graduates. *Economics of Education Review*, **24**(1): 67–83.

Staw, B.M. and S.G. Basade (1993), Affect and Managerial Performance: A Test of the Sadder-but-Wiser vs. the Happier-and-Smarter Hypothesis. *Administrative Science Quarterly*, **38**(2): 304–28.

Thoresen, C.J., S.A. Kaplan, A.P. Barsky, C.R. Warren and K. de Chermont (2003), The Affective Underpinnings of Job Perceptions and Attitudes: A Meta-analytic Review and Integration. *Psychological Bulletin*, **129**(6): 914–45.

Tosi, H.L. (1992), *The Environment/Organization/Person Contingency Model: A Meso Approach to the Study of Organizations*. Greenwich, CT: JAI Press.

Vecchio, R.P. (2005), Explorations in Employee Envy: Feeling Envious and Feeling Envied. *Cognition and Emotion*, **19**(1): 69–81.

Watson, D. and L.A. Clark (1984), Negative Affectivity: The Disposition to Experience Aversive Emotional States. *Psychological Bulletin*, **96**(3): 465–90.

Watson, D. and A. Tellegen (1985), Toward a Consensual Structure of Mood. *Psychological Bulletin*, **98**(2): 219–35.

Weiss, H.M. (1977), Subordinate Imitation of Supervisory Behavior: The Role of Modeling in Organizational Socialization. *Organizational Behavior and Human Performance*, **19**: 89–105.

Weiss, H.M. and S. Adler (1984), Personality and Organizational Behavior. In *Research in Organizational Behavior*, B.M. Staw and L.L. Cummings (eds). Greenwich, CT: JAI Press, pp. 1–50.

Wilshire, B.W. (1968), *William James and Phenomenology: A Study of The Principles of Psychology*. Bloomington, IN: Indiana University Press.

Wood, R.E. and A. Bandura (1989), Social Cognitive Theory of Organizational Managment. *Academy of Management Review*, **14**: 361–84.

Yamagata, S., A. Suzuki, J. Ando, Y. Ono, N. Kijima, K. Yoshimura, F. Ostendorf, A. Angleitner, R. Riemann, F.M. Spinath, W.J. Livesley and K.L. Jang (2006), Is the Genetic Structure of Human Personality Universal? A Cross-cultural Twin Study from North America, Europe, and Asia. *Journal of Personality and Social Psychology*, **90**(6): 987–98.

2. Attitudes, emotions, perception and judgment

PREPARING FOR CLASS

As you prepare for this chapter, most of you are just beginning to adjust to the course that this text supports. Think about the reaction of your classmates to aspects of the class such as the professor, the content, the classroom or this text. Most students in your class have probably already expressed attitudes about one or more of these aspects of the class. You may have heard these attitudes expressed in class or out of class; you may have inferred them, from student behaviors.

1. What are your fellow students' attitudes about these aspects of this course?
2. As you consider those attitudes, try to identify individual beliefs and values that may have contributed to those attitudes.
3. Do you notice different types of student behaviors from individuals with different attitudes?

*   *

One of the major industrial mergers in the late 1990s was between Chrysler and Daimler-Benz. At the time, observers thought that this was a wedding that would benefit both automobile companies: it was to be a merger of equals in that Daimler would benefit by gaining more access to the US auto market, and Chrysler would have access to Daimler technology and financial resources. But the merger failed, and many attribute that to how the attitudes of the German managers differed from those of the US executives. On one side, the Germans had an attitude of superiority, and their actions reflected it. They were also the dominant force in the redesigning of Chrysler's organizational structure. The situation also created feelings of insecurity, fear and loathing on the part of many Chrysler personnel.

What does this experience at Chrysler bode for their merger with Fiat, the Italian automobile manufacturer, in 2010? There is, at least as the merger begins, a different attitude that emanates from the Italian company. It is a more participative attitude that is reflected in the fact that there is a less overbearing presence of the Italians in Detroit, as compared to the Daimler days. And it appears, at least as the two companies move forward, that there is a better consensus and understanding of the goals of the partners (Priddle, 2009).

There is a lot that this example suggests about the content of this chapter. First, the perceptions of all of the parties were used as the basis for attributing attitudes and values to others. Stereotypes also most likely came into play. As an example, when the Daimler managers began to influence how Chrysler was structured, it was consistent with the stereo-type that Germans tend to be dominant persons. Along the same lines, Chrysler staff observed that Fiat managers were less frequently present in Detroit in large numbers. This could have led to an inference that Fiat would be more likely to delegate more responsibility to the American managers.

THE NATURE OF ATTITUDES

Attitudes are psychological tendencies to react in a favorable or unfavorable way toward an object (Eagly and Shelly, 2005). They reflect a person's likes and dislikes toward other persons, objects, events and activities in their environment – almost anything in the world around them. They may also be, in some instances, a behavioral predisposition when they are attitudes about a specific behavior toward the object, such as complying with directions from your boss or leaving work early on Friday. More general attitudes toward physical objects (the Eiffel Tower or London Bridge), specific groups and the like are less likely indicative of behavior (Ajzen and Fishbein, 2005).

It makes sense to study and know about attitudes. Attitudes such as how employees feel about their job and their commitment to the organization are among the most critical consequences that managers can strive to improve, because attitudes and satisfactions also affect different measures of effectiveness. Employee attitudes about their pay and benefits, their co-workers and supervisor, and about work hours and conditions, are among the many factors that both managers and researchers have considered it important to examine. For example, there is research which shows that job-related attitudes are related to important aspects of job performance, such as:

1. Job satisfaction is related to task performance. There is a long history of evidence that shows there is a positive relationship between job

satisfaction and task performance (Vroom, 1964; Iaffaldano and Muchinsky, 1985; Judge et al., 2001). For this reason, a manager should be concerned with employee job satisfaction. Because of its link to performance, one of the key goals in managing behavior in organizations is to create linkages between employees' performance and their satisfaction. Many managerial strategies discussed throughout this book, such as redesigning organizational structures and tasks, are aimed at strengthening this link.

2. Job satisfaction is related to organizational citizenship (contextual performance) dimensions such as lateness, attendance and turnover (see discussion of these concepts in Chapter 3) (Bateman and Organ, 1983; LePine et al., 2002).

3. Organizations suffer significant direct and indirect costs when workers miss work. When they quit, the costs of recruitment, selection and training the new employee to full productivity can be considerable.

Why Attitudes are Important

Attitudes are important because they serve so many useful purposes for people (Katz, 1960). For example, suppose someone on your work team that you admire and look up to comes under attack in a staff meeting by a team from another department. Your positive attitudes toward her and the things she stands for will help you to come to her (and your own) defense. In doing so, you protect your self-image, and have a motive to express the values that you with and your friend espouse. Your attitude toward the attackers could shift toward the negative, providing you with an even stronger justification about how to deal with them in the future. Figure 2.1 shows these and other functions that attitudes serve:

- Providing a frame of reference.
- Reinforcement.
- Expression of values.
- Ego defense.
- Reconciling contradictions.

Providing a frame of reference
Attitudes help us to make sense of the world by giving us a context in which to interpret our world. We selectively perceive only a part of the total world around us. We are likely to select those facts that are consistent with our attitudes, and ignore or discount those that are not. For example, we make sense, rightly or wrongly, about things based on our stereotypes about them. If we have a positive stereotype of the French, then we are

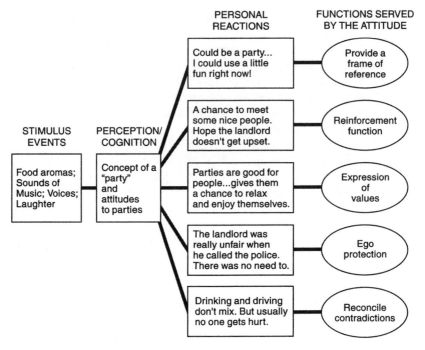

Figure 2.1   What functions attitudes serve

more likely to want to learn more about the country and its people. If this stereotype is negative, then we are likely to avoid those things French. In either case, what we do about understanding the French better will be affected by our attitudes toward them.

The instrumental–expressive function
Attitudes can serve as means to an end. They facilitate the adjustment of the person since we tend to develop and hold positive attitudes toward people, ideas or things with which we have had positive experience, and negative attitudes develop as a result of negative experiences. For example, suppose a person has threatened us in some way. A negative attitude toward such a person can help us to be on guard and protect ourselves when we are around them.

Expression of values
Expressing attitudes through words and actions demonstrates our values and allows us to share them with others and to affect the world in which we live. For example, if we strongly value individual achievement, we

are likely to seek work and have high job satisfaction in an organization that rewards performance through performance bonuses and other merit increases. Similarly, strong democratic values might emerge at work in staff meetings where employees are given a chance to participate in solving a problem or making a decision.

Ego defense

Attitudes help us to maintain our self-image and self-respect. For example, a supervisor might have feelings of superiority regarding subordinates. An attitude that subordinates are lazy and not trustworthy, or that they are not trained well enough to assume much responsibility, tends to enhance the supervisor's feelings of superiority.

Reconciling contradictions

Most of us have some contradictory attitudes or beliefs, yet in many instances these inconsistencies do not cause us to feel uneasy or have a sense of dissonance. This happens when the contradictions between inconsistent beliefs, behaviors or attitudes are reconciled by compartmentalization. We are able to place the contradictions in separate compartments and not connect them, thereby reconciling them. Suppose your new boss treats you in an immature and demeaning way, very different from your previous supervisor. As a result, you become very dissatisfied, and develop a negative work attitude. Yet, at the same time, you are very happy with your family situation, and part of that has to do with the small town in which you live. Do you look for another job in another city? How is such a contradiction reconciled? Compartmentalization occurs when you psychologically separate these two attitudes, compartmentalizing them and taking the position that 'work is work and family is family'.

Sources of Attitudes and Beliefs

Through socialization, we are exposed to countless personal experiences that have lasting effects. Parents, relatives, teachers, friends and many others are critical in shaping your attitudes. They provide reinforcements, they act as models that you emulate, and they serve as sources of information. Other life experiences are also important. For example, having long ago had a bad experience with a sales clerk could affect your attitude toward a whole company or toward the sales profession in general. We learn firsthand that ice cream tastes good, or that it is risky to be late for work. The mass media can also shape our beliefs. The effects of this exposure can be quite subtle. Simple, repeated exposure can cause us to like something; it does not even require the development of a belief or a value. Television has been a particular focus of attention because of its supposed impact on children. For example, playing violent video games increases both aggressive thoughts and behavior in the short and long term (Anderson and Dill, 2000).

A MODEL OF ATTITUDES

Attitudes reflect a person's likes and dislikes toward other persons, objects, events and activities in their environment – almost anything in the world around them. As we are socialized, we develop a whole range of general and specific feelings about objects. This learning process also leads to the development of values. Values underlie attitudes and are usually consistent with them. Then, as things we perceive around us (cognitions) are evaluated against our values and beliefs, we begin to feel a positive or negative orientation toward objects, general and specific. When there are strong positive beliefs about those cognitions that we associate with work, then we will have high job satisfaction. If they are negative, job satisfaction will be low. If they are mixed, then we might have an indifferent attitude about work. For instance, returning to the Chrysler mergers at the beginning of this chapter, the attitudes of the Chrysler employees toward Daimler were initially probably based on general stereotypes of Germans, and perhaps more specific perceptions of Daimler itself. What finally determined their attitudes about the merger, however, came as a result of the specific experiences with the Daimler management and the effects of their decisions on the working conditions of the employees.

Attitudes have cognitive, affective and behavioral components that are related to the object. Figure 2.2 shows that attitudes are tied to values and beliefs, and they precede intentions to behave and actual behavior. Figure 2.3 then shows, for example, the complexity of factors that might affect attitudes toward work, or job satisfaction.

The Object of Attitudes

It is not accurate to say that someone has a good attitude or a bad attitude without specifying the object of the attitude. Attitudes always apply to some identifiable object. The object can be broad and general, such as the government, the Episcopalian Church, a particular country (say, Ireland) or the European Parliament. Objects may also themselves be very specific attitudes toward behavior, such as the attitude toward your specific job, the company in which you work, a sports team of which you are a fan (or their dominant rival), or a specific person.

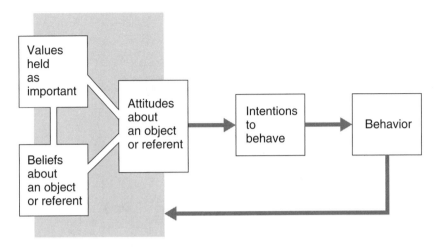

Figure 2.2   A model of attitudes

The Affective Component

The basic way that we refer to attitudes is to say that they are 'positive' or 'negative'. The affective component is the emotional tone, the feelings, generated by or toward the object of the attitude. It simply means that we have some preference – like or dislike – toward the object. In Figure 2.3 the affective dimension of this attitude is a strong, positive emotional orientation toward the 'job'.

The Cognitive Dimension

The affective component of the attitude develops as a result of things that we observe in the world around us that we associate, positively or negatively, with the object of the attitude. These are called the cognitive dimensions of attitude. Figure 2.3 shows some of the cognitions that might be associated with, and will determine, whether your attitude toward work is positive or negative. In this case, you have a positive job attitude that is a result of experiences in the family (mother's work, parents never missing work and being involved with parents in work situations) as well as current positive work experiences, a perception of good future potential. Other cognitions might be your level of pay, the actual working conditions, the parking facilities, the hours that you work, and so on.

What is important is that your specific attitude toward your job will be a function of your perceptions about the job and evaluations about these factors. Another person might have a different set of cognitions associated

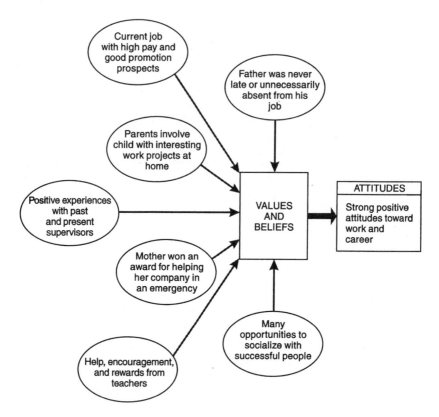

Figure 2.3   Example of the learning and expression of attitudes toward work and career

with work. For example, someone who is not highly committed to the work might focus on the amount of time available for vacation, the hours worked, the level of strict versus loose supervision. The key point is that these relevant cognitions about work may vary from person to person, in large part depending upon their personality and how they view the world.

Values and Beliefs: The Evaluative Element

Attitudes are formed as cognitions are evaluated in terms of your relevant values and beliefs. Values reflect a sense of right and wrong. Values are more general, and perhaps more broad, than attitudes, and they need not have an identifiable object. They define the good life, and identify goals worthy of our aspiration (Myers, 1983). Values are expressed in statements such as 'equal rights for all' and 'hard work is the road to success'.

For example, if you value economic well-being, then the amount of your pay is assessed to determine if it is consistent with the value that you put on 'economic well-being'. If it is, then a belief is formed that pay is a positive factor and it will contribute to the positiveness of the attitude. If it is seen as a negative factor, then cognitions about pay will contribute to the negativeness of the attitude. We know, for instance, that employees who have high positive affectivity whose basic values are not met at work are more likely to leave, while those who find their values are met will remain (George and Jones, 1966).

Beliefs are the thinking component of attitudes. They do not refer to favorable or unfavorable reactions; they only convey a sense of 'what is' to the person (Fishbein and Ajzen, 1975). However, beliefs are not necessarily factual even though they represent the truth for a particular person. Beliefs also can vary in how absolute they are. One might believe that nuclear power plants are all unsafe, or believe that this is only sometimes true.

The Behavioral Dimension

Taking the example of your job satisfaction a bit further, your attitude toward your job might encourage you to take some action. Suppose it is negative and you are frustrated because of what you judge to be low pay and poor working conditions. This is likely to foster intentions, or motivate you to work harder to gain a promotion to a job where pay is higher and conditions are better, or maybe even to seek a job elsewhere. Your choice will depend on which alternative we feel has the greatest likelihood of success.

Attitudes often lead to overt behaviors, but not always. Except for behavior, all other aspects of attitudes are internal to the person; they are not observable. The behavioral component of attitudes is important because people draw inferences about attitudes, beliefs, values and intentions by observing what you say and what you do. For example, if you have a co-worker who has been spending a great deal of time working late at the office, you might infer that he or she has a very positive attitude toward work and the company. However, it could be something else, such as an overdue credit card bill, that leads to your colleague's habit of working late.

Properties of Attitudes

We can now say some things about the properties of attitudes. One is that attitudes have direction, or a focus on the object, whether the object is specific or general. Another property is that they range on a continuum, from very strong to very weak. For example one person may have a very strong positive attitude toward her job, while another's attitude may be very negative. Attitudes have persistence over time. For example, one study showed that job satisfaction was very stable over a five-year time period, even when persons changed jobs (Staw and Ross, 1987a). Finally, there is the condition of equilibrium. This means simply that an attitude does not usually exist in isolation. You do not, for example, have an attitude toward your work that exists independently from other attitudes that might also be linked to work. It is likely, for example, that your attitude toward your place of work is linked with your attitudes toward the work that you do, your co-workers and where you work.

Spotlight 2.1   Employees' attitudes, trust and HR practices

The results of recent studies (Pilati and Innocenti, 2008, 2010; Innocenti and Pilati, 2009; Pilati, Innocenti and Peluso, 2010) confirm the importance of investigating the so-called 'black box' or intermediate set of factors that may contribute to explaining the 'how' of the links between HRM practices and organizational and individual performance. These studies reinforces the optimistic view of the role of HR practices and their impacts on a set of employee attitudes and behavior, highlighting a strong relationship between the two variables. While exploring the black box, the important role of trust in management as a moderating variable in this relationship has also been demonstrated. Results indicate that people differ in their reaction to HRM according to individual conditions, and that these conditions can modify the impact of HRM practices on employee attitudes and behavior. Besides, the studies demonstrated that in situations of low levels of trust in management, HRM practices have a positive impact on some important organizational attitudes and behavior through positive perceptions of work conditions.

These related attitudes form an attitude system and, more than likely, though not always, they will be consistent with each other as well as the specific values, cognitions and beliefs for each specific attitude in a specific attitude system. However, they will also be consistent with other attitude systems to which they are strongly linked. For example, you may have a work attitude system, a family attitude system and a political attitude

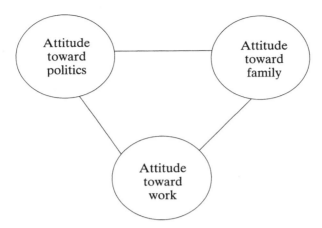

Figure 2.4   Cluster of related attitudes

system. Each of these will include specific attitudes that make up the system; see Figure 2.4. One attitude system might or might not be linked to another. For example, the work attitude system might be very tightly linked to the family attitude system but not to the political attitude system.

This helps us to understand one of the reasons why it is not always easy to change attitudes in ways to increase job satisfaction. As you have seen, attitude toward work may be only one important aspect of the person's complex structure of attitudes. It might be linked strongly to other important ones, making it deeply embedded, and thereby limiting how much managers can succeed in altering the way employees feel and act. However, particular attitudes and satisfactions at work can and do change, sometimes quickly, as events change. An employee who is satisfied and productive one day can become dissatisfied and resentful overnight as a consequence of some managerial action. This is one of the reasons why many organizations pay close attention to attitudes by conducting periodic attitude surveys of their employees.

ATTITUDINAL CONSISTENCY AND COGNITIVE DISSONANCE

The theory of cognitive dissonance is based on the idea that people tend to seek consistency between their behavior and attitudes, beliefs and cognitions (Festinger, 1957; Judge et al., 1944). When there is inconsistency (dissonance), we are motivated to reduce it because we experience discomfort. Dissonance can occur quickly or over a longer period of time. An example of rapid induction of dissonance might be the case in which you are quite happy with your work, and have been for a long time because the specific attitudes that make up the work attitude system (how you feel about the job, the supervisor and the location) are all positive. Then, along comes a new manager and you find that his actions toward the work group are demeaning, demanding and distant, resulting in your attitude toward your boss becoming negative. Now you have a dissonant attitude in the work attitude system that is strong enough to lead you seriously to consider looking for other work. Or, dissonance may be gradually induced. Perhaps you find that new boss is not too bad, but still you are negative; other things begin to change. You learn that while you are well paid, you may be receiving less than others in your job category. Later, you discover that that the top management has engaged in unethical marketing practices. As these different cognitions build over time, your dissonance increases and you eventually become more frustrated and think that you should seek other employment.

Another basic idea of this theory is that we are motivated to explain or justify our behavior, thoughts or feelings. In short, feelings, thoughts and behaviors must each be consistent with one other. One way to deal with the situation above is to modify your overall attitude toward work by reducing your level of job satisfaction. You might cite examples of times when you had problems with the manager, how he deals in negative ways with other workers, or tell others that he is not important to your success. If your work attitude system does become negative, and if at the same time there are cognitive elements that are common with your family attitude system, this could produce dissonance. It has been shown, for example, that there is a strong positive relationship between work satisfaction and life satisfaction (Judge et al., 1944). This means that some cognitive elements will be common in both the work and the life attitude system. For example, one cognitive dimension of your work attitude system and your family attitude system could be 'location'. You like your job because it is located near other members of your family and, at the same time, you are contented because your spouse and family are happy there. This overlap, or spillover, will lead to some discomfort when things at home are going well, but you are dissatisfied at work. However, suppose that there is no overlap of cognitive elements with your political attitude system, as shown in Figure 2.4. This poses no adjustment problems.

Dissonance can arise when there is insufficient justification for what you do. This is called 'decisional dissonance'. Dissonance can be reduced before you take action. Suppose your new boss tells you to reprimand a subordinate, a behavior that you find unpleasant and harsh. If you were ordered to do so, you may have little or no dissonance because your boss has given you sufficient justification (a direct and clear-cut order) to do it. However, in the absence of such an order, the justification may be insufficient. Following the act, the dissonance may remain strong and the motivation to reduce it persists. You would therefore have to rationalize your action. You might justify the reprimand by convincing yourself that your boss wanted you to do what you did, but just did not say so. If the employee has a hostile reaction to the reprimand, it can serve to confirm that he deserved it, reducing your dissonance even further.

Dissonance also arises when there are 'disconfirmed expectations'. If a customer complains about one of our products, dissonance arises because it is inconsistent with our image of the company's reputation. Here again, developing a belief that rationalizes, or explains, the condition can reduce dissonance. We might think that the complaint was triggered by the customer's failure to follow directions in using the product.

Not surprisingly, dissonance is more severe when we are personally involved, such as when our own decisions lead to an unexpected problem. People often refuse to admit that they have made a mistake. Dissonance theory predicts that people may persist in the originally bad decision. They will even repeat it as a way of justifying it, thus compounding the bad decision rather than facing the dissonant admission that they were wrong in the first place (Staw and Ross, 1987a, 1987b; Tosi et al., 1997). When students played a business game in which they allocated funds to different projects, it was found that those students who allocated funds to unsuccessful projects made subsequent further investments in the same unsuccessful project, especially when they felt responsible for the bad decision (Staw, 1976; Tosi et al., 1997).

EMOTIONS AND MOOD

Until recently, for reasons unclear to us, the subjects of emotions and mood had been absent from the field of organizational behavior. The major psychological focus has been on topics such as motivation, job attitudes and organizational justice, positive and negative affect, and cognitive dissonance, for example. Perhaps one reason for this is that there is a negative connotation attached to emotions and moods, that is, that these sorts of responses are not rational. The stereotype of emotional behavior, for instance, is that it is often a quick and extreme response, usually negative, in some situation. So rather than speaking of happiness, love, fear, hatred and passion in organizations, it might be more acceptable to use terms such as job satisfaction or dissatisfaction and organizational commitment instead. This latter language certainly sounds more like what many think should go on in the rational organization.

Object Focused	Time constrained state	Time unconstrained tendency
Yes	Emotion	Attitude
No	Mood	Positive/Negative affectivity

Source: adapted from Clore (2005).

Figure 2.5   Differences between emotions, attitudes, mood and temperament

Emotions

Two recent developments have contributed significantly to the inter-est in the role of emotions in the workplace: the concepts of emotional intelligence (see Chapter 1 on personality, and Chapter 4 on stress) and emotional labor (see Chapter 4 on stress). Emotional intelligence, unlike cognitive intelligence (which more or less means 'how smart you are'), refers to the skills to manage your own feelings as well as the feelings of others. It is the ability to: (1) perceive emotions; (2) access emotions to facilitate better thinking; (3) understand emotions and emotional mean-ings; and (4) regulate emotions (Goleman, 2006a, 2006b). Emotional labor is work with a high emotional content and in which organizations expect members actively to display specific emotions and, as well, try both overtly and covertly to control emotional displays (Fineman, 1993). You can imagine, and we discuss more detail in Chapter 4, that emotional labor can induce a great deal of work stress.

Like attitudes, there is an affective, or feeling, aspect to emotions. Figure 2.5 below shows how they, as well as mood and positive or nega-tive affectivity, are related. Emotions and attitudes are similar because there is some 'object' of an emotion. They differ, however, in an important way: attitudes are not evaluative states, but: 'evaluative tendencies and do not vanish when one stops thinking about the object [while] emotions are ephemeral . . . and temporarily constrained as long as the supporting cognitions, perceptions and [stimuli] are present and vanishing as soon as one is no longer in that state' (Clore, 2005). On the other hand, mood and affectivity (see Chapter 1 on personality) are more general and not 'object'-focused. So, you could be high on positive affectivity (a feeling not limited by time), but be in a bad mood today because you were in an automobile accident this morning. This distinction between attitudes and emotions implies something else: arousing an emotion about something is likely to also act as a stimulus to arouse the attitude toward that object.

An interesting approach is based on the idea that there are some basic, or primary, emotions which when combined with other emotions in different ways can result in more complex emotions (Coon, 1991). The primary emotions are anger, disgust, sadness, surprise, fear, acceptance, joy and anticipation. Some of the complex emotions are, for example, contempt (anger and disgust), remorse (disgust and sadness), disappointment (sadness and surprise), love (joy and acceptance), optimism (joy and anticipation) and aggression (anticipation and anger). Typically these emotions are reflected in facial expressions (smiles or grimaces) and/or behaviors.

The role of emotions in customer–salesperson interaction has been addressed in several studies (Locke, 1996; Rafaeli and Sutton, 1987; Brown et al., 1997). This research is based on the premise that emotions of salespersons emerge as a result of client actions. For example, clerks in busy stores showed more negative emotions than clerks in slower stores (Staw et al., 1994), and positive emotions are displayed when there is higher customer demand (Rafaeli and Sutton, 1990).

Emotions may also be motivational. Staw et al. (1994) showed that employees who express more positive emotions and moods will experience more favorable outcomes in their work. A study by Cote and Morgan found that regulating emotions and amplifying pleasant emotions is related to increased job satisfaction and negative intentions to quit (Cote and Morgan, 2002).

Mood

Both emotions and moods are feelings, or are affective dimensions. But they are different from each other, and they are both different from attitudes, as Figure 2.5 illustrates. Like emotions, moods are not directed at a specific object and they are typically experienced within a limited time, like emotions are. For example, because your boss gave your team negative feedback, you might experience a strong emotion of anger, maybe even hate, toward him. However, at the same time you may be in a generally positive mood, feeling good about your more general work and life situation. After a time, the anger (the emotion) may pass, but you still continue to be in a positive mood.

Sources of Emotions and Mood

The blues song says, 'They call it Stormy Monday . . .' and we all TGIF ('Thank God It's Friday'). These common ideas suggest that emotions and moods are affected by the day of week. If that is so, then it seems reasonable that other common factors may have an effect on moods and emotions. For example (Brief and Weiss, 2002; Clark and Watson, 1988):

1. Experiences away from work. Your son is arrested for driving under the influence of alcohol, for example.
2. Temporal cycles. Positive moods are stronger later in the week (TGIF) and negative moods stronger earlier in the week (Stormy Monday) (Watson, 2000). Emotions and moods may also be induced by cyclical events in your life. For example, the death of a parent, holidays and starting a new job are among stressors assessed by the Social Readjustment Rating Scale (see Chapter 4 on stress).
3. Stress. In Chapter 4, we point out how stressors in the person's psychological environment result in emotional and mood-filled responses. For example, it is well known that role conflict and role ambiguity will lead to frustration. In addition, some of the ways to minimize stress (social support, exercise, changing your cognitive appraisal) may result in positive emotions and moods.
4. Leaders and co-workers. Emotions can be contagious (Barger and Grandey, 2006). Charismatic and transformational leaders induce strong positive emotions in their followers (Erez et al., 2008) and strong negative emotions in their opposition. For example, many of the world's most charismatic persons have been assassinated (John Kennedy, Robert Kennedy, Martin Luther King, Mussolini, John Lennon). And as we have noted above, many actions that supervisors take can have emotional effects For example, making pay decisions for members of the work group can lead to a strong sense of inequity if you feel underpaid relative to your co-workers. And working with others, particularly if they have tendencies toward strong emotions may affect you.
5. Characteristics of the work itself. Being dependent on another's work to achieve success in your own job can be a problem if the other person isn't meeting his or her performance deadlines or performance requirements. We have also mentioned emotional labor above, and will discuss it in more detail in Chapter 4, on stress.

PERCEPTION

Perception is important in this particular chapter because what we observe and how we evaluate it are affected by – and affect – attitudes, emotions and our mood. For example, the cognitive facets of attitudes are those

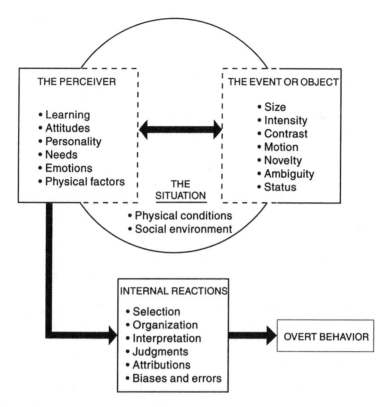

Figure 2.6   A perceptual model

elements in our environment that we 'observe' and associate with other cognitions (or perceptions) to determine the attitude. Perception is the psychological process of creating an internal picture of the external world. It is the way that we organize information about people and things, the attribution of properties to them on the basis of the information and the way we make cause–effect attributions about them. It is how we interpret what information our senses provide to us so as to give meaning to the environment we are in. The resulting interpretation is the perceiver's reality, and even though several people may observe the same environment the perception of it can vary widely from person to person.

In this next section, we focus on the feeling and thinking aspects of perception, with emphasis on just two sensory channels: what we see and what we hear. Then we examine how our perceptions affect behavior. We discuss the perceiver, the event or object being perceived, and the situational context in which the perception occurs. Figure 2.6 illustrates these elements and shows that they interact to determine both the interpretation and the action that takes place.

The Perceiver

The way we perceive is learned, and what we learn affects our perception. For example, an interesting study demonstrated how what we learn affects perception (Labianca et al., 2005). We organize and perceive time as a result of how we learn to 'tell time'. The idea is that we learn to read time in terms of cognitive reference points of 15 minute, or quarter-hour segments, and this affects how we eventually perceive and use time. In the study, individuals worked on a project for an hour (60 minutes) to design and complete a commercial advertisement and record it in one minute (60 seconds). They were placed in a room with the necessary tools, and with an 'official' wall clock hung on a drape to minimize distractions. Some started at prototypical time (for example, 4.00 p.m. or 4.30 p.m.) while others started at atypical times (for example 4.37 p.m. or 4.43 p.m.). The groups that started at the more conventional quarter-hour times performed better than those that started at atypical times. The latter subjects seemed 'lost in time' and felt more time pressure than those who started 'on the hour'.

Spotlight 2.2   Descartes on perception: how do we know wax is wax?

With his famous wax thought experiment, Descartes creates a conundrum for those who believe that perception is reality. When the wax is taken from the bees' honeycomb, it still tastes like honey and has the odor of the flowers from which it came. It is hard and cold, exactly what you would expect from immediately drawn beeswax. But then when that same wax is heated, its character changes: the color, the shape, the size and the feel of it, now much hotter. Essentially the wax has changed from its original form. Descartes then asks if it still wax. Obviously the answer is yes, but he demonstrates with this experiment that the senses, and the perceptions that emanate from them, are not enough to provide a basis for knowing physical objects.

Two processes are at work in perception. The first, selection, is at the heart of the perceptual process, and it is driven by our personal characteristics, attributes of the object itself, and the situation in which perception takes place. For example, Inuits have no concept that corresponds to what most people call snow. They actually perceive different kinds of snow depending on its particular characteristics and its potential uses, and have several concepts for it. There is good reason for this: their survival depends upon snow. This means that out of the many stimuli that bombard people, only a few actually penetrate and become part of their experience and are used in making judgments. The remainder are excluded.

The other powerful mechanism is perceptual organization. The reason is that information has an expected pattern that we have learned from our past experiences: a pattern that might be very general and abstract or very specific and detailed. These patterns are called categories, or schemas. As you are exposed to information in the environment, you tend to group certain stimuli into patterns so that they become meaningful wholes rather than fragmented parts. The way that they are grouped depends upon your schemas. An example is the words that you are now reading. The separate letters are ignored in favor of the whole word. Another example is the inclination to see physical patterns. It takes only three dots for us to see a triangle, and four to see a rectangle or square. Suppose one of your subordinates is late for work and is working slowly, producing below par. You are going to organize these facts in a way that makes sense to you, perhaps that slow work and lateness go together. Perhaps your schema about this set of information is that it reflects lack of caring and indifference. You may explain the behavior, then, in terms of laziness and irresponsibility. You would also seek consistency in surrounding events. Irresponsibility explanations would be reinforced if there was union trouble in the plant and you believed the worker was slowing down under union pressure. However, if there were no union problems and you believed the worker was a loyal employee, it would be more consistent to believe that his behavior was due to a temporary condition, such as an illness.

Physical, emotional and mood states can also shape and determine our reality. When a person is hungry, sights and sounds that point to food tend to become salient. Emotional states can distort perception, as with the example of the level of excitability of eyewitnesses to a crime. Eyewitness perceptions may be so inaccurate that one has to wonder why they are relied on so often (Bradfield and Wells, 2005). Some eyewitnesses report things that never happened, and overlook both small details and glaring stimuli. For example, some may fail to see a bright red shirt or hear an important statement made by a person committing a crime.

The Effects of the Event or Object

Certain attributes of events and objects affect whether they are perceived and how they are perceived:

- Size effects.
- Intensity effects.
- Contrast effects.
- Motion and novelty.
- Ambiguity.
- Characteristics of other people.

Size has an effect: larger objects are more likely to be seen than smaller ones. Intensity of stimuli is another factor: particularly loud noises are likely to be heard, and bright or shining objects will likely be seen. Contrast effects also affect perception, so anything that stands out against its background is more likely to be attended to. Motion and novelty also facilitate perception: a moving object or unusual things draw attention. Experts in advertising creatively manipulate such characteristics of objects and apply them to magazine and newspaper ads, to billboards, and to radio and television commercials.

Ambiguity also has an impact on perceptions. Ambiguous or incomplete events are actually more subject to personal interpretation. Ambiguity is discomforting, and can be reduced by adding meaning to the stimuli or attributing motives to a person associated with the stimuli. For example, after interviewers talk to an applicant for a job, they often draw conclusions that are not justified by the applicant's behavior. They often fill in gaps about the applicant's past experience, and do it in a way that confirms their good feelings or negative suspicions about a candidate with no good reason.

Finally, characteristics of other people affect perception. One example of this is how the status of a person affects our perception of him or her. Higher-status people are more likely to be noticed, and they usually are perceived to be more knowledgeable, accurate and believable.

Situational Effects

Under different conditions, the same cues can easily result in different perceptions. Imagine seeing a person holding a knife in a kitchen in which food is being prepared for a meal. Now imagine the same person holding a knife the same way in the middle of a public demonstration. The knife is often unnoticed in the kitchen setting but would be prominent in the demonstration. Furthermore, your predictions about what might happen would probably be different for each situation.

Perceptions can also be affected by the presence of another person. Suppose you are criticized by your boss in the presence of a higher-level manager. You might conclude that your boss is seeking favor from the higher manager by demonstrating a 'tough' management style. If the higher manager is absent, you are less likely to draw such a conclusion. In short, perceptions occur in a context, which predisposes us to expect certain events and lends an additional ingredient to how we interpret, judge and react.

It is clear, then, that perception plays a huge role in how accurate we are in the conclusions we draw and judgments we make about others. Of particular interest are judgments that distort or misrepresent the facts, or that disagree with the perceptions of others. Distortions and disagreement are at the root of a host of problems in managing people.

JUDGMENT TENDENCIES

In addition to inaccurate perception, other human tendencies lead to inaccurate or unreliable judgments. Optical illusions are a good example of how the actual characteristics of an object are not the same as what they seem to be; see Figure 2.7.

For managers, the most important perceptual biases are those that arise in relationships with other people. There are many such situations at work: performance appraisals, selection interviewing, group meetings, customer relations, and so on. Perceptual biases create distortions that are particularly crucial to understand. Understanding and awareness of these biases could help you avoid the many and frequent errors that may occur when you make a judgment about someone or something. Figure 2.8 shows various ways that we might react to others and the types of errors that can occur.

First Impressions

Strong and lasting impressions of others tend to be formed very early in a relationship. Since early interactions are usually of a short duration, these early impressions are usually based on very limited information. In other words, we use only a few cues when judging others, and then continue to maintain the judgment. This tendency is a critical problem because first impressions are often lasting ones.

There are two reasons why first impressions are so strong: the principles of closure and consistency. The principle of closure is that humans need a

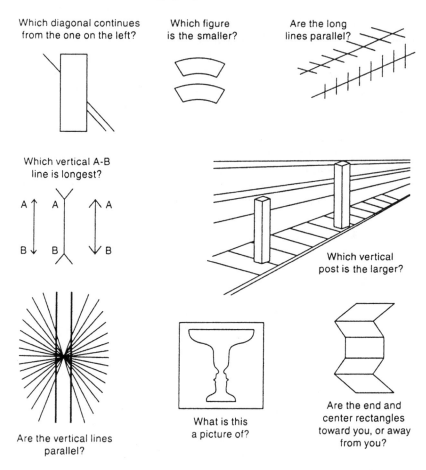

Which diagonal continues from the one on the left?

Which figure is the smaller?

Are the long lines parallel?

Which vertical A-B line is longest?

Which vertical post is the larger?

Are the vertical lines parallel?

What is this a picture of?

Are the end and center rectangles toward you, or away from you?

Figure 2.7   Perceptual teasers

relatively complete conception, or idea, about things. The principle of consistency is that the conception should be congruent with other attitudes, perceptions and beliefs. Suppose you meet someone for the first time. It is very difficult to know most of the things that you should know to form an accurate impression. What happens is that you focus on those cues that strike you as important at the time and then use these as a basis for 'completing' your picture of the person. When this happens, you no longer have limited information, but a fairly full model of the other person, made up of the relatively few cues gathered in your first impression and those that you added to it, which will be consistent with the first information. Later information obtained about the person should be evaluated against this

Figure 2.8   Judgment tendencies

more complete image that you have created, but because you have created this more complete concept now, it becomes difficult to change it when you receive the new information.

Halo: One Characteristic Tells All

The use of one or a few characteristics of a person to affect the evaluation of other characteristics is called the 'halo effect'. For many people there is a particular attribute that they like or dislike strongly in others. For example, if how one dresses is an important concern for a person, it can become a dominant basis to make biased judgments about others – positive or negative – if the halo effect is operating. How another person dresses would determine their overall evaluation. We see this often in the case of employment interviews when the interviewer makes a judgment that a job candidate is dressed in a way that seems consistent with the dress norms of the company. The interviewer assumes that because the candidate is dressed well she will fit well in the firm, and during the interview, has his or her other judgments colored by this factor. The halo effect also has a major impact on performance appraisals, often inflating them by as much as 30 percent (Viswesvaran et al., 2005).

Halo is likely to be related to our own self-image. We tend to have very positive evaluations of those who possess characteristics that we believe we have. A manager who is always on time for work is more favorably disposed toward subordinates who are punctual; they may be negatively disposed toward those who arrive late.

Projection

Projection is a psychological mechanism by which people attribute their own traits to others. Sometimes the trait is one that we like in ourselves. For example, we might attribute potential success to an interview applicant because we discover that she, like us, pays particular attention to spelling and neatness on her resume and other application materials. Sometimes, the trait is one we dislike in ourselves. For example, we might blame a co-worker's mistake on sloppiness when sloppiness is one of our own faults. If others do not possess what we project onto them, our behavior is governed by the false impression, and further misperceptions will likely follow.

Implicit Personality Theory

Statements such as 'honest people are also hard-working', 'late sleepers are lazy', 'quiet people are devious' or 'attractive people are competent' all link together two characteristics of a person. When we make such linkages, we are creating our own implicit personality theory. Any of the linkages could be wrong. Hard work and honesty need not go together. The late sleeper might have a medical problem. The quiet person might simply be shy. Engaging in implicit personality theory is amateur psychology at its worst. For example, a study of how implicit personality theory predicted the evaluation of work outcomes for attractive people found that they were judged more favorably than less attractive persons, whether they were men or women (Hosoda et al., 2003). It is much safer to link two characteristics together only if we witness both characteristics on repeated occasions.

Stereotyping

In stereotyping, we link characteristics of people to characteristics of a group which we associate them with. Surely not all members of a given group possess the characteristic they are said to have, yet stereotyping is common and widespread. It persists because it is useful, and helps us to organize the world around us. Often, however, stereotyping is nothing more than a perpetuation of old myths and prejudices. It is fed by prejudices and ambiguity, and sometimes by fear or threat, and reinforced in many ways. For example, if we know that someone is Italian, we might conclude he is emotional and likes good wine; if he is Irish, we might conclude that he drinks whiskey and is prone to be quick-tempered. Countless other examples exist, often very negative. Ethnic groups, older people, men, women, lawyers, used-car salesmen, or just about any other group can be stereotyped.

Spotlight 2.3   Negative stereotypes about Greek female managers

Perhaps the major problem of career women in Greece is the negative stereotype held about them. This was shown in a study of business students that found that male business students had strong negative stereotypes about women, more so than the stereotypes that women had about other women. The most significant factor that accounted for this difference is gender (Milhail, 2006).

Stereotypes also appear in our language, in words such as 'chairman' or 'cleaning woman'. They are often so embedded in society that they are difficult to change. Think of how women are portrayed in many television commercials and movies. Women's rights organizations spend much time and energy fighting to try to change stereotypes.

It is a fact, however, that members of groups do share certain values and beliefs, and will exhibit similar traits or behaviors. In some cases, therefore, it is quite safe to draw conclusions about people based on their group membership. We are usually correct in concluding that professional athletes are healthy, or that the average weight that women can lift is less than the average man can lift. However, even these generalizations require qualification and have to be carefully stated. For example, there are women who can outperform men in lifting weights.

ATTRIBUTION THEORY: FINDING THE CAUSES OF BEHAVIOR

It is fundamental to human nature to want to explain the causes of our own and others' behavior. An unexplainable event can leave us in a state

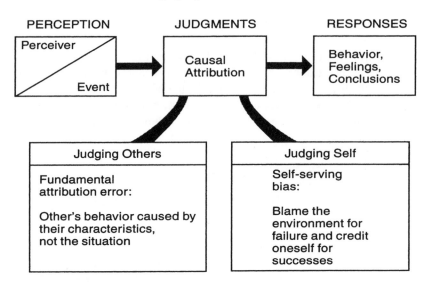

Figure 2.9   A model of attribution theory

of dissonance that motivates us to explain the situation to reduce the dissonance. If we know why something happened, it helps us decide how to react to an event. Suppose our supervisor gives us an unpleasant assignment. If we see the assignment as caused by unfairness, we are tempted to fight it. If we attribute the cause to a higher manager's wishes, we might have a different reaction to the whole situation.

Attribution theory explains why and how we determine these causes. It focuses on key errors people make in attributing causes. The attributions are judgments that subsequently affect our feelings, our behavior and the conclusions we draw about our experiences (see Figure 2.9). Wrong inferences about causation will create problems similar to those created by perceptual errors.

Judging the Behavior of Others

Earlier we pointed out that behavior is determined by the person and the environment, but that when we judge others, we have a strong tendency to attribute causes of behavior to the internal characteristics of the person rather than the environment. This tendency is called the 'fundamental attribution error' (Ross, 1977), overestimating the role of the person relative to the environment as a cause of behavior. Thus if we see people steal, we are more likely to characterize them as dishonest rather than to conclude that their family is starving.

We have a tendency to underestimate the situation as a cause of behavior even when we are told that the person was forced or instructed to behave as he or she did. For instance, if we observe a debate in which participants are assigned to defend a defined position, we will most likely attribute their arguments to their beliefs rather than to the debating rules they are following. Somehow, what people say or do, even under instructions or other situational pressures, leads us to conclude more about them than about the situation. Perhaps this is because we see the situational influences as operating through people and not independent of them.

There are several reasons for the fundamental attribution error. First, if you believe that the other has free choice in the situation, you are more likely to attribute causality to him or her personally. This makes sense, for you can conclude that the person was free to do otherwise, but chose to act as he or she did. Second, you are more likely to attribute internal motives to people when they take action that you view as important, and especially when those actions affect us personally. Suppose someone dented your car in a parking lot but left the scene before you appeared. You would characterize them unfavorably for failing to leave a note or call a police officer. If, however, you seek a situational cause, you might speculate that he or she had to rush home to take care of a dire emergency.

There are several other factors that affect our attributions about others (Kelly, 1973):

1. Consistency. If a person behaves the same way in similar situations, we are more likely to see the behavior as internally motivated, such as when a friend is almost always late.
2. Distinctiveness. Distinctive behaviors are those that are relatively unique to a situation. If a behavior is more distinctive, we are less likely to make internal attributions. If our friend is always on time, we are apt to evaluate a lateness as due to some unforeseen difficulty thrust on them.
3. Consensus. When the person we are judging acts differently than others act in the situation, we are more likely to think of that person's behavior as internally motivated.
4. Privacy of the act. Actions that are taken in the absence of other people are more likely to be judged as internally motivated. When others are present, we might attribute the action to social pressure. When people are alone, we attribute the action to them.
5. Status. In general, higher-status people are seen to be more personally responsible for their actions. They are thought to have more control over their own actions and decisions and do things because they choose to, not because they have to.

One important reason why we often make the fundamental attribution error – as well as the use of first impressions, halo, projection and stereo-typing, and the use of implicit personality theory – has to do with the way that we process information. Recall that we said earlier that perception has to do with how we organize information. We often make these errors because we use 'automatic' information processing. This means that when we recognize some key information, or stimulus, we recall schemas or categories into which that particular information fits, and our judgment is then biased toward the general characteristics of that category. Take the use of stereotypes as an example. Suppose we have a negative stereotype of lawyers and then we learn that a dinner guest is a lawyer. If we auto-matically use our occupational stereotype, then we are likely to attribute all of the negative aspects of the stereotype to him, without ever having taken the time to learn anything more about him. Automatic processing obviously occurs in performance evaluation but it is more likely to occur when a rater observes positive performance of the person being rated. Then they are more likely to attribute other positive characteristics to the person that have not been observed, and to make relatively quick judgments.

To avoid the fundamental attribution error and the other perceptual problems, it is necessary to use a 'controlled' information processing. In the controlled information processing approach, we pause and reflect on the situation as well as the person, and try to identify both the situational forces and the personal causes of behavior before making our judgment. This approach requires searching for more data. While this can complicate and delay matters, it may lead to a more accurate and less biased judg-ment. This is the approach raters used when they had observed negative performance of a person being rated (Kulik and Ambrose, 1993). They took more time and had more accurate recall of the negative aspects of the person's performance.

Judging Our Own Behavior

Self-judgments are affected by a self-serving bias – a tendency to perceive oneself favorably. People credit themselves when they succeed but are also likely to blame external factors when they fail (Sherman and Kim, 2005; Duval and Silvia, 2002). Success is usually attributed to hard work, ability and good judgment. Failure, on the other hand, is attributed to bad luck, unfair conditions or impossible odds. For example, think what happens when you are playing a close golf match. When your opponent makes a long putt, you tell her, 'You're lucky.' When you make a long putt, it is because of your skill. The reason for this is that these self-serving attributions about ourselves are a self-protective motivation (Sherman and Kim, 2005). This motivation is less prevalent among individuals who have made a clear articulation of their personal values. It seems when they do this that they share more group values and this is linked with a reduction of self-serving judgments.

Self-serving attributions and self-congratulatory comparisons operate in many ways. We tend to overrate ourselves on nearly any factor that is subjective and socially desirable (Felson, 1987), seeing ourselves as better than average in intelligence, leadership ability, health, life expectancy, interpersonal skill, and so on. We believe flattery more readily than we believe criticism. We overestimate how well we would act in a given situation and overestimate the accuracy of our judgments. For example, a psychologist who is well known for his work in the development of selection tests and who advocates their widespread use was asked what he thought about a candidate for a position at his department. He had only spent 30 minutes or so with the candidate, who was not selected through the use of any test. When asked what he thought of the candidate, he replied without hesitation, 'We shouldn't hire him. He will never work out here. I could tell it in the first five minutes of our discussion.' This is a good example of how he trusted his own selection judgment without the test, but it is likely that he would not trust the judgment of others unless selection tests had been used.

When we deal with others, we often see our own actions as externally justified, but attribute others' actions to their internal disposition. The objective truth hardly matters, and the self-serving attributions persist even in the face of contrary evidence. You are angered by your boss because you were provoked by a 'stupid' order that he or she gave. However, when your boss is angry with you, it is attributed to his or her 'neurotic personality'. Or, if your team receives negative feedback from the team leader you may think that the poor performance is due to the incompetence or failure of some other team member or that your boss is being too demanding.

Interestingly, the self-serving bias seems to be strongest among people with high self-esteem, especially when they perceive themselves as having the capacity to improve in the context of the situation. When they don't believe they can do better, they attribute their failure to external causes (Duval and Silvia, 2002). Those with lower self-esteem are likely to be more self-deprecating and engage in self-blame rather than blaming external events for failure. They are less likely to exhibit the self-serving bias. On the other hand, when low-self-esteem people have a strong need for respect, they could be more likely than the average person to exhibit the self-serving bias. This is why some people constantly talk about their own activities, exploits and successes. The self-serving bias acts as a boastful cover for their feelings of low self-esteem and is an attempt to gain recognition and thus to enhance self-esteem.

SOME ORGANIZATIONAL IMPLICATIONS OF ATTRIBUTION BIASES

We have already given several examples of how perceptual distortions and attribution biases can affect people at work. Three specific areas that should be especially noted are:

1. Problem solving and decision making.
2. Performance appraisal.
3. Managing workplace diversity.

Problem Solving and Decision Making

Effective management requires making good decisions when solving problems, and effective problem solving requires identifying the most likely cause of the problem. Biased attributions can occur in identifying problems. For example, a committee will blame other groups or departments when problems occur. Here, the self-serving bias can damage cooperation between groups and fail to uncover the true causes of the problem. Another difficulty in problem identification occurs because we tend, when looking at difficult situations, to interpret them in terms of our own experiences and capacity to solve problems. It has been shown, for instance, that when faced with identifying problems to be solved in a complex business situation, managers have a tendency to emphasize more strongly a problem definition that reflects their own functional competence than other functional areas (Dearborn and Simon, 1958; Walsh, 1988). This means, for example, that human resource manager is more likely to perceive a problem to be based on personnel deficiencies, while a production manager is likely to see the problem as having more technical issues that must be solved. The importance of correct problem identification is obvious: trying to solve the wrong problem will not correct the situation.

Performance Appraisal

Attribution biases also operate in performance appraisal. The attribution errors can create serious disagreements between raters and ratees about performance. Some research shows that we look at both effort and ability in evaluating performance, but give more weight to effort (Knowlton and Mitchell, 1980). Effort is weighted higher for both good and poor performance: good performance is rated higher and poor performance lower when effort, rather than ability, is seen as the cause. Thus we are evaluated more on how hard someone who is judging us thinks we are trying. If our boss feels we put in a lot of effort, we will be appraised higher when we succeed. If we are seen as not trying very hard, we will be rated more poorly when we fail. We are also likely to be judged on whether the information that the rater has about us prior to the performance evaluation itself is positive or negative. Raters who had positive information about the performance of work groups tended to attribute more effective behaviors and less ineffective behaviors to the group (Martell and Leavitt, 2002).

Managing Workplace Diversity

Perceptual errors are even more critical problems when ethnic or sex differences are added to the situation. The workforce in the USA is now far more multicultural than ever, but still the number of women and minorities in management jobs is under-represented. One evaluation of the research on selection procedures and performance evaluation shows that minorities are rated lower by supervisors (Martocchio and Whitener, 1992). Hiring biases are also affected by other factors such as gender (Latino women suffer less hiring discrimination than Latino men), the source of recruitment (private employment agencies are more discriminatory), the type of job (there was more discrimination for jobs not requiring college degrees) and location of the job (there was greater bias when selecting for inner-city jobs) (Bendick et al., 1991). However, the bias issue does not only exist in the dominant white male group. For example, a survey of males, females, African Americans, Asian Americans, Native Americans and Hispanic Americans reveals that there is bias and stereotyping of other groups by these groups. In addition, there is bias and stereotyping within their own groups as, for example, the view of women by men within each group (Fernandez, 1991).

Stereotypes are also hard at work when it comes to evaluating men and women. Studies show a tendency to attribute female successes to hard work or luck rather than to ability (Feldman-Summers and Kiesler, 1974). Men, on the other hand, are more protected from adverse evaluations. Interestingly, both males and females make these biased attributions. Men's successes are usually attributed to competence, and their failures to bad luck. From a woman's perspective, it is better if her successes are attributed to ability, rather than to effort or situational conditions. Some recent work showed that when women are successful, they are less well liked and receive more negative criticism than men, especially when they hold positions more characteristically associated with men (Fuchs et al., 2004). Such gender-biased attributions insult women and place them at a disadvantage because they are given less credit than males for their skills, which will have a negative impact on women's careers. It is well known, also, that there is a wage gap, favoring men over women even when women are in comparable jobs and perform as well as men (Ostroff and Atwater, 2003).

SUMMARY

Attitudes, perceptions and judgment tendencies have widespread and important implications in the world of work. Employee attitudes can make a huge difference in the effectiveness of an organization. They affect such things as attendance, retention, work commitments and interpersonal reactions. Perceptions and judgments are critical because they enter into so many work situations: selecting applicants, making assignments, appraising performance, giving feedback, solving problems, and so on.

Attitudes refer to what people like and dislike; they predispose them to act favorably or unfavorably toward an object or event. They function in several ways to help people to adapt to their world. Attitudes are related to beliefs and values. All three are acquired from infancy through our experiences and associations with people, events and the media. Specific attitudes can be learned at any time and apply to any experience. Employers often study employee attitudes about various aspects of their job, because it is known that attitudes affect satisfaction, performance and constructive voluntary contributions to organizational success.

The study of perception is central to understanding how people react. Each of us has certain perceptual tendencies that define the world from our own personal point of view. Values, emotional states, needs and personality all come into play. Characteristics of the object and situation also affect what we select, how we organize what we perceive and how we make interpretations. Most critical are the errors in judgment we make about the world around us. An important tendency is how we make causal inferences about what we perceive. We tend to attribute other people's behavior to their personality rather than to situational forces. When judging ourselves, however, we are more likely to have a self-serving bias. We also attribute our successes not to external forces, but to our own skills and abilities.

GUIDES FOR MANAGERS: MAKING BETTER JUDGMENTS

Making Better Judgments about Attitudes

There are a number of things that we can do to make better judgments about attitudes of others in evaluating their suitability for almost everything that goes on in organizations. For example, in interviews, prospective employees are often asked, 'How do you feel about working here?' or 'How satisfied were you with the type of work that you did in your previous job?' Attitudes are also important when evaluating someone for promotion. We hear comments like, 'He doesn't have a good attitude toward affirmative action' or, 'He just doesn't believe enough in quality to do the job right.' This means that we should be very careful about judging attitudes of others (as well as our own, we might add).

Focus on Specific, Rather than General Attitudes

Rather than generalizing, such as saying that an employee has a good or a bad attitude, it is better to try to focus on employee attitudes in terms of their more specific objects, such as attitudes toward pay, supervision, and so on. This helps you to decide what you have to change in the organization, such as modifying the pay system or training supervisors. There is often very little that you can do about these general attitudes, since they may reflect the positive or negative affectivity of the person.

Notice Depth of Feeling and Behavior

Do not dismiss or underestimate the depth of feeling and the behavior associated with attitudes, values and beliefs. Don't trivialize the attitudes of others by thinking or telling them that their feelings aren't important. Attitudes are very important to the psychological well-being of people and some are strongly held, especially those linked to the person's self-image. More importantly, they may be related to attitudes, values and beliefs that are not directly related to work itself.

Understand how Attitudes Work at Work

Negative attitudes toward the job or the organization may lead an employee to want to avoid work or quit, and they may do so because job satisfaction is negatively related to turnover and to commitment. However, never assume that a satisfied employee is always a productive employee or that a productive employee is satisfied. There is a relationship between attitudes and task performance, and it is statistically significant.

Periodically Assess Employee Attitudes and Satisfaction

It is a good idea for organizations to evaluate attitudes and satisfaction with employee surveys. It is also useful to involve the employees in the design, collection and interpretation of the study. However, never conduct surveys unless you are fully committed to act on the findings and report the actions you have taken.

Accept People's Tendency to Justify, Rationalize and Explain their Beliefs

It helps them to reduce cognitive dissonance, and to appear consistent to themselves and others. However, you should strive to ensure that they understand as clearly as possible what is expected in terms of work performance and that you can accept their attitudes so long as they do not have negative effects on others or on their own performance.

Using Theories of Perception and of the Attributions of Causes and Effects

Theories of perception and of the attribution of causes and effects are also useful to managers. Think about problem solving, for example. We can solve only those problems of which we are aware of, or perceive. But beyond simply recognizing that a problem exists, we are faced with the question, 'What is the cause?' The same is true for evaluating the performance of another. We need to know why performance is high or low. Here are some ways to sharpen your perceptions and attributions.

Don't assume your reality is another person's reality
Perceptions of events (selecting, interpreting, organizing) will vary from person to person, and become each person's individual reality. Many things affect the accuracy of a perception. It pays to seek confirmation of events. If you are part of a group trying to solve a problem, try to find a consensus definition of the situation. Be careful, however, not to be stampeded into an agreed-upon, but wrong, set of perceptions.

Keep the common judgment tendencies in mind
You can reduce the common errors that lead to inaccurate assessments by not rushing to judgments based on stereotyping, halo, and so on. These can be reduced through training and other techniques that seek factual data from several sources. Also remember that the self-serving bias is

widespread and impossible to eliminate; it must be accepted as a factor in interpreting what other people say and do. Also, don't forget that it applies to you yourself.

Fight the fundamental attribution error

Seek environmental or situational causes to explain someone's behavior instead of blaming their personality. This is particularly important wherever judgment tendencies and errors are causing problems, such as when women, minorities or any other employees are unfairly treated as a consequence. Examples may be found in how performance appraisals, task assignments or promotion decisions are made.

CASE : A BAD DAY IN BODENBERG

Geert, plant manager of the Bodenberg facility, sat with his elbows on his desk, holding his head. 'What a day! I've never seen it like this', he said aloud, though he was alone in his office. He was relieved that in a few minutes he could get into his car and head for home. He couldn't remember when it all began, but knew that Karl had burst into his office before he'd finished his first cup of coffee.

'Those guys in Manufacturing wouldn't give you the right time of day!' said Karl, the marketing manager. 'All I wanted was to get this big order scheduled, and you'd think I was asking for the moon. Those manufacturing people are all the same. They hate to touch a thing once a schedule is set.' Geert tried to calm him down, but Karl went on. 'I even tried to talk to Junger. I figured maybe a new guy would help me out. But I should have known better. Last week at the welcoming party for him, I sensed he wasn't any different. I guess I was right. I shouldn't have wasted my time on him.'

Geert told Karl he'd look into the matter, though he knew this wasn't anything new. He also knew he needed to get Manufacturing and Marketing to cooperate more. After answering a few phone calls, Geert strolled out to the Manufacturing area to see what he could find out. He didn't even have to let on that Karl had come to see him. They were hot under the collar in Production, too. Peter Keinegen, manufacturing manager, and Sylvia Greckhamer, chief scheduler, were discussing Karl's visit and turned to Geert for counsel.

Sylvia began, 'I'm not sure how concerned those Marketing people are for manufacturing schedules and costs. They all think we can stop a run and set up for a new order in five minutes. I think they're conditioned to bark three times every time a customer calls. I'll bet half of them let their children tell them what to do!'

Peter had his own ideas as well. He stood up and paced the floor, then in a controlled voice said, 'Marketing needs some appreciation for the total company. I can't figure out why they constantly tie us up in knots. They make impossible promises to customers. They should know better. Where did they get their training? Don't they value what our situation is? I'm pretty sure no one in this company is forcing them to make the delivery commitments they make!'

Geert did what he could to soothe bad feelings, and promised Peter and Sylvia he'd have a meeting in a day or two to discuss these issues. He was particularly upset with Sylvia's attitude. On more than one occasion she had been very critical toward other people. He wondered whether she had what it took to do the job. Much of her performance was good, he admitted. She certainly put in enough hours trying to improve and enforce the manufacturing schedule.

How many perceptual and judgmental tendencies do Geert, Karl, Peter and Sylvia exhibit?

REFERENCES

Anderson, C.A. and K.E. Dill (2000), Video Games and Aggressive Thoughts, Feelings, and Behavior in the Laboratory and in Life. *Journal of Personality and Social Psychology*, **78**(4): 772–90.

Ajzen, I. and M. Fishbein (2005), The Influence of Attitudes on Behavior. In *The Handbook of Attitudes*, D.J. Albarracín, B.T. Johnson and Mark P. Zanna (eds). Mahwah, NJ: Lawrence Erlbaum Associates, pp. 173–221.

Barger, P.B. and A.A. Grandey (2006), Service with a Smile and Encounter Satisfaction: Emotional Contagion and Appraisal Mechanisms. *Academy of Management Journal*, **49**(6): 1229–38.

Bateman, T.S. and D.W. Organ (1983), Job Satisfactions and the Good Soldier: The Relationship Between Affect and Employee 'Citizenship'. *Academy of Management Journal*, **26**: 587–95.

Bendick, M., C.W. Jackson, V.A. Reinoso and L.E. Hodges (1991), Discrimination against Latino Job Applicants: A Controlled Experiment. *Human Resource Management*, **30**(4): 469–84.

Bradfield, A. and G.L. Wells (2005), Not the Same Old Hindsight Bias: Outcome Information Distorts a Broad Range of Retrospective Judgments. *Memory and Cognition*, **33**(1): 120–30.

Brief, A.P. and H.M. Weiss (2002), Organizational Behavior: Affect in the Workplace. *Annual Review of Psychology*, **53**(1): 279–310.

Brown, S.C., W.L. Cron and J.W. Slocum (1997), Effects of Goal-Directed Emotions on Salesperson Volitions, Behavior, and Performance: A Longitudinal Study. *Journal of Marketing*, **61**(1): 39–50.

Clark, L.A. and D. Watson (1988), Mood and the Mundane: Relations between Daily Life Events and Self-reported Mood. *Journal of Personality and Social Psychology*, **54**(2): 296–308.

Clore, G.L.S.S. and S. Schnall (2005), The Influence of Affect on Attitude. In *The Handbook of Attitudes*, D.J. Albarracín, B.T. Johnson and Mark P. Zanna (eds). Mahwah, NJ: Lawrence Erlbaum Associates, pp. 437–90.

Coon, D. (1991), *Essentials of Psychology*. St Paul MN: West Publishing Company.

Cote, S. and L.M. Morgan (2002), A Longitudinal Analysis of the Association between Emotion Regulation, Job Satisfaction, and Intentions to Quit. *Journal of Organizational Behavior*, **23**(8): 947–63.

Dearborn, D.C. and H.A. Simon (1958), Selective Perception: A Note on the Departmental Identifications of Executives. *Sociometry*, **21**: 140–44.

Duval, T.S. and P.J. Silvia (2002), Self-awareness, Probability of Improvement, and the Self-serving Bias. *Journal of Personality and Social Psychology*, **82**(1): 49–61.

Eagly, A.H. and S. Chaiken (2005), Attitude Research in the 21st Century: The Current State of Knowledge. In *The Handbook of Attitudes*, D.J. Albarracín, B.T. Johnson and Mark P. Zanna (eds). Mahwah, NJ: Lawrence Erlbaum Associate, pp. 743–67.

Erez, A., V.F. Misangyi, D.E. Johnson, M.A. LePine and K.C. Halvorsen (2008), Stirring the Hearts of Followers: Charismatic Leadership as the Transferal of Affect. *Journal of Applied Psychology*, **93**(3): 602–16.

Feldman-Summers, S. and S.B. Kiesler (1974), Those Who are Number Two Try Harder: The Effect of Sex on the Attribution of Causality. *Journal of Personality and Social Psychology*, **30**: 846–55.

Felson, R.B. (1981), Ambiguity and Bias in the Self-Concept. *Social Psychology Quarterly*, **44**: 64–9.

Fernandez, P. (1991), Managing a Diverse Work Force. Lexington, MA: Lexington Books.

Festinger, L. (1957), *A Theory of Cognitive Dissonance*. Evanston, IL: Row, Peterson.

Fineman, M. (1993), Organizations as Emotional Arenas. In *Emotions in Organizations*, M. Fineman (ed.). London: Sage, pp. 9–35.

Fishbein, M. and I. Ajzen (1975), *Belief, Attitude, Intention and Behavior: An Introduction to Theory and Research*. Reading, MA: Addison-Wesley.

Fuchs, D., M.M. Tamkins, M.E. Heilman and A.S. Wallen (2004), Penalties for Success: Reactions to Women Who Succeed at Male Gender-Typed Tasks. *Journal of Applied Psychology*, **89**(3): 416–27.

George, J.M. and G.R. Jones (1966), The Experience of Work and Turnover Intentions: Interactive Effects of Value Attainment, Job Satisfaction and Postive Mood. *Journal of Applied Psychology*, **81**(3): 318–26.

Goleman, D. (2006a), *Social Intelligence: The New Science of Human Relationships*. New York: Bantam Books.

Goleman, D. (2006b), *Emotional Intelligence*. New York: Bantam Books.

Hosoda, M., E.F. Stone-Romero and G. Coats (2003), The Effects of Physical Attractiveness on Job-Related Outcomes: A Meta-Analysis of Experimental Studies. *Personnel Psychology*, **56**(2): 431–62.

Iaffaldano, M.T. and P.M. Muchinsky (1985), Job Satisfaction and Job Performance: A Meta-Analysis. *Psychological Bulletin*, **97**: 251–73.

Innocenti, L. and M. Pilati (2009), Employee Work Beliefs, Trust and Human Resources Management Practices. Paper presented at Euram, Liverpool.

Judge, T.A., J.W. Boudreau and R.D. Bretz (1944), Job and Life Attitudes of Executives. *Journal of Applied Psychology*, **79**(5): 767–82.

Judge, T.A., C.J. Thorensen, J.E. Bono and G.K. Patton (2001), The Job Satisfaction–Job Performance Relationship: A Qualitative and Quantitative Review. *Psychological Bulletin*, **127**(3): 376–407.

Katz, D. (1960), The Functional Approach to the Study of Attitude Change. *Public Opinion Quarterly*, **24**: 163–204.

Kelly, H.H. (1973), The Process of Causal Attribution. *American Psychologist*, **28**: 107–28.

Knowlton, W.A., Jr and T.R. Mitchell (1980), Effects of Causal Attributions on a Supervisor's Evaluation of Subordinate Performance. *Journal of Applied Psychology*, **65**: 459–66.

Kulik, C.T. and M.L. Ambrose (1993), Category Based and Feature Based Processes in Performance Appraisal: Integrating Visual and Computerized Sources of Performance Data. *Journal of Applied Psychology*, **78**(5): 821–30.

Labianca, G., H. Moon and I. Watt (2005), When Is an Hour not 60 Minutes? Deadlines, Temporal Schemata, and Individual and Task Group Performance. *Academy of Management Journal*, **48**(4): 677–94.

LePine, J.A., A. Erez and D.E. Johnson (2002), The Nature and Dimensionality of Organizational Citizenship Behavior: A Critical Review and Meta-Analysis. *Journal of Applied Psychology*, **87**(1): 52–65.

Locke, K. (1996), A Funny Thing Happened! The Management of Consumer Emotions in Service Encounters. *Organization Science*, **7**(1): 40–59.

Martell, R.F. and K.N. Leavitt (2002), Reducing the Performance-Cue Bias in Work Behavior Ratings: Can Groups Help? *Journal of Applied Psychology*, **87**(6): 1032–41.

Martocchio, J.J. and E.M. Whitener (1992), Fairness in Personnel Selection: A Meta-Analysis and Policy Implications. *Human Relations*, **45**(5): 489–506.

Mihail, D.M. (2006), Women in Management: Gender Stereotypes and Students' Attitudes in Greece. *Women in Management Review*, **21**(8): 681–9.

Myers, D.G. (1983), *Social Psychology*. New York: McGraw-Hill.

Ostroff, C. and L.E. Atwater (2003), Does Whom You Work With Matter? Effects of Referent Group Gender and Age Composition on Managers' Compensation. *Journal of Applied Psychology*, **88**(4): 725–40.

Pilati, M. and L. Innocenti (2008), Human Resource Practices and Employees' Attitudes: Do Work Experiences Mediate? Paper presented at the annual conference of the British Academy of Management, Harrogate, UK, 9–11 September.

Pilati, M. and L. Innocenti (2009), Worker Participation, Organisational Climate and Change. Bulletin of Comparative Labour Relations, Kluwer Law International, the Netherlands.

Pilati M., L. Innocenti and A. Peluso (2010), Trust and Management Behaviour in the Relationship between Employees and Organisation. Paper presented at 26th Egos Colloquium, Lisbon, 1–3 July.

Priddle, A. (2009), Less Culture Clash with Fiat, Chrysler. *Detroit News*, 2 November, p. 2.

Rafaeli, A. and R.I. Sutton (1987), Expression of Emotion as Part of the Work Role. *Academy of Management Review*, **12**(1): 23–37.

Rafaeli, A.and R.I. Sutton (1990), Busy Stores and Demanding Customers: How Do They Affect the Display of Positive Emotion?. *Academy of Management Journal*, **33**(3): 623–37.

Ross, L.D. (1977), The Intuitive Psychologist and His Shortcomings: Distortions in the Attribution Process. In *Advances in Experimental Social Psychology*, L. Berkowitz (ed.). New York: Academic Press, pp. 220–26.

Sherman, D.K. and H.S. Kim (2005), Is there an 'I' in 'Team'? The Role of the Self in Group-Serving Judgments. *Journal of Personality and Social Psychology*, **88**(1): 108–20.

Staw, B.M. (1976), Knee-Deep in the Big Muddy: A Study of Escalating Commitment to a Chosen Course of Action. *Organizational Behavior and Human Performance*, **16**(1): 27–44.

Staw, B.M. and J. Ross (1987a), Knowing When to Pull the Plug. *Harvard Business Review*, **65**(2): 68–74.

Staw, B.M. and J. Ross (1987b), Behavior in Escalation Situations: Antecedents, Prototypes, and Solutions. In *Research in Organizational Behavior*, L.L. Cummings and B.M. Staw (eds). Greenwich, CT: JAI Press, pp. 37–78.

Staw, B.M., R.I. Sutton and L.H. Pelled (1994), Employee Positive Emotion and Favorable Outcomes at the Workplace. *Organization Science*, **5**(1): 51–71.

Tosi, H.L., J.P. Katz and L.R. Gomez-Mejia (1997), Disaggregating the Agency Contract: The Effects of Monitoring, Incentive Alignment, and Term in Office on Agent Decision Making. *Academy of Management Journal*, **40**(3): 584–602.

Viswesvaran, C., F.L. Schmidt and D.S. Ones (2005), Is There a General Factor in Ratings of Job Performance? A Meta-Analytic Framework for Disentangling Substantive and Error Influences. *Journal of Applied Psychology*, **90**(1): 108–31.

Vroom, V.H. (1964), *Work and Motivation*. New York: John Wiley.
Walsh, J.P. (1988), Selectivity and Selective Perception: An Investigation of Managers' Belief Structures and Information Processes. *Academy of Management Journal*, **31**(4): 873–96.
Watson, D. (2000), *Mood and Temperament*. New York: Guilford Press.

3. Motivation

PREPARING FOR CLASS

Consider three behaviors that are relevant to this course:

1. Your choice of academic major.
2. Your choice of profession that you are pursuing or hope to pursue.
3. How hard you are working in this class.

Note that two of these behaviors involve choices made through some form of decision process and one involves level of effort. After reviewing the motivation theories discussed in this chapter, choose which theories best explain the three behaviors you listed.

1. Were some theories more useful than others in explaining certain types of behaviors?
2. Do the theories complement each other or do they provide very different explanations for behavior?

* *

Francesca is a third-year university student who studies economics. She has recently had the opportunity to study for one semester as part of the Erasmus Project. She knew that this was a chance to come face to face with students from different cultures and to improve her skills in the English language.

During the time away she took a course and passed an exam on the global banking industry. When she returned to her home university she asked to have the exam validated and included in her record. The Records Office told her that this couldn't be done because the course was not part of the program in which she participated. However, she could ask the professor responsible for the course at her university to validate the course for her. So she did.

It was evident from the course syllabus that listed the texts, the exams, the number of credits and the comprehensiveness of the course that it was similar to one at her own university, and perhaps even more comprehensive and better designed. Despite this, the instructor refused to validate her course and concluded the discussion by saying: 'Listen, young lady, I do not want waste my and your time: these are rules and policies which the university applies. As far as I am concerned, I consider our conversation over.' Francesca, sad and disappointed, resigned herself to the decision.

This case is a situation where a student perceives an injustice that can have a strong motivational effect on her, not only because of the professor's reply to her request, but also because of the processes, policies and procedures of the university. We return to this example later, in our discussion of organizational justice theory.

For most managers, the words 'motivation' and 'performance' go together. Motivation is a seductive subject for many managers who believe in it for many reasons, some right and some wrong. One reason is that work motivation is an important value in Western society. In Western society in general, and particularly in the USA, there has been a historical stress on the 'work ethic'. The work ethic belief – that work is good and that it should be valued – is so strongly ingrained in some that if they do not have an opportunity to work, they have psychological and social problems. Health statistics from areas experiencing long and extensive lay-offs show increases in anxiety and depression, and often suicide.

Second, many managers believe that the improved performance resulting from motivation is free. Imagine that you hire a worker for $10 per hour who produces five units per hour. The unit labor cost is $2. If the worker has the potential to produce ten units each hour and does so without the need to buy new equipment, the unit labor costs drops to $1. To make such a gain with improved equipment would cost money; through motivation it seems to be free. However it is not the case that improvements can be made through motivation without cost. A highly motivated workforce only comes with good selection, sound compensation practices, training and the use of good human resource management practices, all of which 'cost'.

Third, motivation is an explanation of why some organizations are more productive than others. Suppose you take a tour of two breweries and there are no identification signs to inform you whether you are in the Coors brewery or one owned by Anheuser-Busch Inbev. The equipment looks very similar. The two buildings look alike. If there are any differences in productivity and the equipment is the same, it is only logical to conclude that these differences arise because of the people involved. The problem with this perspective is that it generally attributes the responsibility for poor performance to the worker, and ignores the possibility that the management is poor.

MOTIVATION AND PERFORMANCE

Consider this situation: Lance Roberts has a burning desire to be a good tennis player. He spends hours practicing, reads all the instructional magazines, regularly takes lessons, and plays almost every day. Blaine Davis is one of Lance's regular weekly matches. Every Wednesday afternoon they play and Blaine usually wins. It is especially frustrating to Lance because Blaine hardly practices and plays only twice, at the most three times, each week.

This example illustrates that performance (or results) is a function of two things: motivation and ability. This is the basis of a very fundamental relationship for understanding human performance in organizations:

$$\text{Performance} = f(\text{Ability} \times \text{Motivation})$$

Figure 3.1 shows how these three factors are related. On one axis is performance, and on the other, motivation. The lines in the figure represent the abilities of both men. They show that Lance has less tennis ability than Blaine. Therefore, if both are equally motivated (say at point X), then Blaine will always win. Lance will only win when he has high motivation (at point Y) and Blaine is not highly motivated to perform (near point Z).

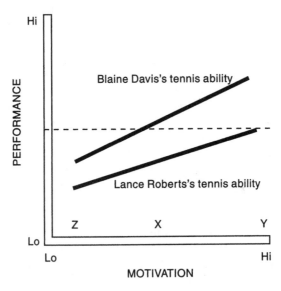

Figure 3.1   Relationship between performance, motivation and ability

What Do We Mean by Performance?

Performance results from mental or physical effort. Performance levels can be stated in terms of quantity or quality, and require some subjective judgment by a manager. A particular level of performance may be judged as 'high' by one person, but the same level may be only 'satisfactory', or perhaps 'unsatisfactory', for another. It is a little more complicated when we think about job performance because most jobs have several distinct elements and therefore require several different types of performance.

Spotlight 3.1 Developing performance competence: Zen and archery

A way to think about developing competence and internal motivation at something is described by Eugen Herrigel, a German philosophy professor, in his book *Zen in the Art of Archery*. Being no longer necessary in wartime because of the development of firearms, archery in Japan has become an art, a spiritual exercise and very ritualistic. The process of becoming a Zen archer is much more than developing the motor skills of nocking the arrow, taking aim at a target, then letting the arrow fly. For the Zen archer it is a natural process in which the archer loses himself:

Zen is the 'everyday mind,' [it] is no more than 'sleeping when tired, eating when hungry.' As soon as we reflect, deliberate, and conceptualize, the original unconsciousness is lost and a thought interferes. We no longer eat while eating, we no longer sleep while sleeping. The arrow is off the string but does not fly straight to the target, nor does the target stand still. Calculation which is miscalculation sets in [and the] archer's confused mind betrays itself in every direction and every field of activity. (Suzuki, in *Zen and the Art of Archery*, Herrigel, 1981 [1953]: vii).

What the archer must do is develop the capacity to shoot without thinking, and in a way detached from the process. The archer learns that the focus must be on the target, but the objective is not to hit the center. Through concentration and breathing exercises, the archer learns to relax his muscles as much as possible, forgetting the strain in the hands and the arms, and the direction of the arrow. The archer must become detached from these physical and material things and the become detached so that the arrow is released without tension, as the 'bamboo leaf . . .

> bends lower and lower under the weight of the snow. Suddenly the snow slips to the ground without the leaf having stirred. Stay like that until the shot falls from you', the Master said. But the most important thing that the archer learns is to aim not really at the target, but at his internal 'I'. When these things are learned, the target will be centered and will be struck by the arrow (Herrigel, 1981 [1953]).

The different elements are called performance components, relatively discrete subtasks or behaviors that require different abilities and which might have different motivational predispositions. Jobs have two major types of performance components – task performance components and contextual performance components:

- Task performance components are the activities required to do the work itself. For example, a plant manager must have the ability and the motivation to manage production and quality levels, prepare work schedules, order supplies, deal with subordinates and run departmental meetings.
- Contextual performance components are behaviors that go beyond task performance and are essential if organizations are to excel, because success depends on employees going beyond formal task role (Borman and Motowildo, 1993).

These performance components are also referred to as prosocial or organizational citizenship behavior (Borman and Motowildo, 1993; Organ, 1988: 888), and reflect the extent to which a person is willing to go beyond the norms of performance and involvement of his or her work role (Organ, 1988: 888). They are:

- Altruistic behavior.
- Conscientious behavior.
- Sportsmanlike behavior.
- Courtesy.
- Civic virtue.

Ability

Ability is the capacity to carry out a set of interrelated behavioral or mental sequences to produce a result. For example, to play the piano requires that you be able to read music, understand chord structures and have the manual dexterity to finger the keyboard. Generally, it is easy to see ability differences between two individuals; it is often apparent among individuals who perform similar jobs.

It is also important to remember that any specific individual has different abilities. A person may be a highly skilled architect but have very low communication skills. Since most job performance is multidimensional, it follows that the person who is assigned to do the job must have adequate ability for each different performance component. For example, the plant manager's job involves scheduling work, dealing with subordinates (handling grievances, supervision, and so on) and running departmental meetings. Each of these separate activities requires different skills, and a person can be good in some and poor in others.

The Role of Technology

Technology refers to the methods, tools, facilities and equipment a person uses in performing a task. Technology interacts with ability to affect performance, but in different ways. For example, auto workers 'use' a complex production system with highly independent activities to manufacture a car. An artist's technology may be a canvas, paint and brushes.

Most task performance components involve the use of some technology, but for some of them, technology is more important than for others. For example, the technology of the production line is critical for the task performance component 'managing production levels' of a plant manager's job. However, for the task performance component 'dealing with subordinates', the impact of technology is minimal; human skill is more important.

Since technology plays different roles, it is useful to think of any specific task as being either skill-dominated or technology-dominated. In skill-dominated tasks, individual skill is the most important factor. A fashion designer's job is an example of skill-dominated work. Giving a designer better equipment is likely to have only a marginal effect on performance, just as giving Blaine and Lance, our tennis players, better clubs, balls and shoes will probably not improve their game very much because tennis, like most sports, is a skill-dominated task.

Contrast this with assembly-line work, an example of a technology-dominated task. Only limited human skills are required in the job; technology is the most important factor. Figure 3.2 shows how technology can affect performance. Here you have enough motivation and ability to perform at a minimum level; for instance, to start the machine. From there

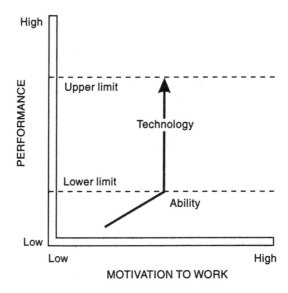

Figure 3.2   Technology-dominated work

on, the equipment determines how well the job is done. The lower and upper limits of performance are set by the technology. When technology sets such limits, one cannot expect performance to increase simply because one obtains competent or more motivated people.

There are several important things to learn when viewing performance in this way.

1. Specific and different abilities are required for the various task components of a job. A person may be more talented in one performance component and less in another. A quarterback for a football team may be an excellent passer but a very poor runner.
2. A person may be more motivated (willing to put forth more effort) for one performance component than others; the plant manager, for example, might rather manage production and quality than spend time in dealing with subordinates.
3. For some performance components, significant levels of technology may be required to achieve results. For example, required production levels in a plant cannot be achieved unless the appropriate equipment is operating effectively. Technology is not critical, however, in running a meeting; for this, human skill is most crucial.
4. Technology and human skill may be interchangeable. When technology is substituted for human skill, it often leads to more predictable

and dependable performance. Consider a task as simple as making coffee. Until the introduction of automatic coffee makers, making a good cup of coffee required a great deal of skill. With the automatic technology, it is a task that a child can do.

What Do We Mean by Motivation?

The term 'motivation' has both a psychological and a managerial connotation in the field of organizational behavior. The psychological meaning of motivation refers to the internal mental state of a person which relates to the initiation, direction, persistence, intensity and termination of behavior (Landy and Becker, 1987). It determines what you do at work (the direction), how hard you work (the intensity of your behavior) and how long you work (the persistence) (Kanfer, 1990). The source of motivation can be intrinsic or extrinsic. Intrinsic motivation leads to behavior that can be thought of as being for its own sake rather than because you expect to receive something for it (Pinder, 2008), and is usually likely to make you feel more competent and self-determining (Deci, 1971). When your actions are driven by rewards controlled or applied by other sources, it is called extrinsic motivation.

The managerial meaning of motivation refers to the activity of managers to select persons who have high intrinsic motivation, or to induce others to produce results desired by the organization or, perhaps, by the manager through the application of extrinsic rewards. In this context, we might say: 'The role of every manager is to motivate employees to work harder or to do better.' The managerial concept of motivation is illustrated in Figure 3.3, which shows the relationship between motivation, ability and performance for two football teams about to play each other. For simplification, we assume that the teams are equal in personal motivation (at level 2), but that they differ in overall ability as shown by the diagonal lines in the diagram. Suppose the coach of the Blues takes the game between the teams lightly because of the Oranges' superior ability. He gives the team only a little boost to level 2.23. The coach of the Scarlets recognizes the Grays' superior ability and inspires his team to put forth a great deal more effort. If the coach of the Grays can move the players to a high level of motivation (to level 4), they will win the game despite having lower ability.

In Chapter 1 (on personality), we said that motivation is linked to our affective dimension. Because of personality differences, you can expect that there will be different emotions, needs, preferences and values for different people. These will guide their actions in situations that they face. This is because a person's behavior, or performance, is a result of what the person is (in terms of ability and personality dispositions) and the specific situation. Further, as we say below, how we perceive the situation is a function

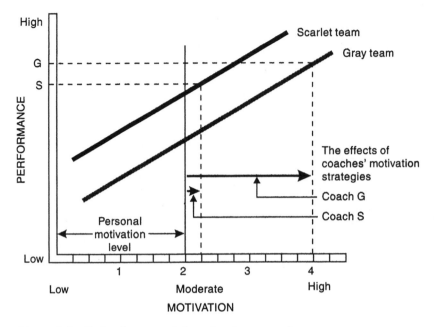

Figure 3.3   Role of managerial motivation strategies

of our personality, values and emotions. The 'ultimatum game' is a clear example of how motivations are influenced by emotion. In the 'ultimatum game' two players have to decide how to split an amount of money given to them. However, only one player can propose the amount to be given to the other, and the second person can only accept or reject the proposal. If the proposal is rejected, the game ends. Rationally, the offer, although though it might seem unfair, should be accepted, but often anger and pride will push the second actor to refuse, feeling wounded and offended.

Classes of motivation theories
Any motivation theory attempts to account for the reasons why people behave as they do and the processes that cause the behavior:

- Content theories focus on 'what' motivates behavior.
- Process theories focus on 'how' behavior is motivated.

We use this distinction between content and process theories of motivation because it highlights the main orientation of a particular formulation about motivation. However, content theories have some process orientation, and process theories usually have some content dimensions. For example, content theories usually focus on a human need of some type. The strength of that need – and the specific way that a person wishes to satisfy it – are usually learned through socialization, a process that can be understood in reinforcement theory terms. As you study the theories in this chapter, you will see that these two orientations – content and process – are present in each of them.

MOTIVATION: THE CONTENT THEORIES

Content theories of motivation emphasize the reasons for motivated behavior; that is, 'what' causes it. A content theory would explain behavioral aspects in terms of specific human needs or specific factors that 'drive' behavior. For example, you might say that: 'Joan is motivated to work for higher pay', or, 'John did that because he has a high need for power.' In this section, we discuss four different content theories:

- Need theory and, in particular, Maslow's need theory and ERG theory.
- Herzberg's two-factor theory.
- The job characteristics approach.
- McClelland's achievement–power theory.

It is important to point out at the outset, however, that a motivational approach that works in one cultural context may not work in another because of differences in values and preferences. For example, a large US company operating in 46 countries with more than 20 000 employees found significant differences in preferences and motivations of its employees (Sirota and Greenwood, 1971). In the English-speaking countries, individual successes are emphasized more than security. The French-speaking countries tend to give greater importance to the safety of the work rather than to challenging objectives. In Northern European countries free time is the most important thing, and there is greater attention to the needs of employees and less to those of the organization. The Latin countries, Germany, Italy and South European countries give greater emphasis to the safety of the work and fringe benefits. Japanese employees give more importance to good working conditions and a pleasant working environment.

Need Theories

Need theories of motivation assume that people act to satisfy their needs. A need (or a motive) is aroused when the person senses that there is some

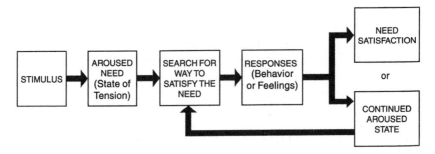

Figure 3.4   A needs approach to motivation

difference between the present (or, perhaps, a future) condition and some desired state. When a 'need' is aroused, the person feels some tension and acts to reduce it. This sequence is shown in Figure 3.4.

Suppose a manager tells you about a vacancy at a higher organizational level and that the position will be filled by the most productive worker in the group. This may arouse your desire for advancement, achievement or more pay. If your need is aroused, you will search for ways to satisfy it. You might work harder, which is what the manager wanted. If your harder work leads to a promotion, then the need is satisfied. If it does not, the desire for promotion may be suppressed and lead to frustration or you might decide to seek a job elsewhere.

Ways to satisfy needs are learned through socialization, and so people differ with respect to the needs that are important to them. We learn through experience that some situations are more rewarding than others, and seek these out; other situations, we try to avoid.

Need theory is elegant in its simplicity and appeal. If, as the theory suggests, people are concerned with satisfying their needs, then all that has to be done is to provide for need satisfaction opportunities in the workplace. Yet, for a very simple reason, this is not so easy to translate into practice: a particular need may be satisfied in different ways for different people. For example, one person's need for self-esteem may be satisfied by being recognized as the best worker in a department; another may find this need satisfied by others' recognition of his or her dress style – being acknowledged as the sharpest dresser in the group.

Maslow's need theory
In organizational behavior, the most popular need theory of motivation by far is the one developed by Abraham Maslow (1943). He believed that human needs could be categorized into five categories:

Spotlight 3.2 Aristotle on motivation

Aristotelian concepts ideas underlie the dominant motivation theories in organizational behavior. Aristotle believed that motivation is the result of a desire, a human appetite, that is related to some outcome. The object of desire can be either real or apparent, and initiates movement toward the object. The images of the object are a result of mental perceptual processes. The perception of the object as resulting in pleasure or pain drives human behavior. According to Aristotle the principle of the pleasure and the avoidance of pain is the basis of the motivation. Expectancy theory, for example, is based on an Aristotelian principle: motivation results mainly from internal expectations of the potential consequences that are a result of various actions. These expectations are the main source of motivation. From Aristotle's point of view, what people feel and the way in which they act depend on the value, positive or negative, that they themselves determine, and the causes that attach to the subsequent consequences that they believe will follow. High 'positive' expectations, for example, can push people to more effort in the hope of achieving the desired results. Consequences that are perceived as 'negative' will lead to apathy or expulsion [from the mind].

---

1. Physiological needs are the basic requirements for survival. Humans must have food to live, and shelter is necessary. Physical well-being must be provided for before anything else can assume importance for a person.
2. Safety needs reflect a desire for protection against loss of shelter, food and other basic requirements for survival. Security needs also involve the desire to live in a stable and predictable environment. It may also involve a preference for order and structure.
3. Belonging needs reflect the person's desire for love, affection and belonging. The need to interact with others and have some social acceptance and approval is shared by most people. For some, this need may be satisfied by joining groups. Others may find sufficient affection from their family members or other individuals.
4. Esteem needs are those human desires to be respected by others, and for a positive self-image. Individuals strive to increase their status in the eyes of others, to attain a good reputation or a high ranking in a group. Self-confidence is increased when self-esteem needs are

satisfied. When self-esteem needs are thwarted, feelings of inferiority or weakness often result.

5. Self-actualization needs are the individual's desire to do what he or she has the potential of doing. The desire for self-actualization is the 'highest-order need'.

These basic needs are arranged in a hierarchy of needs. Maslow hypothesized that unsatisfied needs dominate the individual's thoughts and are reflected in what the person is concerned about. The higher-order needs (belonging, esteem and self-actualization) are not important until the primary, or lower-order needs (safety and physiological) are at least partially satisfied. Maslow also feels that a person is not motivated by a need that is satisfied. Once a need is satisfied, the person is concerned with the next level of the need hierarchy. A person seeks to move up the hierarchy of needs, generally striving to satisfy the need deficiency at the next-highest level.

ERG theory

ERG theory is similar to Maslow's approach, though there are important differences. In ERG theory there are three, not five, basic need categories (Alderfer, 1972). They are existence needs, relatedness needs and growth needs (hence the label ERG):

- Existence needs encompass Maslow's physiological and security needs for material things.
- Relatedness needs include security needs for interpersonal matters, love and belonging needs, and needs of an interpersonal nature.
- Growth needs focus on the need to confirm personal esteem and self-actualization.

Like Maslow's theory, ERG theory states that unsatisfied needs will dominate behavior, and that once a need is satisfied, higher-order needs are desired. For example, the less existence needs are satisfied, the more their satisfaction is desired. As they become satisfied, relatedness needs become more desired. Growth needs continue to be desired even as they are satisfied. Unlike Maslow's theory, ERG theory makes two further statements:

- The less relatedness needs are fulfilled, the more existence needs will be desired.
- The less growth needs are fulfilled, the more relatedness needs will be desired.

Table 3.1   Basic elements of two-factor theory

Hygiene factors	Motivators
1. Technical supervision	1. Responsibility
2. Interpersonal relations: peers	2. Achievement
3. Salary	3. Advancement
4. Working conditions	4. The work itself
5. Status	5. Recognition
6. Company policy	6. Possibility of growth
7. Job security	
8. Interpersonal relations: supervisor	

This implies that if a person is deprived of a higher-order need or does not have the potential to satisfy it, he or she will focus on lower-order needs. In other words, he or she will regress on the need hierarchy.

Herzberg's Two-Factor Theory

The application of need theory to motivate people poses problems for managers, because it is difficult to translate needs into management strategies. Research by Herzberg et al. (1959) provided some guidance for managers in solving this problem. Their study challenged a long-held assumption about how a person's work satisfaction affected performance and motivation. Before, it was assumed that if a person was dissatisfied with part of the job (for example, pay), then all that had to be done was to improve the factor (increase pay). This would lead to higher satisfaction, greater motivation and higher performance. However, Herzberg and his co-workers concluded that there are two sets of factors (hence the name 'two-factor' theory) that affect people in the workplace, each of which works in different ways. These are hygiene factors and motivating factors (Table 3.1).

Hygiene factors create dissatisfaction if they are not present. If they are present in a job setting, dissatisfaction will be lower, but satisfaction will not be high. Hygiene factors are associated with the context of a job. They include working conditions, status and company policy. A complete list is given in Table 3.1. Therefore, according to the two-factor theory, providing fringe benefits, nice offices and good vacation plans serve mainly to minimize dissatisfaction and to keep people in the organization; they do not lead to higher motivation or better performance.

Motivators are related to high satisfaction and willingness to work harder. When they are present, these job factors may induce more effort, but if they are absent, it will not produce dissatisfaction in most people.

Motivators are associated with the content of the job. They are factors such as responsibility and achievement; see Table 3.1. Therefore, a person in a challenging job is likely to be satisfied and motivated to perform better. However, the lack of challenging work does not cause dissatisfaction, merely the absence of satisfaction. A person who is well paid will not be dissatisfied; however, high pay will not lead to motivation.

This theory became popular with managers because it gave them direction in managing motivation. For instance, if worker dissatisfaction is seen as the major problem, then the hygiene factors must be improved. To improve performance, the manager must work on the motivators, and this means changing the nature of the work to make it more challenging and intrinsically rewarding. That means that the person experiences good feelings of growth and status as a result of doing a good job.

Herzberg's work has been the subject of much research and controversy. First, the results may be a consequence of method bias. He used the incident recall method, an approach in which subjects are asked to think of a good work experience, or to think of a bad work experience. With this method there is a tendency for the person to attribute good experiences to themselves, as when they did a good job, and bad experiences to others or to the context, as when their supervisor prevented them from doing a good job. This could account for why the particular hygiene and motivating factors were discovered. Studies which used other methods, such as questionnaires, reached different conclusions (Pinder, 2008). Second, individual differences are not considered. For example, self-confidence and skill may both affect whether a job is seen as challenging. A highly skilled systems analyst may find it challenging to design the information system for a new plant, while an equally intelligent person with less computer competence may find the same assignment frustrating.

Even with these problems, the two-factor theory made an important contribution. It did provide some guidance to those who design jobs, and it was widely used by practicing managers. Of more importance, though, is that Herzberg's research directed attention in a very dramatic way to the role of the work itself as a factor that affects worker motivation and performance.

The Job Characteristics Approach

One motivational approach that helps to solve the problem of translating 'needs' into management strategies is called the job characteristics approach, also called the job design approach. Working from Herzberg's idea that the work itself is an important motivating factor, Hackman and Lawler (1971) set out the first structure of the job characteristics model,

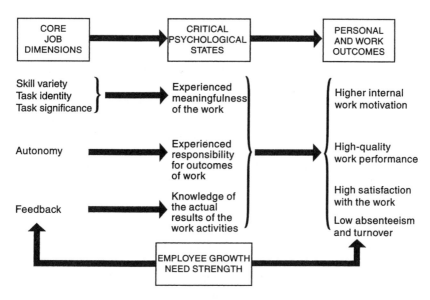

Figure 3.5   The job characteristics model: the relationships among core job dimensions, critical psychological states and work outcomes

which is the basis of the job design approach to motivation. Based on this premise, the job design approach says that when specific job characteristics are present: 'employees will experience a positive, self-generated response when they perform well and that this internal kick will provide an incentive for continued efforts toward good performance' (Hackman and Suttle, 1977). There are four key elements in the job design approach (1976):

1. Work outcomes.
2. Critical psychological states.
3. Core job dimensions.
4. Growth need strength.

As shown in Figure 3.5, there are four important work outcomes in this model:

1. Internal work motivation is how motivated the person is by the work itself, rather than external factors such as pay and supervision.
2. Quality of work results from people having meaningful jobs. Individuals will produce fewer errors, lower numbers of rejected parts and lower scrap rates. The job characteristics approach does

not suggest that people will produce more, although productivity may increase if an output level is maintained and work quality is improved.

3. Job satisfaction is a third outcome that is affected by the characteristics of work.

4. Absenteeism and turnover are the final set of outcomes in the job characteristics model. Both absenteeism and turnover can be quite expensive for firms when they are high and out of control.

The four work outcomes are affected by three critical psychological states that give the person a kick out of doing the work when performing well in a job:

1. Meaningfulness of work occurs when the person believes that it counts for something, that is, that it is important either to the person or to someone else. For instance, most US Peace Corps volunteers believe that their work is 'the toughest job you will ever love'. This feeling exists even though a volunteer's work may be a very ordinary task, at a very low pay level, and in very undesirable working conditions. Most volunteers believe that their work makes an important difference, however small, to someone. It certainly makes a difference to the volunteer.

2. Experienced responsibility for outcomes of work occurs when a person believes that he or she is personally accountable for the results of work. This is also the case for Peace Corp volunteers. Usually volunteers are working alone or with only a few others. They know that they are responsible for the success or failure of projects.

3. Knowledge of results is when a person can personally judge the adequacy or inadequacy of work performance. Obtaining knowledge of results is not as simple as it sounds. For instance, the project directors for those Mars missions that successfully landed mobile devices on Mars only had feedback about how well they did when the vehicles were on Mars and began transmitting pictures. For the prior several years that they worked on the project, they had no idea about whether or not the project would be successful.

High levels of meaningfulness, responsibility and knowledge of results exist when certain core job characteristics are present. There are five core job dimensions:

● Skill variety.
● Task identity.

- Task significance.
- Autonomy.
- Feedback.

Different core job characteristics contribute to different psychological states:

- Work meaningfulness is affected by skill variety, task identity and task significance.
- Experienced responsibility is a function of autonomy.
- Knowledge of results is determined by feedback.

Skill variety is how many different abilities and capacities are required for the performance components that make up the person's job. A clerk in a secretarial pool who only types outgoing letters has a job that is of a low skill variety. A personal secretary to the chief executive officer (CEO), however, may use several different skills such as typing and dealing with different people from both inside and outside the organization.

Task identity is the extent to which a person is responsible for the whole job, from beginning to end.

Task significance is the effect that work has on others, either in their work or in their lives. This occurs when the person can link his or her task to some value created for the customer.

Autonomy is the freedom that a person has in the job. High autonomy is the freedom to determine when, how and where a job is to be done. When autonomy is high, so are perceived feelings of responsibility.

Feedback is the information that a person receives about the results of the job. One source of feedback is from other workers or supervisors. Another form of feedback may be from the job itself; a basketball player has immediate feedback – when a shot goes through the hoop or it misses.

These job characteristics do not affect everyone the same way. A person's growth need strength is very important. Growth need strength is the extent to which a person desires to advance, to be in a challenging position and, generally, to achieve. If you have high growth strength and have a job high on the core dimensions, you are more likely to experience high internal motivation, high satisfaction, high work quality, and low turnover and absenteeism than if you have low growth need strength (Spector, 1985).

Job enrichment
Job enrichment is a motivational approach based on the job characteristics model (Hackman et al., 1975) is aimed at increasing skill variety, task identity, task significance, autonomy and feedback so that workers will

have more meaningful jobs, a greater sense of responsibility and more feedback. In the job enrichment approach, there are five basic ways to redesign jobs, as shown in Figure 3.5, to increase their motivating potential and affect the core job dimensions, critical psychological states, and personal and work outcomes (Hackman et al., 1975):

1. Combining tasks. Narrow tasks, especially those that are 'fractionalized', should be combined into larger, more complex tasks. If the new task is too large for one person, it may be assigned to a team. Combining tasks increases skill variety and task identity.
2. Forming natural work units. Tasks should be grouped into work units so that as much of the work as possible can be performed in the same organizational group. This leads to a sense of ownership of the job, increasing task identity and task significance.
3. Establishing client relationships. It is a good idea, when possible, to link the worker with the purchaser of the product or the service. Since the worker cannot often interact directly with a customer, it may be possible to devise ways that the customer can give the worker feedback. If client relationships can be established, skill variety, autonomy and feedback should improve.
4. Vertical loading. The job should be enriched by vertical loading (adding responsibilities from higher organization levels) as opposed to horizontal job loading (adding more tasks from the same level). Vertical loading gives the person more responsibility and control at work, which should lead to an increase in the level of perceived job autonomy.
5. Opening feedback channels. There are two ways to provide feedback: job-provided feedback occurs when the person knows how to judge performance from the job itself; management feedback comes from the supervisor or from reports such as budgets and quality reports. Removing obstacles to increase job-related feedback will improve performance.

McClelland's Achievement–Power Theory

An important motivational model, useful particularly in understanding leadership was developed by McClelland (1965). Two important concepts that underlie achievement–power theory are motives and the force of motives on behavior. Motives are a person's 'affectively toned associated networks arranged in a hierarchy of strength and importance' (McClelland, 1975). There are three needs, or motives, that are at the center of this approach:

1. The need for achievement.
2. The need for power.
3. The need for affiliation.

The two most important, discussed in detail below, are the achievement motive and the power motive.

The need for achievement

The achievement motive is the extent to which success is important and valued by a person. The strength of the achievement motive is related to socialization experiences. For example, if your early success experiences were very rewarding, we would expect you to have high achievement motivation. If these success experiences were not rewarding, another motive (say, power) may have a more dominant place in your motive cluster.

One person's achievement motive may differ from another's in terms of level and area of focus. Rewarded success in school may lead to high academic achievement motives, while rewarded success in a part-time job might lead to work achievement motives. For example, someone high in work achievement may be driven by this motive to be successful in the firm; a person with a high academic achievement motive may be driven to be successful in an area of science and not seek organization success.

When the achievement motive is generalized, a person wants to succeed in everything. For the high achiever, the achievement motive is toward the top of the motive hierarchy and only minimal achievement cues are necessary to generate the positive feelings of potential success and, therefore, increase the likelihood of trying to succeed. Here are the sorts of cues and conditions that activate achievement motives (McClelland, 1965):

- Success must come from your own efforts, not from those of others or from luck. High achievers wish to take personal responsibility for success.
- The situation must have an 'intermediate level of risk'. This means that it will be challenging, but not impossible. If the risk is so high that success is impossible, you will avoid it. If it is so low that the task is easy, you would avoid it because it is no real challenge.
- You want concrete feedback about success, because you want to keep track of how well you are doing. You would try to avoid situations where there can be any doubt about their achievement.

Successful entrepreneurs have high achievement motives – those high in achievement motives play a 'one man game that need not involve other people' (McClelland, 1975; Collins et al., 2004). The entrepreneurial situation in business has most of the characteristics that arouse the achievement motive. Entrepreneurs know that if they win or lose, they are responsible, accountable and in charge.

The need for power

Interestingly, it was initially thought that successful managers would have high achievement motivation that would lead to better work performance, faster promotion and, ultimately, to high levels of management. It was discovered that many top-level executives did not have high achievement motivation, but instead they had high power motives (McClelland, 1975).

The power motive is your need to have an impact on others, to establish, maintain or restore personal prestige or power (McClelland, 1975). It can show up three different ways.

1. You could take strong aggressive actions towards others, give help to others, try to control or persuade others or try to impress them.
2. You might act in a way that results in strong emotions in others, even though the act itself is not strong.
3. This motive can be reflected by a concern for your reputation and, perhaps, doing things that would enhance or preserve it.

The power motive may take one of two different forms: personalized power or socialized power. Personalized power is adversarial. Those with a personalized power orientation prefer person-to-person competition in which they can dominate. To them, life is a win–lose game and the law of the jungle rules; the strong survive by destroying the weak. They drink somewhat heavily and gain considerable satisfaction from power fantasies while under the influence of alcohol. These persons are high in the power motive but low in self-control and inhibition (McClelland, 1965).

Those with a socialized power orientation want to exercise power for the good of others, to be careful about the use of personal power, plan carefully for conflict with others, and know that someone's win is another person's loss. They have high self-control and prefer a more disciplined expression of their power motivation than those who have a personal power orientation

Men and women high in the power motive have similar characteristics (McClelland, 1975; Winter, 1988). They hold organization offices, prefer jobs in power-oriented careers (such as business, teaching and journalism), prefer to be highly visible in their organizations and tend to acquire prestige possessions. One important difference is that men with high power motives tend to drink heavily, while women do not.

The need for affiliation

The need for affiliation is very much like Maslow's belonging need. Those high in the need for affiliation have a strong desire for affection, belonging to groups, social support, attention, emotional support and praise.

Since motives are an aspect of the personality and they develop as the personality emerges, we can say that these motives can take on different levels of importance, or dominance in the person's need hierarchy. The result can be thought of as a 'motive profile'. The idea is that the dominant motive has the highest position in the hierarchy, and that motive will have the strongest effect on behavior. McClelland suggests several profiles that might be found in managerial or leadership roles (McClelland, 1975). For example, the person with the 'leader motive' pattern has strong socialized power motives, low affiliation needs and high self-control. The 'empire builder', a person who builds empires and strong organizations, has a high need for socialized power, a high need for control, a low need for affiliation and high inhibition in the use of power. Those who build a power base in close groups, relying on loyalty, have a 'personal enclave' focus. They seek to secure power through close personal ties. They have high needs for power, high needs for affiliation and low inhibition in the use of power.

MOTIVATION: THE PROCESS THEORIES

A second group of motivation theories is called the process theories. Process theories of motivation focus on how behavior change occurs, or how a person comes to act in a different way. There is less emphasis on the specific factors (or 'content') that cause behavior. For example, a content theory would lead you to say that, 'Increases in pay can improve satisfaction and performance', while a process theory would explain, one way or another, how that happens. For example, reinforcement theory would lead you to say that 'Performance will increase if the consequence of high performance is a positive reinforcer'. In this case, the reinforcement of the high-performance behavior with the desire consequence is the process by which performance improves. As you come to understand the concepts in these theories, you will see the dominant process orientation and the less prominent, but still present, content aspects of each. Four process theories are discussed in this section:

1. Reinforcement theory.
2. Expectancy theory.
3. Goal-setting theory.
4. Organizational justice theories.

Reinforcement Theory

Reinforcement theory is one of the most important and, perhaps, most complicated of the motivation theories. As we said in Chapter 2, it is very useful to understand not only how personality develops, but also how rewarding or punishing behavior affects performance and satisfaction. A good deal of research supports reinforcement theory. Research done in the workplace, though more complicated because there are just too many factors that prevent the linking of consequences to behavior, also supports reinforcement theory. There are two key concepts in reinforcement theory:

1. The types of reinforcement consequences.
2. Reinforcement schedules.

Types of reinforcement consequences
In reinforcement theory, several types of consequences can occur:

1. Positive reinforcement.
2. Negative reinforcement (avoidance).
3. Punishment.
4. Extinction.

Figure 3.6 shows the nature of each type of consequence and its effects on the probability of a behavior recurring.

Positive reinforcement occurs when desirable consequences are associated with a behavior. A positive reinforcer increases the likelihood that the behavior will recur in the future. Figure 3.7 shows how a manager might use positive reinforcement to improve the quality of your work. When you produce a report, she could point out that it was much better than your previous work and could provide positive reinforcement through praise ('You did great!'). If this continues, the stimulus ('Do good work') will eventually lead to fewer problems with your reports.

Negative reinforcement occurs when an undesirable consequence is removed. It also increases the likelihood that the behavior will occur again. Suppose that you work in a very noisy plant and find that wearing earplugs reduces your discomfort from the noise. This should lead you to associate noise (in the plant) and the use of earplugs. The removal of the noise is a negative reinforcer as it strengthens the association between the stimulus (working in high noise) and the response (wearing the earplugs). This is also called avoidance learning. We engage in the response to avoid a negative effect. Just as you stop at a red light to avoid a ticket and fine, so at work you may work hard to meet job standards to avoid negative

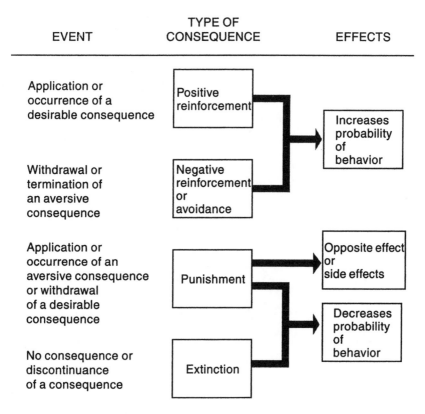

Figure 3.6 Types of consequences and their effects

consequences. Part (b) of Figure 3.7 shows what you might do to avoid negative criticism from your boss.

Some managers think that negative reinforcement is a good way to manage people at work: that is, employees who engage in undesirable behavior should expect something to happen to them. However, there can be some difficulties with this approach. First, it creates a tense environment – it is difficult to work day after day where the main motivation is to prevent unpleasant outcomes. Second, relationships often deteriorate when another person, particularly your supervisor, represents a constant threat to be avoided.

Punishment can take two forms. Negative consequences (undesirable things) can be applied to a response, or positive consequences (desirable things) can actively be taken away. Part (c) of Figure 3.7 shows how you could be punished when your reports are not well done. Your boss may be very critical and reprimand you. The figure also shows how punishment

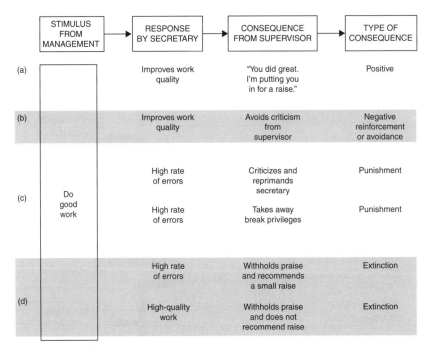

STIMULUS FROM MANAGEMENT	RESPONSE BY SECRETARY	CONSEQUENCE FROM SUPERVISOR	TYPE OF CONSEQUENCE
(a)	Improves work quality	"You did great. I'm putting you in for a raise."	Positive
(b)	Improves work quality	Avoids criticism from supervisor	Negative reinforcement or avoidance
(c) Do good work	High rate of errors	Criticizes and reprimands secretary	Punishment
	High rate of errors	Takes away break privileges	Punishment
(d)	High rate of errors	Withholds praise and recommends a small raise	Extinction
	High-quality work	Withholds praise and does not recommend raise	Extinction

Figure 3.7   Examples of consequences in a work setting

Spotlight 3.3   Epicurean needs

'Epicurean delights' is a phrase often associated with things that bring you great gratification, such as good food and drink, as well as other hedonistic pleasures. The philosopher Epicure's ideas were a bit more complicated, though pleasure is an important element. He distinguished between natural needs and unnecessary needs. Some natural and necessary needs must be met for happiness while others must be met for the health of the body. Unnecessary needs should be eliminated.

The Epicurean School is based on the principle that human beings, by their nature, seek pleasure and try to avoid pain. Real pleasure, Epicure argued, is produced not only by pleasant emotions and feelings, but also by avoiding pain. True pleasure is in the state of *ataraxia*, or a genuine state of serenity and tranquility.

can be applied by withdrawing positive consequences. Here, the contingent result of a low-quality report is taking away your extra break privileges. In both instances, the response, 'poor reports', should decrease.

There is an important distinction between punishment and negative reinforcement. When you are punished, you learn to prevent negative consequences by withholding behaviors. For example, you do not criticize your boss if she treats you unfairly, because you are afraid you might be fired. In negative reinforcement, you learn to do things (perform responses) that stop a negative consequence from occurring. You might learn to avoid certain situations at work where you might be made angry by your boss (Stajkovic and Luthans, 1997).

Certainly punishment can affect behavior at work, but it should be a last resort. Reprimands and firing may have to occur, but it is best to try to correct the behavior first. Positive reinforcement is a much better alternative, and many examples exist of its effective use in improving performance and attendance (Locke et al., 1981). There are some serious problems with using punishment:

- It needs to be carefully handled. It cannot be too mild, nor too severe – its magnitude should fit the crime.
- It should be linked to the undesirable behavior and applied as close in time as possible. Punishment is more effective if it encourages an incompatible response or a desirable substitute response.
- It can have an opposite effect and actually become a positive reinforcer. A subordinate who is punished may in fact feel rewarded by having angered his boss or by gaining the attention and support of fellow workers.
- Punishment can have undesirable side-effects. For instance, punishment can reduce the frequency of desirable behaviors. It contributes to a fearful environment in which people may stop taking initiative or trying new things, or they might cut back on bringing problems to their boss's attention.
- It may address a symptom and not the cause of the undesirable behavior. If the cause persists, the behavior will probably persist.
- The manager cannot control how other employees interpret the punishment. It is often the punished employee who controls the information that other employees receive about it. They return to the workplace and give their own interpretation of the situation. If they lack accuracy and completeness in their tale, or if they distort their report to save face, the punishment will not serve as an example to others. This is ironic, because managers often punish to set an example but may end up at the mercy of misinformation and rumor.

Extinction is another way to change behavior. It involves stopping a previously established reinforcer, either positive or negative, that is maintaining a behavior. Managers may extinguish a response of a worker by not reinforcing it for an extended period of time; the response then becomes less frequent and eventually stops. Part (d) of Figure 3.7 shows two examples of extinguishing behavior. In one case, your supervisor withholds both praise and punishment when your reports are not well done. In the other, praise and rewards are withheld when you do a good report. In both cases, the response rates may decrease, but one is desirable behavior and the other one is not.

Managers should be very sensitive to the wide array of possibilities of extinction in the workplace. Employees should not learn that good behaviors have little or no consequences. For instance, when there is no distinction between rewards for average performance and outstanding performance, you soon learn that high levels of performance do not pay off. In short, you have been extinguished from doing more than average or minimal performance. Another interesting case of extinction is when you seek feedback on your performance. You might be told: 'I thought you knew you were doing well; I haven't been on your back, have I?' A boss who manages by saying little or nothing to the good employee could well be fostering mediocre work performance.

Reinforcement schedules
Reinforcement schedules are the timing and frequency that consequences are associated with behavior. They are important because they affect how long it takes to learn a new behavior and how resistant the behavior is to change. Five types of reinforcement schedules are shown in Figure 3.8:

1.   Continuous schedules.
2.   Fixed-interval schedules.
3.   Variable-interval schedules.
4.   Fixed-ratio schedules.
5.   Variable-ratio schedules.

In a continuous reinforcement schedule, a response is reinforced (or punished) each time it occurs. For example, when learning a new job, an instructor may be constantly present to respond in a reinforcing manner each time a worker does the right thing. It is not easy to apply a continuous schedule in work situations, because it requires the constant presence of someone else; supervisors cannot use continuous reinforcement or punishment schedules unless they monitor subordinates closely. This level of monitoring is probably not advisable, except for short periods where

CONTINUOUS SCHEDULE

Every Response Reinforced; Rapid Learning and Extinction

	FIXED	**VARIABLE**
INTERVAL (Time)	FIXED INTERVAL Reinforcement at fixed times. Learning fairly slow and connected to time. Moderately resistant to extinction.	VARIABLE INTERVAL Reinforcement at varied, perhaps unpredictable times. Learning is slow and activity high.Very resistant to extinction.
RATIO (Responses)	FIXED RATIO Reinforcement after a fixed number of responses. Learning slow, activity high, and pauses after reinforcement. Moderately resistant to extinction.	VARIABLE RATIO Reinforcement after a varying number of responses. Learning slow, response rule steady and very high. Very resistant to extinction.

Figure 3.8   Schedules of reinforcement and their effects on learning and extinction

a supervisor is coaching or training an employee on a specific task. Close monitoring creates an unfavorable climate if subordinates feel they are constantly watched, and it can have negative effects on the satisfaction and productivity of work groups.

In a fixed-interval reinforcement schedule, a response is reinforced after a fixed amount of time has elapsed. These schedules result in irregular performance rates, with behavior at its highest rate closer in time to when the reinforcement occurs. For example, when performance appraisals are scheduled every six months, employees are likely to work harder as the time for appraisal nears. Pay is another example because it is generally given at a regular time of the week or month. It is difficult to say exactly what pay reinforces, but it is unlikely that paychecks reinforce performance because pay is often not a function of performance. The most probable effect of a regular paycheck is to reinforce attendance (if pay is reduced for lateness) or to deter people from quitting.

In a variable-interval reinforcement schedule, the period of time between reinforcements is not constant. Variable-interval schedules are common in work settings. Supervisors often visit work sites at irregular intervals. Consider the example of a security guard who dare not leave his post because his supervisor checks on him at irregular intervals.

The problem with variable-interval schedules is that they might also result in the wrong behavior. If subordinates are rewarded by a visit from the boss, the visit might inadvertently reinforce an undesirable act. Suppose the boss makes an unscheduled visit and tells an employee what a good job she is doing, but arrives at the site just after the employee has returned late from a work break. The employee may feel that she is the victim of inconsistent signals or may feel some resentment, for example: 'Why wasn't she here when I did so well the other day?'

In a fixed-ratio reinforcement schedule, a certain number of responses must occur before a reinforcement follows. A piece rate payment system is an example of a fixed-ratio schedule at work. The employee is credited with additional pay for increments of productivity. Additional pay is received, say, for each dozen cartons packed or for every three vehicles sold. Fixed-ratio schedules can produce high rates of response that continue so as long as the reinforcement remains powerful.

With a variable-ratio reinforcement schedule, the number of behaviors necessary for a reinforcement varies. You might be reinforced after one response or after several, and the number of required behaviors changes. This schedule produces a very high and steady rate of response, typically without predictable pauses or bursts of behavior. Gambling and fishing are good examples of variable-ratio schedules. The pay-off occurs at unpredictable times and sustains behavior over long periods. Hundreds of lottery tickets might be bought before a large winning ticket comes along, but there are always small prizes randomly won while you are hoping – and still buying. Likewise, it may take many casts before a fish is hooked.

Variable-ratio schedules occur at work when managers reward irregularly, either by accident or by design. Some companies have tried to implement them formally by using lotteries to reduce absenteeism, For example, in one company employees with perfect attendance records for six months are eligible for a draw in which a new car is the prize. Unless the reinforcement occurs or its perceived likelihood remains, it will not affect behavior. Extinction would take place if the employee attends regularly but never wins a prize.

One approach to changing behavior, called behavior shaping, involves reinforcing small increments of behavior that are in the direction of desired behavior until a final desired result is achieved. Behavior shaping can be used in all kinds of learning, not just when we are trying to extinguish or overcome old habits. Shaping requires that we break down a desired response into components and think of the desired behavior as a sequence of the components. Then if we can encourage a part of the behavior any-where in the sequence, it can be reinforced. This continues until the complete behavior is learned. For example, suppose that a manager in your department has been resisting the use of personal computers in his unit. You believe that the reason for his resistance is simply that he is afraid he will not be able to use them easily. Here are some ways that you can begin shaping his behavior so that he will eventually introduce personal computers:

- Take him to the office of another manager who has successfully introduced computers so that he can see the benefits that her department gained.
- Assign him a simple task that requires the use of a computer on which he works with a supportive and helpful computer user.
- Ask him to prepare a brief report on the costs, benefits and user-friendliness of different computers. Throughout this process, you would encourage and positively reinforce any behaviors consistent with your overall goal of introducing computers.

Transfer of learning occurs when behavior learned in one situation occurs in another situation. Sometimes the transfer is appropriate, but sometimes it is not. Suppose you take a job in a company in which there are relaxed standards of dress. So long as you are productive and dress neatly, you can succeed. If you change jobs and join another firm with a more formal dress norm, the way you dress may no longer be acceptable, and you could suffer the consequences despite your good work. What you learned in the first company about appropriate dress style transferred negatively to the second. For learning to transfer, it is necessary to have similar conditions to those that existed when the behavior was learned. For example, the use of similar or identical equipment at work as that used in training aids the transfer of learning from the classroom to the workplace. It also helps to maintain the reinforcements and feedback that took place in training.

Cognitive evaluation theory: effects of extrinsic rewards on intrinsic motivation

Intrinsic motivation is the drive to perform that comes from a person's internalized values and beliefs that the task is rewarding in and of itself. Intrinsic rewards are 'self-administered'; the good feelings one has while working or when the task is completed. These include experiencing a sense of autonomy, personal growth and task accomplishment when the job is well done.

Cognitive evaluation theory suggests that the use of extrinsic rewards, as is the usual case in using reinforcement theory, might have a negative effect on intrinsic motivation (Pinder, 2008). This is an intriguing argument, because it states that if a person receives extrinsic rewards for performing an intrinsically motivating task, then the intrinsic task motivation will decrease. Suppose you play golf for the university team. You practice hard and play your best because, within yourself, you enjoy the challenge of winning and the competition of the game. The extrinsic rewards are weak, few and far between. After college, you become a professional player and begin winning large sums of money in tournaments. Your motivation (the cause of your effort) changes from intrinsic to extrinsic. Now you do it for the money. The reason for this is probably due to the way a person attributes causality to his or her actions:

> If external pressures on an individual are so high that they would ordinarily cause him to perform a given task . . . then the individual might infer he is extrinsically motivated . . . In contrast . . . if the external rewards are extremely low or nonsalient, the individual might then infer that his behavior is intrinsically motivated (Staw, 1976).

There is some research that supports this idea. It shows that when people working on intrinsically motivating tasks were later paid for them, they chose later to work on less intrinsically motivating tasks (Herzberg et al., 1959). This means that there could be negative effects of extrinsic rewards.

However, later studies have been more helpful in understanding the results of these studies and how they may be used in work settings. First, the negative effect of extrinsic rewards on intrinsic motivation seems to operate for interesting jobs and not for uninteresting ones. Therefore, if we assume that most work in organizations is not highly interesting, then there is no problem. Certainly most work in factories and in offices is not very interesting, and most people wouldn't do them without pay (an extrinsic reward) (Staw, 1976). Second, pay serves more purposes than just an extrinsic, contingent reward. There are strong norms about the importance and meaning of pay. It is a way for people to keep score of how they compare to others and how they are valued by the organization. In industrial organizations where: 'extrinsic reinforcement is the norm . . . tasks may often be perceived to be more interesting when they lead to greater extrinsic rewards' (Staw, 1976).

Positive reinforcement programs

Positive reinforcement programs – also called 'organizational behavior modification' (OB Mod) programs – are based on reinforcement concepts. They seek to improve performance (that is, to change behavior) by changing the stimulus (antecedents) and the consequences (reinforcers and punishments). These motivational strategies, based on reinforcement theory, have been used in some of the very largest and best-managed organizations, and have led to major improvements in productivity, reductions in turnover and improved safety (Luthans et al., 1981; Orpen, 1982). These firms used praise, recognition and other non-direct compensation (time off or freedom to choose activities) as reinforcers for production workers, which proved quite effective in bringing about improvements in attendance and increased performance (Hamner and Hamner, 1976). Other firms have designed reward systems to encourage managers to pay more attention to long-run, rather than short-run, interests of the organization (Tosi and Gomez-Mejia, 1989).

Positive consequences from an organization can take many forms. One of the strongest is praise and recognition for good work. Others are money (when it is a consequence of good performance), some autonomy in choosing work assignments, opportunities to improve one's status and self-esteem and, lastly, power to influence co-workers and management.

Positive reinforcement is good rewards management. It shifts the emphasis and energy of the manager toward a larger number of employees, rather than focusing the attention and time mainly on poorer employees. It can be handled in a way that makes all but the worst employees feel that the organization recognizes and appreciates their effort and contribution.

There is some good evidence for the effects of OB Mod in organizations (Stajkovic and Luthans, 1997). This tells us that it is more effective in manufacturing organizations than in service industries. In these manufacturing cases, the use of financial reinforcement and other types of reinforcement produced positive results. Interestingly, however, there was no difference in the effects between complex reinforcement packages and those that were non-financial interventions. This would suggest that the most effective managerial approach is to use the non-financial reinforcements and not become involved in the extra cost, 'time and effort to apply the [financial reinforcements]' (Stajkovic and Luthans, 1997).

This same research also shows that financial reinforcers seemed to work better in service organizations. However, they are far more effective when they are combined with social reinforcers. Still, the effect of these social reinforcers was very high, justifying a recommendation that they may well be used alone with good results.

Expectancy Theory

The basic idea of expectancy theory is that you will work (put forth effort) to do those things that will lead to the results (outcomes) that you

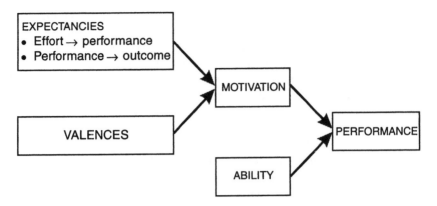

Figure 3.9   Some key concepts in expectancy theory

desire. This is a rational approach to motivation that implies that people make an assessment of the costs or benefits of the different alternatives that they have, and then select the one with the best pay-offs (Vroom, 1964).

Suppose a real estate agent has two different ways to approach selling houses:

- He could spend a lot of time telephoning prospective buyers.
- He could wait until prospective buyers come into the office.

What he does depends on his preference for certain outcomes and the expectations about those outcomes. If he estimates that calling prospective buyers has a high probability (an expectation) of earning a substantial bonus, and there is a low expectation of earning the bonus if he waits for them to come to the office, the motivation to call prospects is much higher. According to expectancy theory, the salesman would choose the work behavior, telephoning prospective clients.

We must know some other things about the salesman before we can predict his behavior with expectancy theory. For instance, we assumed that the salesman values the income and that he feels he can succeed if he tries to sell. However, there are other outcomes associated with both success and failure. For example, failure or success will affect opportunities for advancement, personal satisfaction with work and, perhaps, relationships with other members of the sales staff. Finally, there is the question of ability. A person with high selling ability will be more successful than one with lesser skills, given similar levels of motivation. These elements of expectancy theory are shown in Figure 3.9.

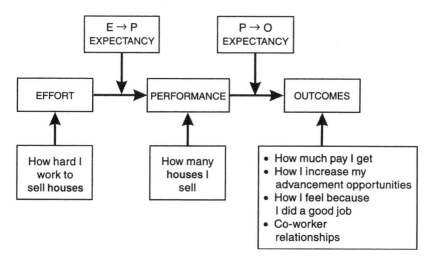

Figure 3.10   Effort–performance and performance–outcome expectancies

An expectancy is an individual's estimate, or judgment, of the likelihood that some outcome (or event) will occur. It is a probability estimate and can range from 0 (impossible) to 1 (certain). If the salesman believes that to sell one house it is necessary to show houses to five potential buyers, the expectancy is 0.20.

There are two kinds of expectancies (see Figure 3.9):

1. The effort–performance expectancy (E → P) is the person's belief about the level of effort made and the resulting performance that it will lead to. For the salesman, the effort–performance expectancy is the relationship between, 'how hard I work to sell homes', and 'how many homes I sell'.
2. The performance–outcome expectancy (P → O) is the expectation that achieving a given level of work performance will lead to certain outcomes. High P → O expectancies, particularly with respect to attaining rewards, are necessary for high performance. This is called the performance–reward linkage, and if it is not made, then we should not expect a person to make an effort.

Figure 3.10 shows four possible outcomes for the salesman's performance, 'how many homes I sell':

1. 'How much commission I will receive.'
2. 'How I increase my advancement opportunities.'

3. 'How I feel because I did a good job.'
4. Co-worker relationships.

All these outcomes affect the level of motivation. As an illustration, a salesperson may feel that if he works hard, high performance will result ($E \rightarrow P$). This may have a high probability of increasing income and self-esteem, but a low probability of improving relations with co-workers. These several outcomes of performance (pay, advancement, self-esteem, and co-worker relations) are all $P \rightarrow O$ expectations.

'Valence' is the strength of the person's preference for a particular outcome, that is, not all outcomes are equally valued by a person. Valences are anticipated satisfactions (or dissatisfactions) that result from outcomes, or the different degrees of pleasantness (or unpleasantness) of outcomes. So when an outcome has a low positive valence, you will not exert much effort to attain it. The salesman may have a strong desire for some outcomes but not for others. He may, for example, wish to have the pay increase and the advancement, but avoid antagonizing co-workers.

Goal-Setting Theory

Goal-setting theory is based on a simple premise: performance is caused by a person's intention to perform (Locke, 1997). Goals are what a person is trying to accomplish or intends to do, and according to this theory, people will do what they are trying to do. What follows from this is quite clear:

- A person with higher goals will do better than someone with lower ones.
- If someone knows precisely what he or she wants to do, or is supposed to do, that person will do better than someone whose goals or intentions are vague.

These are the two basic ideas that underlie the four propositions of goal-setting theory:

1. There is a general positive relationship between goal difficulty and performance. This, however, does not hold for extremely difficult goals beyond one's ability. Difficult goals lead to better results than easy goals. This has been shown time after time in very different research settings, using students, workers and managers (Tubbs, 1986).
2. Specific goals lead to higher performance than general goals. This is a particularly important point to remember because managers have a tendency to set goals that are too general for their subordinates

(Carroll and Tosi, 1973). The findings from studies with students, keypunch operators, marketing personnel, production workers and laboratory personnel show that individuals given 'specific, challenging goals either outperformed those trying to do their best', or surpassed their own previous performance when they were not trying for specific goals (Locke, 1997).

3. Participation is related to performance through goal acceptance and commitment, and information sharing. Participation in setting goals does not directly affect performance but it can increase goal commitment and, ultimately, performance, particularly if it leads to some real choices about the way to achieve a goal as well as information about the goal and the task (Erez et al., 1985). This means that participation is a complex process. It cannot be limited only to narrow areas in which superiors want to have subordinates set goals, but must be more broadly based. Participation must also be realistic, in the sense that subordinates have some choices about ways to perform the task, the goal levels, and what information they need to perform the task (Scully et al., 1973).

4. Feedback about performance with respect to goals is necessary. Clear goals and feedback about performance are both necessary for higher performance. A person must know whether the desired level of performance has been achieved. In a study of telephone service personnel that compared the performance of two groups of workers, the group that had goals and received feedback performed better than the group that only had goals. The goals–feedback group had lower costs and a better safety record. And when individuals receive positive feedback about goal achievement, they are likely to subsequently set higher goals; but when they receive negative feedback about performance they adjusted subsequent goals downward (Ilies and Judge, 2005).

One personality dimension that seems related to the effects of goals on performance is the sense of self-competence. One measure of self-competence, a general one, is self-esteem. Self-esteem has been found to interact with goals to affect performance. Managers with high self-esteem reported that they worked harder toward performance goals than those managers who had low self-esteem (Carroll and Tosi, 1973). Another is self-efficacy, the individual's belief that he or she can perform a task successfully. In a large number of goal-setting studies, self-efficacy has been shown to be an important factor affecting goal success (Locke, 1997; Bandura and Locke, 2003).

Overall, the Big Five traits (discussed in Chapter 1 on personality) are also good predictors of goal setting, as well as other motivational approaches. A very strong positive relationship exists between conscientiousness (a proxy for motivation) and goal setting; and a very strong negative relationship was found between goal setting and neuroticism (Ilies and Judge, 2005).

Management by objectives

As a managerial motivation strategy, goal setting has a prominent place in management by objectives (MBO). This is is a process in which a manager and a subordinate work together to set the subordinate's goals, relying on a participative approach to goal setting. It is probably the most popular and most widely implemented approach to managerial motivation since the 1950s. Many of the largest firms in the USA and Europe – among them companies such as Service America, Black & Decker, ARAMARK and Tenneco – have made systematic efforts to build MBO into their management philosophy.

Goal-setting theory is the underlying basis of MBO, and from that theory we know that there are three specific process components of a sound MBO system:

1. Goal setting.
2. Feedback.
3. Participation.

However, trying to use these processes on an organization-wide basis as MBO means that each must be done in such a way that the individual members of an organization work with one another to identify common goals and coordinate their efforts in reaching them. This makes it a much more complicated matter than simply setting goals with specific individuals without regard for the more broad organizational context within which these goals are set.

This leads to the major problem that many organizations have when trying to implement MBO: it is not strongly supported by management throughout an organization (Rodgers and Hunter, 1991). If some managers use it and others do not, then the positive effects are unlikely to occur (Carroll and Tosi, 1973). When the top management is strongly committed to building an objectives-oriented approach into its organizational culture and philosophy, the pay-offs can be very high. Organizations with a culture of high commitment to MBO report an average productivity gain of 56 percent in the first several years; in firms with a low implementation commitment, the gain is only 6 percent, a dramatic difference (Rodgers and Hunter, 1991). In addition, the job satisfaction of those managers who use MBO increases, regardless of the degree of organizational commitment or the increase in productivity.

The responsibility for developing this commitment to MBO lies with the top management. Typically, it begins with the development of strategic organizational goals by the CEO and the board of directors. Once these strategic organization goals are developed, functional subunit goals (marketing, production, and so on) are then prepared, usually in the form of general plans. These are then communicated to the next-lower levels. This process continues down through the organization through a series of cascading meetings between superiors and their subordinates and work groups, until there is an unbroken chain from the top management level to the lowest levels of supervision.

Two things must be done for MBO to be effective: it is necessary to implement it organization-wide; and each manager and subordinate must be willing and able to work with goal setting. A superior and a subordinate attempt to reach a consensus:

- What goals the subordinate will attempt to achieve in a given time period.
- The means by which the subordinate will attempt to accomplish the goals.
- How and when progress toward goals will be assessed.

Later, during the following period, the superior will review performance, possibly quarterly, along with a final performance at the end of the year.

Other considerations in goal-setting theory
One problem with this theory is the way it deals with goal complexity. In all the laboratory studies, goals were set for simple tasks. Even many of the field experiments generally studied relatively low-level, simple tasks such as typing or loading trucks. Work goals for managers and professionals are much more complicated. We simply do not know from goal-setting theory, for instance, how a manager sets priorities and makes choices between tasks for which goals have been set that are likely to differ in specificity and difficulty. In fact, a review of the research on goal setting showed that goal specificity and goal difficulty had weaker effects for more complex tasks than for simple tasks (Locke and Latham, 1990).

There is some recent research that suggests how goal-setting problems can develop in an organization. One study found that when a person had dual goals of high difficulty, the cumulative demands could exceed the person's capability and result in abandonment of one of the goals, to the detriment of the other (Schmidt and Dolis, 2009). There can be other dysfunctional effects of goal setting. There can be a tendency, when goals are not met, for a person to engage in unethical behavior that might lead to goal attainment (Schweitzer et al., 2004).

Organizational Justice Theories

Organizational justice approaches to motivation are based on perceptions of how justly or fairly you are treated at work (Colquitt et al., 2001):

- Distributive justice is the degree to which persons believe that they are treated fairly and equitably with respect to work outcomes, or how much they put into work and how much they gain from it. This is the basis for equity theory.
- Procedural justice is the extent to which people believe they are treated fairly in terms of how decisions are made about things that affect them in the workplace.

Outcome justice theory

Equity theory is based on the premise that people are motivated to maintain fair relationships with others and to rectify unfair relationships by making them fair (Adams, 1965). A fundamental premise is that individuals compare themselves to others and want their efforts and achievements to be judged fairly relative to them. This idea is different from other theories that explain motivation by intrapersonal comparisons (for example, 'what I have now' compared to 'what I would like to have'); equity theory explains motivation by interpersonal comparisons ('what I have now' compared to 'what others have'). That means that the concern in equity theory is outcome justice, or how you perceive your organizational outcomes relative to the contributions that you, and others, make to gain them. In other words, equity theory focuses on how you evaluate your outcome relative to how you evaluate the outcomes of others. There are three key factors used in explaining and understanding motivation in equity theory:

1. Inputs.
2. Outcomes.
3. Referents.

Inputs are what you bring to the job, such as age, experience, skill and seniority, and contributions to the organization or group. They can be anything that you believe to be relevant to the job, and that should be recognized by others. Outcomes are things that you perceive to be received as a result of work. Outcomes may be positively valued factors such as pay, recognition, promotion, status symbols and fringe benefits. They may also be negative: unsafe working conditions, pressure from management and monotony. In equity theory, a referent is the focus of comparison for the person – either other individuals or other groups. For example, as a department manager, you might compare yourself to 'Paula Dawkins', one of the other department managers, or to all the department managers in your firm.

Perceived inequity (or equity) is based on the comparison of two ratios of outcomes to inputs. Equity occurs when your ratio of outcomes to inputs is equal to the ratio of the referent (Paula), as shown in the following equation.

$$\frac{\text{Outcomes (yours)}}{\text{Inputs (yours)}} = \frac{\text{Outcomes (Paula)}}{\text{Inputs (Paula)}}$$

Underpayment inequity occurs when you believe that your inputs are at least equal to Paula's but your outcomes are less than hers. You gain less from the job than Paula does, relative to what you both contribute. This underpayment results in dissatisfaction that stems from anger at being under-rewarded and is likely to lead to a reduction in the quality of work (Kanfer, 1990; Cowherd and Levine, 1992), counterproductive behavior such as theft (Greenberg, 1990, 1993) and lower performance (Greenberg, 1988).

There is also overpayment inequity. If Paula assesses her outcomes in the same way that you evaluate them, she experiences overpayment inequity. This means that she believes that she gains more from the job relative to her referent (you, in this case). Overpayment inequity leads to dissatisfaction, just as underpayment inequity does, but in this case the dissatisfaction results from feelings of guilt that the person (in this case, Paula) develops. The dissatisfaction, whether it arises from guilt or anger, will cause the person who experiences it to do something to bring the situation into a state of equity. For example, when a group of managers were assigned higher-status offices than their current position warranted, they increased their performance (Greenberg, 1988). Similar increased levels of performance were found in a study of workers who remained in a firm after downsizing and had seen their co-workers released (Brockner and Wiesenfeld, 1996). If co-workers were terminated because of low performance, those remaining thought that they had performed more favorably on the assignment than those terminated. When co-workers were terminated on a random basis, the remaining workers worked harder, increasing their inputs, as equity theory predicts.

When inequity is perceived, a person is likely to take some action to restore equity, and thus to bring these ratios into balance. This is especially so for those who have strong moral values, a strong conscience and high ethical standards (Vecchio, 1981). Here are some of the different ways of achieving an equitable balance:

- Change the inputs. One way for you to restore equity is to reduce your inputs. You might lower your organizational commitment, put in fewer hours, and not be as concerned with quality as you had been in the past. If Paula experiences overpayment inequity, she could increase her inputs by trying to raise the quality of her work or increasing her effort.
- Change outcomes. Another way to reduce your feelings of inequity is to try to gain more out of your work. You might seek a pay raise, try to increase your power or seek more privileges. Paula might alter her outcomes by refusing a pay increase (unlikely) or by taking on less intrinsically satisfying work.
- Rationalize the inputs and outputs and psychological distortion. You could increase your outcomes by rationalizing that your job has higher status or is more important than you earlier believed. You could psychologically distort inputs by changing your attributions about how much effort you put into the job, believing that you do less than you formerly believed. Paula might also 'convince' herself that her job is more important than yours. A study found that workers who were forced to take a pay cut but remained on the job elevated the perceived importance of their own work (Greenberg, 1989).
- Psychological distortion. Physical distortion of the other person's outcomes and inputs is also possible. You may rationalize that Paula's actual contributions are not as great as yours, but that she has done so well because she had the advantage of being a woman during a time when the company was under pressure to treat women more favorably. This would make her inputs seem greater and bring the ratios into balance.
- Leave the situation. You may decide to move to another job. Then in the new setting, you escape the inequity and may find a fairer situation.
- Act against the other person. You might try to convince Paula to work harder, thus increasing her inputs. Alternatively, you may be able to decrease her outcomes by a political strategy in which you undermine the confidence others have in her, so that she leaves the company.
- Change the referent. You may find it easier not to compare yourself to Paula. If you can find another person in the firm who seems to

have a similar ratio of outcomes to inputs as you, you will reinstate a sense of equity, your satisfaction will increase, and your anger will decrease.

Procedural justice theory

Procedural justice theory focuses on another facet of justice that affects motivation and satisfaction: how you make judgments and your perceptions about whether you believe that the way that decisions are made are fair. Perceptions of procedural justice are related to higher levels of organizational commitment, job satisfaction and organizational citizenship behavior, or contextual performance (Folger and Konovsky, 1989; Ball et al., 1994).

Procedural justice theory is a relatively new motivational approach, but an important one. If you think about it for a minute, you will realize that decisions that affect you – decisions about your pay, your advancement, your work assignment, and so on – are made in the organization where you work. There are organizational systems of rules, policies, procedures and operating systems through which these decisions are made and then implemented. Very often, managers believe that simply because they are following these specified procedures, rules and policies in making decisions, those who are affected by them will accept the decisions and actions as reasonable, fair and equitable.

There could be nothing further from the truth. Though managers might think that the use of standard procedures and policies is fair, there are still feelings of unfairness when managerial action does not result in an outcome favorable to the person, or when the procedures are seen as unfair. Three factors have to be present to have a sense of procedural justice (Brockner and Wiesenfeld, 1996). The first is process control, or the extent to which you believe that you are allowed to present your position and justify your case before a decision is made. Process control was present in Francesca's case above, as we have seen that she was able to bring information about her previous course to her advisor. In unionized organizations, the grievance procedure permits you some level of process control since you are allowed to provide evidence favoring your position at every step in the process.

A second factor is decision control: the amount of influence you have in the decision-making process. In Francesca's case, the decision was made by her advisor and she was unable to have any influence in the decision outcome itself. One way that she might have been able to exert some influence would be if there were some sort of appeal process in which she might ask a committee to review the advisor's decision and, at the same time, be able to designate a representative to be on that committee.

Managing organizational behavior

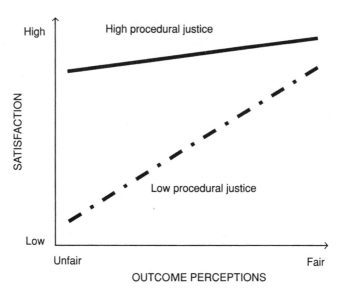

Figure 3.11   The interaction of procedural justice and outcome justice

The third factor that affects perceptions is interactional justice: whether the decision and the decision-making process are fully explained to you and whether you are treated with respect and dignity during the decision process (Brockner and Wiesenfeld, 1996). It is a reasonable prediction that if Francesca had been given the 'It's our policy' explanation, she would not have perceived that there was procedural justice.

The interaction of outcome justice and procedural justice
It is quite obvious that the effects of procedural justice on personal reactions depend on whether the result (the outcome) is favorable or unfavorable and, vice versa, that the favorability of any outcome will have an effect on the perceptions of procedural justice (Brockner and Wiesenfeld, 1996). Figure 3.11 shows how these two different justice concepts are related to each other and how they affect the satisfaction of the reactions of those affected. It shows that when the outcome is favorable to a person, then there is high satisfaction, whether or not the procedure was fair. To return to our example of Francesca, suppose that she was given credit for the course she wished to transfer, a decision that is highly favorable to her. She is likely to be similarly satisfied with the procedure that the advisor used to make the decision, whether it was fair and whether it was consistent with the university's policies. Now suppose that the decision was made not to accept the transfer credit, a much less favorable outcome

for her. Figure 3.11 shows that if she thought the procedure was unfair ('We won't accept this because it is our policy not to do so!'), then she will have much lower satisfaction than if, say, she was able to appeal to a committee, appoint one member as her representative, and present her case personally to them.

Spotlight 3.4   Motivation and culture

Motivational approaches that work in one culture may not work in others because of differences in values and preferences. For example, one large US company operating in 46 different countries with over 20 000 workers found major differences in worker preferences (Sirota and Greenwood, 1971):

- In English-speaking countries, individual achievement was more strongly emphasized than security.
- French-speaking countries tended to place greater importance on security and less on challenging work than the English-speaking countries.
- In Northern European countries, leisure time was more important; there was higher concern for the needs of employees and less for the needs of the organization.
- Latin countries, Germany and Southern European countries put more emphasis on job security and fringe benefits.
- Japanese employees put a stronger emphasis on good working conditions and a friendly work environment.

SUMMARY

Several motivation theories have been discussed in this chapter. Need theories, a class of content theories, suggest what motivates people. They give clues to managers about what they can change so that increased employee performance and satisfaction as well as organizational effectiveness can result. Maslow's need hierarchy approach, and achievement–power theory, are examples of need theories. The job characteristics approach describes ways that work itself can be modified to build in more motivational power. It suggests a number of strategies designed to activate and satisfy the needs of employees at all levels.

The remaining approaches to motivation emphasize the process of motivation – how it occurs. Reinforcement theory, also discussed in Chapter 2, explains behavior and its persistence in terms of consequences associated with the behavior. Expectancy theory is based on the premise that a person will make an effort toward behavior that leads to desirable results. It is a rational approach that suggests people seek to enhance their pay-offs. Expectancy theory calls for the management of factors to improve performance and ways to reward it. Equity theory states that people are motivated to maintain fair relationships with others and to rectify unfair ones. A number of conditions can trigger feelings of inequity at work, and these trigger reactions such as withholding performance, seeking better pay-offs or leaving the field. Goal-setting theory predicts how well people perform, based on the characteristics of goals they have. Difficult and specific goals and feedback have been consistently associated with high performance.

It is important to note here, though, that there is no one best theory of motivation and some seem better suited to deal with certain topics than others: need theories are most widely used to study satisfaction and work effort; reinforcement theory focuses on effort, performance, and absenteeism and turnover; expectancy theory can be used to predict job and organization choices and withdrawal behavior; goal-setting theory has been related to choice behavior and performance.

Further, since these different theories have psychological bases and concern the same variable, human behavior, it is only logical that they can be related to one another. Expectancies, for example, develop as a result of previous learning experiences. Learning theory may also explain the development of particular motives. Strong achievement needs may result from the positive reinforcement of success experiences in early life. In fact, this is exactly the point we make in Chapter 2 in the discussion of learning and personality. In the final analysis, understanding each of these different approaches is useful because it gives the manager several ways to look at problems. As a result, he or she may arrive at better solutions more quickly and effectively.

GUIDE FOR MANAGERS: USING MOTIVATION THEORIES AT WORK

There are several useful ideas for managers in this chapter. Perhaps the most important is that they must recognize that their primary role is to manage performance, and that low levels of motivation can be one of many factors that contribute to poor performance. There are several indicators that one can check to determine whether there are performance problems. For example, a manager should be aware of:

- Increased absenteeism in the work group.
- More grumbling or complaining than usual.
- Increased tardiness of those in the unit.
- Significant changes in performance, up or down.
- Major shifts in attitudes or in the level of commitment.

These are only indicators that there is a problem to be managed, a problem that may have its source in something other than worker motivation. For example, it is possible that the low performance is a result of deficiencies in ability that may require additional training or, perhaps, shifting a person out of his or her current position and finding a replacement with the skill to perform the job. It is also possible that some of the indicators above may be attributable to the work context. For example, performance problems are often attributable to equipment beginning to have problems, though these problems may not be immediately obvious to the manager. In this case, surely the solution to poor performance is to fix what is wrong. Once these questions have been addressed and the conclusion is that there are motivational issues that need attention, there are several things that can be done to increase motivation.

Create an Intrinsically Rewarding Work Environment

This can be accomplished by making the job more challenging and interesting while at the same time increasing the autonomy and responsibility of workers.

Define Clear and Challenging Work Goals

The manager should ensure that subordinates know what level of performance is expected in some measurable, quantifiable terms if possible. These goals must be attainable. Unattainable goals have an $E \rightarrow P$ expectancy of zero, and very difficult goals have low $E \rightarrow P$ expectancies.

Remove Barriers to Performance

By providing adequate resources, training workers, or removing unnecessary bureaucratic constraints, the E → P expectancy can be increased.

Clarify What is Appropriate Performance

There are often several ways to achieve a goal. For example, cost reduction might be achieved by effective control of all costs or by omitting preventive maintenance programs. A subordinate should know what is considered the preferred way to achieve reduced costs. Clarifying such performance-level expectations for subordinates is an important aspect of the coaching role of the manager.

Reward Performance

Extrinsically rewarding good performance can modify the P → O expectancy of a person. Extrinsic rewards are administered by someone else and include, for example, pay, advancement and fringe benefits. To the extent that high rewards follow good performance, one can expect an employee to engage in such performance more frequently.

Link the Reward to the Behavior

This can be accomplished by first clarifying what might constitute outstanding performance. The connection can also be made by rewarding very soon after performance or by verbally explaining why the employee is being rewarded.

Fit the Magnitude of the Reward to the Magnitude of the Behavior

A small reward such as a brief word of praise is insufficient for a rather substantial contribution by an employee. It is also possible to overreact to performance, such as putting a story about the employee in the company newspaper and throwing a party when the performance was not sustained or outstanding. This rule requires some judgment.

Better Performers should be Rewarded more than Average Performers

Who complains when every employee gets the same reward treatment? The best performers do, and there is not much that can be said to the best employees when they have not been differentially recognized. Who complains when the best employees are rewarded better? The poorer performers are more likely to make inquiries. Thus, when using such discrimination in rewards, the manager needs to prepare for questions raised by the poorer employees and attempt to improve their performance.

Reward more Often

Many managers are stingy with rewards, either because they are embarrassed to give them or because they fear the employee might become 'spoiled'. Good rewarding does not mean giving employees whatever they want whenever they want it. Good rewarding is based on the existence of performance standards, and if the reward is linked to performance, it need not lead to the spoiling effect.

Reward after Performance

Avoid rewarding before the behavior takes place. For example, suppose a supervisor grants a merit raise to an employee and explains to the employee that the raise is an act of good faith and that the employee will improve on their unacceptable performance in the future. This might work on the rare occasion that the employee agrees that he or she needs to shape up, and really respects the supervisor. Usually, however, the reward will act as a reinforcement for past behavior. The employee might conclude that his or her behavior couldn't have been that bad, or the boss would never have granted the merit pay.

Reward People with What They Value

It is important to remember that individuals differ in what they value. A group of employees may have a wide range of preferences. Knowing what those preferences are, the manager may be able to tailor some rewards to the specific values of employees; unless someone values a reward, it is not likely to affect their behavior. There are several ways to discover what people value. One is to use consequences that are widely valued, such as praise, a smile or recognition. Another is to ask people. A third is to observe how a person uses their free time on and off the job to find out what they like or dislike.

Administer Rules and Policies Fairly

Rules and policies should be applied in a consistent, fair and impartial way. Inconsistent application will surely result in feelings of favoritism, unfairness and dissatisfaction by those who are negatively affected by decisions that they think have been made differently for others.

Provide Due Process for Your Staff

When a person has a complaint or criticism, every attempt should be made to provide a fair hearing. If there is a union involved, you should follow the bargained procedure. If there is not, but there are organizational policies that specify a procedure, follow them. If there are neither, then use your good judgment to treat the complaint as you would want yours treated.

CASE: FRANCK PIETRI'S RAISE

It was Friday afternoon and Franck Pietri, a computer programmer at the Lock & Sons Company, was feeling nervous. So was his boss in the nearby office, Mr Buttersby. The time had come for Pietri's first annual performance appraisal interview.

Franck felt he had performed well in the first year, especially in the past six months. But it was always hard to tell what Mr Buttersby thought, because he was usually busy, as well as being the quiet type. He didn't know how he felt about some of the mistakes he had made or how many of them he knew about. Franck did try to make some of his recent improvements apparent to Mr Buttersby, but he hadn't said much about them either.

Before inviting Franck into his office, Mr Buttersby had reviewed the year and concluded that Franck needed a lot of improvement. His early mistakes had been costly in time and money to the company. But he had shown some progress. The question was whether to give Franck a merit raise and, if so, how much. Mr Buttersby disliked appraising performance, but he look a deep breath and called Franck into his office.

After a friendly greeting, Mr Buttersby pointed out Franck's good work and attitude. He told him how much he appreciated a recent program that Franck had written, which Franck took as a pleasant surprise. He was also pleased to know that Mr Buttersby thought he had a good attitude.

Then the blow fell. Mr Buttersby began to recount several of Franck's early errors, especially the time he was late with an inventory control program that took a long time to debug. After ten minutes of this, Franck became quite tense, because he was getting hit with more surprises and wasn't given much of a chance to defend himself.

But much to Franck's surprise and relief, Mr Buttersby informed him that he was going to give him a merit increase anyway. He said, 'Despite the fact that we both know you didn't have a good first year, the merit increase gives you an incentive to improve the coming year. It's our way of saying we have faith you can earn this raise by better and better performance.'

With that, the appraisal interview ended. Franck went back to his desk pleased about the merit money, but feeling a bit bewildered. A number of things were still bothering him.

1. Did Mr Buttersby use good learning and reinforcement techniques in Franck's first year? Explain. What effect did this have on Franck?
2. Will the merit raise act as an incentive for Franck to improve performance, or will he view it as a reward for past performance?

3. Franck is likely to experience cognitive dissonance because he received two conflicting messages: he was told he didn't have a good year, and he was given a merit raise. How can Franck reduce this dissonance?
4. How would you use expectancy theory and reinforcement theory to improve Franck's performance?

REFERENCES

Adams, J.S. (1965), Inequity in Social Exchange. In *Advances in Experimental Social Psychology*, L. Berkowitz (ed.). New York: Academic Press, pp. 267–99.

Alderfer, C. (1972), *Existence, Relatedness, and Growth: Human Needs in Organizational Settings*. New York: Free Press.

Ball, G., L.K. Trevino and H. Sims (1994), Just and Unjust Punishment: Influences on Subordinate Performance and Citizenship. *Academy of Management Journal*, **37**(2): 229–323.

Bandura, A. and E.A. Locke (2003), Negative self-efficacy and goal effects revisited. *Journal of Applied Psychology*, **88**(1): 87–99.

Borman, W.C. and S.J. Motowidlo (1993), Expanding the Criterion Domain to Include Elements of Contextual Performance. In *Personnel Selection in Organizations*, N. Schmitt and W.C. Borman (eds). San Francisco, CA: Jossey Bass.

Brockner, J. and B. Wiesenfeld (1996), An Integrative Framework for Explaining Reactions to Decision: Interactive Effects of Outcomes and Procedures. *Psychological Bulletin*, **120**(2): 189–208.

Carroll, S.J. and H.L. Tosi (1973), *Management by Objectives: Applications and Research*. New York: Macmillan.

Collins, C.J., P.J. Hanges and E.A. Locke (2004), The Relationship of Achievement Motivation to Entrepreneurial Behavior: A Meta-analysis. *Human Performance*, **17**(1): 95–117.

Colquitt, J.A., D.E. Conlon, M.S. Wesson, C.O.L.H. Porter and K.Y. Ng (2001), Justice at the Millennium: A Meta-analytic Review of 25 Years of Organizational Justice Research. *Journal of Applied Psychology*, **86**(3): 425–45.

Cowherd, D.M. and D.I. Levine (1992), Product Quality and Pay Equity Between Lower-Level Employees and Top Management: An Investigation of Distributive Justice Theory. *Administrative Science Quarterly*, **37**(2): 302–20.

Deci, E.L. (1971), The effects of externally mediated rewards on intrinsic motivation. *Journal of Personality and Social Psychology*, **18**: 105–15.

Erez, M., P.C. Early and C. Hulin (1985), The Impact of Participation of Goal Acceptance and Participation. *The Academy of Management Journal*, **28**(1): 50–66.

Folger, R. and M. Konovsky (1989), Effects of Procedural and Distributive Justice on Reaction to Pay Raises. *Academy of Management Journal*, **32**(1): 115–30.

Greenberg, J. (1988), Equity and Workplace Status. *Journal of Applied Psychology*, **73**(4): 606–14.

Greenberg, J. (1989), Cognitive Reevaluation of Outcomes in Response to Underpayment Inequity. *Academy of Management Journal*, **32**(1): 174–85.

Greenberg, J. (1990), Employee Theft as a Reaction to Underpayment Inequity: The Hidden Costs of Pay Cuts. *Journal of Applied Psychology*, **76**(5): 562–9.

Greenberg, J. (1993), Stealing in the Name of Justice: Informational and Interpersonal Moderators of Theft Reaction to Underpayment Inequity. *Organizational Behavior and Human Decision Performance*, **54**(1): 81–104.

Hackman, J.R. and E.E. Lawler (1971), Employee Reactions to Job Characteristics. *Journal of Applied Psychology Monograph*, **55**: 259–86.

Hackman, J.R. and G.R. Oldham (1976), Motivation Through the Design of Work: Test of a Theory. *Organizational Behavior and Human Performance*, **16**: 250–79.

Hackman, J.R. and J.L. Suttle (eds) (1977), *Improving Life at Work: Behavioral Science Approaches to Organizational Change*. Santa Monica, CA: Goodyear Publishing.

Hackman, J.R., G.R. Oldham, R. Janson and K. Purdy (1975), A New Strategy for Job Enrichment. *California Management Review*, **17**: 57–71.

Hamner, W.C. and E.P. Hamner (1976), Behavior Modification on the Bottom Line. *Organization Dynamics*, **4**: 8–21.

Herrigel, E. (1981 [1953]), *Zen in the Art of Archery*. New York: Random House.

Herzberg, F.A., B. Mausner and B. Snyderman (1959), *The Motivation to Work*. New York: John Wiley.

Ilies, R. and T.A. Judge (2005), Goal Regulation across Time: The Effects of Feedback and Affect. *Journal of Applied Psychology*, **90**(3): 453–67.

Kanfer, R. (1990), Motivation Theory and Industrial and Organizational Psychology. In *Handbook of Industrial and Organizational Psychology*, M.D. Dunnette and L. Hough (eds). Palo Alto, CA: Consulting Psychologists Press, pp. 75–170.

Landy, F.J. and W.S. Becker (1987), Motivation Theory Reconsidered. In *Research in Organizational Behavior*, L.L. Cummings and B.M. Staw (eds). Greenwich, CT: JAI Press, pp. 1–38.

Locke, E.A. (1997), The Motivation to Work: What We Know. *Advances in Motivation and Achievement*, M. Maehr and P. Pintrich (eds). **10**: 375–412.

Locke, E.A. and G.P. Latham (1990), *A Theory of Goal Setting and Task Performance*. Englewood Cliffs, NJ: Prentice Hall.

Locke, E.A., K.N. Shaw, C.M. Saari and G.P. Latham (1981), Goal Setting and Task Performance: 1969–1980. *Psychological Bulletin*, **90**: 125–52.

Luthans, F., R. Paul and D. Baker (1981), An Experimental Analysis of the Impact of Contingent Reinforcement on Salespersons' Performance Behavior. *Journal of Applied Psychology*, **66**(3): 314–23.

Maslow, A.H. (1943), A Theory of Human Motivation. *Psychological Review*, **50**: 370–96.

McClelland, D.A. (1965), Toward a Theory of Motive Acquisition. *American Psychologist*, **20**: 321–3.

McClelland, D.A. (1975), *Power: The Inner Experience*. New York: Irvington.

Organ, D.W. (1988), *Organizational Citizenship: The Good Soldier Syndrome*. Lexington, MA: Lexington Books.

Orpen, C. (1982), The Effects of Contingent and Noncontingent Rewards on Employee Satisfaction and Performance. *Journal of Psychology*, **110**(1): 145–50.

Pinder, C. (2008), *Work Motivation in Organizational Behavior*, 2nd edn. London: Psychology Press.

Rodgers, R. and J.E. Hunter (1991), Impact of Management by Objectives on Organizational Productivity. *Journal of Applied Psychology*, **76**(2): 322–36.

Schmidt, A.M. and C.M. Dolis (2009), Something's Got to Give: The Effects of Dual-Goal Difficulty, Goal Progress, and Expectancies on Resource Allocation. *Journal of Applied Psychology*, **94**(3): 678–91.

Schweitzer, M.E., L. Ordonez and B. Douma (2004), Goal Setting as a Motivator of Unethical Behavior. *Academy of Management Journal*, **47**(3): 422–32.

Scully, J.A., S. Kirkpatrick and E.A. Locke (1973), Locus of Knowledge as a Determinant of the Effects of Participation on Performance, Affect and Perception. *Organizational Behavior and Human Decision Processes*, **62**(3): 276–88.

Sirota, D. and M.J. Greenwood (1971), Understanding your Overseas Workforce. *Harvard Business Review*, **49**(1): 53–60.

Spector, P.E. (1985), Higher-Order Need Strength as a Moderator of the Job Scope–Employee Outcome Relationship: A Meta-Analysis. *Journal of Occuptional Psychology*, **58**: 119–27.

Stajkovic, A. and F. Luthans (1997), A Meta-Analysis of the Effects of Organizational Behavior Modification on Task Performance. *Academy of Management Journal*, **40**(8): 1122–49.

Staw, B.M. (1976), *Intrinsic and Extrinsic Motivation*. Morristown, NJ: General Learning Press.

Tosi, H.L. and L. Gomez-Mejia (1989), The Decoupling of CEO Pay and Performance: An Agency Theory Perspective. *Administrative Science Quarterly*, **34**: 169–89.

Tubbs, M.E. (1986), Goal Setting: A Meta-Analytic Examination of the Empirical Evidence. *Journal of Applied Psychology*, **71**(3): 474–83.

Vecchio, R.P. (1981), An Individual Difference Interpretation of the Conflicting Predictions Generated by Equity Theory and Expectancy Theory. *Journal of Applied Psychology*, **66**: 470–81.

Vroom, V.H. (1964), *Work and Motivation*. New York: John Wiley.

Winter, D.G. (1988), The Power Motive in Men and Women. *Journal of Personality and Social Psychology*, **54**(3): 510–19.

4. Stress and its effects in organizations

PREPARING FOR CLASS

As you prepare for this chapter, team up with another student who is taking this course and with whom you are willing to discuss the issues involved in this activity. Independently, both of you should answer these three questions:

1. Write a general description of the level of stress you are feeling in your life at this time.
2. What are the main aspects of your life that are contributing to the stress you are feeling? (Look at the 'Sources of Stress' section below for a list of the types of events that can lead to stress.)
3. List the activities that you do to manage your own stress.

Now, compare your answers with those of your teammate:

1. Are the stressors in each of your lives similar?
2. Do you have different ways of managing the stress?
3. Can either of these aspects explain the differences or similarities in the stress you said you were feeling?
4. Where there are differences? Can they be explained by the individual differences mentioned in the text?

* *

Valerie was thinking about her recent interview with her new boss, just after the organization had gone through an extensive process of organization change that had involved the whole firm for which she works:

> I felt threatened from the beginning, when they said we were downsizing. I can't think of a more stressful time in my whole career than the change that we have experienced over the past 12 months. I thought in the past that I would remain with this organization until retirement. Then the change. How would I have paid my mortgage if I had been one of those who were released? Right now I have problems with sleep and I can't eat. I spend most of my time trying to understand what happened. Even now, when we are told is that there will

be no more changes, I am still very skeptical. I feel like a different person, with different feelings about the organization and even my colleagues here. I'm just more pessimistic.

Valerie is describing her emotional reaction to a significant change in the workplace. It is the kind of change that has a major impact on the patterns of organizational life, it affects individual motivation to work, and consequently it has effects on attitudes toward the organization and the way people see themselves. They often wonder about their future and the organization to which they belong. This emotional reaction to change is normal, since the uncertainty created by a restructuring is a major source of stress and has a significant effect on the organization's well-being.

Working life can be very rewarding and motivating. It provides a great deal of satisfaction and rewards, both intrinsic and extrinsic. But at the same time, work can be stressful and create a lot of negative emotions. These occur because of interaction with others, whether they are colleagues, department heads or other employees. Very often at work there is conflict, argument and problems which we have to face. We can find different forms of problems such as verbal abuse, sexual harassment, bullying among colleagues and mobbing, a new and genuine phenomenon, all of which undermine the basic health of people in organizations. In general, organizations recognize these issues and try to solve them by creating high-involvement organizations and constantly monitoring the organizational climate.

In this chapter we examine the meaning of stress, its causes, how it is manifested by individuals, some personality factors that are important, and how it can be managed. However, while the emphasis is on work-related stress, we also discuss some extra-work considerations because we believe that stress may emanate from many sources and has effects beyond the workplace.

Stress is pervasive, it has no respect for national or state borders. In Japan the word *karoushi* means sudden death due to excessive work. A study by the European Campaign for Health and Safety at Work on the quality of work in Europe reports (Takala, 2008):

- More than 28 percent of workers experience the burnout syndrome.
- Work-related stress accounts for more than 25 percent of absences of at least two weeks in the form of various health problems.
- According to 1999 figures, work-related stress costs the EU member states at least 20 billion euros a year.
- The service sectors, particularly the socio-health sector, are the most affected.
- Younger workers, older workers and temporary workers are the groups most at risk.

Stress also extracts a very high cost in the United States (Schwarz, 2004). For instance, it is estimated that:

- 75 percent of visits to family physicians are stress-related;
- stress in the workplace is estimated to cost the United States more than $300 billion per year; and
- stressed workers incur health care costs that are, on average $600 (46 percent) higher than other employees.

It can be very costly for work organizations because critical levels of stress can result in lower work performance, lower worker well-being, increased absences and higher health care costs (Potter et al., 2007; Ganster et al., 2001).

However, the effects of stress are not always negative. Each of us has experienced a stress-inducing situation that was a positive learning experience. For instance, preparing to take your first examinations at university might have been very stressful. As the time came closer you became more tense, worried about the exams and studied harder. When you walked into the classroom and took your seat, you had butterflies in your stomach and your palms were sweaty. If you were well prepared, these reactions disappeared when you started on the exam and found you could solve the problems or answer the questions. You learned that you were able to perform well in examinations, and as a result, later exams were not as stress-inducing as the first. Even performing poorly could be a positive developmental experience if you learned where you went wrong, what your limits are, and how to do better next time. You became stronger, and the next time you faced the examination situation, you knew what to do. Over time, exams could become less and less stress-inducing.

A MODEL OF STRESS AND COPING

Stress has a number of different connotations, or meanings. For instance, you might feel that the situation you are in (that is, your work) is very stressful – you feel more pressure than you prefer in your work or life environment, but you are dealing well enough with it. Or, you might feel 'stressed out' – you are physically and/or psychologically drained from the situation or the people that surround you. You are more depressed, have lower self-confidence, feel more anxious, are smoking or drinking more, your blood pressure is going up or you are more frequently absent from or late for work.

We define stress as a psychological or physical state of an individual that develops because the individual is faced with situations that tax or exceed available resources (internal or external), as appraised by the person involved (Lazarus, 2000a). It results as we interact with the environment, objective and psychological, in which there are stimuli called stressors, which could be a result of:

1. Harm or loss that has already occurred.
2. A threat of some harm or loss that may occur in the future.
3. A challenge, meaning that there are difficulties that the person believes he or she can overcome with persistent effort (Lazarus, 2000b).

Some stressors can be chronic, constant conditions that we face at work and at home. Other stressors may be acute, in the sense that they are time-limited major events that we face. It can also happen that an acute stressor leads to other circumstances that might become chronic. For example, a death of a brother, an acute stressor, might create relatively permanent feelings of depression that occur when we visit the family home and see his bedroom, now empty.

The Stress Environment

Figure 4.1 shows how we conceptualize stress in this chapter. Stressors exist in the objective environment, which contains those conditions in which you are embedded and that may affect you. Working conditions, other people, noise and heat are all examples of possible stressors in the work environment. Non-work elements such as social pressures, demands from spouse and children, and community problems may also act as stressors, and they can certainly affect what happens on the job. These are important pressures because the relationship between work and family and other critical aspects of a person's life must be resolved.

The psychological environment is the way that you experience the objective environment. For instance, if you are in a job that requires dealing with people outside the organization (a fact of the objective environment), you are likely to feel more incompatible job demands or role conflict (an aspect of the psychological environment) than someone who works completely within the organization.

The Cognitive Appraisal: What You Tell Yourself about Stressors

Where does the psychological environment come from? A useful way to think about that is the 'general adaptation syndrome' (Selye, 1974). The first thing that happens when stressors are perceived is an alarm reaction: physiological changes that warn the body it is under pressure. Adrenaline

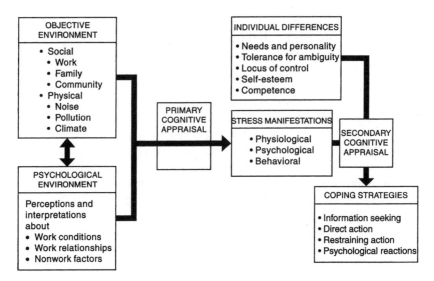

Figure 4.1   A model of stress

flow increases, blood pressure rises and muscles become tense. Next there is the resistance stage: when the body tries to restore its balance it expends physical and psychological energy and people use different physiological, psychological and biological ways to resist stressors. The final stage is the exhaustion stage. Over time, the stressors may use up all of your psychological and physiological energy. If the resistance is not successful, you simply wear out. When you reach the exhaustion stage, both physical and mental illness may occur.

However, what happens under stress depends upon the individual. Some people are more sensitive to the presence of stressors; some use more effective coping mechanisms. And you cannot necessarily tell how a person is responding to stress by outward appearances. In stressful situations, some are 'hot reactors' and experience dramatic physical changes (Eliot and Dennis, 1989). Blood pressure shoots up, heart rate may increase or decrease, and blood vessels may become more or less resistant to blood flow. Other people are 'cool reactors': under stress their bodily functions change at rates more or less appropriate to the situation. At the same time, both the hot reactor and the cool reactor may appear to be very calm on the outside. The hot reaction may overstimulate the body's nervous system and lead to arterial spasms and other circulatory problems. It also causes the body to increase its production of adrenaline, potentially a serious problem because adrenaline stimulates both physical and mental activity, and the person may become addicted to it. That is,

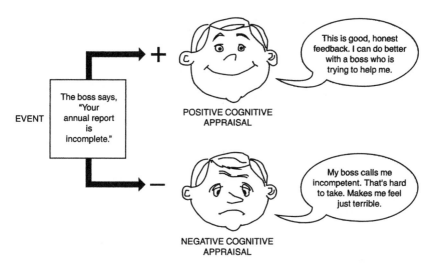

Figure 4.2   The effects of two different cognitive appraisals of the same event

the person is able to operate best only under conditions of an adrenaline surge.

The psychological environment is a result of the primary cognitive appraisal: the way you assess the significance of the various aspects of the environment (Lazarus, 2000b; Cooper and Dewe 2004). How they are actually judged depends on the person, so that one person could feel stressed while another feels neutral. The primary cognitive appraisal determines the intensity and quality of the individual's emotional response (Lazarus, 2000a). When your primary cognitive appraisal is positive, you will have emotions such as pleasure and joy and feel relaxation. When your environment is appraised as stressful, you will experience negative emotions such as anxiety, fear and so forth. Suppose your boss says to you, 'Your annual report is incomplete.' You may appraise this event in one of at least two ways, as shown in Figure 4.2. You might believe: 'My boss called me incompetent! He shouldn't do that. I can't stand to be called incompetent.' Such a cognitive appraisal may lead to feelings of job anxiety, low job satisfaction, and frustration because you are not sure how to improve your report-writing skills. Another, but positive, way to appraise the same event is: 'I am a human being and I have some faults. I am not perfect. This is good feedback. I am going to strive to do better.' This may lead to more constructive actions to deal with exactly the same event.

We know that these sorts of processes are important because they do have effects on how you feel about yourself and your work. Research has shown, for instance, that when persons have negative and dysfunctional thoughts and thought processes, they are more likely to be less satisfied with their jobs, as well as feel that they are not in good physical and mental health (Judge and Locke, 1993). However, it is possible to alter these negative thought processes by cognitive restructuring. This is done by:

1. Identification of positive and negative thoughts and statements.
2. Substitution of positive thoughts and statements for the negative ones.

This will increase self-efficacy and lead you to believe that you have the ability to perform the task or to cope with the stress. Suppose, for instance, that your first reaction to feedback from your boss might cause you to feel quite stressed. However, if you reappraise the situation and cognitively restructure it, you might conclude after all that you are not incompetent. You could, therefore, affect the strain you experience by what you think and tell yourself about the situation.

Strain

When these stressors, or demands, exceed the person's resources and results in negative physiological, psychological or behavioral responses by the individual, we say that the person experiences strain. Strain occurs when a stressor produces negative responses in the person. Strains may be physiological, psychological or behavioral reactions that are triggered by the cognitive appraisal of the situation. We also discuss another, important type of strain called burnout.

Physiological strains

Bodily functions change when you are stressed. These changes may be immediate or long-term reactions. When a stressor is recognized, an immediate biochemical bodily reaction initiated by the brain leads to an increased flow of adrenaline. In response to stressors, blood sugar increases, the heart beats faster, muscles tense, perspiration increases and all senses become heightened.

The longer-term physical reactions are, perhaps, more of a problem. As you experience stress over long periods, the body begins to show signs of wear and tear. Serious health problems such as coronary heart disease and cardiovascular illness have been associated with occupational and organizational stressors (Karasek et al., 1981). Other specific illnesses associated with stress are ulcers, hypertension (high blood pressure), headaches and migraine headaches. There is some belief that even illnesses not normally associated with stress, such as cancer, can be due to stress because stress leads to a breakdown in the body's immune system and this will increase susceptibility to other illnesses (Segerstrom and Miller, 2004).

Psychological strains

Psychological strains are the ones that we conventionally associate with stress. These emotions, thoughts and feelings may be work-specific or non-work-oriented. There are several work-specific strains that result from work stressors. For example, nurses who experienced more frequent and intense work stressors were more depressed, had greater work anxiety and were more hostile toward co-workers (Motowidlo et al., 1986). Other work-specific responses are lower job satisfaction, lower confidence in the organization, anxiety about work and career, increased alienation and lower commitment to work (Kahn and Byosiere, 1992).

Non-work-oriented responses are either short-term or long-term changes in the individual's psychological state. When these effects persist, they may reflect a change in personality, which is in itself a coping response. Some of these non-work psychological responses are lower self-confidence (or self-esteem), denial of the situation, an increased sense of futility, neuroticism, tension, general anxiety, irritation, hostility and depression.

Behavioral strains

People may act differently when they are under stress. They may use more alcohol, smoke more and change their eating patterns. Stress has also been associated with increased absenteeism; lateness at work; poor performance; reduced work concentration, composure, perseverance and adaptability; and lower work quality (Kahn and Byosiere, 1992). Stressed individuals are also less interpersonally effective. When exposure to stress resulted in higher depression for a group of nurses, they were less tolerant with doctors and showed less warmth toward other nurses. Highly stressed persons are more aggressive toward others, they are more competitive, and group cohesiveness is lower (Cohen, 1980). Communication with others may also be reduced. All these responses may be part of a more general coping syndrome of withdrawal from others, avoiding contact, and rejecting influence attempts from those who may be exerting pressure.

Burnout: a special type of job strain

When it was first used to describe a form of strain, it referred to persons working in human services jobs and education, but has now been applied to a wide range of occupations such as the military, police, managers and clerical work. 'Burnout is a prolonged response to chronic emotional and interpersonal stressors on the job, and is defined by the three dimensions of exhaustion, cynicism, and inefficacy' (Maslach et al., 2001). It can lead to lower job performance and lower well-being, both physical and psychological. We described exhaustion earlier as part of the 'general adaptation syndrome', occurring if resistance is not successful. You wear out as, over time, the work stressors use up all of your psychological and physiological energy. With burnout, however, the exhaustion leads to two other reactions. One is cynicism, which takes the form of depersonalizing yourself from your work, especially your clients, customers and co-workers, by creating greater psychological distance. The other reaction to exhaustion is a sense of inefficacy, or feelings of lower self-worth and competence.

Coping Strategies

Coping strategies are the way that you handle either the stressors or yourself when you experience strain. If you are sensing a stressor either consciously or unconsciously, you choose a way to respond to it. This occurs through a secondary cognitive appraisal process, which is different from the primary cognitive appraisal in which one becomes aware of the stressor (Lazarus, 2000b).

There are two functions of coping (Lazarus, 1980, 2000b). The first is problem solving; you may try to change the environmental stressor or your own behavior so that the stressor is less likely to occur or to be so severe. For instance, suppose you feel stress because you constantly receive negative feedback about your performance. If you are actually doing well, you might be able to change this feedback by making sure that your boss receives the correct information about your performance. You might also change the feedback by improving your performance if you have not been up to par.

The second is emotion-focused function, or managing the physiological and emotional reactions to stress; 'for example, by avoiding thinking about the threat or reappraising it – without changing the realities of the stressful situation' (Lazarus, 2000b).

There are four different strategies to cope with stress (Lazarus, 1980):

1. Seeking information.
2. Direct action.
3. Restraining action.
4. Psychological coping reactions.

Information seeking is trying to find out what the stressors are and what causes them. Because uncertainty is a property of stress, information seeking can be productive if the result is reduced uncertainty. However, it is possible that 'ignorance is bliss'. Sometimes the truth may be quite disruptive. Stress was found to be higher for employees who actively sought and obtained information about a major organizational change which might have had negative effects on them.

Spotlight 4.1 Stress management interventions in the EU: examples from Ireland, Poland, Finland and Denmark

Stress has been recognized as a leading cause of lost productivity in the European Union. For example, it is estimated that in Ireland the costs of absenteeism could be as high as €793 million per year. Ireland, like other countries in the European Union, has undertaken serious efforts to deal with the costs of stress.

In Finland, for instance, they have designed a health survey to identify 'higher-risk' participants who, when they are known, receive feedback about the stress levels they are experiencing and are invited to participate in stress management programs.

A similar program was instituted in Denmark. When employees were identified as having high stress, they were offered the opportunity to participate in a multidisciplinary stress management program which dealt with identifying relevant stressors, how to change coping strategies to be more effective, and other approaches to stress management. When they evaluated the results for those who participated in this program, they found that sick leave dropped from 53 percent to 17 percent. Notably, when those participants were compared to a control group which had not participated, it was found that they had a significant decrease in depression symptoms.

A similar program was introduced in Poland. A series of sessions were held over a ten-week period in which the participants learned about stressors, how to identify conditions that led to strain, and to develop their own strategies to change their work context and their own reactions to the stressors. Those who participated in the Polish program were found to increase their positive coping styles significantly, to decrease negative coping styles and, if they had a tendency to overuse one negative coping style, it decreased later (see Netterstrøm and Bech, 2008; Taimela 2007a, 2007b).

Source: www.sfa.ie/Sectors/SFA/SFA.nsf/

Direct action may take several forms. When experiencing job stressors, you may work harder, take pills, drink more, change jobs, or change the environment in some way. You might try to escape it by removing yourself from the immediate danger, or you might choose to respond by taking direct or indirect actions to remove the stressors. A study of truck drivers revealed that they coped with the strains of their work by quitting and looking for other forms of work (de Croon et al., 2004). Another form of direct action is to seek and develop social support (Zellars and Perrewe, 2001). Acceptance and help from others may buffer the effects of the stressors as well as help you to find more constructive solutions. If you are experiencing stress because of conflicting demands from your boss, you might seek out an older colleague (perhaps a mentor) with whom you can discuss the problem, and find a solution that helps.

Restraining action is dealing with stress by doing nothing, especially when taking action might lead to other, less desirable outcomes. For example, acting on an immediate impulse to a problem at work might lead to a person becoming so angry when another person is promoted that he or she might resign in haste. This could result in serious upheaval to family, a significant change in a person's career, and other undesirable results. Waiting before doing something is probably a more effective way to cope with such stress.

Psychological coping reactions are very common ways to cope with stress. Emotions, and often subsequent behavior, are determined in part by what the person says to himself or herself about the situation. Denial of the existence of a problem, psychological withdrawal from the situation, and other defense mechanisms may change the perceptions of the objective environment so much that the perceived environment is one in which the person can operate more comfortably, at least in the short run. When psychological coping modes distort reality and are used extensively, they may represent a poor adjustment to stress. For example, a person who consistently has a difficult time performing a job, but denies the failure or attributes it to wrong causes, may continue to stay in an unsuccessful situation. In the long run, this may diminish both self-esteem and job performance.

SOURCES OF STRESS

Stress is a result of the transaction and interaction between the person and the environment. In this section, we discuss environmental stressors. Some are in the objective environment, most are part of the psychological environment. We distinguish between 'work factors' and

---

Spotlight 4.2 Stoicism and managing stress

Epictetus, one of the most important Stoic philosophers, was a freed Roman slave who had his own school of philosophy in Greece when he was banished from Rome, with other philosophers. His philosophy offers ways to cope with stress in life. He says that in our lives, some things are in our control and some are not. Those things which we can control are our opinions, actions toward things and desires for those things. We can't control things like property, our body, our reputation (what others think about us) and governments. If you worry about things that are not in your power, you will always be hindered, but if you focus on those things that you control, you won't be hindered by others. Do nothing involuntarily and suffer no harm (Epictetus, 1991).

'non-work factors' which are sources of stress, as well as individual differences that affect our propensities to react to stressors or how we cope with stress.

Work Factors

There are good personal and organizational reasons to reduce stressors in the work context. For the person, work can be hazardous to your mental and physical health, an idea that is not consistent with the Western work ethic that work is rewarding and valued in and of itself. For the organization, work-induced stress has serious financial effects, as we noted earlier in this chapter. In this section, five work-setting stressors are discussed:

1. Occupational factors.
2. Role pressures.
3. Participation opportunities.
4. Responsibility for people.
5. Organizational factors.

Occupational factors

The demand–control approach by Karasek and his colleagues is a helpful way to understand why some jobs are more stressful than others (Karasek et al., 1981). They studied work factors and coronary disease,

Figure 4.3 Stress at work

since coronary disease is considered to be related, in part, to stress. Those jobs with the highest levels of coronary disease have two common characteristics: they are high in 'psychological demands' and low in 'decision control' (see Figure 4.3). People in these jobs are constantly under pressure from others, say a customer, and they must respond in a way that the other person wishes, not in the way they would like to. Consider a waiter. When the customer is ready to order, the waiter must be there. Food cannot be delivered until the cook prepares it. The waiter is in the middle between the cook and the customer, and subjected to demands from both while having little control over the situation. High-demand, low-control jobs are shown in the lower-right quadrant of Figure 4.3. Cooks, assembly line workers, firefighters and nurses have higher coronary disease risks. One study of nurses in the high-risk quadrant found they had lower job satisfaction, higher blood pressure and higher levels of salivary cortisol. Blood pressure is typically associated with coronary risk, and cortisol is associated with reduced immune reactions and depression. These nurses also carried stress reactions to home after work, increasing their chances of longer-term negative health effects. Studies have shown, however, that the effects of job demands and control depend upon the person's self-concept. Those with higher self-efficacy tend to experience fewer negative effects than those with higher self-efficacy (Schaubroeck et al., 2000, 2001).

The demand–control model has been used in many studies to assess the effect of work strain on employees. A extensive review of this research indicates that many of these studies support the model's basic concept, that working in high-demand, low-control jobs is related to lower well-being, lower job satisfaction, more job-related psychological distress and more burnout (van der Doef and Maes, 2000).

'Emotional labor' is another occupational source of stress that has some similarity to the demand–control model. In some organizations, employees are expected to exhibit friendly attitudes, to be smiling, to act cordially, and to manage anger and fatigue whether they are dealing with customers directly or by phone. When this is seen by the management as strategically critical, the organization will try to influence and exert control over emotional displays by the worker through processes of selection, socialization and training (Fineman, 1993). Hochschild has called this the 'management of the heart' (Hochschild, 1979, 1983).

We see examples of emotional labor all around us. There are several specific examples of firms who engage in this sort of training. For example, McDonald's Hamburger University trains its managers not only how to manage a fast food franchise, but also how to act in ways that will increase customer satisfaction (Rafaeli and Sutton, 1987, 1990). It is well known that employees at Disney who deal with the public are required to act and dress as if they are 'on stage' at work. One Disney employee recounted how his effort to control facial expression and tone of voice, and remember the numerous procedures, was a source of considerable stress to him. He developed a number of personal coping strategies such as increasing emotional distance from Disney visitors, automatic replies, and a procedural litany that, he thought, sometimes had undesirable effects on the perception of Disney visitors. The result generally, however, is that as customers we see the 'plastic smiles' that are obviously not sincere, and we usually participate in a sort of 'dance' that implies acceptance.

For some, emotional labor can be a stressor and result in negative psychological effects such as burnout, frustration, anger and emotional exhaustion, as well as physical effects such as hypertension, sleeplessness and fatigue. However, negative effects of emotional labor do not appear

---

Spotlight 4.3   Empowering emotional labor (for eldercare nursing staff) in Sweden

In Sweden they have made an attempt to increase the motivation of nurses involved in helping the elderly by a three-step program sponsored by several government and private agencies. The program involves:

- A competence program, directed at increasing the skills of the nurses.
- The creation of worksite competence circles to support a learning organization.
- Local worksite projects to ensure that the focus of activity is on things relevant to the local community.

There are local community groups as well as groups in each facility to support this initiative. Evaluations of the program have demonstrated positive and sustainable results (Petterson et al., 2006; Swedish Work Environment Authority, 2003).

---

to be a problem for extroverts or for those with high core self-evaluations (Judge et al., 2009; Kammeyer-Mueller et al., 2009).

Role pressures

Individuals are more effective at work when they are clear about what is expected of them and when they do not have severe role conflict and role ambiguity at work (Kahn et al., 1964). Role conflict and role ambiguity are both associated with a broad set of negative work reactions, including higher job tension and anxiety, lower job satisfaction, lower organization commitment and a higher propensity to leave an organization (House and Rizzo, 1972; Byiosiere and Kahn, 2004; Tubre and Collins, 2000). A moderately negative relationship also exists between individual performance, role conflict and role ambiguity (Jackson and Schuler, 1985; Tubre and Collins, 2000).

Role conflict occurs when a person is in a situation where there are pressures to comply with different and inconsistent demands. If the person complies with one demand, it is difficult or impossible to comply with other demands. Suppose a student has a Tuesday evening history class in which the instructor schedules an exam, but then finds out that her statistics exam is to be given during the same Tuesday evening class period. She cannot do both exams.

The particular type of role conflict depends on the sources of the demands. An 'intrasender' role conflict is inconsistent expectations from a single person. A manager, for instance, may expect you to increase production but does not give you the necessary additional resources. Often managers resort to this kind of demand when there are cost-cutting drives or other programs to increase efficiency.

'Intersender' role conflict occurs when two or more individuals place incompatible demands on a person. For example, the quality control manager of a plant may expect the production supervisor to reject more units of the product, while the production manager wants increased production output and therefore fewer rejections.

Person–role conflict occurs when organizational demands are in conflict with one's values. An example of this is the whistleblower. Whistleblowers call public attention to unethical or illegal actions by an organization, even though there can be great personal costs, often because they are motivated by personal beliefs about ethical responsibilities. In most organizations, person–role conflict is not likely to be a serious problem, since individuals who have serious personal differences with organizational values would probably discover this early in their organization socialization and leave.

There are two types of role ambiguity – the uncertainty about the expectations of others. Task ambiguity refers to uncertainty about the work requirements themselves. This is common, for example, when you take a new position and are trying to learn how to do the job. It also occurs when responsibilities are not clear because of vague job descriptions or unclear instructions from a manager. Social–emotional ambiguity is uncertainty about how you are evaluated by another person. This happens when work standards are unclear and performance judgments are subjective. It is also a problem when someone does not receive feedback from others.

Stress can also result if you are overworked or if you are underworked. Role overload occurs when the work requirements are so excessive that they exceed the limits of time and/or ability. Role underload is when work does not make use of a person's abilities. For security guards and receptionists, where the person is underutilized, their jobs do not require many different skills. Persons in such jobs characterize them as boring and monotonous. This kind of work is associated with higher levels of absenteeism, lower job satisfaction and alienation.

Challenges and hindrances Not all role pressures result in negative strains. Some may have some positive effects. Research shows that when a stress situation is appraised as being challenging (challenge stress) managers were more motivated, performed better, were more satisfied and less likely to seek work elsewhere (Cavanaugh et al., 2000; LePine et al., 2005). However, when the stressful situation was appraised as being a hindrance (hindrance stressors) managers were more likely to seek work elsewhere and have lower job satisfaction. Challenge stressors have positive motivational effects because it is likely that the cognitive appraisal is that the person is able to meet the stressor demands and that doing so will lead to desired outcomes. Hindrance stressors, on the other hand, lead to an appraisal that the person is unable to meet the demands and, therefore, will be less motivated. Challenge stressors are (Cavanaugh et al., 2000):

- The number of assigned projects.
- Amount of time at work.
- The quantity of work to be done with deadlines.
- Time pressure.
- Responsibility of the job.

Hindrance stressors are:

- The dominance of politics in the situation.
- Role ambiguity.
- Excessive bureaucracy.
- Job insecurity.
- Career blockage.

Participation opportunities
Managers who report higher levels of participation in decision making feel much lower stress, job anxiety and threat than those who report low participation (Tosi, 1971). Participation is important for two reasons:

- Participation is associated with low role conflict and low role ambiguity (Kahn and Byosiere, 1992).
- Participation gives you the feeling of some control of the stressors in the environment, reducing the effect of stressors compared to when you have no real or perceived control (Cohen, 1980).

Responsibility for people
Responsibility for others may lead to stress at work. As a manager, your effectiveness depends on those who work for you. If for any reason you do not have confidence in them or in your ability to manage them, then you are likely to experience stress because you do not perceive that you

have control over the situation. In addition to that, responsibility for others calls for making decisions about pay, promotion opportunities and career paths of others, and exerting a good deal of influence over their lives.

Organizational factors
The organization itself affects stress. For instance, it has long been argued that when organizations are restrictively bureaucratic, this does not maximize human performance potential; others believe that when they are too unstructured they are more likely to release human productive capacity (Argyris, 1964; Presthus, 1978). Five characteristics of organizations that can be stressors are:

1. Organizational level.
2. Organizational complexity.
3. Organizational change.
4. Organizational boundary roles.
5. Organizational justice.

At top organization levels, executives experience role overload; they have responsibility for others, and there is often a good deal of conflict and ambiguity present in the job. Managers tend to have more time constraints and efficiency problems. The very characteristics of the managerial role, such as constant interruptions, short times on any one activity, and so on, make effective use of time difficult. Workers at lower levels are more likely to have role overload and role conflict due to conflicting demands from supervisors and lack of resources (Parasuraman and Alutto, 1981).

Regarding organization complexity, excessive rules, requirements and complicated networks that exist in large organizations can be stressful. Role strain tends to become increasingly a problem as work becomes more specialized, more levels of supervision are introduced and more complexity is added (Kahn and Byosiere, 1992).

When there are organizational changes that modify your job and responsibilities so that you have to accommodate to them, stress reactions are possible. Some changes reduce a person's job security, status and power. Mergers, acquisitions, retrenchment and downsizing will create uncertainty, job anxiety and higher stress.

An organizational boundary role is one in which you must interact with, and be accountable to, others in your own organization at the same time that you are interacting with persons from other organizations who place demands on you. This is more stressful because you are subjected to role conflict which emanates from both internal and external sources. For example, sales personnel must meet customer demands at the same time that they must satisfy company requirements.

Organizational justice (or injustice) may also play a role in stress (Vermunt and Steemsma, 2001; Judge and Colquitt, 2004) (see Chapter 3 on motivation). For example, perceptions of procedural justice and relational justice are related to occupational strain, as well as moderating the relationship between job control and strain (Elovainio et al., 2001).

Non-Work Factors

Suppose that two administrative assistants have been working for you for several years. They may both have very similar work assignments, and both be exposed to the same set of work stressors in their objective work environment. How will this affect them? They are likely to experience different levels of stress and will exhibit different stress responses because:

1. They may make different cognitive appraisals of the same objective environment.
2. Personality differences may account for their different reactions.
3. One may be experiencing stressors in the non-work environment, such as divorce, the recent death of a parent, a very ill child or marital difficulties, that are not in the environment of the other.

In this subsection, we show the relationship of stress responses to some of these non-work environmental factors such as life structure changes and social support.

Life changes
Some of the natural flows of life can induce stress, both acute and chronic. For instance, most of us will experience the death of a parent, a spouse or a close family member and we all face the prospect of changing jobs. Any of these may be acute stressors since they are often major events and time-constrained. One approach to assessing the impact of these stressors is the 'Social Readjustment Rating Scale' (Holmes and Rahe, 1967; Scully et al., 2000). The scale lists over 40 stress-producing events and changes that most people will experience at one time or another in their life, and the weight of the impact they have that indicates the difficulty of coping, or dealing, with the events. Table 4.1 shows, for example, that the death of a spouse is very stressful; changing jobs less so. The non-work events are more severe stressors than the work events. Basically, the idea is that if you accumulate a large number of stressor points in a relatively short period, you are more

Table 4.1   Relative difficulty of adjustment to selected life changes

Non-work		Work	
Event	Weight	Event	Weight
Death of spouse	100	Fired at work	47
Divorce	73	Retirement	45
Jail term	63	Business readjustment	39
Death in close family	63	Change in responsibilities	29
Marriage	50	Trouble with boss	23
Death of close friend	37	Change in hours/working conditions	20
Wife begins/stops work	26		

Source: Holmes and Rahe (1977).

likely to show a stress reaction. High life stress is related to how individuals seek information on coping with stress-inducing events. Studies show that when faced with high life stress, individuals tended to seek help off the job (Weiss et al., 1982). They seek help from friends, take continuing education courses, or seek a new job. When faced with work stress, people tend to seek help from others at work, looking to workers and superiors.

Chronic stressors
These are things that are relatively constant in a person's life. The Hassles Scale measures them. This scale contains items that describe relatively minor, 'but sometimes very disturbing, daily annoyances that can impair morale, social functioning and health' (Lazarus, 2000b). Some examples of hassles are being late for work, not getting enough sleep, and receiving a lot of junk email. Daily hassles can be more important sources of negative health outcomes than the sorts of acute stressors measured by the Social Readjustment Rating Scale (ibid.).

The 'daily grind' is another chronic stressor that has been studied (Fuller et al., 2003). Daily stressful events over time resulted in increased and cumulative perceived strain. An interesting finding is that events which were positively associated with strain on one day seemed to dissipate and were negatively associated with strain the next day.

Social support
Social support is the communication of positive feelings of liking, trust, respect, acceptance of one's beliefs and, sometimes, assistance from others who are important people in one's life. It is important because it affects a person's psychological environment (Kahn and Byosiere, 1992). When

Spotlight 4.4   Work–life balance in Hungary

There are many stressors in a person's environment outside of work and it is necessary that these work and non-work stressors be balanced. Many EU countries have addressed this by introducing family-leave-related policies that facilitate the resolution of these issues. A recent study in Hungary, a recent EU member, found that the resolution of these problems is more difficult than in longer-term members. The perceptions of family-friendly policies in Hungary are gender-related. Men and women view the problem differently and anticipate that the problem is better handled by individuals rather than by the organization (Toth, 2005).

you have social support, events may seem less stress-inducing because the resources that you draw on are greater – help from others – and therefore the demands of the environment can be met and you are less likely to experience burnout (Zellars and Perrewe, 2001). For example, while perceptions of organizational injustice are related to stress, the effect is not as strong when there is less work–family conflict (Judge and Colquitt, 2004) and the reason may be perhaps as simple as the fact that you have some help in dealing with pressure. This is particularly the case when your conversations with those in your support system tend to be positive and focus on personal interests and concerns instead of engaging in 'gripe' sessions (Zellars and Perrewe, 2001).

Individual Differences and Stress

We have already told you something about the role of individual differences and how they relate to stress in Chapter 2. Now we turn to a specific set of them:

- The self-concept and hardiness.
- Locus of control.
- Type A/B behavior patterns.
- Ability.

The self-concept and hardiness
Individual self-perceptions affect the way that you handle stressful life events. One of the more important facets of self-perception is self-efficacy,

that is, the way that you perceive and evaluate your competence to perform your task. High self-efficacy is related to lower burnout (Maslach et al., 2001). It also affects the way that people handle demanding jobs. People who are high in self-efficacy are less likely to experience negative physical effects of work stress such as high blood pressure (Schaubroeck et al., 2001). There is also evidence that a sample of American bank employees with low self-efficacy had more negative reactions when they had high levels of control over their job (Schaubroeck et al., 2000).

The concept of hardiness is a bit more complex than that of self-esteem. 'Hardy' persons tend to feel more in control, less alienated from themselves, have a clear sense of personal values and goals, are confident of their abilities and are more oriented toward challenge and adventure (Kobasa, 1979; Rhodewalt and Agustsdottir 1984). Hardy persons cope with stress and burnout better than those who are not (Maslach et al., 2001). Over 800 executives in a large public utility were studied to find out if those who experienced a high degree of stress without falling ill were more 'hardy' than those who become sick under stress (Kobasa, 1979). Life stress was measured for the managers using the 'Social Readjustment Rating Scale'. Recent illnesses of each executive were also assessed to determine how often and how severely each had been sick. Lastly, 'hardiness' was assessed. Executives who experienced high stress but low levels of illness were more hardy than those who experienced high stress and had high illness rates. Here is an example of how a hardy executive might respond to a job change:

> The hardy executive does more than passively acquiesce to the job transfer. Rather, he throws himself actively into a new situation, utilizing his inner resources to make it his own . . . [He has] an unshakable sense of meaningfulness and ability to evaluate the impact of a transfer in terms of a general life plan with its established priorities. (Kobasa, 1979)

These findings are supported in recent research which showed that persons high in self-esteem, self-efficacy and hardiness reported that they had more positive responses (less strain) to stressors than those who were low in hardiness (Bliese and Britt, 2001).

Locus of control
To have real or perceived control over stressors is related to reduced stress levels and active coping responses (Kahn and Byosiere, 1992). Specifically, the locus of control has been shown to moderate stress reactions. Internals – that is, persons with an internal locus of control (see Chapter 1) – believe that they can influence their environment, that what they do and how they do it determines what they attain. Externals – those with an external

locus of control – believe that they have little influence over the environment and that what happens to them is a matter of luck, fate or due to the actions of others (Rotter, 1966). Internals manifest stress in different ways from externals. Internals faced with a stressor are more likely to believe that they can have a significant effect on outcomes, while externals are more likely to acquiesce, to be passive and to see events as more stressful. When faced with stressors, internals are less likely to become burned out (Maslach et al., 2001).

Type A/B behavior pattern

Those who are hard-driving, highly competitive, impatient with others, irritated when they are in situations that they believe prevent them from achieving their goals, and strive to accomplish more and more in less and less time, manifest a Type A behavior pattern. The Type B behavior pattern is the opposite. Those who exhibit this pattern tend to be less aggressive, less competitive and more relaxed.

Different responses to stress have been linked to the Type A behavior pattern and the Type B behavior pattern (Kahn and Byosiere, 1992). Physiologically, Type As tend to have more extreme bodily responses to stress and to recover more slowly than Type B individuals. Those who are Type A are more likely to have a higher incidence of risk factors associated with cardiovascular disease as well as having a higher incidence of coronary disease itself. They have higher pulse rates when faced with challenging tasks, and also tend to have elevated blood pressure when their self-esteem is threatened (Matteson and Ivancevich, 1980). In a study of a new plant start-up, Type A workers reported more sexual problems and a higher frequency of headaches (Zahrly and Tosi, 1988).

Behavioral responses to stress for Type A individuals may contribute to the more extreme physiological responses. For example, when they have perceived control of the situation they perform better, but behaviorally they are less able to handle conflict through accommodation (Baron, 1989). Type A individuals tend to smoke more and are more impatient, act in aggressive ways and report higher levels of physical problems (Puffer and Brakefield, 1989).

Psychologically, Type A persons experience more subjective stress in their environment that is moderately uncontrollable or uncontrollable. When exposed to stressors they are more angry, time-pressured and impatient. They also respond more cognitively to stressful situations: they are more likely to use denial and suppression than a Type B person. They are also more likely to have high rates of burnout (Maslach et al., 2001).

One reason for these different reactions is that the Type A may internalize stress and, perhaps, failure. When they fail, they try again and again to solve the problem. If they are not successful, they feel that they did not try hard enough, leading to greater frustration and annoyance. They feel ineffective and attribute the failure to themselves.

Ability

There is not much evidence to show how task competence affects responses to stress, however it is reasonable to think that it does. Some research does indirectly support this: in stressful conditions, supervisors with more experience perform better than those with less experience (Murphy et al., 1992). We also know that in times of crisis, experts are called in to solve problems. For example, a physician trained in trauma medicine knows what to do in a serious automobile accident emergency, whereas a psychiatrist may not; and professional athletes are regularly involved in competition with severe time pressures and extreme performance demands. There are at least four reasons why those with high ability may perform better in stressful situations:

1. One is that through extensive repetition and practice, they learn what to do and, perhaps more importantly, are able to focus intensely on relevant factors, not extraneous ones.
2. It is less likely that they will experience role overload. The greater the ability, the more one can do.
3. They tend to know their upper limits. They are therefore better able to assess their likelihood of success in stress-inducing situations. You will recall that stress occurs in situations that are uncertain and important. The high-ability person will probably face less uncertainty than the low-ability one.
4. High-ability people have more control over a situation than low-ability people, and situational control affects how a person responds to stressors.

Research on social facilitation can tell you something about the effects of ability, performance and stressors. Social facilitation refers to the effect of the presence of other people on performance. In the presence of others, some people perform very well, whereas others do not. The difference has to do with the person's ability: high-ability people tend to do better in the presence of others, whereas those with low ability seem to do worse.

Political skills may also make a difference in coping with stress. Political skills refer to the person's ability to use power effectively and to maneuver skillfully in the organization. When persons with low political skills were faced with role conflict, they reported higher anxiety, complained more and had higher increases in blood pressure than those with high political skills (Perrewe et al., 2004).

SUMMARY

Stress is a major determinant of health problems, both physical and mental; and much stress comes from the work setting. Since stress depends on the relationship of a person to the environment and what is happening in that environment, you must look for the causes of stress in the person as well as environmental forces. The objective environment is the actual context in which you live, both at work and away from it. The psychological environment is the way that you experience the objective environment. Different people might psychologically experience the same job conditions in quite different ways because they have different needs, concerns and personalities, and therefore appraise the situation differently.

We also know that an individual can experience too much stress or too little stress. Too much stress may cause poor health, absenteeism, emotional breakdowns and other dysfunctional behaviors. If there is too little, the motivation of the individual will be inadequate. The organization can manage stress in a situation by careful selection of personnel and by the manner in which the work of individuals is arranged or designed. The selection approach – selecting 'internals' rather than 'externals', those with high self-confidence, those who are flexible rather than rigid people, and high-ability people – can reduce the amount of stress experienced by individuals in the organization. In designing work, it appears that stress may be lower if employee decision control over work is higher, if there is less ambiguity about what is to be done on the job, and if a person does not have to comply with different and inconsistent demands.

GUIDE FOR MANAGERS: DEALING WITH STRESS

There are several ways to manage stress. It may be possible to change the objective environment to remove a stressor or to alter the psychological environment that you experience. Perhaps it is possible to alter the stress symptoms in some way so that they will not have debilitating long-run effects. All of these general approaches work, and the most effective way to manage stress may be a broad attack on several dimensions.

Personal Approaches to Stress Management

Stress can be managed, at least in the sense that you can avoid stressful conditions, change them or learn to cope more effectively with them. There are so many ways to do this that an extensive discussion of each is beyond the scope of this chapter. However, some that are currently thought to be useful and seem particularly relevant to organizational stress are discussed here.

Manage the environment in which the stressor exists
Change some activity or behavior to modify the environment. Suppose you are experiencing high stress from work. One way to resolve the problem may be by changing jobs within the company or by leaving the firm.

Managing your life can diminish stress and its symptoms
Many stress-inducing situations occur because of poor personal planning and time management. For example, students often have test anxiety because they do not believe they have enough time to prepare for tests. Here is a typical scenario. A student has two mid-term examinations scheduled in the next week. Because both exams cover a lot of material, the student begins to worry, especially if it is important to get good grades. She goes to one of her instructors to ask for permission to take a 'make-up' exam at a later date. The reason given is, 'I don't have time to prepare.' In cases like this, the anxiety can easily be avoided or at least reduced by preparing earlier in the term, instead of waiting until the last minute.

Change your cognitive appraisal of the environment
You can restructure the way that you think about and appraise the environment by telling yourself that the situation is not as destructive as when you felt stress from it. You can also change your behavior at work, perhaps by performing your job in a different way. Relaxation, meditation and biofeedback are a few of the mind-clearing approaches that you might use. These approaches either detach you from the stressor or help you to

focus on other, less stressful situations. They may also have important and positive effects on physiological stress symptoms. For example, relaxation approaches can reduce hypertension and heart rates.

Get help

Counseling and psychotherapy have long been used to solve stress-induced problems. A second party trained in mental health intervention works regularly with the person to determine the source of stress, help modify his or her outlook, and develop alternative ways to cope. Often this is done by helping a person gain enough self-confidence and self-esteem to try a different way of coping with stress.

Therapists and counselors use many different approaches. These methods tend to be based on learning theory and the use of internal or external reinforcements. They are behavioral self-management tools to help you monitor, facilitate and modify your own behavior. The role of the therapist is to teach you these methods and then withdraw so that you can use them independently.

Develop social support

Having a group of close friends is helpful. They may provide a listening ear, a less biased assessment of the situation, some help in working your way out of a stressful situation and, finally, they may suggest ways to change your behavior so that it is more adaptive.

Improve your physical condition

Being in good physical condition will help you deal more effectively with stress. Proper exercise, a wise diet and not smoking will result in positive physiological effects for anyone. Heart rate decreases, blood pressure is generally reduced, and the body becomes more resistant to pressures.

Organizational Approaches to Stress Management

Many organizations realize that if they can reduce the number and intensity of stressors or help employees cope more effectively with them, there should be increased performance, reduced turnover and absenteeism, and substantial reductions in costs. This problem can be attacked through the implementation of employee wellness programs and by management practices which modify the work environment.

Employee wellness programs

Since the mid-1990s an increasing number of organizations have instituted some type of employee wellness program, including stress management.

These programs include health risk assessments, exercise facilities and programs, individual counseling when employees feel job or personal strain, clinics to deal with the use of alcohol, and regular seminars and lectures.

Implement management practices to improve the work environment
There are several ways that some work stressors can be affected by good management practices:

- Improving communication with employees will reduce uncertainty. This is a way to lessen role ambiguity and may also have direct effects on role conflict if better communication clarifies lines of responsibility and authority.
- Effective performance appraisal and reward systems reduce role conflict and role ambiguity. When rewards are clearly related to performance, the person knows what he or she is accountable for (reduced role conflict) and where he or she stands (reduced role ambiguity). When a good coaching relationship between a superior and a subordinate exists along with the performance appraisal system, the person may perceive more control over the work environment. He or she may also sense some social support for the task of getting the job done well.
- Increasing participation in decision making will give the person a greater sense of control over the work environment, a factor associated with less negative reactions to stress. There is a strong relationship between participation and job satisfaction, role conflict and role ambiguity. Increasing participation requires decentralization of decision making to more people, and delegation of responsibility to those who are already accountable for work performance.
- Job enrichment gives the person more responsibility, more meaningful work, more control, more feedback. Uncertainty will be reduced, greater control over the work environment will be perceived and there will be more variety. Job enrichment increases motivation and encourages higher work quality, especially among those with high growth needs.
- An improved match of skills, personality and work is also a way to manage stress at work. There is nothing so frustrating as being placed in a job that you can't handle and do not have the potential to perform well (Motowidlo et al., 1986). Similarly, some jobs involve a good deal of stress just because the work is set up that way (Karasek et al., 1981). For these tasks, organizations should seek highly skilled and competent persons with personalities that help them cope effectively.

CASE: BARCELONA'S TEACHERS

When researchers studied stress among school teachers in Spain they found that, like other European workers, there was a high rate of stress in this occupational group (European Agency for Safety and Health at Work, 2002). However, the study also found ways to cope with stress. Stress was dealt with most effectively by adopting proactive strategies, including positive thinking, that can have an important role in alleviating mental pressure while addressing the root problems. The researchers analyzed the level of adrenaline and noradrenaline of 165 teachers from Barcelona during the late summer, when tensions are increasing because of exams and other factors; and then again in September, after the holidays, when stress levels are usually lower.

The researchers found that the main cause of stress resulted from situations that teachers were not able to control, often for lack of information or assistance. The common problems were 'having to do things that I do not approve of', 'lack of information on how to implement the changes', 'conflicting instructions' and 'lack of assistance from parents in connection with disciplinary problems'.

Teachers who simply accepted these problems without trying to find solutions were found to have higher stress levels and symptoms of stress, as measured by increased levels of adrenaline and noradrenaline. On the other hand, those teachers who used active strategies, such as positive thinking and cognitive restructuring, had lower levels of stress.

Eliminating the causes of stress in organizations is certainly important, but these results show that it is possible provide short-term help to people on how to adopt more active strategies to cope with stress problems. Training in stress management can also reduce prejudices about stress, strengthen the networks of social assistance and facilitate the exchange of best practices within organizations.

Discussion:

- In this case, was it important to recognize that there is work-related stress? Why?
- How has the risk assessment and identification of its causes helped the organization?
- Which coping strategies have been implemented?

REFERENCES

Argyris, C. (1964), *Integrating the Individual and the Organization*. New York: John Wiley.

Baron, R.A. (1989), Personality and Organizational Conflict: Effects of the Type A Behavior Pattern and Self-Monitoring. *Organizational Behavior and Human Decision Processes*, **44**: 281–96.

Bliese, P.D. and T.W. Britt (2001), Social Support, Group Consensus and Stressor–Strain Relationships: Social Context Matters. *Journal of Organizational Behavior*, **22**(4): 425–36.

Byosiere, P. and R. Kahn (2004), Stress in Organizations: Overview, Reflection and evaluation of the Kahn–Byosiere Model. *International Journal of Psychology*, **39**(5–6): 503.

Cavanaugh, M.A., W.R. Boswell, M.V. Roehling and J.W. Boudreau (2000), An Empirical Examination of Self-reported Work Stress among US Managers. *Journal of Applied Psychology*, **85**(1): 65–74.

Cohen, S. (1980), After Effects of Stress on Human Performance and Social Behavior. *Psychological Bulletin*, **88**: 82–108.

Cooper, G.L. and P. Dewe (2004), *Stress: A Brief History*. Oxford: Blackwell Publishing.

de Croon, E.M., J.K. Sluiter, R.W.B. Blonk, J.P.J. Broersen and M.H.W Frings-Dresen (2004), Stressful Work, Psychological Job Strain, and Turnover: A 2-Year Prospective Cohort Study of Truck Drivers. *Journal of Applied Psychology*, **89**(3): 442–54.

Eliot, R.S.S. and L. Dennis (1989), *Is It Worth Dying For? How To Make Stress Work For You – Not Against You*. New York: Bantam Books.

Elovainio, M., M. Kivimaki and K. Helkama (2001), Organizational Justice Evaluations, Job Control, and Occupational Strain. *Journal of Applied Psychology*, **86**(3): 418–24.

Epictetus (1991), *The Enchiridion* (transl. George Long). Amherst, NY: Prometheus Books.

European Agency for Safety and Health at Work (2002), Preventing Psychosocial Risks at Work. http://osha.europa.eu/en/publications/reports/104.

Fineman, M. (1993), Organizations as Emotional Arenas. In *Emotions in Organizations*, M. Fineman (ed.). London: Sage; pp. 9–35.

Fuller, J.A., J.M. Stanton, G.G. Fisher, C. Spitz Muller, S.S. Russell and P.C. Smith (2003), A Lengthy Look at the Daily Grind: Time Series Analysis of Events, Mood, Stress, and Satisfaction. *Journal of Applied Psychology*, **88**(6): 1019–33.

Ganster, D.C., M.L. Fox and D.J. Dwyer (2001), Explaining Employees' Health Care Costs: A Prospective Examination of Stressful Job Demands, Personal Control, and Physiological Reactivity. *Journal of Applied Psychology*, **86**(5): 954–64.

Hochschild, A.R. (1979), Emotion Work, Feeling Rules, and Social Structure. *American Journal of Sociology*, **85**(3): 551–75.

Hochschild, A.R. (1983), *The Managed Heart: Commercialization of Human Feeling*. Berkeley CA: University of California Press.

Holmes, T.H. and R.H. Rahe (1967), The Social Readjustment Rating Scale. *Journal of Psychosomatic Research*, **11**: 213–18.

House, R.J. and J.R. Rizzo (1972), Role Conflict and Ambiguity as Critical Variables in a Model of Organizational Behavior. *Organizational Behavior and Human Performance*, **7**: 467–505.

Jackson, S.E. and R.S. Schuler (1985), A Meta-Analysis of Research on Role Ambiguity and Role Conflict in Work Settings. *Organizational Behavior and Human Decision Processes*, **36**: 16–38.

Judge, T.A. and J.A. Colquitt (2004), Organizational Justice and Stress: The Mediating Role of Work–Family Conflict. *Journal of Applied Psychology*, **89**(3): 395–404.

Judge, T.A. and E.A. Locke (1993), Effect of Dysfunctional Thought Processes on Subjective Well-Being and Job Satisfaction. *Journal of Applied Psychology*, **78**(3): 475–91.

Judge, T.A., E.F. Woolf and C. Hurst (2009), Is Emotional Labor more Difficult for Some than for Others? A Multilevel, Experience-Sampling Study. *Personnel Psychology*, **62**(1): 57–88.

Kahn, R.L. and M. Byosiere (1992), Stress in Organizations. In *Handbook of Industrial and Organizational Psychology*, M.D. Dunnette and L.M. Hough (eds). Palo Alto, CA: Consulting Psychologists, pp. 571–650.

Kahn, R.L., D.M. Wolfe, R.P. Quinn and R.A. Rosenthal (1964), *Organizational Stress: Studies in Role Conflict and Ambiguity*. New York: John Wiley.

Kammeyer-Mueller, J.D., T.A. Judge and B.A. Scott (2009), The Role of Core Self-Evaluations in the Coping Process. *Journal of Applied Psychology*, **94**(1): 177–95.

Karasek, R.A., D. Baker, F. Marxer, A. Ahlbom and T. Theorell (1981), Job Decision Latitude, Job Demands, and Cardiovascular Disease: A Prospective Study of Swedish Men. *American Journal of Public Health*, **71**: 694–704.

Kobasa, S. (1979), Stressful Life Events, Personality, and Health: An Inquiry in Hardiness. *Journal of Personality and Social Psychology*, **37**(1): 11.

Lazarus, R.S. (1980), The Stress and Coping Paradigm. In *Models for Clinical Psychopathology*, C. Eisendorfer, D. Cohen and P. Maxin (eds). New York: Spectrum, pp. 175–98.

Lazarus, R. (2000a), Towards Better Research on Stress and Coping. *American Psychologist*, **55**(6): 665–73.

Lazarus, R. (2000b), *Stress and Emotion*. New NY: Springer Publishing.

LePine, J.A., N.P. Podsakoff and M.A. Lepine (2005), A Meta-analytic Test of the Challenge Stressor–Hindrance Stressor Framework: An Explanation for Inconsistent Relationships among Stressors and Performance. *Academy of Management Journal*, **48**(5): 764–75.

Maslach, C., W.B. Schaufeli and M.P. Leiter (2001), Job Burnout. *Annual Review of Psychology*, **52**: 397–422.

Matteson, M.T. and J.M. Ivancevich (1980), The Coronary Prone Behavior Pattern: A Review and Appraisal. *Social Science and Medicine*, **14**: 337–51.

Motowidlo, S.J., J.S. Packard and M.R. Manning (1986), Occupational Stress: Its Causes and Consequences for Job Performance. *Journal of Applied Psychology*, **71**(4): 618–29.

Murphy, S.E., D. Blyth and F.E. Fiedler (1992), Cognitive Resources Theory and the Utilization of the Leader's and Group Member's Technical Competence. *Leadership Quarterly*, **3**: 237–54.

Netterstrøm, B. and P. Bech (2008), The Effect of a Multidisciplinary Stress Programme on Sick Leave. Presented at the Work, Stress and

Health Conference: Health and Safe Work through Research, Practice and Partnerships. APA/NIOSH, Washington, DC.

Parasuraman, S. and J.A. Alutto (1981), An Examination of the Organizational Antecedents of Stressors at Work. *Academy of Management Journal*, **24**: 48–67.

Perrewe, P.L., K.L. Zellars, G.R. Ferris, A.M. Rossi, C.J. Kacmar and D.A. Ralston (2004), Neutralizing Job Stressors: Political Skill as an Antidote to the Dysfunctional Consequences of Role Conflict. *Academy of Management Journal*, **47**(1): 141–52.

Petterson, I.L., H.Å. Donnersvärd, M. Lagerström and A. Toomingas (2006), Evaluation of an Intervention Programme Based on Empowerment for Eldercare Nursing Staff. *Work Stress*, **20**(4), 353–69.

Potter, P.T., B.W. Smith, K.R. Strobel and A.J. Zautra (2002), Interpersonal Workplace Stressors and Well-being: A Multi-wave Study of Employees with and without Arthritis. *Journal of Applied Psychology*, **87**(4): 789–96.

Presthus, R. (1978), *The Organizational Society*. New York: St Martin's Press.

Puffer, S.M. and J.T. Brakefield (1989), The Role of Task Complexity as a Moderator of the Stress and Coping Process. *Human Relations*, **42**: 199–217.

Rafaeli, A. and R.I. Sutton (1987), Expression of Emotion as Part of the Work Role. *Academy of Management Review*, **12**(1): 23–37.

Rafaeli, A. and R.I. Sutton (1990), Busy Stores and Demanding Customers: How Do They Affect the Display of Positive Emotion? *Academy of Management Journal*, **33**(3): 623–37.

Rhodewalt, F. and S. Agustsdottir (1984), On the Relationship of Hardiness to the Type A Behavior Pattern: Perception of Life Events Versus Coping With Life Events. *Journal of Research in Personality*, **18**: 212–23.

Rotter, J. (1966), Generalized Expectancies for Internal vs. External Control of Reinforcement. *Psychological Monographs*, **80**: 609.

Schaubroeck, J., J.R. Jones and J.L. Xie (2001), Individual Differences in Utilizing Control to Cope with Job Demands: Effects on Susceptibility to Infectious Disease. *Journal of Applied Psychology*, **86**(2): 265–78.

Schaubroeck, J., S.S.K. Lam and J.L. Xie (2000), Collective Efficacy versus Self-efficacy in Coping Responses to Stressors and Control: A Cross-cultural Study. *Journal of Applied Psychology*, **85**(4): 512–25.

Schwarz, J. (2004), Always on the Job, Employees Pay With Health. *New York Times*, 25 September.

Scully, J.A., H. Tosi and K. Banning (2000), Life Event Checklists: Revisiting the Social Readjustment Rating Scale after 30 Years. *Educational and Psychological Measurement*, **60**(6): 864–76.

Segerstrom, S.C. and G.E. Miller (2004), Psychological Stress and the Human Immune System: A Meta-analytic Study of 30 Years of Inquiry. *Psychological Bulletin*, **130**(4): 601–30.

Selye, H. (1974), The Stress of Life. New York: McGraw-Hill.

Swedish Work Environment Authority (2003), *Systematic Work Environment Management: Guidelines*. Work Environment Authority, Publication Services. Also at http://www.av.se/dokument/inenglish/books/h367eng.pdf.

Takala, J. (2008), European Risk Observatory: More and More People Face Psychosocial Risks at Work. http://osha.europa.eu/en.

Taimela, S., A. Malmivaara, S. Justen, E. Läärä, H. Sintonen, J. Tiekso and T. Aro (2007a), The Effectiveness of Two Occupational Health Intervention Programs in Reducing Sickness Absence among Employees at Risk: Two Randomised Controlled Trials. *Occupational Environmental Medicine*, 6 August.

Taimela, S., S. Justen, P. Aronen, H. Sintonen, E. Läärä, A. Malmivaara, J. Tiekso and T. Aro (2007b), An Occupational Health Intervention Program for Workers at High Risk for Sickness Absence: Cost-effectiveness Analysis Based on a Randomised Controlled Trial. *Occupational Environmental Medicine*, online 12 October.

Tosi, H.L. (1971), Organizational Stress as a Moderator of the Relationship between Influence and Role Response. *Academy of Management Journal*, **14**(7): 22.

Toth, Herta (2005), Gendered Dilemmas of the Work–Life Balance in Hungary. *Women in Management Review*, **20**(5): 361–75.

Tubre, T.C. and J.M. Collins (2000), Jackson and Schuler (1985) Revisited: A Meta-analysis of the Relationships between Role Ambiguity, Role Conflict, and Job Performance. *Journal of Management*, **26**(1): 155–69.

van der Doef, M. and S. Maes (2000), The Job Demand–Control(–Support) Model and Psychological Well-being: A Review of 20 Years of Empirical Research. *Work and Stress*, **13**: 87–114.

Vermunt, R. and H. Steensma (2001), Stress and Justice in Organizations: An Exploration into Justice Processes with the Aim to find Mechanisms to Reduce Stress. In *Justice in the Workplace: From Theory To Practice*, R. Cropanzano (ed.). Manwah, NJ: Erlbaum, **2**: 27–48.

Weiss, H.M., D.A. Ilgen and M.E. Sharbaugh (1982), Effects of Life and Job Stress on Information Search Behaviors of Organizational Members. *Journal of Applied Psychology*, **67**(1): 60–66.

Zahrly, J.H. and H.L. Tosi (1988), Antecedents of Stress Manifestations. National Meetings, Academy of Management.

Zellars, K.L. and P.L. Perrewe (2001), Affective Personality and the Content of Emotional Social Support: Coping in Organizations. *Journal of Applied Psychology*, **86**(3): 459–67.

5. Decision making

PREPARING FOR CLASS

Using the Internet or your local library, search for discussions of major historical decisions that have affected the USA and the EU; Watergate, Bay of Pigs, American and European involvement in Iraq, Chernobyl, or any of the incidents discussed in this chapter. Consider these questions:

1. Are there common themes across these different decision contexts?
2. What went wrong with the decision-making process?
3. How much was 'luck' a factor in the eventual outcome?

Think about problem solving in a group or organization with which you are involved. Consider these questions:

4. How are problems identified?
5. Who makes input on possible solutions to the problem?
6. How are decisions reached about how to resolve those problems?
7. By what criteria is the effectiveness of those decisions evaluated?

*   *

Two of the persistent and dominant themes around the subject of decision-making in organizations are the importance of the role of the chief executive officer (CEO) and that decision making is a rational process followed by actors to optimize firm performance. We think that the persistence of these ideas stems from the dominance of classical and neo-classical economics in which the entrepreneur/CEO is a rational decision maker and will act in rational ways in response to market forces. This 'ideal' model is pretty far from the reality of how decisions are made. In Table 5.1 we briefly describe eight myths about decision making.

Myth 1: CEOs make strategic decisions. It is a common belief that strategic decisions that affect the organization are made at the highest levels, and more often by the CEO. Actually these major decisions take shape from processes of negotiation, bargaining and dealing with coalitions or

Table 5.1   Myths vs. reality in organization decisions

Myths	Reality
1. CEOs make strategic decisions	Strategic decisions are made by several key actors, often at different level of the organization
2. A single team makes all of the big decisions	Most strategic decisions involve several high-level groups, not just one
3. The executive team is a body of equals	Some top management team members are relied on more than others.
4. Team members should always adopt a CEO perspective	In many instances top-management team members are more focused on the functional units that they manage
5. Decisions are made in rational ways	Decisions are complex social, emotional and political processes
6. Managers analyze, and then decide	Decisions are often non-linear sequences, with solutions often arising and selected before careful analysis and assessment of alternatives
7. Managers decide, and then act	Decisions are often formed through an interactive process of choice and action
8. Managers tend to be highly aware of what is going on in decision-making	Decisions are taken with 'limited awareness'

Source: Adapted from Bazerman (2005), Roberto (2005).

managers in the firm (Roberto, 2005). In short, the CEO may make and ratify the final decision, but it often emerges from decision-making micro-processes at various levels of the organization.

Myth 2: A single team makes all of the big decisions. A lot of attention has been paid to the 'top management team', usually thought of as the key group of advisors, including the CEO, that makes major decisions. It is more likely that instead of a single group, there are several subgroups, each made up of a different set of top managers who advise the CEO on diverse decisions.

Myth 3: The executive team is a body of equals. There is usually a status and power hierarchy within each top management team, giving some members more influence than others. In addition, it is likely that depending on the problem, the CEO may rely on the team member who is thought to be the most reliable.

Myth 4: Team members should always adopt a CEO perspective. It isn't likely that all team members can take the broad view that the CEO must take. Often a team member will be more concerned with his or her own unit or functional area of responsibility.

Myth 5: Decisions are made in rational ways. The concept of organizational rationality is that decisions are made which will maximize firm performance, and after a careful analysis of information. This is a pretty commonsense notion that implies that smart people, before deciding, think carefully, collect data, analyze the data and then decide, using intuition and experience. But as we discussed in Chapter 2, few of us are immune to the cognitive biases in all stages of analyzing problems and making decisions. A classic example is the 'sunk-cost bias', a decision to increase time, money and resources already invested in an earlier decision. There appears to be a sort of 'no-return threshold' where it is difficult for the decision maker to recognize that the sunk costs are greater than the gains of abandoning the earlier wrong decision, an issue we examined in Chapter 2 on attitudes: that is, the escalation of commitment.

Social pressures also play an important role in decision making, especially for those with a strong need for affiliation (Chapter 3), or with the desire to meet the expectations of others. Emotions also play an important role, providing energy and motivation to make choices or, in some cases, paralyzing decision making completely. Finally, political motivation (see Machiavellianism, in Chapter 2) may have positive or negative effects through the creation of coalitions, lobbying or other tactics.

Myth 6: Managers analyze, then decide. The traditional problem-solving technique is to: (1) identify and define the problem; (2) collect data and information; (3) identify alternative solutions; (4) evaluate the various alternatives; then (5) select an action to be taken. However, it is been shown in research that the process is often non-linear: activities such as evaluation of alternatives, problem definition and data collection may take place concurrently (Drucker, 1967; Simon, 1977; Eisenhardt and Bourgeois, 1988).

Myth 7: Managers decide first, act second. While it makes sense to think that decisions are made first and action follows, that is not necessarily the norm. Take the case of a company which pursues a strategy of diversification. You might think that managers at some point take the decision to penetrate new markets and launch new products by investing in new technologies. In reality this decision is not always deliberate, but can be part of an emerging strategy and, as such, without a precise beginning and end. Decisions are often more a back process of an action: a sort of sense-making process, '*ex post* rationalized' (Weick, 1995).

Myth 8: Managers recognize the relevant factors when making decisions. Because many managerial decisions have significant implications for the success or failure of the organization, there is a tendency to think that they are made after careful consideration of the important factors involved. Some have argued, though, that when these critical decisions are made the manager may be in a state of 'bounded awareness', a tendency to fail to recognize information that is readily available (Bazerman and Chugh, 2006).

This can occur when you are too highly focused on a specific task. One reason is that decision makers often prefer readily available information that they believe is necessary for choosing, instead of identifying other information that might lead to a better decision. Bounded awareness might also occur because of the 'success syndrome', the case when an organization has been very profitable in a particular market segment and ignores threats from external organizations or technologies in its environment.

This is very clearly shown in a study by Neisser (Neisser, 1976; Neisser and Hyman, 2000). The subjects were asked to watch two videos in which three actors played with a ball. In one video the players wore white shirts and in the other, dark shirts; otherwise, the videos were identical. One other cue in both videos was a woman, walking in the background with an open umbrella. The viewers were asked to count the number of times the ball passed from one player to another. Because they were focused on counting the number of passes of the ball, only 21 percent of them 'saw' the woman, though she was clearly visible.

The 'success syndrome' may also lead to bounded awareness. A firm which has been successful with a specific product or a particular technology may hinder its awareness of information in its environment. For example, the study of the Swiss watches industry by Tushman and Rosenkopf (1992) showed how that industry, having controlled the watch market for years, had the technology of quartz movements before anyone else but failed to use it, and left the development of quartz watches and that market to Japanese firms. A more recent example is British Petroleum (BP) and how a set of decisions led to the disastrous oil spill in the Gulf of Mexico in 2010. In the late 1980s, BP was an average oil company, but a series of strategic acquisitions resulted in rapid growth in size and profitability (Lyall, 2010). This success was a result of the mergers, but also serious cost-cutting efforts, which some in the industry believe led to less concern for safety. Then there were a series of accidents: an explosion at a Texas refinery in 2005, a major spill on the north slope of Alaska, and a near calamity when an oil platform almost sank in the Gulf of Mexico in July 2005. However, it seems that the success of BP over its recent history overshadowed some safety considerations as it consistently took risky approaches to save time and keep costs low (Lyall, 2010). Many attribute the Gulf spill to this success syndrome and the subsequent risky choices BP made.

Decision making is an important process in any organization, as it is in everyday life. One person from whom you want to get the best possible decision is your doctor – your life could depend upon it. But even the best trained and experienced physicians can get it wrong. For example, consider the case of Martin Ferry, a bricklayer who went to see his doctor, Dr St Clair, complaining about strong chest pains after finishing his usual three mile morning run. Martin was a very healthy man. He was 40 years old, fit and trim from running and exercising since he was 20, there was no family history of heart problems, he didn't smoke, drank very little – and only red wine. The chest pains sounded like a heart attack, but Dr St Clair, after an electrocardiogram, a chest X-ray and blood tests that were 'normal', sent him home, telling him it was probably a strained muscle. The next day when St Clair arrived at the hospital he found that Martin had come into the emergency room in the middle of the night after experiencing a heart attack. Why did the doctor, with all the tests, miss the diagnosis? Because Martin looked very healthy, he was fit, there were no family history clues, and so forth, so Dr St Clair relied on his intuition – that someone in such good physical condition, with no indication of heart problems, was typically unlikely to have a heart attack. This isn't unusual: physicians usually have two or three diagnoses in mind within a few minutes after meeting a patient, and these are based on the patient's complexion, posture, eye movements and other stimuli (Groopman, 2007). So most doctors use 'heuristics' – intuition or rules of thumb – in diagnosing patient problems.

Managers, when they make decisions, are no different from doctors. Like doctors, their decision-making environment is an important one to consider, especially for those who believe that organizational decision making is usually a rational, reflective process that is a significant aspect of their day. The manager, like a doctor, as a reflective, systematic planner and decision maker is folklore and myth (Mintzberg, 1975). The fact is that managers work at an unrelenting pace and are strongly oriented to action, not to reflection (Mintzberg, 1973). Many managers feel they cannot afford the luxury of long, involved decision-making processes, as their environments became increasingly complex. Managers report spending more time making decisions than planning for those decisions. Modern business environments demand that they are able to process large amounts of information and balance the needs of multiple constituencies within an often very stressful environment. Little time is left for careful information gathering, yet decisions made can be costly in terms of lives and money.

Several classic dramatic events provide insight into decision-making environments in complex information contexts. The 1986 Challenger disaster, the decision by the United States to go to war in Iraq, and the BP corporate strategy for oil exploration are all examples of how day-to-day decisions can converge with catastrophic consequences. As we discuss these cases throughout this chapter, what will become strikingly clear is that there are similar causal factors in each case.

What happened in the Challenger disaster? The Rogers Commission determined that the direct cause leading to the deaths of seven astronauts was the failure of the joint between the two lower segments of the right solid rocket motor (Rogers Commission Report, 1986). However, the report also highlights four other important contributing causes that provide an interesting insight into the nature of decision making in high-pressure environments:

1. Serious flaws in the decision-making process.
2. Launch constraints waived at the expense of safety without being reviewed by all levels of management.
3. One organization within the space center having a propensity to try to deal with serious problems internally rather than communicating them to other decision-making levels in the organization.
4. Reversal of an earlier decision by the management of a major contractor to recommend against the launch, after pressure from a major customer.

The Challenger example illustrates human decision-making situations with critical consequences. Like other cases discussed in the chapter, managers were confronted with numerous decision-making opportunities where there was information available that would have helped them make a decision that may have avoided the disaster. However, those opportunities were missed and key information was overlooked because of some very common problems that occur in decision-making processes.

Of course, many decisions are not as complex or consequential as those highlighted in the Challenger decisions and the development of BP's corporate strategy. However, you make decisions in every function you perform as a manager. Herbert Simon, Nobel Prize winner for his work on decision making, says that management and decision making are virtually the same thing (Simon, 1976). The consequences of poor decisions may affect many parties, including the decision makers themselves. Managers have even been held personally liable, and criminally charged for failure to meet social and legal responsibilities for worker safety.

Sometimes decisions are made very easily and quickly, often without us even thinking about them. For example, if our company policy is to take returns, 'no questions asked', we accept it when a customer decides not to keep a purchase. This is a policy of many companies that sell online. For example, a young student recently bought a pair of designer shoes from an online vendor. When they arrived she discovered that they were the wrong size. She called the seller and was told to return them in the packaging that was sent with her order. This was a very easy decision for the sales agent. At other times, decision making can be a stressful process and cause considerable anxiety, in part because we are all often reluctant decision makers, especially in the case of important decisions. In one Peanuts cartoon, Linus said to Charlie Brown: 'No problem is so big or so complicated that it can't be run away from!' (Janis and Mann, 1977). Not surprisingly, people do not always deal systematically with an important decision. They might overreact and plunge headlong and headstrong into it. They might also show great resourcefulness in avoiding the decision.

In this chapter, we discuss problem solving and decision making. We describe characteristics of the process and explore individual and group decision making. Emphasis is given to the difficulties that arise and to methods for improving the process outlined in the model.

INTUITION, JUDGMENT AND DECISION MAKING

Overall, decision making is an exercise of values. When facing complex and difficult choices, where the costs and benefits are high, emotion can dominate over reason. Your values, attitudes, personality and perception enter the decision process in all of its stages. They affect what you perceive to be (or not to be) a problem, and how you approach solving it. Sometimes you will take a very deliberate and step-by-step approach, as Dr St Clair did when he ordered tests and examined Martin. Other times, you will use your intuition, as Dr St Clair did when he concluded that Ferry's pain was not a heart attack, but a strained muscle. We tend to think of these types of decisions as 'intuition', and not what we usually think of when we discuss decision making in a book about management. Instead, we think of decision making as a more deliberate, reasoned process of making choices.

These two approaches to decision making, intuition and reasoning, as different ways of making decisions, are integrated into a comprehensive approach to decision making developed by Kahneman and Tversky (see Kahneman, 2003) and illustrated in Figure 5.1. They show how perception, intuition and reasoning are related to both the process and the content of arriving at choices.

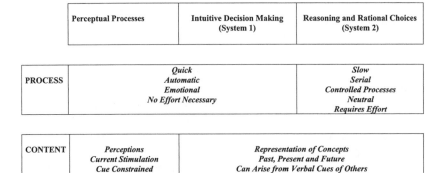

	Perceptual Processes	Intuitive Decision Making (System 1)	Reasoning and Rational Choices (System 2)
PROCESS		*Quick* *Automatic* *Emotional* *No Effort Necessary*	*Slow* *Serial* *Controlled Processes* *Neutral* *Requires Effort*
CONTENT		*Perceptions* *Current Stimulation* *Cue Constrained*	*Representation of Concepts* *Past, Present and Future* *Can Arise from Verbal Cues of Others*

Source: Adapted from Kahneman (2003).

*Figure 5.1   The role of process and content in intuitive and rational
decision systems*

As Figure 5.1 shows, intuition (System 1) is based on impressions that
result from perceptions, thoughts and stimuli, or they may be triggered
by ideas, concepts or language; they aren't voluntary or explicit. Intuitive
choices are usually quick and spontaneous; we usually don't know why we
make them (Kahneman, 2003). Reasoning (System 2), which is more like
what we mean by decision making in this chapter, is more controlled and
deliberate. It may be a result of the same things that precipitate an intuitive
decision, but it also results from more deliberate and thoughtful processes.
One of its purposes is to: 'monitor the quality of both mental operations
[and intuition] as well as overt behavior' (Kahneman, 2003).

Here is how this process worked for Dr St Clair and Martin Ferry.
When Martin entered the office, Dr St Clair quickly perceived several
things about him. Martin looked trim and healthy, young and muscular;
St Clair guessed he was in pretty good health. As he talked with Martin, St
Clair's hunch was that there were two or three things that might be wrong
with him (Groopman, 2007). With these cues, his intuition told him that
there was probably not much wrong with Martin – System 1 was in play.
Then System 2 kicked in for St Clair. He began his examination, checking
the liver, heart and other parts of the body that might give him more information. Then, 'Let's get some facts.' So he ordered the usual series of tests.
When they came back, all within the normal range, his System 2 told him
that nothing was wrong, so back to System 1 – he sent Martin home. And
we know what happened that night. But why? How could this happen?
St Clair took every precaution with his diagnosis, but he did miss some
things. Ferry was experiencing unstable angina (chest pains) that might

not show up on the tests or the X-rays, so the examination and tests didn't indicate a heart problem. As a result, St Clair used his intuition (System 1) that nothing was wrong, and sent Ferry home.

BIASES IN INTUITIVE DECISION-MAKING

The decision-making model of Kahneman and Tverskey (Kahneman, 2003) (shown in Figure 5.1) helps us to understand what happened. Martin Ferry was a casualty of bias that is not unusual in decision making when System 1 is in play. Dr St Clair relied on a heuristic, or a decision short-cut, to make his diagnosis, as many of us do when we make decisions. When you use these short-cuts, errors can occur. Some of these biases identified by Kahneman and Tversky are (see also the section on attribution theory in Chapter 2):

The Representative Bias

This is the bias that crept into Dr St Clair's diagnosis of Martin Ferry (Groopman, 2007). It occurs when your decision is based on stereotypes or similarity to other circumstances. In evaluating Ferry, St Clair appears to have been affected by factors such as his appearance (trim and in good condition), his age, and the results of the physical examination.

The representativeness bias often appears in selection decisions. For example, if you have recently hired two or three new software designers from Midwest University and you are about to hire another person, you might base your choice on the fact of your earlier successful choices. Or, if you ordering dinner in a new Italian restaurant you might order spaghetti with clam sauce because you had the same dish in another restaurant earlier and judged it to be excellent. This could be a mistake, especially if the chef is not the same.

The Availability Bias

Recently, Jennifer Smith received a negative performance evaluation. She was told that her performance was not up to standard, and the main reason that her supervisor Linda gave was that Jennifer had failed to meet an important deadline that cost the division a substantial loss of income last month. Jennifer was upset, of course, because throughout the year she had met all other deadlines and, in fact, received a lot of positive feedback from Linda. Linda was affected by the availability bias. This means that Linda used a recent and a vivid event that was fresh in her memory to determine her evaluation. This is a heuristic that results from the ease with with information comes to mind, such as information salience, very vivid cues, or something that is particularly relevant and important to the decision maker (Kahneman, 2003).

The Affect Bias

Jennifer may have also been a victim of the affect bias, or the fact the Linda simply did not like her. Or, if they had a good relationship and Linda liked Jennifer, she might have evaluated her positively, disregarding any of the negative things that Jennifer might have done. Thus, the decision is based on the positive or negative feelings that the decision maker has toward the person or the situation.

Anchoring

The anchoring bias occurs when a decision is based on a single factor which is used as a basis for a decision. Essentially, we start with some given factor, or value, and then we adjust it to arrive at a judgment. One study examined the anchoring effect on charitable donations. When simply asked for a donation, people found it hard to determine what an acceptable amount would be. However, when some amount was suggested, if it was reasonably low, then there were very substantial increases over the rate of giving than when no amount was suggested (Briers et al., 2007). Another example is the halo effect, when we make a judgment about a person's ability to perform a number of tasks based upon how well he or she performs a single job. Or we judge a person to have the best qualifications for a position based on the fact that he or she graduated from a famous and important university.

Framing

Decisions may also be affected by how a situation is framed, or the way the person perceives the decision context. One of the classic examples of framing is in the work of Kahneman and Tversky (Kahneman, 2003) in which they gave people the following choices: A – a certain gain of $240; or B – a 25 percent chance of gaining $1000 and a 75 percent chance of getting nothing.

The rational decision maker would select Alternative B because the expected value is $250, which greater than the expected value of Alternative A, or $240. Over 80 percent selected A, the certain alternative.

Another example of framing is how President Bush presented the justification for the war in Iraq. There were many possible reasons advanced by critics, among them President Bush's sense that the Iraqi government had attempted to assassinate his father, getting control of oil in the Middle East, and the economic effects of the Iraqi government changing the way that oil was paid for from dollars to euros. However, the reasons that he presented were that:

- Iraq had violated UN resolutions.
- Iraq had weapons of mass destruction.
- Saddam Hussein was a cruel dictator.

Obviously, framing the decision this way gained a great deal more support than would have been the case had other justifications been given.

Other Decision Biases

There are other ways to think about decision biases that we discussed earlier in Chapter 2. Some of these are:

1. The fundamental attribution error (Ross, 1977). This is overestimating the role of the person relative to the environment as a cause of behavior.
2. The consistency bias. If a person behaves the same way in similar situations, we are more likely to see the behavior as internally motivated, such as when a friend is almost always late.
3. The consensus bias. When the person acts differently than others act in the situation, we are more likely to think of that person's behavior as internally motivated.
4. The privacy bias. Actions that are taken in the absence of other people are more likely to be judged as internally motivated. When others are present, we might attribute the action to social pressure. When people are alone, we attribute the action to them.
5. The status bias. In general, higher-status people are seen to be more personally responsible for their actions. They are thought to have more control over their own actions and decisions and to do things because they choose to, not because they have to.
6. The self-serving bias. This is the tendency to perceive oneself favorably. People credit themselves when they succeed, but blame external factors when they fail (Zuckerman, 1979). Success is usually attributed to hard work, ability and good judgment. Failure, on the other hand, is attributed to bad luck, unfair conditions or impossible odds.

Biases aren't always bad. These biases tend to come into play in System 1, or when we use our intuition. But intuition isn't necessarily bad, nor does it does it mean that you will make a bad decision. Experts often make split-second decisions that are correct. Herbert Simon provided one of the classic examples – and explanations – for this when he explained how grand master chess players are able to look at a chess board and make very quick decisions about their moves, while amateurs take more time (Simon, 1987). The reason why the grand master is so good is that they have learned, over time, how to process relatively large amounts of information about the chessboard and, hence, have it stored in their brains. The amateur, on the other hand, doesn't have the same amount of information readily available, so he or she must go through a more careful and slow analysis. Both masters and amateurs demonstrated this in a study in which a chessboard was set up in some standard games and then studied by them. The pieces were then removed and both groups were asked to reproduce the board. The masters were almost 100 percent correct in placing the pieces, while the amateurs got very few on the right square. But the interesting part came next. Instead of being set up as in standard chess games, the pieces on the board were randomly placed. The board was then viewed by both the masters and the amateurs, the pieces removed again – and this time, the masters were no better than the amateurs at placing the pieces on the correct squares.

This tells you that intuition is not something that comes as a gift, but rather after one has spent a long time studying something and developing competence. Then making decisions comes quick and looks easy. This is why many doctors make correct diagnoses very quickly (though in most cases they want to check because health, and maybe even life, is involved) and many of our mothers and grandmothers, when making their favorite family recipes, tell you that it was 'just a little of this and a little of that' in the pot. They knew from experience what a 'little of this' was and didn't have to measure or to look at a recipe.

CHARACTERISTICS OF THE DECISION PROCESS

There are certain characteristics common to decision-making processes that are useful to consider. These are apparent in the catastrophic outcomes of decisions discussed in the introduction, as well as in everyday decisions that we make within organizations.

Decisions within Decisions

Often we incorrectly focus on the final decision made as the result of a process. In many cases, the final decision is just one of several decisions that were made and which had a significant impact on the success of the outcome. For Martin Ferry, Dr St Clair made a series of decisions about the results of Martin's tests, his history and his physical appearance that were important in both setting the stage for subsequent decisions, but that also established a precedent. These are the decisions within the decisions: decisions not to pass on concerns to higher levels of management; decisions to stop consideration of alternative solutions at a premature point.

Small Decisions Accumulate

The fact is that many decisions we make are trivial, or seem to be so, and are made very quickly. Yet the consequences of a series of small decisions can accumulate into a serious problem. Think about how Dr St Clair approached the diagnosis of Martin Ferry. There were a series of decision points: the electrocardiogram, his blood pressure and his family history pointed in a direction different from the real problem. The cumulative effect of all of these led St Clair to conclude that Ferry had strained a muscle. What a mistake!

This characteristic is evident in even more common organizational situations. Picture an employee who postpones a call to a customer so as to arrive home on time. Another employee overlooks a detail on that customer's order because he has a headache. Later, a shipping clerk leaves the order off a truck rather than make an extra effort to load it. Taken together, these minor decisions can add up to the loss of a major account.

Decisions are Partial or Temporary Solutions

It is almost impossible to prevent errors in decision making. Most decisions, therefore, never completely solve a problem. Even if they come close, the solution often contains seeds of new problems requiring attention. Since decisions are imperfect, they are partial solutions. This means that it is necessary to follow up on important decisions and to be prepared to modify them.

Decisions as Organizational Politics

Organizational politics can show up in decision making in several ways. For example, often decisions to promote one person instead of another may be based on personal factors such as how well the candidates are liked or disliked by the decision maker. We see this in the 'good-enough theory of promotions'. Once a pool of candidates has been identified, then the person who is promoted is the one with the 'right attitude', and that is defined by the decision maker, even though that person may not be the best of all others in the pool. Strategic decisions also have political implications. For example, one large US automobile company decided in the early 1990s not to pursue hybrid engines. One of the underlying reasons was that to move in that particular direction would have influenced the board of directors' decision about the selection of the next CEO. One faction was in support of the hybrid power source and another was not. Had the hybrid strategy been followed, a completely different group of managers would have been the dominant power coalition.

MODELS OF DECISION MAKING

There are different ways, or models, for thinking about decision making. Attempts to show how people 'should' make a decision are called rational or normative models of decision-making. These models are called rational because they assume that decision makers apply a carefully applied set of criteria or rationale for their decisions. They assume that the process is rational as well. The term 'normative' is used because these models are based on observation of the actual errors that decision makers tend to commit. Certain errors are very common, and in normative models an attempt is made to prevent or reduce them. The administrative decision-making model, a second approach to decision making, was described by Herbert Simon in an attempt to provide a more accurate picture of how managers deal with routine and non-routine problems. It also incorporates human tendencies into the process tendencies that often lead to poorer-quality decisions. A third approach, the garbage can model of decision making, is based on the premise that some decisions aren't made to solve a problem, but rather are choices that have already been made and are in search of a problem to which they can be applied, when it is convenient to do so. Fourth, a cybernetic model shows us that some decisions are taken in a systematic, trial-and-error way to discern the best way among the possible choices. Finally, the 'deliberation without attention model' explains how decisions that are taken without thinking appear to be instinctive.

The Rational or Normative Model of Decision Making

Normative models are also called rational or economic models. They have several characteristics. A decision maker should adhere to them even though human abilities and the availability of information put limits on what can be done. Figure 5.2 shows the steps that are commonly considered important in the rational decision-making model.

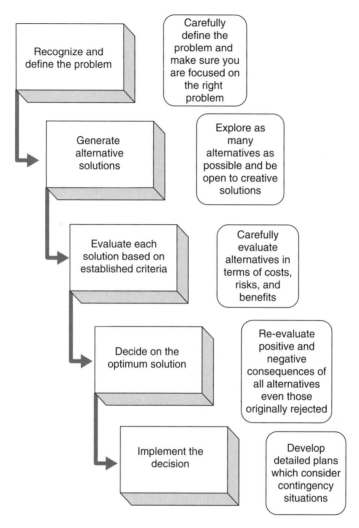

Figure 5.2   Rational model of decision making

In the rational model, decision making usually begins with a judgment that a problem exists or a change is needed. Sometimes the problem is an uncomfortable or negative condition that you want to eliminate, such as Dr St Clair's problem in deciding what to do with the chest pain that Martin Ferry complained about. A problem can also exist when you set a goal, because a goal also represents a desire to improve on a current condition. A manager setting a sales goal considers the new sales level to be preferable to the present level. The problem is how to attain the new sales goal.

Spotlight 5.1   Sir Francis Bacon on the scientific method

Francis Bacon was an English philosopher, statesman and lawyer. He famously said: 'Knowledge is power.' One of his most important contributions was to popularize the Baconian method, or what is now called the 'scientific method', to solving problems. He insisted that there be planned, systematic ways to study issues and to arrive at the appropriate solution. The Baconian method is still the dominant approach to solving problems and making decisions.

Once a problem is recognized and defined, alternatives are sought that could eliminate the negative condition or achieve the goal. Alternatives are activities that you believe will lead to a better state of affairs. For example, Dr St Clair had at least two alternatives: he could have admitted Martin to the hospital and treated him for a heart attack; or he could have sent him home, telling him to rest until he felt better. When you generate alternatives, you make assumptions or predictions that certain outcomes will follow. The relationship between alternatives and their outcomes is not a simple one. One alternative can result in a single outcome or several outcomes, or more than one alternative could be required to achieve a single desired outcome. Some outcomes are intended, while others are unintended side-effects. For example, a total effort to win a ball game can cause unintended injury to a player who takes some unnecessary risks.

You have to use criteria to evaluate the various alternatives that you are evaluating. Among the most common criteria used are feasibility, time, cost and personal acceptability. Criteria will usually vary from person to person, and it is not always clear what criteria are being used. Dr St Clair, in looking at his examination, applied conventional medical criteria and arrived at a choice of which alternative cause was the most likely cause of the chest pain. Once the choice is implemented, it becomes possible to evaluate once again, and this is what the doctor should have done because re-evaluation can uncover faulty implementation or reveal that errors were made at an earlier stage of the decision process.

The normative approach is a way for managers to improve their approach to decision making. To optimize decision quality, the normative approach requires that you follow these steps:

1. Explore a broad range of alternative courses of action.
2. Survey all possible objectives sought and the values relevant to the choice to be made.
3. Carefully evaluate the positive and negative consequences in terms of costs, risks and benefits.
4. Search further for new information to evaluate alternatives further.
5. Account for new information and inputs, even when it might not support a preferred course of action.
6. Re-evaluate positive and negative consequences of all known alternatives, even those originally judged unacceptable, before making a final choice.
7. Develop a detailed plan of implementation, including contingency plans to handle risks or new problems should they arise.

The Administrative (Heuristic) Model of Decision Making

Researchers who study what managers actually do have questioned the usefulness of normative models. They suggest that the process is much less systematic than the rational process suggests (Simon, 1957; March and Simon, 1958). Two key concepts form the basis for the administrative model of decision making: bounded rationality and satisficing.

One concept is bounded rationality. This means that decision makers are able to recognize only a limited number of alternatives and are aware of only a few consequences of each alternative. Human abilities are fallible and limited, information is never perfect, and money and time add limits as well. These contextual constraints place pressures on managers to circumvent the rational decision-making process by making decisions more efficiently.

Often, in response to a problem, organizations will begin a search for 'fixes' to that particular problem. This will often result in the introduction of a new 'program' which focuses on the most easily identified (or accepted) cause of the problem. When these routines and programs exist, decision makers need not generate a large listing of alternative responses to a problem and perhaps do not even consider alternative definitions of the problem. Pressures due to cost and time may limit the number of options decision makers want to consider. Instead, as alternatives are suggested, they are compared to a set of minimally acceptable criteria. The first alternative that meets those criteria is selected. This process is called satisficing.

Suppose, for example, that as a manager you are dissatisfied with the quality of performance appraisals in your department. It would take considerable time and effort to uncover and define elements of this problem.

Spotlight 5.2   Danish managers take a different
                approach to decision making than
                French managers

Danish managers have a different approach to decision making
than French managers. French managers tend to take a more
rational approach to decision making. These French managers
appear to value intellect and creativity in making their decisions.
Apparently they seem more concerned with any actual decision
making, as opposed to implementing the decision. This is usually
left to lower organizational levels. However, the French tend to
have tight controls at these low levels, ensuring that the decision
is effectively implemented. On the other hand, Danish managers
tended to use more 'heuristics'. Their tendency is to satisfice,
rather than optimize. Unlike the French, the Danish managers
tend to be more pragmatic and results-oriented, following through
to the stage of implementation. They apparently do not follow
through as extensively in the control process (Schramm-Nielsen,
2001).

It would also be a major effort to review alternative appraisal systems
and thoroughly evaluate each one. Many complications would arise, and
many questions would be unanswerable. This is a situation in which some
information is unavailable. Alternatives are not easy to identify and are
difficult to select. Your ability to be rational is limited by these complexities, and your decisions will be imperfect. In this situation, there are many
opportunities to satisfice, such as choosing a rating form that looks quite
adequate enough rather than comparing the form to all possible alternatives. Satisficing is called a heuristic approach because decisions are based
on procedures and rules of search. Heuristics are practical rules and are
often based on common sense to solve certain types of problems. It seems
that in everyday life we tend to choose satisfactory outcomes rather than
maximizing the expected utility of a decision (March and Simon, 1958).
For example, the owner of a small retail store could determine prices by
evaluating information on total demand of the market of the store and
relating this to a range of different prices. She could then set a price that is
more in line with both her preferences and preferences of this market. She
then applies her profit margin percentage (a heuristic decision) for each
product sold.

The Garbage Can Model of Decision Making

Many forces in organizations complicate decision making. For example, problems are redefined and decisions modified as different people become involved in the process over time. Even with normative approaches, organizational forces will have an effect. One approach to understanding organizational decision making that considers these effects is the 'garbage can model', or 'organized anarchy' (Cohen et al., 1972). The garbage can decision process consists of four elements:

1. The participants with their various priorities.
2. Problems to be solved.
3. Solutions to be chosen and applied.
4. Decision opportunities.

The participants in complex organizations are the many decision makers with different goals and problems. They have limited time and energy, and cannot involve themselves in all decisions. So their involvement depends on their individual needs, goals and availability. The participation of decision makers can be direct, in that they are directly involved or responsible for resolving the problem. Alternatively they can be indirectly related to the decision and can influence outcomes. Decision makers may also vary in the priority with which they view the problem. Consider what occurs within cross-functional teams, that is, teams whose members come from different functions within the organization. While members may bring more ideas and perspectives to the discussion of the problem, they can also bring a different and perhaps competing set of priorities.

Within the decision context, various participants may view the problems differently or may, in fact, actually be working on a different set of problems. They also have ideas that they would like to see adopted. Sometimes these ideas are solutions in search of a problem, rather than a problem in search of a solution. For example, remember the case of Jennifer and Linda discussed earlier. Linda had decided long ago that she did not want Jennifer in her group because they had personal differences, but it is difficult to fire someone for that reason. So, she looked for an opportunity to take action against Jennifer and when it came up, Linda did so.

Timing is also an important element in this model. The organization is a fluid structure in which people, problems and solutions flow together and apart at different times. Decisions result from a disorderly convergence of these elements, heavily determined by patterns of timing and opportunities (March and Weissinger-Baylon, 1986).

The garbage can model is most likely to operate when situations are ambiguous, methods for achieving goals are not well understood, and organizational units are scattered and loosely linked together. This approach is also more likely to operate when an organization has many departments, committees and task forces, each with vague or overlapping responsibilities. It is also likely to appear in a decision environment with multiple participants representing multiple subunits with varying responsibilities and loyalties.

The Cybernetic Model: Trial and Error

Problems can arise for which you have no experience to solve. To arrive at a final decision you adopt a 'trial-and-error' approach. You apply a solution, and if it doesn't work, you continue until you find one that does. Those decisions that work for a particular problem become a repertoire of potential actions that you apply when you are faced with identical or similar decision problems. Those that don't work are cast aside and not used. Essentially, the choice of alternatives in decision making is the imitation of successful actions. For them to work, you must be able to recognize the characteristics of the situation, recognize the similarity to the earlier problem, review the possible solutions for that situation, then apply the solution. An example of a cybernetic approach to decisions could be the sharing between firms of organizational or technological know-how. This is often approached and arrived at by 'benchmarking' and 'best practices' imitation. Cybernetic approaches are effective in that they can produce significant effort savings in solving problems, but it should be obvious that they are limited to contexts in which decision-making situations occur with similar characteristics over time.

Deliberation without Attention: The Unconscious, Intuitive Model

How, for instance, does a surgeon decide in a few seconds that a patient's life is at risk, and what action is necessary to reduce that risk? Or how does a Formula One race driver decide when to try to overtake cars ahead? Or how does the fireman decide on a high-risk action to save a life? These decisions appear to be instinctive and unconscious and made without thinking.

A more recent idea which supports the use of intuition in decision making is the 'deliberation-without-attention model' of Dijksterhuis et al. (2006). They argue that conscious thinking is rule-based and precise and works very well when decisions are relatively simple, but that unconscious or intuitive choices are more effective when decisions are complex. The 'deliberation-without-attention' hypothesis is that:

A choice between two objects for which one or two attributes are important . . . is simple, whereas a choice between objects for which there are many attributes are important . . . is complex. Conscious thought is hypothesized to lead to good choices in simple matters . . . [but] that unconscious thought is expected to lead to better choices . . . under complex conditions (Dijksterhuis et al., 2006: 1006)

The hypothesis was supported in research by Dijksterhuis and his colleagues (Dijksterhuis and van Olden, 2006). They had a group of students make choices from a list of problems involving simple choices, and a longer list of more complex decisions. The subjects made purchasing decisions for different products such as clothing, kitchen equipment, furniture and accessories furnishing for the home. Some groups of students were given time to think, while others were distracted and had less time to think. They found that for simple and minor decisions, better results were achieved after careful thought and evaluation of their choice. For more complex choices, better solutions were obtained by students not thinking at all and choosing instinctively, unaware of their thoughts.

The researchers' explanation is that in complex situations, with a great deal of information to be considered, the brain is able to maintain an overall, systemic view to examine relevant aspects quickly and to formulate the most valid choice at the time. It is likely that the result is a choice unconsciously dictated by a mix of past experience, knowledge and understanding of the current situation. So, it seems that in the case of highly complex decisions it is preferable not to not think too much, but to proceed instinctively.

This is an interesting idea: that instinct can be an excellent guide to follow in complex and difficult decision-making situations, and should not be dismissed because these experiments were based on consumer choices and may seem, even for the complex decisions, to be relatively simple cases. Two concepts, discussed earlier in this chapter, provide some confirming evidence for this argument: the intuition (earlier in this chapter) of Dr St Clair as he started his examination of Martin Ferry, and the 'automatic information processing' of chess masters, as described in the work of Herbert Simon.

IMPROVING INDIVIDUAL DECISION MAKING

As we look at individual decision making, we can describe how people typically behave, including the errors they make. Once we understand these behaviors, we can turn to ways to improve individual decision making. Thus, while this discussion follows the steps in the rational process, it provides equally useful ideas for dealing with issues suggested by non-rational models of decision making as well. Many of these decision-making concepts are also used later to discuss the process as it occurs within groups (see Chapters 6 and 8).

Improving Problem Selection and Definition

As managers, someone else often makes us aware of a problem. This can result in us spending considerable time and resources towards resolving a problem that may in reality not exist, or that may be a symptom of a larger problem. That is why problem selection and definition are so important. We said earlier that perception has to do with how we organize information (see Chapter 2), and we also pointed out that decision biases lead to errors because we use 'automatic' information processing. This means that when we recognize some key information, or stimulus, we recall schemas or categories (for example, stereotypes) into which that particular information fits, and our judgment is then biased toward the general characteristics of that category. To avoid these decision errors it is useful to use a 'controlled' approach to information processing, in which we pause to reflect on the situation as well as the person and try to identify both the situational forces and the personal causes of behavior, before making our judgment.

Issues in problem selection and definition
The choice of which problems to work on and the definition of a problem both provide a chance for errors in decision making. Here are some common errors in recognizing, choosing and defining problems:

1. Biases in our perceptions make us aware of some problems and unaware of others. We block out or ignore problems based on our needs, values and personalities.
2. Event sequences dictate what we select to work on. Problems are often dealt with in the order in which they arise.
3. Problems that we perceive as emergencies, and problems that we feel are solvable, take priority over other problems.
4. We tend to be overly reactive. Given a choice between reflective planning and action, we will usually take action.
5. Problems are often poorly defined. Definitions may be inaccurate, incomplete, and not creative.
6. The way we define a problem may lead to a built-in solution that takes the focus away from the problem itself.
7. We often leap to solutions long before the problem is even moderately well defined.
8. A problem may be defined in a way that threatens others.

How to improve problem selection

A number of steps can be taken to prevent problem selection from being dominated by our perceptions or by the order in which problems happen to arise. The first is to recognize that nothing is a problem until someone calls it that. A problem is nothing more than a conclusion that things are not the way they ought to be. It might be wise, therefore, to check out our perceptions with others before concluding that a problem exists that is worth taking action upon.

Problem selection can also be improved by making lists of problems and prioritizing them. One technique for doing this is to scan and monitor the environment periodically for both problems and opportunities. This may identify conditions that need attention, such as a drop in product quality or new market opportunities.

Value clarification is a process by which we express and clarify the particular values that we hold, especially when they may impact a particular decision. For example, suppose you are considering introducing a new product and you personally value innovation and believe a new product is needed. Others, however, value more highly the reliability and reputation of existing products. Value clarification can lead you in any number of directions. You could seek value consensus, or they might choose to exploit diverse values by working on both new and old products.

Improving problem definition

We can improve problem definition by properly framing the situation in a way that leads to good solutions. There are several things that we can do. The first is to work toward a thorough definition. A second is to avoid the tendency to jump prematurely into solutions before the problem is completely defined. The third comes into play if you fail to do one of the first two. That is, if you have a solution in mind, ask yourself to link that solution back to some aspect of the problem. In other words, when a solution occurs to you, ask yourself how it relates to the problem at hand. This forces you to go back to the problem definition rather than develop the solution. Improving problem definition can help you to obtain and use facts and information that are less ambiguous. When information is ambiguous, managers are more prone to react to threats and to ignore opportunities.

One way that you can provide a better definition of a problem is to determine its causes. Investigate any events that might be related to the problem. Is there a pattern to the occurrence of the events? Does the problem occur at consistent times or within consistent situations?

Improving, Generating and Evaluating Alternatives

The normative model tells us to generate, explore and examine all possible solutions in a thorough and exhaustive manner, and to estimate the probabilities and values of all possible outcomes. Methods and criteria are established for evaluating and comparing alternative solutions.

Improving and generating alternatives

Even when extensive efforts are made to do this, errors creep in:

1. Alternative solutions are evaluated prematurely. We tend to react positively or negatively to an idea as soon as it arises.
2. Because we evaluate solutions prematurely, idea generation is curtailed. An incomplete set of possible solutions is generated because evaluation works against the generation of alternatives. Satisficing is one result.
3. We do not use the definition of the problem as a source of additional solution ideas.
4. A variety of blocks interfere with our search for a solution. Perceptual blocks put blinkers on our creative thinking; social and cultural values limit our thoughts; and patterns of thought keep us in mental ruts.
5. We often fail to make our evaluation criteria explicit before using them to judge alternatives. Sometimes we are not even aware of the criteria ourselves.
6. It is difficult to deal with both the value of a solution and the probabilities associated with it. Both are important, but we may ignore one or the other. In other words, if a solution is high risk, we may ignore its value and potential.
7. Emotions can lead to self-deception. We can psychologically rationalize or justify an alternative that we strongly prefer.
8. We sometimes rush into making a decision when there may be no need to do so. All we need to do is ask whether postponing a decision could have some benefits.

Improving solution generation

The way in which solutions and ideas are generated makes all the difference in the effectiveness of our decisions. Here are some techniques that you can use to assist in the process.

One important practice is to separate idea generation from idea evaluation. This suggestion is based on the idea that when you evaluate an idea, you cut off the generation of others. A positive evaluation is more harmful than a neutral or negative evaluation. If you are neutral toward or dislike an alternative solution, you have an incentive to generate another one, but if you like an alternative you might stop your search right there.

Brainstorming requires that you let your mind run free and avoid evaluating what you say or think, and do the same for others (Osborn, 1957). All ideas are considered valuable. Using other people to generate additional ideas can often be well worth the effort. First of all, more ideas will result. More importantly, perhaps, these others may not suffer the same perceptual or experience blocks as ourselves. As a matter of fact, lack of experience with the problem may be an advantage. In decision making, experience can work for or against you. It is useful for evaluation, but it puts limits on your ability to see a problem from different perspectives.

Social and cultural blocks are also difficult to overcome. In fact, we may not wish to ignore values that put moral and ethical limits on our decisions. These limits, referred to as 'bounded discretion', operate in all of our decisions, directly and indirectly. While bounded discretion is a critical component of behaving ethically, occasionally considering outrageous solutions may spin highly creative ones.

Managers need to be aware of the mental models they use (Senge, 1994). These are assumptions and generalizations about how the world works that affect how we react to that world. These models may also affect our approach to problem resolution. Many of us tend to view problems in terms of linear relationships (Senge, 1994). When looking for causes of problems, we look for the action that occurred immediately preceding the problem surfacing. We then assume causality and go about focusing on a factor that may not be the cause, or that may be unrelated to the problem. The key is understanding the relationships that exist, and our assumptions about those relationships.

Improving solution evaluation
Eventually every idea has to be tested. First, an idea must pass your mental and emotional scrutiny. You can, in some cases, try ideas out before full commitment is made. These tests can take many forms, such as further discussions, computer simulations or the full-scale construction of a test model, as is done with airplanes.

Another step can be taken to organize alternatives into different clusters before evaluating them. Suppose a manager is deciding how to reduce plant accidents. Alternatives might fall into distinct categories, such as machinery improvements, changing work hours, employee training, and so forth. These clusters may then be evaluated for easier decision making.

Another often overlooked step is to establish criteria to use for evaluating alternatives. Criteria are not easy to establish, but doing so and making them explicit can help decision making immeasurably. Criteria can then be weighted by importance before the process goes further.

Applying criteria to alternatives can be very complicated. For example, suppose you were looking for a job and salary is one of your criteria. If a job is lacking in that criterion, it is eliminated; for example, jobs that fall below a certain salary level are eliminated regardless of how well they meet other criteria. Another complicating factor can be introduced by considering probabilities: lower-probability events would carry less weight. A number of decision-making techniques apply both probabilities and values.

Solution evaluation is also improved if you know your personal tendencies. Some people take more risk and are more oriented toward seeking success. They are more likely to ignore what can be lost, and rather than protect themselves against losses they will choose alternatives to maximize gain. Others will avoid the risks of maximum gain and will seek smaller but safer gains. Others may focus on losses rather than gains: their main motivation is to prevent losses, even if it means losing the chance of gaining something. This is a failure-avoidance strategy and leads to conservative decision making.

Improving Decision Implementation

Some decisions are implemented easily once we have made a decision. Even a complex decision can have a simple implementation. For example, a company might consider many factors in deciding whether to buy from a particular supplier. Once one is selected, an order can be easily placed. Other decisions may require more complicated implementation. Consider the case of a company that decides to expand into a new product line. The decision is just the beginning of a long process. Hundreds of new problems will have to be solved to prepare the new product. The long and detailed process from design to production, to sales and distribution of the product, will require attention.

The ease of implementation will depend on how often we have implemented a decision in the past. If we have been through it many times, implementation can be a routine matter. However, we are often in new territory when we carry out a decision, and when this is the case, we are always faced with new problems requiring new decision.

Problems in implementation
Post-decisional dissonance can impede implementation of a solution. After a decision has been made, people may waver and hesitate. As the decision is executed, anxiety can overcome good judgment. The decision

maker can become extremely cautious and overly vigilant. Feelings of regret can set in. Minor setbacks can become signals of concern and evoke new uncertainties about the original decision.

Perceptual errors and cognitive dissonance can also follow a decision. If people are positively disposed toward a decision, they may ignore information that suggests the decision is not working, and interpret events to support their original choice. In terms of cognitive dissonance theory, people are motivated to reduce feelings of dissonance. Suppose you strongly favor a particular solution, but information that is unfavorable to your choice creates dissonance in your mind. It is likely to be ignored or distorted to support your original choice. The opposite can happen if you are opposed to a decision: information favorable to that decision may be distorted.

People make decisions and sometimes stick to them over time, even if they are bad decisions. This is called 'escalation of commitment' (Staw, 1981; Whyte, 1986). People become trapped or locked into a course of action for several reasons (Staw, 1981; Staw and Ross, 1987). They resist admitting that they have made an error, so as to appear competent or consistent; they can save face by holding to their original position. They may feel that changing their position will be viewed as a sign of weakness and make them more vulnerable to criticism or exploitation. People may also feel that their original decision was a good one that will contribute to an improved situation. Escalation of commitment can then occur, such as when people pour money into a failing business or when they refuse to admit they are wrong in an argument. Escalation can be a potentially costly behavior if you are wrong (Staw and Ross, 1987). In some situations, escalation of commitment is less likely when:

1. The resources to stay with the decision are depleted.
2. The responsibility for the bad decision is shared, or when people feel that more than one person was the cause.
3. The evidence is strong that negative things will continue to happen (Garland and Newport, 1991; Whyte, 1991).

Improving implementation and evaluation
You have to accept the fact that post-decisional conflict is natural, and not repress or ignore it. Such conflict is quite common because many decisions are complex and involve a good deal of risk or uncertainty. There are at least three ways to resolve post-decisional conflict.

1. Stick with the original decision, to reaffirm it. After weighing the evidence, you proceed as planned.

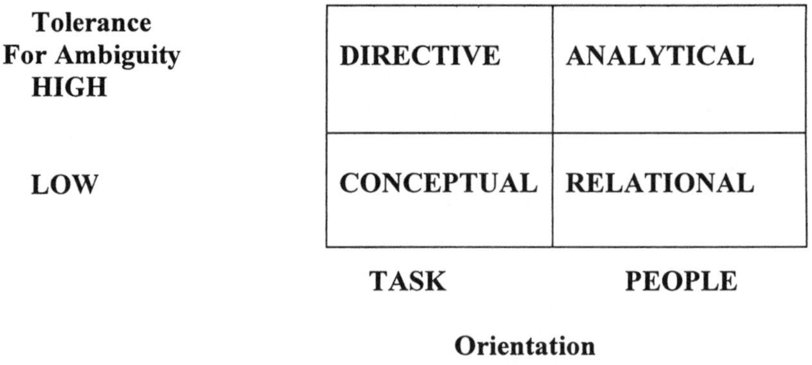

Tolerance For Ambiguity HIGH	**DIRECTIVE**	**ANALYTICAL**
LOW	**CONCEPTUAL**	**RELATIONAL**
	TASK	**PEOPLE**

Orientation

Source: Adapted from Rowe and Watkins (1992).

Figure 5.3 Personality and decision style

2. Modify or curtail implementation. It might be possible to stay with the original decision but slow down a bit in implementing it.
3. Undo the original decision. When the costs and risks of continuing outweigh the benefits of the original decision, it might be wise to drop or change the original choice rather than escalate commitment.

In general, it is wise to consider how common escalation of commitment is and to analyze your own decision-making processes to make sure that it has not overtaken your judgment. As a decision maker, you can work diligently to seek information of all kinds. This posture of active openness can help to overcome tendencies to pursue feedback selectivity during implementation. Another strategy is to give all information fair and thorough consideration, rather than deny it or rationalize it away. It takes considerable effort to seek pros and cons actively, and to evaluate all sides of an issue.

Decision-Making Style and Individual Differences

The decision models we have analyzed show how individuals approach making choices as a function of the situation, the degree of structure in the problem, the amount and quality of information, and the clarity and understanding of objectives. The way that a person usually makes these choices is also obviously related to one's personality. Figure 5.3 shows a two-dimensional model that shows how personality is related to decision styles (see Figure 5.3) (Rowe and Boalgarides, 1992). One dimension is the person's tolerance for ambiguity: whether you prefer well-structured contexts or can function effectively under conditions of high ambiguity. The other dimension is whether the person has a stronger orientation toward people or toward the task.

A person with a low tolerance for ambiguity and task orientation tends to use a directive approach. They make decisions relatively quickly, focusing on the short term. They are also likely to have a strong need for power (McClelland, 1975).

An analytical decision style is characteristic of a person with a task orientation and with higher tolerances for ambiguity. They are high in need for achievement in the form of challenges (McClelland, 1975). They seek more information and alternatives before making a decision. They know how to confront a new decision context, but they may appear to be slow and deliberate because they want to achieve the most rational result possible.

The conceptual decision style is typical of those who are high in need for achievement that is reflected by recognition from others. They have a high tolerance for ambiguity and a strong people orientation, as opposed to task orientation. They often try to broaden the boundaries of the problem and seek creative solutions to the problem.

Finally the relational decision style is one in which the decision maker seeks to build consensus of those involved in the process. This is typical of a person with a strong need for affiliation (McClelland, 1975). They have a strong people orientation and a relatively low tolerance for ambiguity that is reduced by achieving consensus.

This model is a useful way to think about personality and a dominant decision-making style. However, as we noted in earlier chapters, while a person may have strong behavioral tendencies because of personality and attitudes, he or she may take a different approach to decision making, depending on the situation.

SUMMARY OF IMPROVING INDIVIDUAL DECISION MAKING: A CALL FOR SYSTEMS THINKING

The practice of systems thinking is useful in resolving problems that occur throughout the decision-making process (Senge, 1994). Systems thinking means that you look for interrelationships among variables within the decision space. For example, a university president was concerned about the declining level of enrollment at her university. Since the traditional student population came either directly from the area's high school or transferred from the local community college, she focused on the enrollments at those 'feeder' institutions. As a result, her strategy for increasing enrollments was to focus on attracting more students from the area high school and community college. Extensive funds were spent on marketing the university as the right place for those particular students to study. Unfortunately, this narrow view of the problem ignored a growing market segment that has more mature students returning to universities and colleges across the country. Structural factors such as the lower number of students in the population enrolling directly from high school limited the eventual success of her strategy. However, when she considered the possibility of attracting other types of students, and students coming from other areas, she was able to view different possibilities in problem definition and, as a result, solution implementation. Systems thinking encourages us to look for alternative or contributing causes of the problem, and alternative solutions.

Spotlight 5.3   Culture and decision making

Decision-making is affected by the decision maker's time horizon. Long- versus short-term patterns of thought reflect a culture's view about the future (Hofstede et al., 1990). The short-term orientation, a Western cultural characteristic, reflects values toward the present, perhaps even the past, and a concern for fulfilling social obligations. Long-term thought patterns, characteristic of Asian countries, reflect an orientation toward the future, belief in thrift and savings, and persistence. In countries with a long-term orientation, planning has a longer time horizon. Firms are willing to make substantial investments in employee training and development, there will be longer-term job security and promotions will come slowly; and they are likely to develop long-term relationships with suppliers and customers.

IMPROVING GROUP DECISION MAKING

As we will discuss in the chapters on groups (Chapter 6) and conflict (Chapter 8), organizations frequently use teams, committees, task forces and other types of groups in all stages of the decision process. Usually this involvement or participative management philosophy is an attempt to find better decisions and more commitment by including employees in decisions that affect them, spreading responsibilities for decision making to all employees, not just managers.

Sometimes group decision-making works well, and sometimes it does not. Several things are necessary for success. One is that the group norms

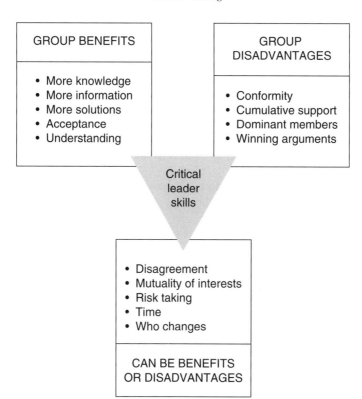

GROUP BENEFITS

- More knowledge
- More information
- More solutions
- Acceptance
- Understanding

GROUP DISADVANTAGES

- Conformity
- Cumulative support
- Dominant members
- Winning arguments

Critical leader skills

- Disagreement
- Mutuality of interests
- Risk taking
- Time
- Who changes

CAN BE BENEFITS OR DISADVANTAGES

Figure 5.4   Benefits and disadvantages of group decision making

place a higher value on critical analysis than on consensus of the members (Postmes et al., 2001). This is even more likely to be the case when there is a strong orientation to share information. To succeed, the commitment to group decision making must be genuine. In addition, various skills are needed. First, as managers we must learn the steps and techniques of good decision making discussed in the first part of this chapter. Knowledge of group and team dynamics is essential too. We need to know the benefits and disadvantages of group decision making over individual decision making. Finally, leadership is needed to guide the process so that effective decisions have a chance of emerging.

Benefits and Disadvantages of Groups

Using groups for decision making has both benefits and disadvantages (Maier, 1967). These are shown in Figure 5.4. To a large degree, making them an asset depends on the skill of the leader. Compared to individuals, groups have more knowledge and information. Groups also generate a larger number of approaches to a problem, and members can knock each other out of ruts in their thinking. Group participation can increase understanding and acceptance of the decision, and the commitment to execute it. Managerial decisions often fail because of faulty communication of the decision to those who must implement them. Employees often lack knowledge of rejected alternatives, obstacles, goals and reasons behind the decision. These problems can be overcome when a group is involved in the entire process.

A disadvantage of group decision-making lies in social pressure for conformity. The majority can suppress good minority ideas, or a desire for consensus can silence disagreement. Some solutions, good and bad ones, accumulate a certain amount of support. Once support for a solution reaches a critical level, it has a high probability of being selected and other solutions are very likely to fail. Even a minority can build up support for a solution by actively asserting themselves. Thus, decisions can emerge from this support, rather than from their quality. Members who are hard to control and who persuade, threaten or persist in their point of view also can dominate groups. A final disadvantage of groups occurs when it becomes more important to avoid disagreement or to win an argument than to make a good evaluation of alternatives. Avoidance of disagreement and arguments prevents open and objective discussion. We discuss some of these social pressures later in Chapter 8 on conflict.

Some factors can be either benefits or disadvantages depending on the skill of the group leader. If the leader suppresses disagreement or allows it to create hard feelings, it can damage the solution. However, if the leader treats disagreement as acceptable, it can generate innovative solutions. The leader can also make a difference by emphasizing either conflicting or mutual interests. Mutual interests should be explored at all stages of decision making, beginning with the problem definition.

Consensus development begins in the process of seeking mutually acceptable solutions, but the leader has to work hard to probe areas of mutual concern. Unless he or she does so, conflict among members might lead to a poor solution. The leader can also affect the level of risk that a group takes: it can be guided toward a very safe and conservative decision, or one that is riskier and more innovative.

Time can also be an asset or a liability. Groups generally take longer than individuals to make decisions. Even if both take an hour to decide, a group of five people has spent five work hours. Leaders who permit rushing to save time can risk losing acceptance and may reduce the quality of the decision. A final factor that can help or hinder a decision is, 'Who changes their mind in the group?' If the person with the worst ideas changes their mind, the decision will be better, but if the person with the best ideas is forced to change, the decision will be worse.

Deciding When to Use a Group

Not every decision that we make can – or should – be made by a group. Managers can make the decision alone or involve others in the decision process. They can assign the responsibility to an individual, a committee or a task force. The question is, under what conditions is it best to use a group?

Quality and acceptance as criteria

Quality and acceptance are useful in deciding whether to engage a group in decision making (Maier, 1967). The quality of a decision refers to the feasibility and technical aspects of a problem and calls for the use of facts, analysis of data and objectivity. Acceptance of a decision, on the other hand, deals with feelings, needs and emotions, and is subjective in nature.

Decisions can be classified into several types, depending on whether quality, acceptance or both are important factors. With some decisions, quality is more important than acceptance. These problems are usually technical or scientific in nature, such as how to control pressure in a valve, or devising a test to select among vendors' products. When quality is the main concern, you are not likely to become emotionally involved in the outcome or decision, so as a manager, you need only find experts with the knowledge and experience to find a quality solution. They can research, develop and test technically feasible solutions. Facts and analysis will dominate decision making.

With other problems, however, acceptance may be the most important criteria. For example, deciding who works overtime is an acceptance issue, assuming that all of the candidates for overtime are able to do the work. Other changes that might involve workplace procedures, or that will significantly impact a particular group and require their efforts for successful decision implementation, increase the importance of the acceptance criterion.

Other problems involve both quality and acceptance: deciding how to increase productivity, introducing new methods or equipment, reducing absenteeism or developing new safety standards. Here quality solutions are essential, and those affected by them will have strong feelings about them. The decision could fail unless employees accept it and can commit to its implementation. An example of a decision in which both qualtity and acceptance were important was the way that the Pathfinder mission to Mars would land the Sojourner Mars Rover vehicle. The project team

A.   Is there a quality requirement such that one solution is likely to be more rational than another?
B.   Do I have sufficient information to make a high-quality decision?
C.   Is the problem structured?
D.   Is acceptance of decision by subordinates critical to effective implementation?
E.   If I were to make the decision by myself, is it reasonably certain that it would be accepted by my subordinates?
F.   Do subordinates share the organizational goals to be attained in solving the problem?
G.   Is conflict among subordinates likely in preferred solutions? (This question is irrelevant to individual problems.)

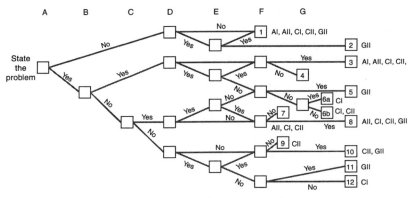

Figure 5.5   The Vroom–Yetton decision model

had essentially three alternatives: to land with a parachute, to land with retro-rockets as were used in the lunar landing, or to use airbags. There was a great deal of discussion, much of it very heated, as to what would be the best way, and there were factions that favored different modes of landing. Finally, the decision was to use a combination of methods. The atmosphere of Mars was entered with the Sojourner in a capsule, then a parachute was used, and finally the Rover hit the Mars surface in an airbag device – successfully (Spear, 2007).

The general rule to use is: 'Whenever acceptance is critical, the manager must at least consider using a group for the decision process. Unilateral decisions by the manager run the risk of being misunderstood or rejected.' Even though shortage of time could argue against participation, group decision is the best way to achieve acceptance.

The Vroom–Yetton model

A useful model for deciding whether to use a group has been developed by Vroom and Yetton (1973) (see Figure 5.5). They propose five different types of decision making, which vary according to the amount of sub-ordinate influence. At one extreme is unilateral decision making by the manager; this is a quick and efficient way to make a decision. At the other extreme is participative decision making.

These five decision styles are listed below. Notice that, as the decision approach moves from AI toward GII (A stands for autocratic, C for consultative, and G for group), the amount of subordinate influence over the final decision increases:

1. AI: You make the decision with currently available data.
2. AII: Necessary information is obtained from subordinates, but you still decide alone. Your subordinates' role is to provide information data only; they have nothing to do with generating or evaluating alternatives.
3. CI: You discuss the problem with relevant subordinates individually. Then, without bringing them together, make a decision that may or may not reflect their input.
4. CII: You share the problem with subordinates in a group meeting, gathering ideas and suggestions, then make the decision alone, which may or may not take the input of the group meeting into account.
5. GII: Problems are shared with the group. In this case, you would be using the participative management style. Your role is to provide information and help, facilitating the group's determination of its own solution rather than the solution preferred by the manager.

This model can help you to decide which of these five decision-making methods to use. The most effective style depends on seven situational characteristics, described below.

SC1: The importance of decision quality   How important is it to achieve a high-quality solution? If there is no quality requirement, then any acceptable alternative will be satisfactory to management, and the group can make the decision. For example, groups can decide how to accomplish or assign routine tasks where quality is not critical.

SC2: The extent to which the decision maker has the necessary information   There are two kinds of information that make an effective decision: preferences of subordinates about alternatives; and whether there are rational grounds to judge the quality of alternatives. When you do not know your subordinates' preferences, participation can reveal them. If you know your subordinates' preferences, but the problem is such that an individual decision is more likely to produce a better solution than that of a group, then clearly the situation calls for you to make the decision alone.

In what kind of situation is a group likely to make a better decision than an individual? Research indicates that an individual can do as well as a group when either the problem has a highly verifiable solution, or the solution requires thinking through complicated interrelated stages, keeping in mind conclusions reached at earlier times. A group is superior when the problem is complex, has several parts, and the group members possess diverse but relevant talents and skills. Insight and originality can then more likely be obtained from a group than from an individual.

SC3: The extent to which the problem is structured   In structured problems the alternatives, or at least the means for generating them, are known. Standard procedures used in most organizations give individuals all or most of the information they need. In an ill-structured problem, the information may be widely dispersed through the organization. Different individuals will probably have to be brought together to solve the problem or to make a joint decision. For example, a computer assembly worker can figure out how to assemble the components given a set of instructions and specifications, but may need to consult with others if a new material or component is involved.

SC4: The importance of subordinates' acceptance   Acceptance by subordinates is not critical where a decision falls within the boundaries of the psychological contract. In this case, carrying out the decision is a matter of simple compliance. The more commitment required from subordinates in the carrying out of a decision, of course, the more important subordinate acceptance becomes.

SC5: The probability that an autocratic decision will be accepted   If a decision is viewed as within the legitimate authority of a manager, it will be accepted by subordinates without participation.

SC6: Subordinate motivation to attain organizational goals   Sometimes the objectives of superiors and their subordinates are not compatible. Then participation in decision-making may be more risky than in situations where the goals are congruent. Participative decision making works best where there is mutual interest in the problem.

SC7: Subordinates' disagreement over solutions   Subordinates may disagree among themselves over prospective alternatives. The method used to reach a decision must facilitate resolution of the disagreement, and thus group involvement is necessary.

All of these situational characteristics are presented in the form of questions in the Vroom–Yetton model, shown in Figure 5.5. The questions are answered on a yes–no basis. The decision tree format establishes the sequence of the questions to be answered by the manager. At the end of every path in the decision tree is one or more alternative approaches for making the decision.

Problems with Group Decision Making: Groupthink and Polarization

Groups can make poor decisions because they fall into a pattern called 'groupthink' (Janis, 1972). The need for consensus and cohesiveness assumes greater importance than making the best possible decision. It happens when the group collectively becomes defensive and avoids facing issues squarely and realistically. When you understand how groups can affect members, it is easier to know how many of the decisions with tragic outcomes occur. NASA leaders may have framed the decision to launch Challenger as a choice between two outcomes (Rogers Commission Report, 1986). One was damage to the public perception of the reliability of the shuttle program because of the numerous delays that had already been experienced. The other was the potential safety issues occurring from launching in temperatures where performance of the seals was questionable. Additional pressure and negative consequences on NASA were assured if they chose to delay the launch further. There was a possibility, and subsequent discussion reinforced that possibility, that the launch would be successful. The result of the decision to launch Challenger demonstrates the dangers inherent in group decision-making.

In groups there is often pressure for conformity from those who hold a majority view, on the minority of group members with a different position. Much of this pressure occurs during the social interaction of discussing the issues. The result of this pressure is a fascinating phenomenon found in groups: they often tend to take more extreme positions, either more risky or more conservative, than the individuals in the group might take. What might cause a group to shift to a more extreme position compared to individuals? The answer provides a powerful lesson on social influence.

In group decision-making contexts, individuals usually have inclinations about a decision before they enter the group discussion. In general, group discussion tends to strengthen these inclinations. The social process of the group discussion causes a person who favored a particular decision before a group discussion to feel even stronger after the discussion. This process, called polarization, refers to the tendency that the average group member's position on an issue will become more extreme as the result of group discussion. It occurs as subgroups form of members who have similar opinions on an issue, but opinions that differ from others. Through the decision process, these subgroups become further apart on the issue. For example, suppose the Human Resources (HR) Department favors a

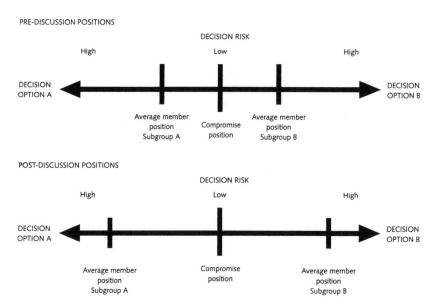

Figure 5.6   Effects of polarisaion on decision risk

new appraisal system for first-line supervisors, but these supervisors are against any change. As both sides meet to discuss the issue, polarization predicts that the HR Department members will strengthen their inclinations favoring the new system, while the supervisors will strengthen their biases against the change. This would create an even larger gap between the two groups. Figure 5.6 shows what will happen if this same process occurs within a group contemplating alternative decisions that have increased risk as the decision options becomes more extreme. Prior to the discussion, the average pre-discussion positions of subgroup members were closer to the compromise position. However, notice that after the meeting, polarization causes the group members' position to move, on average, towards a preference for a riskier decision.

This strong consensus in groups, especially when a bad decision is made, is called 'groupthink'. Some of the more famous examples of groupthink are found in high-level government decision-making groups, several of which were studied by Irving Janis, a psychologist, who asked the question: 'Why do smart people do dumb things?' (Janis, 1972):

- President Kennedy and his colleagues decided to invade Cuba at the Bay of Pigs, despite good information that the attempt would fail and damage the USA's relations with other countries.

- President Richard Nixon and his staff proceeded with the Watergate burglary of the Democratic election headquarters and continued with its subsequent cover-up, despite its serious risks and implications.
- Decision makers, in deciding to launch the space shuttle Challenger in 1986, ignored negative information.

When groupthink occurs, those in the group:

1. Have an illusion of invulnerability. The group acts as if it is protected from criticism. This gives members too much optimism and encourages extreme risk-taking.
2. Tend toward rationalization. The group members tend to explain away facts or ideas that press them to reconsider their position.
3. Have illusion of morality. This is a belief that the group is acting in the name of goodness, and causes inattention to ethical consequences.
4. Engage in stereotyping. Rivals or enemies outside the group are treated as evil, too stupid to negotiate with, or too weak to harm the group.
5. Exert pressure for conformity. Group members are pressured to go along with the group's illusions and stereotypes. Dissent is suppressed as contrary to group expectations.
6. Practice self-censorship. Group members become inclined to minimize their own feelings of doubt or disagreement.
7. Have illusions of unanimity. Silence comes to imply agreement. Perceptions develop that unanimity exists.
8. Have self-appointed 'mind guards'. Some members act to protect the group from adverse information.

Causes of groupthink

There appear to be three key causes of groupthink (Baron, 2005). First, it often occurs in highly cohesive groups, those in which there is very strong social identification among the members. Members have a strong sense that they are in the group for a particular, shared reason. When there is strong social identification, members will listen to each other's ideas when they are put forth. It also means that deviating too far from the dominant group position could be punished. Second, salient norms are also a prerequisite for groupthink. For example, the key staff members of the second Bush cabinet all had a very similar and strong view about the necessity of invading Iraq that eventually pervaded the White House during Bush's administration. Such strong and salient views among group members will lead to polarization, resulting in a strong defense by the group when its decision comes under criticism. Finally, there will be low group situational self-efficacy. This means, especially for critical problems, that group members individually may lack high confidence to reach a good solution. All of these factors may be exacerbated when the group faces an important problem and there is high stress, as when an important decision is needed but hope is low for finding a solution other than the one desired by the leader or other influential members. Such factors can combine to create disastrous conditions. Consider a situation where a plant manager and his subordinates are under pressure from headquarters to complete a rush order from a customer. They might easily convince themselves that machine breakdowns, employee fatigue or union resistance will not become an issue. Dissenting members of the team might be pressured to conform, and withhold their opinions.

Groupthink and polarization can be key factors in conflict, and there are several managerial solutions to minimize the problem. To reduce polarization, it may be wise to avoid premature meetings of subgroups for and against an issue. It is also helpful to mix membership within groups, or occasionally to invite outsiders or people with different ideas into meetings whenever feasible. Any action that calls for a focus on the total organization mission might reduce the tendency towards groupthink and polarization. Just making members aware of this tendency may cause members to develop procedures to minimize the impact of polarization in leading their group to make a riskier decision.

SUMMARY

Decision making is often an imperfect process that requires new decisions to compensate for prior decisions. The basic process includes defining the problem, generating and evaluating alternative solutions, choosing among solutions and implementing the decision. Both evaluative and creative behaviors are important in all stages. At each step, a number of errors can be made that reduce the effectiveness of a decision. People frequently define problems too narrowly, or fail to generate sufficient alternatives. Premature and incomplete evaluation is also common. Because of such errors, many ideal models and techniques for better decision making have been suggested. These can help decision making significantly, but rarely produce perfect, lasting solutions.

Groups that make decisions commit many of the same errors that individuals make. Therefore, it would serve a group well to follow the suggestions offered by ideal models of decision making. One of the first steps consists of deciding when or whether to involve a group in decision making. Group decision making increases the opportunity to gain group acceptance and commitment to a decision, and groups can have a larger reservoir of ideas. However, it takes practice and skill to overcome the disadvantages of groups, such as pressures to conform. A skilled group leader can make a great difference in solution quality and acceptance, not only by overcoming disadvantages but also by bringing out the best that the group has to offer.

GUIDE FOR MANAGERS: IMPROVING GROUP DECISION MAKING

The greatest responsibility for group decision making is in the hands of the group leader, who is in a critical position to affect the quality and acceptance of a decision. When you are the leader of a decision-making group you have to be like an orchestra leader: you do not play an instrument, but rather you conduct and guide group members (Maier, 1963).

The leader has to focus on the group decision-making process as well as on the actual content of the decision. The leader who focuses on process does things to urge members to define the problem well, helps them to generate alternative solutions, and so on. In focusing on process, the leader sees to it that members participate freely and that disagreements are handled appropriately. The leader can affect content by holding to high standards of quality and acceptance and by preventing the group from making unworkable decisions. Many leaders become too involved in the content of a group decision, because they typically know a good deal about the problem at hand and have a natural tendency to offer their ideas and to contribute directly to the decision. Yet it is a mistake to do so, especially if the process goes unattended. Shifting your focus to the group process takes practice. You must unlearn past thinking habits and practice the acceptance of dissent and experimentation in decision making (Osborne, 1957). Here are some things you can do to manage the group decision-making process (Maier, 1963).

Define the Problem Fully and Accurately

You must overcome the tendency of the group to define problems too quickly or simply. Ask members how they view the problem, and what they feel caused it. Probe the group and work toward a thorough definition. As the group members speak, record their ideas on a chalkboard or on flip charts. The group can be asked to differentiate symptoms from more basic, underlying causes. It is better to put the problem in situational rather than personal terms. For example, it is unwise to state the problem as how to get Charley to work evenings. Depersonalizing helps members to respond to various aspects of the problem with more objectivity.

Group members will still move off the problem too quickly. Some will begin to offer solutions too early. When this happens, you must turn the solution statement back into a problem definition and remind the group, 'We are not ready for solutions yet', or say, 'How does the solution relate to the problem?'

Use the Problem to Generate Solutions

A good definition of a problem can be put to productive use. Each element of the definition can be a source of solution possibilities. All you have to do is to keep the group working to generate ideas that respond to all of the problem elements. In this way, you not only encourage various solutions but also help to ensure thoroughness. Solutions are less likely to be incomplete if all the problem elements are attended to.

Prevent Premature Evaluation of Solutions

The process of idea-getting is blocked by idea evaluation. This is especially true when group members quickly agree on a solution and adopt the first acceptable solution that arises. The leader and members should see to it that evaluative statements are withheld until idea generation is at least adequate.

Gain Consensus

Eventually, group members need to evaluate their ideas and arrive at a decision that they can live with. You can help in several ways here. You can summarize the group's progress to help make sure that the group is ready to make the decision. You can also get members to develop criteria to evaluate the alternatives they generated. Questioning where the group agrees or disagrees on any matter before them can directly test consensus. You may have to organize and present a review of the group's work in order to adequately test and gain a true consensus.

Avoid Leader Solutions

A group leader, especially one who has formal authority, should avoid offering solutions to the group. This may be difficult for you to do. You usually want to express your opinions in these situations. The problem is that a superior's idea is evaluated by group members on the basis of the source of the idea and not on its worth. Objective evaluation loses out to concern over how the boss will react if the idea is supported or challenged. It is rare that a boss is treated as a peer. You will get better solutions from groups when they are given no time to prepare or think about a problem (Maier, 1963). When you prepare, you tend to think of solutions that you later find difficult to keep to yourself.

Value Disagreement and Chaos

There is more value in disagreement than in quick agreement. When group members agree, solution generation often comes to a close. If a disagreement occurs, however, solution generation is still alive. Train people that if things don't make sense, they should speak up. People in the group should raise their own white flag when they are falling into the trap of reacting without thinking. This is most likely in four situations:

1. When we expect something.
2. When we want something.
3. When we are preoccupied with something.
4. When we finish something.

This means that you should embrace chaos (Weick, 1995, 1998). Accept that within chaotic contexts, there is pattern. Always look for clues to the pattern and consider numerous methods of problem resolution. Looking, for example, at the Challenger failure and the BP oil spill, consistent mistakes were made, mistakes that decision-makers should be trained to notice when they might occur so that they can avoid them. Leaders squelch disagreement when they say: 'If we're going to argue, we'll never get this problem solved.' Statements such as this, frustrated sighs or other non-verbal cues soon tell group members to avoid disagreement. Ideas are accepted because no one wants to incur disfavor.

Disagreements can be made to pay off. This is done when the leader accepts and probes a disagreement. The leader can say: 'Phyllis, your idea really contrasts with John's. Tell us what you have in mind, and then we can get John's point of view.' This tells the group that it is acceptable to disagree, and no one will be punished for doing so. It also opens the door to new ideas. Often the disagreement can be traced to different definitions of the problem, or to goals that the group had not considered earlier. Probing disagreement can prevent the rubber-stamping or the avoiding of ideas. Managers should program disagreement into discussions with the use of the devil's advocate role or by asking for counter-proposals (Cosier and Schwenk, 1990).

CASE: WHAT WILL I STUDY?

Giorgio is a very precise person: when he has to make a decision, he wants as much information as possible. For example, as he was choosing the college in which he would study at the university, he was confounded. As he began looking at the information from the university he thought he would attend, he thought that were so many different fields of study: accounting, economics, literature, chemistry and psychology, for example. He eliminated some areas: he thought that medicine required too much study and he didn't like the sight of blood; biology and mathematics required too much skill with numbers for him; and physics was too complex.

Being such a precise decision maker, he spent a good deal of time thinking about the criteria he would use to evaluate different courses. He had a pretty clear set of ideas that were important to him:

- What would life be like when he finished university?
- What was the image of the university?
- How far was the university from his home?
- What would be the expenses if he lived away from home?
- What fees were required at the university?
- How many students were enrolled in the different fields?
- Were there many exams and were they difficult?
- What would the job opportunities be after graduation?

As he read over his list, Giorgio realized that there were many other criteria that he could list, but decided that this was enough. He then began to weight the various criteria to compare the different alternatives. As he was doing so he realized that many factors (for example, the image of the university and job opportunities after graduation) were not easily measured, and it might take a long time to get much good information for him to weight these factors properly.

So, he decided to talk with Michael and Jessica, his best friends and schoolmates, with whom he had studied on many evenings. Michael, a bright young man, very good at mathematics, who had applied to study physics, made it clear that in order to be rational, Giorgio's starting question should be: 'Do I want to continue studying, or do I want a job just now?'

For each of these alternatives, Michael told him that he should identify several subalternatives relating to the different types of work and the possible paths of study, comparing and evaluating them with as many of the possible criteria he could think of (for example, thinking about life, opportunity costs, time, passion, effort, prospective and current salary levels, the dynamic nature of the labor market, new jobs, and so on). Giorgio could then develop a mathematical model and a computer simulation to arrive at a Pareto-optimizing solution.

All of this gave George a headache; he was even more confused. But then he spoke with Jessica and everything became clear. Jessica was going to study geology, not only because she had a strong passion for the environment and ecological problems, but also because she believed that there would be ongoing emergencies in the world and, thus, the possibility of finding a job after graduating was very strong. At the same time, the classes in geology were not very large, so she felt she would be able to work more closely with her professors. Finally, but not least, she applied to the University of Perugia, a beautiful Italian town with a beautiful campus. George, who also had a strong feelings for Jessica, had no more doubt: he would become a geologist.

Discussion

- What kind of decision-making process gave George use?
- What was your decision making process when selecting a field of study?
- Which do you think is more effective, yours or his?

REFERENCES

Baron, R.S. (2005), So Right It's Wrong: Groupthink and the Ubiquitous Nature of Polarized Group Decision Making. In *Advances in Experimental Social Psychology, Vol. 37.*, M.P. Zanna (ed.). San Diego, CA: Elsevier Academic Press, pp. 219–53.

Bazerman, M.H. (2005), *Judgment in Managerial Decision Making*, 6th edn. New York: John Wiley & Sons.

Bazerman, M.H. and D. Chugh (2006), Decisions Without Blinders. *Harvard Business Review*, **84**(1): 88–97.

Briers, B.P., M. Pandelaere and L. Warlop (2007), Adding Exchange to Charity: A Reference Price Explanation. *Journal of Economic Psychology*, **28**(1): 15–30.

Cohen, M.D., J.G. March and J.P. Olsen (1972), A Garbage Can Model of Organizational Choice. *Administrative Science Quarterly*, **17**: 1–25.

Cosier, R.A. and C.R. Schwenk (1990), Agreement and Thinking Alike: Ingredients for Poor Decisions. *Academy of Management Executive*, **4**(1): 69–74.

Dijksterhuis, D. and Z. van Olden (2006), On the Benefits of Thinking Unconsciously: Unconscious Thought can Increase Post-Choice Satisfaction. *Journal of Experimental Social Psychology*, **42**(5): 627–31.

Dijksterhuis, A., M.W. Bos, L.F. Nordgren and R.A. van Baaren (2006), On Making the Right Choice: The Deliberation-Without-Attention Effect. *Science*, **311**(5763): 1005–7.

Drucker, P.F. (1967), *The Effective Executive*. Oxford: Elsevier.

Eisenhardt, K.M. and L.J. Bourgeois (1988), Politics of Strategic Decision Making in High-Velocity Environments: Toward a Midrange Theory. *Academy of Management Journal*, **31**(4): 737–70.

Garland, H. and S. Newport (1991), Effects of Absolute and Relative Sunk Costs on the Decision to Persist with a Course of Action. *Organizational Behavior and Human Decision Processes*, **48**: 55–69.

Groopman, J. (2007), *How Doctors Think?* New York: Houghton Mifflin.

Hofstede, G., B. Neuijen, D.D. Ohayv and G. Sanders (1990), Measuring Organizational Cultures: A Qualitative and Quanitative Study Across Twenty Cases. *Administrative Science Quarterly*, **35**: 286–316.

Janis, I.L. (1972), *Victims of Groupthink*. Boston, MA: Houghton Mifflin.

Janis, I.L. and L. Mann (1977), *Decision Making: A Psychological Analysis of Conflict, Choice and Commitment*. New York: Free Press.

Kahneman, D. (2003), A Perspective on Judgment and Choice: Mapping Bounded Rationality. *American Psychologist*, **58**(9): 697–720.

Lyall, S. (2010), In BP's Record, a History of Boldness and Costly Blunders. *New York Times*, 12 July.

Maier, N.R.F. (1963), *Problem-Solving Discussions and Conferences: Leadership Methods and Skills*. New York: McGraw-Hill.

Maier, N.R.F. (1967), Assets and Liabilities in Group Problem Solving: The Need for an Integrative Function. *Psychological Review*, **74**: 239–48.

March, J.G. and H.A. Simon (1958), *Organizations*. New York: John Wiley.

March, J.G. and R. Weissinger-Baylon (1986), *Ambiguity and Command: Organizational Perspectives on Military Decision Making*. Marshfield, MA: Pitman Publishing.

McClelland, D.A. (1975), *Power: The Inner Experience*. New York: Irvington.

Mintzberg, H. (1973), *The Nature of Managerial Work*. New York: Harper & Row.

Neisser, U. (1976), *Cognition and Reality*. San Francisco, CA: W.H. Freeman.

Neisser, U. and I.E. Hyman (2000), *Memory Observed: Remembering in Natural Contexts*, 2nd edn. New York: Worth Publishers.

Osborn, A.F. (1957), *Applied Imagination*. New York: Charles Scribners Sons.

Postmes, T., R. Spears and S. Cihangir (2001), Quality of Decision Making and Group Norms. *Journal of Personality and Social Psychology*, **80**(6): 918–30.

Roberto, M.A. (2005), *Why Great Leaders Don't Take Yes for an Answer: Managing for Conflict and Consensus*. Philadelphia, PA: Wharton School Publisher.

Ross, L.D. (1977), The Intuitive Psychologist and His Shortcomings: Distortions in the Attribution Process. In *Advances in Experimental Social Psychology*, L. Berkowitz (ed.). New York: Academic Press, pp. 435–94.

Rowe, A. and J. Boalgarides (1992), *Managerial Decision Making*. New York: Macmillan Publishing Company.

Rowe, A.J. and P.R. Watkins (1992), Beyond Expert Systems: Reasoning, Judgement, and Wisdom. *Expert Systems with Applications*, **4**(1): 1–10.

Rogers Commission Report (1986), U.S.C.S.S.h. 99-967, Editor. U.S. G. P. O: Washington, DC, p. 216. http://history.nasa.gov/rogersrep.

Schramm-Nielsen, J. (2001), Cultural Dimensions of Decision Making: Denmark and France Compared. *Journal of Managerial Psychology*, **16**(5–6): 404–23.

Senge, P.M. (1994), *The Fifth Discipline*. New York: Doubledary/Currency.

Simon, H.A. (1957), *Models of Man*. New York: John Wiley.

Simon, H.A. (1976), *Administrative Behavior: A Study of Decision Making Processes in Administrative Organization*. 3rd edn. New York: Free Press.

Simon, H.A. (1977), *The New Science of Management Decisions*, 2nd edn. 1977, Englewood Cliffs, NJ: Prentice-Hall.

Simon, H.A. (1987), Making Management Decisions: the Role of Intuition and Emotion. *Academy of Management Executive*, **1**(1): 57–64.

Spear, A. (2007), Determining the Most Effective Way to Land a Vehicle on Mars, H.L. Tosi (ed.). Gainesville, FL.

Staw, B.M. (1981), The Escalation of Commitment to a Course of Action. *Academy of Management Review*, **6**: 579–87.

Staw, B.M. and J. Ross (1987), Behavior in Escalation Situations: Antecedents, Prototypes, and Solutions. In *Research in Organizational Behavior*, L.L. Cummings and B.M. Staw (eds). Greenwich, CT: JAI Press, pp. 55–69.

Tushman, M.L. and L. Rosenkopf (1992), Organizational Determinants of Technological Change: Toward a Sociology of Technological Evolution. *Research in Organizational Behavior*, **14**: 311.

Vroom, V.H. and P.W. Yetton (1973), *Leadership and Decision Making*. Pittsburgh, PA: University of Pittsburgh Press.

Weick, K.E. (1995), *Sensemaking in Organizations*. Foundations for Organizational Science. Thousand Oaks, CA: Sage.

Weick, K.E. (1998), The Vulnerable System: An Analysis of the Tenerife Air Disaster. In *New Challenges to Understanding Organizations*, K.H. Roberts (ed.). New York: Macmillan Publishing Company, pp. 173–98.

Whyte, G. (1986), Escalating Commitment to a Course of Action: A Reinterpretation. *Academy of Management Review*, **11**: 311–21.

Whyte, G. (1991), Diffusion of Responsibility: Effects on the Escalation Tendency. *Journal of Applied Psychology*, **76**: 408–15.

Zuckerman, M. (1979), Attribution of Success and Failure Revisited, or the Motivational Bias is Alive and Well in Attribution Theory. *Journal of Personality*, **47**: 247–87.

6. Groups and teams

PREPARING FOR CLASS

Consider the groups or teams that you have been associated with in your sports, academic or professional experience. Make two columns on a sheet of paper. In one column, list those teams that you believe were effective; in the other column, list those teams that were not effective. With these two lists in mind, consider these questions:

1. What criteria did you use when you distinguished effective teams from ineffective ones? Were they subjective or objective measures of performance? Were your criteria based on the level of success the team/group achieved or was it the process and experience of working with this particular team?
2. As you look at your list of effective teams, are there any characteristics of the environment that these teams or groups operated in that are similar and that may explain their success? Are there similarities within the environments among the teams or groups you determined were ineffective?
3. Develop your own model of group or team effectiveness. While you can consider the components from Figure 6.4 in this chapter, use your own experience to develop a model that you feel helps to explain why some groups or teams are effective, and why others are ineffective.
4. Based on your personal experiences working in groups and teams, develop your own ideal profile of a team, focusing on the underlying functioning characteristics, interpersonal dynamics and personality of team members.

* *

Teams are so important that some organizations have adopted a strategy of acquiring other organizations as a means of buying human talent – specifically buying a smaller company to acquire new product teams. At all levels in countless organizations, teams and teamwork seem to be a part of the strategy to become more productive and competitive. Self-managed teams, cross-functional teams, product teams and virtual teams – teams that rely on information technologies for communication and may never meet face to face – are all commonly used in the modern workplace. However, the use of this potentially powerful management tool has had mixed effectiveness and often been met with high cynicism. Some have said that half of the decisions reached by teams are never implemented, and the other half should not have been implemented.

Why are some teams effective and other teams ineffective? What factors within the organizational environment influence that effectiveness? Are there leadership strategies that can be implemented along with teams that would increase their chance of success? This chapter reviews what we know about group and team effectiveness, and in Chapter 7 (on conflict) we point out some serious problems that can occur in groups and teams.

GROUPS AND TEAMS: DEFINITIONS

If you were to see 20 passengers on a bus, would you call them a group? Are the thousands of runners in the New York Marathon a group? And would they be different from runners in a relay team? The marathon runners share the same objective, but we wouldn't call them a group or a team because each runner is independent. But the relay runners are a team. Each person has the same objective and they must work together to achieve it. Each must contribute by running at full speed, attend to the time, and encourage other team members. That is different for the marathon runners.

A group is defined as two or more people who interact and are dependent upon each other to achieve some common objective. Patients in a doctor's waiting room or passengers on a bus do not constitute a group, because while they may have some interaction, they do not depend on each other. Without interdependence, several people in proximity to one another are referred to as a collection. People in collections are usually aware of one another, such as in a movie theater.

The term 'team' has gained increased popularity in organizations. Researchers who study groups often use this term when studying the same processes. Teams are a special form of group that have highly defined tasks and roles, and demonstrate high group commitment (Katzenback and Smith, 1993). In this chapter, we use the terms 'team' and 'group' interchangeably. However, there is much discussion about team issues in Chapter 8 on conflict. It would help you a great deal to read that chapter along with this one.

WHY GROUPS FORM

Before we begin our discussion of group factors that influence the overall effectiveness of groups and teams, we should consider the factors that influence group formation. People join groups for a variety of reasons and are often willing to endure great hardships and financial costs in order to belong to a group. However, in many common organizational situations, individuals often have little choice about the groups and teams to which they are assigned. Understanding the basic theories of group formation can help us to understand groups we associate with willingly, and more carefully analyze those we associate with because of our job requirements. Figure 6.1 shows the factors critical for group formation:

- Personal characteristics.
- Interests and goals.
- Potential to influence.
- Opportunity for interaction.

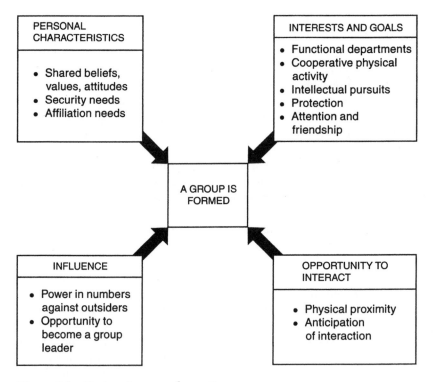

Figure 6.1   Factors in group formation

Personal Characteristics

Our social groups, which we usually join willingly, are often formed with those who share our beliefs, values and attitudes. It is much easier to interact with those who share our attitudes: it permits us to confirm our beliefs, to deal with others with minimal conflict, and to express ourselves with less fear of contradiction. In our earlier discussion of the development of our beliefs, attitudes and values, we discussed the role that association and interaction with others has in reinforcing these structures (Chapter 1). Groups also form around political philosophies and parties, ethnic and religious affiliations, or factors such as gender, age or intelligence. While a common notion is that opposites attract, research into group formation does not confirm that conclusion.

Over time, our work groups can also have many of the same characteristics of our social groups. While the beliefs, attitudes and values of group or team members may not be consistent initially, socialization can have a strong influence on their development over time. Organizations that use intensive socialization processes often attempt to develop in members the factors required for group formation. Early socialization processes in the military emphasize the need for new recruits to value the importance of the group for their social and security needs.

Interests and Goals

Shared goals that require cooperation are a powerful force behind group formation. Managers organize employees around functions such as sales, production, accounting or maintenance. If people in these groups also have similar characteristics, the basis for group formation and cohesion may even be strengthened.

Individuals may form their own groups or teams to achieve common goals. Common interests can include physical activities such as golf, football or basketball. Groups may also form due to shared interests in personal or professional development, such as among individuals who are interested in learning more about a particular subject or in learning a new skill.

Interests and common objectives that give life to new groups may also be functional as emotional needs are satisfied. Many people derive security and a sense of protection from the membership of a group (see Chapter 3 on motivation) and this explains the birth of a group in the presence of threats or pressure.

One formal group found in organizations is a union. Employees may be more prone to join a union if they perceive that the union has the ability to meet their needs and act in their interests.

Potential to Influence

Many managers have been approached by a group of workers with a complaint or a request. The work group knows that a manager might be more prone to listen when any complaint is prefaced with a 'we' instead of an 'I'. Unions, associations and public committees have more negotiating power than the single members. Co-worker support may be necessary to gain attention and action. Groups also provide opportunities for individual members to influence each other. In an informal organization, the role of informal leader can be very important to some employees. If an employee can gain acceptance as an informal leader, he or she can satisfy many personal needs and gain visibility that could even boost his or her career.

Opportunity for Interaction

Individuals often form groups with others just because their jobs force them to be in close contact. Physical proximity and interaction permit relationships to develop and this can lead to friendships and group formation. We often associate with groups that developed from relationships that began in college dorms, apartment complexes and work organizations.

Interaction and group formation can be influenced in an organization, for example through the design of office space. Pathways and barriers can affect group membership and identification. People are more likely to form groups with others in their vicinity. Managers often cooperate with architects to design space so as to foster interactions. Employees who work closely together can be located near each other to increase interaction and allow the needed cooperation to take place.

TYPES OF GROUPS

We are all members of some type of group. Since birth, most of us have been members of a common group, our families. As we grew, we participated in groups or teams formed in our schools, neighborhoods and work organizations. Each group added to our knowledge of how to behave in group settings and we learned that roles and expectations may differ, based on the type of group or team and its objectives. There are several common types of groups:

- Reference groups.
- Formal groups, for example functional groups and task groups.

- Informal groups.
- Virtual teams.

Reference Groups

Reference groups, or primary groups, are groups that shape our beliefs, values and attitudes. These groups are formed of members whom we trust enough to rely on for testing ideas and giving feedback, guidance or support. They serve as standards of comparison against which we evaluate our own behavior. A person facing a decision might draw on a reference group's values, or talk with someone in that group, before making a choice. Our family, our running partners, a local volunteer group, or a work team can also be reference groups.

A primary group is one with which we identify, even though we may not be a member. We are more likely to affected by a primary group. The expectations of the group might lead a person to increase production, to 'take to the streets', take part in a strike or participate in a meeting. You might be able to predict better the behavior, values and attitudes of a person if you know the primary groups with which they identify.

Formal Groups

Formal groups are those created as part of the formal organization structure. The formal organization is the hierarchical structure and the various departments that exist within that structure. Formal organization is reflected in the goals, policies, rules and procedures that are designed to accomplish the organization's tasks. Any group that is purposely designed into this configuration is a formal group.

One form of formal group, a functional group, is comprised of individuals who accomplish similar tasks within the organizational structure. Functional groups exist for an unspecified period of time. Many organizations organize around functional groups assigned to related work activities such as accounting, marketing, production, research and development (R&D) or other related task groupings. Universities are usually organized into functional groups called departments.

Task groups are groups that are used to accomplish a specific organizational goal. They are usually established by the organization and exist for a specified period of time. In task groups, social benefits for members are secondary or may even be absent. Committees, project teams, quality circles, task forces and employee participation teams are all organizational task groups. They usually have a defined purpose, deadlines to meet, specific work assignments and a reporting relationship in the organization. Some task groups are relatively permanent; others are temporary groups.

Informal Groups

Informal groups arise out of individual needs and the attraction of people to one another. While outside the normal structure of the organization, these groups can have a significant effect on organizational performance. Membership is usually voluntary and is based on common values and interests. Sometimes the origin of these groups is social in nature.

Social or interest groups are a type of informal group. Social groups exist primarily to provide recreational or relaxation outlets for members. For example, friends may eat together at work or socialize after work. Most softball teams, bowling groups and gourmet clubs exist so that people can enjoy themselves in good company. Sometimes work goals could be involved, as might be the case for a company sports team or computer club, but the work is secondary to the social benefit.

On other occasions, an informal group develops in response to the organization, such as when workers band together to protest an unpopular management action. This case is an example of a clique, which may include people from the same hierarchical level (horizontal cliques) or from different hierarchical levels. The key factor is that they share a common interest.

Informal groups arise at work because many employees are concerned about their freedom at work, about control over their jobs and about establishing good relationships with others (Katz, 1965). Informal groups may develop to bypass company rules or to enhance the members' power. They might consist of people who also like and trust each other and perhaps interact outside work in a church group or neighborhood.

Informal groups can be both effective and powerful. This may explain why some managers view them with doubt and suspicion. They tend to see informal groups as disruptive and potentially harmful to the formal organization. Some managers seek ways to gain the support of informal groups and informal leaders to reduce their threat or to enhance some company purpose.

Since informal groups are an inevitable component of behavior in organizations, as managers we should attempt to work with these groups so that they contribute to, rather than subvert, organizational goals. Informal groups serve basic needs for employees and are just as important, enduring and rewarding as the relationship that employees have with the formal organization. The informal group can become a problem when it conflicts with some formal purpose, but even this is not necessarily bad. It may signal some error on management's part or be a symptom of a poor relationship with employees.

Virtual Teams

In most cases, work groups, whether they are functional groups or task groups, physically meet together to work on their problems (see also Chapter 8, on conflict, for a more extensive discussion of these problems). Virtual teams don't do that; instead the virtual team members are located in different physical locations and use electronic technology, particularly the Internet, to communicate. In the past, virtual teams communicated by telephone conferencing. Now, however, organizations are increasingly reliant on virtual work arrangements with individuals who work in different buildings or even different countries.

While much of what we know about groups and teams applies to virtual teams, the very nature of this form of team structure creates new advantages and challenges for management (Cascio, 2000). One advantage is that they can span time and distance constraints. For example, a virtual team meeting is not constrained to have everyone in town on the day of the team meeting. Team members can 'virtually' be anywhere and still be active participants in meetings. Another advantage is that these teams can take advantage of the expertise of an individual who works in another location.

Suppose that the production line of the Toledo manufacturing plant has a history of frequent breakdowns. In response, plant management has appointed a virtual task team to solve this problem. This would allow the involvement of a troubleshooter from the manufacturer of the equipment, and a foreman from a similar plant in Germany that has had the same problems. This example also highlights a third advantage in that virtual teams can significantly reduce costs. The travel costs for members who are widely separated geographically would be quite high. A fourth advantage of virtual teams is improvement in the processes used to create team reports. In traditional teams this can be a cumbersome and time-consuming process, one in which a copy of a document is sent to all team members and then one person consolidates all of the inputs. With virtual technologies, all members can have synchronous and asynchronous access to documents. Virtual team members from Detroit and Tampa could simultaneously work on a document, and that same document would be available for a team member in Tokyo.

A major disadvantage of virtual teams is the lack of physical interaction, so that many key elements of communication are eliminated (Cascio, 2000). There are fewer verbal and non-verbal cues, and as a result, information that we traditionally rely on to infer meaning from communications is also missing. In consequence, there is evidence that virtual teams may have difficulty in developing the level of trust necessary to become a high-performing team. Virtual teams are more likely to develop higher levels of trust when three conditions exist. First, there is a social period where members introduce themselves and provide background information. Second, there must be clear roles for members. Finally, virtual team members must maintain and demonstrate positive attitudes about the team's tasks (Jarvenpaa et al., 1998).

Like traditional teams, training is critical for effective performance of virtual teams. In some ways, virtual team members require similar skills as those for traditional teams. However, because of the use of technology, managers need to understand the limitations and advantages of virtual technologies as a communication medium. Therefore, team members must be competent to use the specific technologies that support team activities. Members also need to be trained in behaviors relevant for the virtual environment. Since traditional communication cues are limited in the virtual environment, members may need to learn new skills to communicate effectively as part of a virtual team. These skills, including collaboration, socialization and communication (Jarvenpaa et al., 1998), as well as a strong openness to experience, are necessary for high-performing groups (Colquitt et al., 2002). Collaboration skills are behaviors such as exchanging ideas without being critical, and ensuring that member ideas and input are tracked and summarized for accuracy. Socialization skills include using team member names in electronic greetings, soliciting feedback on process, express appreciation for the ideas of others and volunteering for necessary roles. Communication skills include responding in a timely manner to email, using chat functions when available, addressing the entire team in communications, and insuring that local translators are used when language issues may be a factor.

GROUP AND TEAM EFFECTIVENESS

Figure 6.2 introduces a model of group effectiveness. Groups and teams exist within an environment that can influence their performance. This group performance environment includes the combined effects of industry, organization and group factors that form the unique context within which the group operates. These environmental effects on group effectiveness are often beyond the control of the group or team. In addition to environment, the group processes that exist within the group also affect group effectiveness. The combined effect of internal group processes occurring

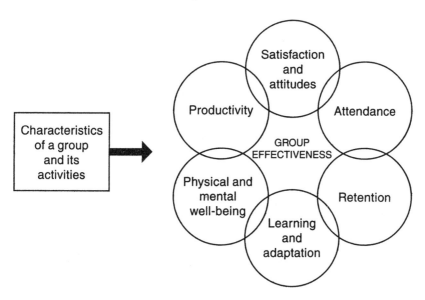

Figure 6.2   Measures of group effectiveness

within the group performance environment determines the overall group effectiveness. Group effectiveness occurs when there is high group performance as well as changes in group members' attitudes and behaviors.

Spotlight 6.1   Teams and problem-based learning in Sweden

Problem-based learning is the structured group approach which involves participants in continuous problem solving to facilitate learning. In a study by Areneson and Ekberg, the objective was to promote change, in particular enhancing the health of the person in the workplace and giving them tools to solve workplace problems. In a group, a problem that got in the way of individual well-being was selected. Using brainstorming, the group then decided how to work on the problem. They worked to articulate solutions and then sought to implement them. After this intervention had taken place, participants were more self-conscious and self-aware. They had higher self-esteem and greater insight about workplace conditions. Finally, they felt more self-directed and had a better sense of both the formal and informal organization (Areneson and Ekberg, 2005).

Our model suggests that, in addition to influencing effectiveness through influence on group processes, the elements that comprise the group performance environment can influence effectiveness directly through factors beyond the control of the group. Notice that, in addition to the influence that the environment can have on group processes in Figure 6.1, there is also an arrow pointing directly towards the measures of group effectiveness. Despite how effective a group's internal processes may be, there may be environmental factors beyond its control that will be stronger determinants of its overall effectiveness. This is common in team sports such as football where effectively performing teams do not win the championship because they do not have enough talent to succeed. Likewise, teams that have very high levels of individual talent are often unsuccessful because of group internal processes such as a lack of team cohesion, such as the French football team in the World Cup competition in 2010.

Group Performance Environment

The environment within which groups or teams function may be critical in determining their ultimate success or failure, because effectiveness can be affected by factors outside of the control of the group or team (Mohrman et al., 1995). We consider here three major influences on the group environment:

- Industry.
- Organization.
- Group.

Industry factors

There are two external industry factors that influence team success: (1) characteristics unique to a particular industry; and (2) industry turbulence. Many who study team effectiveness believe that teams may be more successful in certain types of industries. For example, teams may be more effective in knowledge or service industries because of the unique aspects of the work setting. In these industries, where work is less routine, more judgment is required and that judgment may benefit from access to the additional information and feedback mechanisms that can be provided by teams. In manufacturing industries, the routine nature of some tasks may make employee involvement activities such as the use of teams less effective (Cohen, 1994; Smith and Comer, 1994; Mohrman et al., 1995).

The amount of turbulence that an industry faces can also influence a team's success. For example, a highly effective team may develop an excellent new product but it may fail because of turbulence in that product's potential market. Actions by competitors to introduce new technologies or to develop alternative products, or significant changes in consumer tastes, all can adversely affect a team's effectiveness in ways outside of its control. Not surprisingly, studies have found that team effectiveness is higher for teams formed in industries that are in growth markets (Halebilian and Finklestein, 1993).

Organizational factors

In any organization, group or team success can be affected by:

- Organizational culture.
- Reward structure.
- Training.

Organizational culture   An organization that has the concept of teams built into its culture is the Ferrari Race Group. In Formula One circles, Ferrari holds a special place and mystique for many fans. For example, when the Ferrari Test Team is testing a car:

> the Reds are watched with special attention . . . [team members] can feel it from the way people approach you in the hotel in the evening or the way they look at you at an airport check-in. And you can also feel the sense of pride when you put on your team kit when you are at the track (Ferrari, 2010).

The Test Team is now a very important component of the Ferrari organization as its role has grown over the past several years from just five mechanics to 60 members with a diverse range of specialties that are required for the success of the Ferrari cars. For example, when the Ferrari was outfitted with Bridgestone tires the team added engineers, mechanics and logistical support for this new component.

The Test Team is now an integral part of the Ferrari team culture, fitting in with the race team with the goal of improving Ferrari performance. One interesting aspect of this fit is how the Test Team took over many of the functions previously handled by the Race Team, which at one time was responsible for testing. Now the Race Team and the Test Team work closely together to form a smooth working relationship. The Test Team knows its role: while the Race Team operates on a strict schedule, the Test Team flexibly adopts to the needs of the Race Team and often asks the drivers to participate in their work. The result is a culture of mutual respect and trust (Ferrari, 2010).

The reward structure   Another aspect controlled by the organization is the reward structure. Does the organization have a system of rewards that encourages the cooperation required for successful team performance? There is considerable debate as to whether individual rewards are more appropriate to encourage team performance or whether team reward systems should be used. Organizations use a wide variety of monetary and non-monetary rewards in team contexts. One study found that, in companies using teams to improve quality, monetary rewards were often restricted to less than $500 to allow organizations to give out more of these types of rewards. Rewards are often linked to improvements in customer satisfaction or other measures of overall product quality (Balkin, 1997).

Training   Training is an obvious need for the Ferrari Test Team. Team members have to know their technical responsibilities as well as how to function as an effective group. While these individuals may have important technical skills to contribute to the team when they arrive, their placement on the team may have dysfunctional consequences if they lack the appropriate team skills. Training programs that can achieve this can include team-building activities to build member confidence and trust in each other, conflict resolution skills, or a variety of other useful team skills.

Group factors

A final set of factors that contribute to the group performance environment are those factors specific to the group. This subsection considers those factors that may influence group effectiveness but that are, in some cases, determined by managers who are not part of the group itself.

Task design   One aspect, task design, considers the nature of the task assigned to the group or team. One component of task design considers clarity of the goals and tasks that are either assigned to the group or that the group or team itself establishes. Groups are often formed with specific goals such as improving the quality of a particular product or resolving a specific problem. Groups can also be formed with less specific goals such as improving the general quality of work life or improving issues within the workplace. Just as in our discussion of individual goal setting in Chapter 3, group performance is improved when the group is handed specific and difficult goals.

A second component of task design considers the amount of coordination the group must have with others in achievement of its assigned tasks. We consider two potential task characteristics here. Autonomy refers to the degree of freedom and independence that the team has to conduct its activities. Teams that operate autonomously are also called self-managed teams. Autonomy appears to have both positive and negative effects on measures of team effectiveness. While autonomous workgroups appear to have more positive attitudes towards the organization, this may lead to higher turnover and absenteeism (Cordery et al., 1991). The research is contradictory at this point but one possibility is that autonomous groups work better in organizations operating in environments that are more turbulent (Smith and Comer, 1994).

Interdependence is determined by the amount of coordination with, or approval from, others that the team needs to complete its assigned tasks. Ferrari's leadership is obviously concerned with the characteristics of the tasks assigned to the Test Team. Its response was to give the team total control over developing the ideas and implementing the solutions for testing, but also required relying on the Race Team for input.

Group structure and status A second factor specific to the group is the structure of the group and the status of members within the group. Group structure refers to the roles and relationships among the members and to the forces that maintain the group's organization. As groups develop and pursue their purposes, certain structural characteristics emerge. Structure is dynamic and changes over time. It can also contribute to the overall effectiveness of the group, as many of these structural components are linked to important group issues such as the structure of the rewards and the amount of training the team receives in team processes. A detailed understanding of structure and status issues is important to improve our ability to manage and work in teams. In addition, many decisions, including the determinations of key roles such as leadership, and other factors of team structure, are often determined by the organization and are out of the control of team members.

People in small task groups engage in certain key functions and assume individual roles. Roles are defined in terms of expectations that members hold and communicate about each other's behavior. Groups expect each member to perform his or her role in a certain way. There are several different types of roles in groups, and each one has different implications (Bales, 1953):

- Task roles.
- Socio-emotional roles.
- Leadership roles.
- Role complications.
- Disruptive actions and roles.

Some group member roles are based on the behaviors required to accomplish a particular group task. While we discussed the importance of task clarity as a component of the group performance environment, task and role clarity among group members is also critical. In general, members have to clarify goals, give and seek suggestions and opinions about the task, and help the group to succeed. For example, research by LePine and his colleagues has shown several ways in which the members help lower-performing members (LePine and Van Dyne, 2001; Jackson and LePine, 2003). They can compensate for the lower performer, recommend training, help motivate them, or in some cases reject them. Specific task roles grow out of the purposes of the group and the goals that are established. It follows then that the better the groups' goals are defined, the more clearly will specific roles be determined.

Many complications arise in role assignments. In some situations, managers external to the group may make role assignments, and at other times, group members may make their own assignments. In either situation, poor planning of assignments causes gaps or duplication of effort, which later slows the group down or detracts from effective performance. When the group assigns tasks, sometimes a member will quickly volunteer for what he or she feels is a 'choice' assignment. Other members are then faced with less desirable work. Some members want to do work that is easy for them, while others want to learn a new skill. It is probably impossible to please everyone in assigning tasks. Groups contemplating task assignments may benefit from open and careful consideration of both the desires and the abilities of group members. Figure 6.3 highlights techniques for making task assignments in different conditions of team member desires and abilities.

As the group works on the task and as members grow used to one another, other issues come into play. People give and receive help. They reward or punish each other, and give or receive feedback. Tensions develop that need releasing. Joking and laughter are not uncommon, nor are disagreements and arguments. People turn to each other for acceptance and understanding. All of these are examples of the socio-emotional activities and roles of groups. Socio-emotional needs of members are important, yet most groups do not deal adequately with them.

Task and socio-emotional roles are not entirely independent, and they both affect all aspects of group effectiveness. Dissatisfied members may perform their assignments poorly, or they might quit the group or psychologically withdraw. These reactions also affect retention and cohesion. When attention is paid to the socio-emotional activities within a group, that group can be more effective. Actions that show support and acceptance of others contribute a great deal. Listening and showing understanding make people feel positively toward each other. For example, when a person is not performing to standards, other group members may compensate by picking up some of the person's work load, help in trying to

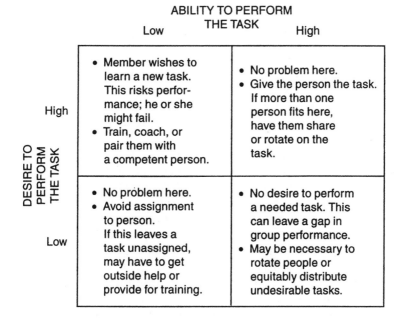

Figure 6.3   Dilemmas and techniques in making task role assignments

motivate them, suggest training and, if these fail, reject the person (LePine and Van Dyne, 2001; Jackson and LePine, 2003).

Leadership   Leaders control many factors that contribute to group effec-tiveness. They determine many of the design features of the team or group that we have been discussing. Leadership, within the group and external to the group, can influence reward systems, task assignments, task clarity and other important aspects of the performance environment. Leaders who reward individual accomplishments are likely to find that the teams are less effective if those rewards contribute to competition within the team or group. Leaders can influence the group through the clarity with which they understand the organization's goals for the group and how they communi-cate that vision to group members. Leaders can also determine the structure and autonomy afforded to the group as well as how resources are allocated.

Groups may have leaders who are skilled at task functions and other leaders who are skilled at socio-emotional functions. It is rare that one leader has the skills to provide leadership in both areas. As a result, dif-ferent people may perform leadership within a group at different times. A study of work teams found that groups which relied on leaders, rather than peer support, tended to perform better, cooperate more and provide constructive ideas when the leadership role was rotated among members (Erez et al., 2002).

Role complications   Groups face many problems that require constant attention, especially in the early stages of group development. Most groups adequately handle task issues, particularly if they make good individual assignments that match member desires and skills. On the other hand, most groups struggle when faced with role difficulties and when group members act disruptively.

One role complication arises when members experience role ambiguity; this occurs when people feel uncertain about what is expected of them or when they are not sure what behaviors will earn them acceptance or rejection. Group members can also experience role conflict; this results when a person feels difficulty in meeting conflicting demands, and can take several forms. A person can be a father, a manager, a friend, a husband, a fund-drive chairman and a Little League coach, all at once. The demands of these roles compete with one another for time and commitment. Within a single role such as manager, conflict can arise from pressure to act in a way that conflicts with the person's values, and from pressure to meet the expectations of others whose requests conflict with one another. Role ambiguity and role conflict were discussed in Chapter 4, on stress.

Spotlight 6.2   Team building for collective coping in Belgium

Using a team-building approach called Collective Coping has been an effective way to help managers deal with common problems that they face at work. The Collective Coping approach to dealing with problems was instituted in a local government agency in Belgium. In the team building, participants outlined common problems, analyzed the problems and their causes, and then developed collective actions and strategies. They then returned to their workplace and implemented what they had learned in team building. By the end of the team-building exercise, the managers were very satisfied with the process and had intentions of continuing with it in the future (Hoedemakers and Pepermans, 2007).

A final role that surfaces in some group environments is when one member acts in a disruptive way that not only interferes with the task but may also disrupt the social processes of the group. A group member might force his or her ideas on others, and refuse to see different points of view, often generating defensive or aggressive behavior in others. You have probably had experience working in a group where there was a disruptive member. Perhaps even in your work for this course, you are in a group that has a member who disrupts group effectiveness. Is there a member of your group who comes in late for group meetings, does not complete assignments on time, or interjects comments that causes the group to lose track during a meeting? It is not easy to cope with this type of disruption or to correct it. If the disruptive behavior is rooted in the basic personality of an individual, it is more difficult to handle. Skillful leaders might take disruptive people aside and try to bring about a change. The entire group could also confront a disruptive individual and appeal to his or her sense of fairness and goodwill. If this fails, the group may threaten to ostracize the individual. Sometimes the group might just have to ignore, or work around, the difficult member. Another technique is to seek help from outside the group, perhaps from a higher authority. Few managers who use groups in their workplace, or professors who use groups in their classes, have not had occasion to help groups to deal with a disruptive member.

Group member status One aspect of group structure is the hierarchy it often creates within the group. While the hierarchy does help to bring order and control to the group, it is also a way for people to acknowledge and express status differences between each other. These distinctions can be sources of inequity and concern among group members. Group member status is the relative position or standing of a person in a society or group. It is an index of rank or worth. Like norms, status is a common social force, and often it is habitually accepted. Status is quite apparent and easily identifiable. Here is a partial list of factors that we might use to accord status to a person:

- Title or position.
- Education, knowledge or expertise.
- Awards or prizes earned.
- Income.
- Ownership of resources or property.
- Personal attributes such as appearance, size, dress, age or sex.
- Behavioral clues such as work or recreational activities.
- Interpersonal clues such as communication patterns or reactions.
- Physical location in relation to others.
- Cultural identification or nationality.
- Physical surroundings, such as home or office.

From the list, we can see that status is accorded people on the basis of their accomplishments and characteristics, on the nature of their interactions with others, and on the conditions of the situation in which they work and play.

Status is rooted in what is culturally valued and results from the evaluation of others. Studies have examined the status of occupations. At the top of the lists are college professors, physicians, Supreme Court justices, scientists, architects and the clergy. Various managers, some salespeople, nurses, actors and musicians fall in the middle ranks. Lowest-ranked occupations include trash collectors, newsboys, waiters and waitresses, coal miners and gas station attendants.

Achieving status is not a simple process. Some factors are within an individual's control, such as how hard he or she works, but some are obviously not controllable, such as family background. In a small group, someone with more education, a respected title or a fine reputation would probably be accorded high status immediately. However, people can also earn status in a group through their contribution and relationships with others. They could become a respected member or even the group leader.

Can your status change? Factors that determine status depend a great deal on the situation. A short person will have difficulty achieving status on a basketball team or any activity where height counts, but size need not prevent him or her from becoming a national hero or movie star. Status can also have very specific limits. A group of physicians might grant an architect status, but not for his or her knowledge of medicine. In a fair-minded society or group, people can improve their status and earn great respect by providing any valued activity. As long as there are opportunities for an individual to contribute, there is potential for status improvement.

Status distribution in a group is usually uneven: those with high status have disproportionately more than those with low status. This is often a source of conflict within the group. If status were derived from factors such as member competence or contribution, it would be more acceptable. However, status is usually derived from factors that often have little to do with competence or contribution. Furthermore, contributions or competence are quite differently valued. For example, many groups will value a person who actually writes the first draft of a report rather than a person who made skillful contributions to the ideas contained in the report.

It may be reasonable that some contributions are more valuable than others, but if differences are overplayed, group cohesion and individual feelings can suffer considerably. These difficulties worsen when group members disagree on the value of contributions and on the status distribution across members. Status incongruence can occur when members are given either more or less status than others feel they deserve.

Group composition   A final component of the performance environment is the composition of the group itself. Groups that form naturally, such as a social group, have much more discretion over different aspects of group composition than do members of a group within a typical organizational setting. Factors such as group size and group member diversity are important components that influence overall group effectiveness.

Groups can vary widely in size, and size in turn affects member behavior. Groups of two or three are sufficiently unique that they deserve special attention. Larger groups show different effects. Dyads are groups that consist of two people. In this case, no third person is available for an opinion or for help when a disagreement arises. As a result, tensions frequently arise between the two people because they have no outlet, and negative feelings tend to remain unresolved. People in dyads seem to sense this and tend to avoid giving strong opinions or acting in a way that might lead to disagreement. In dyads, opinions are sought more frequently than they are given. Dyads avoid disagreement because it can lead to failure, and this may foster consensus even when it does not exist. Do these characteristics of dyads sound like any marriages or significant relationships of which you know? You should notice that the problems described are similar to those that couples experience. In organizational settings, if two people assigned to a dyad cannot deal with disagreement, it may be wise to change group size.

Triads are groups of three people and pose other problems of their own. Suppose Alan, Betty and Cathy are on a project team and are assigned to solve a problem. Alan makes a suggestion. Betty agrees wholeheartedly, but Cathy disagrees. The instant Alan and Betty agree, Cathy faces difficulty: the odds are two against one, and Cathy has had no chance to think about it. What choices does Cathy now have? She can go along with Alan and Betty, hoping to have her way another time. If she does not, Cathy must confront the other two or try to sway one or both of them. Now suppose instead that Betty disagrees with Alan; Cathy faces a new bind. Does she side with Alan or Betty? Does she assume the more difficult task of trying to resolve the disagreement, or does she simply withdraw and let the matter sit?

Events like this are a natural consequence of the triad. This is why people often leave triad meetings with considerable tension. Even when people are congenial, repeated imbalances in interactions occur. The triad has very high potential for power struggles, unplanned and planned coalitions, and general instability. Managers should probably avoid the use of triads, especially when the task calls for frequent interaction and influence opportunities. On the other hand, triads can be more effective than two-person problem-solving groups. They are likely to propose more solutions and solve problems more quickly (Laughlin et al., 2006).

Small groups are of interest because many of the team structures found in organizations are representative of a small group: that is, work teams, project teams, committees and taskforces. There is general consensus among group researchers that a small group has a membership from four to 15 members.

If groups are much larger, it is much more difficult for people to interact. Fewer than ten people can conduct a discussion quite adequately. In larger groups, individuals sense the interaction problems and may become less involved and withhold their ideas. Consider your experience in large classes. Do you notice that class members often avoid speaking up because they intuitively know that everyone cannot do so?

There are other considerations in determining the optimum size for group effectiveness. There should be an odd number of members, as even-numbered groups are more likely to have deadlocks. Because of this groups of five, seven or nine members are more effective.

There are four other factors about group size that we should consider:

1. Participation.
2. Satisfaction.
3. Subgroup differentiation.
4. Performance.

In larger groups, there is less opportunity to participate. In addition to the natural inhibitions that people experience in groups, the amount of time available to a person to talk is reduced as size increases. Members of larger groups are also more likely to feel that there is a negative climate for organization justice (Colquitt et al., 2007).

People in smaller groups are generally more satisfied. Positive aspects of group participation like increased interaction and shared goals all positively relate to member satisfaction. In smaller groups, it is easier for members to feel that they have contributed to the group's success.

To manage a larger group, it must often be differentiated into subgroups. This is a natural tendency as group size increases. Control also becomes a problem as groups grow in size, so it is natural for norms and rules to develop. Larger groups even formalize communication by using written memos to supplement face-to-face discussion.

The effect of size on performance depends on the task characteristics. If adding more people to a task helps rather than hinders effectiveness, then size is an asset to performance. If the people work independently, such as in a typing pool, more people usually means more productivity. Size can also be a benefit for some interdependently performed tasks (Hirschfeld and Berneth, 2008; LePine et al., 2008). When the size of groups is increased, errors in problem solving can be reduced. A larger group can be beneficial because people can check work for possible errors.

The research on the effects of group diversity on performance often offers conflicting results. When diversity is defined as difference in personalities, gender, attitudes and background, there is a positive effect on creativity and decision making (Jackson et al., 1995). For example, male-dominated teams were more likely to make overaggressive, less rational decisions than groups in which women were significantly represented (LePine et al., 2002). However, when diversity is defined as cultural diversity, initial performance of culturally diverse groups is often poorer. However, that performance may improve over time when compared to less diverse groups (Watson et al., 1993).

Perhaps diversity may initially cause difficulty as groups deal with values, belief and attitudinal differences during the initial stages of group development. This may imply that diverse groups may be less efficient in the short term, but may improve in the long term (Cohen and Bailey, 1997). The best conclusion from the research on diversity is that more research needs to be done, but increasing the heterogeneity of the group may initially complicate the group formation processes. This puts added pressure on managers and leaders to teach all team members' effective team behaviors that would improve the group processes.

Development of Mature Groups

One factor that may strongly influence the effectiveness of a group is its maturity. Group maturity can be thought of similarly to individual maturity. As individuals, we develop confidence in ourselves and increase our emotional stability over time, partly through our education and interaction with others. Just like individuals, some groups are slower to mature and some never reach full maturity. Groups go through stages of development, shown in Figure 6.4 (Tuckman, 1965). Early in the life of a group, members engage in behaviors useful for forming the group and orienting members. Often a period of conflict or 'storming' follows the initial forming stages and the polite behaviors that were associated with that stage. The group often struggles in this stage. In the next phase, the group is better organized and more cohesive, sometimes referred to as 'norming'. As the group continues to mature, it will still have relationship difficulties to resolve if it is to mature fully into a high-performing team.

Forming

For a group to succeed, it needs to become organized. Initially, there is an initial orientation period called 'forming'. Members try to find the

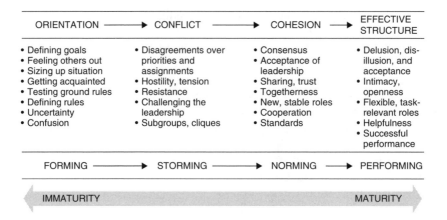

ORIENTATION ⟶	CONFLICT ⟶	COHESION ⟶	EFFECTIVE STRUCTURE
• Defining goals • Feeling others out • Sizing up situation • Getting acquainted • Testing ground rules • Defining rules • Uncertainty • Confusion	• Disagreements over priorities and assignments • Hostility, tension • Resistance • Challenging the leadership • Subgroups, cliques	• Consensus • Acceptance of leadership • Sharing, trust • Togetherness • New, stable roles • Cooperation • Standards	• Delusion, dis- illusion, and acceptance • Intimacy, openness • Flexible, task-relevant roles • Helpfulness • Successful performance
FORMING ⟶	STORMING ⟶	NORMING ⟶	PERFORMING
IMMATURITY			MATURITY

Figure 6.4   Stages in group development

purposes of the group and begin to establish its activities and priorities. Much of the early conversation revolves around learning the group's cognitive territory by identifying common objectives, methods of working and internal rules. There is also a need to define relational territories, as members get to know each other and are very likely to be seeking roles they might fill, as well as testing the ground rules for behavior.

This early stage can be chaotic and uncertain. When a formal leader appointed by the organization exists, pressure is exerted on him or her to guide the group through this stage. In the absence of a formal leader, the group might select one or simply allow one to emerge.

Storming

In the forming stage there is little to disagree about, but when the cognitive and relational issues are resolved a conflict stage, called 'storming', usually emerges. This is a delicate stage because there is high potential for conflict. There can be leadership crises and subgroups can form. Conflict is not necessarily bad at this stage, but good conflict management practices are necessary. If a group successfully resolves these conflicts, it is more likely that it will mature, moving into a cohesive stage. If consensus develops around goals and leadership, and a sense of liking and trust develops, individuals begin to feel cohesive and express a readiness to move ahead into the 'norming' stage.

Norming

'Norming' is characterized by a high level of internal confrontation among members as they can question each other and argue, but can come to agreement because they have developed the capacity to deal with such internal issues. If there are some who can't or won't be integrated into the group, they may leave the group or develop a resigned attitude that we have called 'indifferent' in Chapter 1.

Performing
If a group gets through these stages, its members move into dealing with problems concerning the structure of the group. This stage is called the 'performing' stage. Here, they face problems that stem from interpersonal relationships, such as intimacy and openness. These operate on at least two levels. One level is how well the group deals with emotional tensions that arise out of dissatisfaction of its members. For example, do members feel free to say that they are being unfairly treated? The other level is how idea generation is affected. Unless the participants can freely offer alternative definitions of a problem and differing solutions, problem solving and decisions will suffer. Other types of conflict can occur, that we discuss in Chapter 8.

If the group is successful in maturing beyond the conflict stage, a stage of acceptance is achieved. Subgroups become less important. Communication increases and the needs of individuals are more freely expressed. When the task and the emotional needs of group members are handled well, the group has achieved full maturity. Mature groups: (1) accept feelings in a non-evaluative way; (2) disagree over real and important issues; (3) make decisions rationally and encourage dissent, but don't force members or fake unanimity; (4) have an awareness of their process; and (5) members understand the nature of members' involvement. Mature groups are not that common.

SUMMARY

People spend enormous amounts of time working within groups, as groups and teams become more common in work settings. Groups and teams tend to form around people with similar attitudes and beliefs, and among those who share common interests and goals. Group formation is also facilitated when people need the power of numbers to influence others or to accomplish a task. However, even the opportunity to interact can cause a group to form.

We have proposed a model of team and group effectiveness and have discussed the three factors that form the environment within which groups operate. Group performance is strongly affected by the context within which the group operates. We have considered factors from the industry

Spotlight 6.3   Cultural differences and groups

Individualism–collectivism refers to whether individual or collective action is the preferred way to deal with issues. In cultures oriented toward individualism – such as the USA, the UK and Canada – people tend to emphasize their individual needs and concerns and interests over those of their group or organization; while the opposite is true in countries which score high on collectivism, for example Asian countries such as Japan and Taiwan. In a collectivist society, you are expected to interact with members of your group. It is almost impossible to perceive a person as an individual rather than one whose identity comes from groups with which that individual is associated (Brislin, 1993). For that reason, when visiting a collectivist society, it is useful to carry business cards that clearly identify your organization and status within that organization.

Often firms in collectivist societies will make decisions without regard for the personal needs of those affected, if it is thought that the decision is good for the organization. For instance, employees may be arbitrarily transferred to other locations with little concern for how such a transfer will affect the person or the family. This happened to a Taiwanese manager who was directed to enter an MBA program in the USA. He went against his wishes; his wife was about to have a child, and when the child died in birth, he was not allowed to return to Taiwan. He was told that it was not in the company's interest to allow him to do so, and that he should just learn to bear with the situation.

Certain work behaviors may also be affected. For example, in an individualistic society such as the USA, there is a tendency for people to shirk when tasks are assigned to a group, as opposed to when tasks are assigned to individuals. This tendency is not present in the collectivist country of Taiwan (Grabrenya et al., 1985).

and organization as well as those specific to the group. Within the industry, characteristics unique to that industry and the market within which it operates can influence effectiveness. Organizational aspects such as culture, systems of reward and training are also critical factors to group success.

Factors specific to the group include aspects of the task design, group structure and composition. The basic building blocks of group structure are the functions and roles assumed by its members. A balance of task and socio-emotional roles tends to aid success. Disruptive individual roles can threaten the group at any time. One of the key problems is the success of the leadership roles that members take. Another central aspect of group life is the status accorded to each of its members. Status can be a force that contributes to group success, or it can create difficulties that prevent the group from developing into an effective unit. Groups vary in size, but typically small groups range from four to about a dozen people. The smaller dyads and triads have distinct and different characteristics. Larger groups have a tendency to organize into smaller subgroups to facilitate effectiveness.

GUIDE FOR MANAGERS: CREATING A GOOD TEAM ENVIRONMENT

This chapter has focused on the influences of the environment on a team's effectiveness. Throughout the chapter we discussed environmental factors that can impact teams. In most cases, those factors are within the control of managers who want to increase the effectiveness of teams within their organizations. Here are some specific suggestions for doing that.

Instill Within the Organization and the Organizational Culture the Value of Groups and Teams to Organizational Success

Organizations like Monarch Marking Systems and Saturn have embedded the use of teams within the company's culture. Supporting the use of teams through vision statements, allocation of resources and developing team-based reward systems all contribute to team success.

Develop Selection Approaches for all Employees that Value Team Skills of Newly Hired Employees

Employees who come from industries and organizations where teams were not used may have difficulty in adjusting to a team-oriented environment. Many organizations focus on technical skills but we suggest you also consider interpersonal and team skills as part of your selection criteria.

Implement Organizational Training Programs to Ensure Team Skills are Taught to Employees Who May Participate in Teams or Groups

Behaviors required in team environments are quite different from those needed in other environments. Do not assume that employees are aware of the tools needed to be a successful team member. Training is also important for individuals who will lead teams or groups. Group leadership requires a complex set of skills and knowledge to be successful.

Develop Reward Structures that Reward Team Performance or Encourage Team-Oriented Individual Behaviors

Compensation programs that provide individual incentives are likely to foster competition rather than cooperation.

Provide Clear, Specific and Difficult Goals for the Team or Group

Teams need to understand what they are being asked to do. Where possible, clearly identify effectiveness metrics that will be used to measure team performance.

Consider the Amount of Interdependence Required by the Group or Team

We recommend erring on the side of allowing the group to operate more autonomously. This prevents groups from being hampered by cumbersome organization structures and processes. It also fosters increased creativity.

Establish Group Size Carefully

Unless there are strong reasons to do otherwise, groups of two and three should be avoided. Beyond this, odd-sized groups of fewer than ten members are best, particularly if interaction is required for effectiveness. If groups must be larger, they should be broken into subgroups as a means to facilitate interactive problem solving.

Allow Group Members to Select Other Members Whenever Possible

Interpersonal attractiveness can create a strong force toward cohesion and cooperation. Likewise, replacements should be selected carefully so as to minimize disruption. However, diversity of group members should be a factor when creativeness is an important goal.

Provide Groups With as Many Opportunities for Success as Possible

Participation in goal formation, special assignments and other methods can give groups a sense of involvement. Successful achievement has a powerful impact on all aspects of group effectiveness. Opportunities for success are especially useful for newly forming groups: success helps to keep them on a track toward maturity as opposed to dissolution.

Empower Teams to be More Responsible, More Self-Sufficient and Self-Managing

Expect teams to identify, select and solve problems on their own as much as possible, and to evaluate the quality of their own work. Help the group to cross-train members and to share and rotate leadership. Minimize supervisory interventions.

CASE: THE SAME OLD STORY

Recently, the Dixon Company had reorganized its 30 factory workers into work teams of five persons. Dixon manufactured various-sized storage units and handcarts for industrial use. The work was often done to customer order and the storage units and carts were designed by engineers to meet special customer needs for size and strength.

Before using work teams, two supervisors kept track of all orders and the blueprints that the engineers and designers developed for special jobs. The supervisors would assign individual workers to different tasks, depending on what was needed. The 30 workers were all capable of just about any task needed to build and assemble the parts that went into storage units and carts. However, from moment to moment, they never knew which task they would be assigned.

Before teams were formed, morale in the plant was low. Absenteeism and lateness were increasing. The quality of work was not too bad, but a number of errors were found each week that could easily have been prevented. Most of the workers were skilled and experienced, and had been with Dixon for at least three years. The pay was good, and so were benefits, but still Dixon was not perceived as a great place to work.

There were several reasons why morale, attendance and quality were suffering. These were uncovered by an outside consultant, who eventually recommended that the work teams should be formed. The consultant said that workers disliked not knowing their assignments until the last minute. The workers felt that supervisors gave more pleasant tasks as rewards, and unpleasant ones as punishments. Most often, they never completed a job they had started. They were also upset because some of their fellow workers knew how to hide from the supervisors at the right time. Others were treated with favoritism. Another problem was that every worker knew he could build any storage unit or handcart if he had the blueprint and was left alone to do the work.

The work teams were immediately popular. Teams were formed taking into consideration the workers' own choices of fellow team members. They were given the job orders, blueprints and deadlines, and set free to work. Team members were allowed to work out their own method of assigning tasks within the group. Management said that teams were not to be used as an excuse to reduce productivity, or else the old method could be reinstituted. Productivity did not diminish, and absenteeism and lateness began to decrease. Fewer quality errors were found.

One day, the consultant returned to see how things were going. Two of six teams were quick to complain, 'We're back to the same old story.' The consultant soon found out why they were upset. In both cases, the supervisor had entered the team area and reassigned one or more of the team members to a different task. The supervisors had good reasons, they claimed. The customer had called and requested that the order be rushed, and they were only trying to meet the new deadline. However, the workers saw things differently. They wondered if the supervisors really supported the team concept.

- Did the supervisors do the right thing when the customer's deadline moved up? Explain.
- What happened in the teams when they were set up? What norms were likely to develop, for example?
- How would you explain the improvements in absenteeism, lateness and productivity?

REFERENCES

Areneson, H. and K. Ekberg (2005), Evaluation of Empowerment Processes in a Workplace Health Promotion Intervention Based on Learning in Sweden. *Health Promotion International*, **20**(4), 351–9.

Bales, R.F. (1953), *Interaction Process Analysis: A Method for the Study of Small Groups*. Reading, MA: Addison-Wesley.

Balkin, D.B. (1997), Rewards for Team Contributions to Quality. *Journal of Compensation and Benefits*, **13**: 41–6.

Brislin, R. (1993), *Understanding Culture's Influence on Behavior*, Fort Worth, TX: Harcourt Brace Jovancovich.

Cascio, W.F. (2000), Managing a Virtual Workplace. *Academy of Management Executive*, **14**(3): 81–90.

Cohen, S.G. (1994), Designing Effective Self-Management Teams. In *Advances in Interdisciplinary Studies of Work Teams*, M. Beyerlein (ed.). Greenwich, CT: JAI Press, pp. 239–90.

Cohen, S.G. and D.E. Bailey (1997), What Makes Teams Work: Group Effectiveness Research from the Shop Floor to the Executive Suite. *Journal of Management*, **23**: 239–90.

Colquitt, J.A., R.A. Noe and C.L. Jackson (2002), Justice in teams: Antecedents and Consequences of Procedural Justice Climate. *Personnel Psychology*, **55**(1): 83–109.

Colquitt, J.A., J.R. Hollenbeck, D.R. Ilgen, J.A. LePine and L. Sheffard (2002), Computer-Assisted Communication and Team Decision-Making Performance: The Moderating Effect of Openness to Experience. *Journal of Applied Psychology*, **87**(2): 402–10.

Cordery, J.L., W.S. Mueller and L.M. Smith (1991), Attitudinal and Behavioral Effects of Autonomous Group Working: A Longitudinal Field Study. *Academy of Management Journal*, **34**: 464–76.

Erez, A., J.A. Lepine and H. Elms (2002), Effects of Rotated Leadership and Peer Evaluation on the Functioning and Effectiveness of Self-managed Teams: A Quasi-Experiment. *Personnel Psychology*, **55**(4): 929–48.

Ferrari (2010), *The Ferrari Test Team*, http://www.thescuderia.net/testteam.shtml.

Grabrenya, W., Y.J. Wang and B. Latane (1985), Social Loafing in an Optimizing Task: Cross Cultural Differences Among Chinese and Americans. *Journal of Cross Cultural Phycology*, **16**: 223–42.

Halebilian, J. and S. Finklestein (1993), Top Management Size, CEO Dominance, and Firm Performance: The Moderating Poles of Environmental Turbulence and Discretion. *Academy of Management Journal*, **36**: 844–63.

Hirschfeld, R.R. and J.B. Berneth (2008), Mental Efficacy and Physical Efficacy at the Team Level: Inputs and Outcomes among Newly Formed Action Teams. *Journal of Applied Psychology*, **93**(6): 1429–37.

Hoedemakers, C. and R. Pepermans (2007), Stimulating Collective Coping: Conceiving Training for Managers. In S. McIntyre and J. Houdmont (eds), *Occupational Health Psychology: Key Paper of the European Academy of Occupational Health Psychology*, 7th edn. Castelo da Maia, Portugal: Edicoes ISMAI, pp. 111–13.

Jackson, C.L. and J.A. LePine (2003), Peer Responses to a Team's Weakest Link: A Test and Extension of LePine and Van Dyne's Model. *Journal of Applied Psychology*, **88**(3): 459–75.

Jackson, S.E., K.E. May and K. Whitney (1995), Understanding the Dynamics of Diversity on Decision-Making Teams. In *Team Decision-Making Effectiveness in Organizations*, R.A. Guzzo and E. Salas (eds). San Francisco, CA: Jossey Bass, pp. 204–61.

Jarvenpaa, S.L., K. Knoll and D.E. Leidner (1998), Is Anybody Out There? Antecedents of Trust in Global Virtual Teams. *Journal of Management Information Systems*, **14**(4): 29–64.

Katz, D. (1965), Explaining Informal Work Groups in Complex Organizations: The Case for Autonomy in Structure. *Administrative Science Quarterly*, **10**: 204–21.

Katzenback, J.R. and D.K. Smith (1993), *The Wisdom of Teams: Creating the High Performance Organization*. Boston, MA: Harvard Business School Press.

Laughlin, P.R., E. Hatch, J. Silver and C. Boh (2006), Groups Perform Better Than the Best Individuals on Letters-to-Numbers Problems: Effects of Group Size. *Journal of Personality and Social Psychology*, **90**(4): 644–51.

LePine, J.A. and L. Van Dyne (2001), Peer Responses to Low Performers: An Attributional Model of Helping in the Context of Groups. *Academy of Management Review*, **26**(1): 67–84.

LePine, J.A., J.R. Hollenbeck, D.R. Ilgen, J.A. Colquitt and A. Ellis (2002), Gender Composition, Situational Strength, and Team Decision-Making Accuracy: A Criterion Decomposition Approach. *Organizational Behavior and Human Decision Processes*, **88**(1): 445–75.

LePine, J.A., R.F. Piccolo, C.L. Jackson, J.E. Mathieu and J.R. Saul (2008), A Meta-analysis of Teamwork Processes: Tests of a Multidimensional Model and Relationships with Team Effectiveness Criteria. *Personnel Psychology*, **61**(2): 273–307.

Mohrman, S.A., S.G. Cohen and A.M. Mohrman (1995), *Designing Team-Based Organizations: New Forms for Knowledge Work*. San Francisco, CA: Jossey-Bass.

Smith, C. and D. Comer (1994), Self-Organization in Small Groups: A Study of Group Effectiveness Within Non-Equilibrium Conditions. *Human Relations*, **47**: 553–73.

Tuckman, B. (1965), Developmental Sequence in Small Groups. *Psychological Bulletin*, **63**(6): 382–99.

Watson, W., K. Kumar and L.K. Michelson (1993), Cultural Diversity's Impact on Interaction Processes and Performance: Comparing Homogenous and Diverse Task Groups. *Academy of Management Journal*, **36**: 590–602.

7. Communications in organizations

PREPARING FOR CLASS

Before you read this chapter think about your experiences in the following situations:

1. You were in a foreign country and didn't understand the language at all. How did you communicate to the waiter what you wanted to eat for lunch? Did you know what you were ordering?
2. At work, your supervisor told you that you were doing a 'good job', but when the time came for your performance appraisal, she told you that there were several areas in which your were 'below average'. Why do you think that happened?
3. One of your fellow students came up to you after class and asked, 'Are you angry with me? What did I do that caused you to avoid me in the corridor before class?' You thought about this a bit and replied, 'I didn't do it intentionally. I was talking with our professor and didn't see you. Sorry.' What would lead to such a conclusion by your fellow student?

* *

Julia and Marie could feel that the temperature in the meeting room was hot, not because of the heat, but because of what was emanating from Francois, the chief executive officer (CEO) of Parnasse, a small publicity firm in Paris that in the last ten years had developed a worldwide reputation for its creative ways of getting the message of mid-size French high-technology companies disseminated all over the globe. Julia and Marie had started with Francois at the beginning, and now they were both heads of departments with 20 employees in each. They had never seen Francois like this. His face was red, he was nodding his head, held between his hands, up and down. And on the table were the operating statements for the last fiscal year. They both knew that the news wasn't good. They had anticipated problems, but now they knew. Francois didn't say a word. He glared at everyone in the room, then walked out. Everyone in the room knew and understood that Parnasse had had a bad year. Francois hadn't said a word, but had communicated precisely what he meant to convey to his team.

Communication is the process by which meaning is exchanged between individuals through a common system of symbols, signs or behavior. Meaning is the shared understanding of the message (Pearson et al., 2007). Of course it is fairly simple to understand how a company like Parnasse might use the tools of its industry to communicate with the customers of its clients. We can also understand communications at work, giving orders to others, receiving orders and information from our boss, reading procedures and policies that we have to implement, or communicating with customers about some problem that they have had with our product.

Spotlight 7.1   When I say what I mean, do you mean what I say? Deconstructionism and the meaning of language

If communication is defined as the transmission of meaning, postmodernism confuses the issue. Postmodernists argue that since conceptions of the world are socially constructed, then the meaning of words themselves must be a function of cultural and symbolic elements that the writer or speaker has experienced. As such, a reader or listener with different experiences would have a different view of the world, which may be equally valid, though significantly different. Thus you can't really be sure what words mean, but rather the meaning is what the reader or listener interprets it could be – which becomes the basis for the reader or listener's meaning. This is what the term deconstructionism, a key concept of postmodernism, means. This poses a communication problem because if different people have different meanings for the same term (say, for example, 'leader') then they cannot meaningfully communicate about leadership. This means that it is possible to conclude that 'a text has no univocal meaning', and that the interpretation could proceed ad infinitum. This is a view challenged by Umberto Eco in *The Limits of Interpretation* (1990). He argues that there are social and cultural parameters that proscribe unlimited interpretations and, in fact, do result in meaning.

But the fact is that communications is so endemic in our everyday life that we often fail to recognize it. For example, from the time you rise in the morning you are bombarded with information that you process to get the day started. When you look into the mirror after getting out of bed, your reflection communicates something about how you slept and what you think you need to do to 'clean up' for the day. As you drive to work you listen to the news of the day that informs you about important local, national and world events, and you hear commercials trying to convince you to buy something. When you approach a stoplight, the color of the light of informs you that you should stop or that you may continue. When you arrive at work your colleagues greet you, then you open your email to get the day's instructions from your boss. All of these are different ways that people are communicating with you, hoping that you will understand what they intend, or how they intend for you to respond.

There are a number of ideas that we've introduced in earlier chapters that will help you with this chapter. One group of helpful ideas is concepts from learning theory that appear in Chapter 1 on personality. Stimuli trigger behavior or affective responses, but a stimulus must be perceived, and perception is necessary for communication to occur. Similarly, the discussion of perception helps you understand how we organize information about people and things, the attribution of properties to them on the basis of the information, and the way we make cause–effect attributions about them. You will also find that communication is involved in virtually everything organizational that is discussed in this book, from leadership and management to managing conflict in organizations.

COMMUNICATION IN ORGANIZATIONS

We can draw on the example, again, of the Challenger explosion in 1986 as a dramatic example of both internal and external communication failure. An investigation revealed that some engineers at Morton Thiokol, which built the shuttle rockets, had expressed serious technical reservations about a launch in cold weather (Rogers Commission Report, 1986). This information, however, never reached the higher command levels of NASA, who made a bad decision and gave the go-ahead for the flight (see Chapter 5 on decision making for more about this disaster). Poor communications can hinder innovation and cause delays in bringing new and needed products to markets. Communication deficiencies may keep work projects that should be initiated off a manager's personal task agenda. Some organization difficulties arise because problems are not reported to others; over time, they become crises and much more difficult to resolve. As a consequence, many decisions fail because they are not based on adequate information.

While it is obvious that communication can occur in many different contexts (interpersonal, between groups and cultures, and so forth) it is especially important in organizations because they are human communities in which the members are tied together in complex relationships. In this chapter we focus on internal communications, though obviously there is a lot of other communication with external parties such as customers, suppliers, government agencies and others who are involved with the organization. The nature of these relationships, both internal and external, is influenced by the quality of communications and therefore it is not surprising that the effectiveness of organizational communication can contribute to organization effectiveness.

Communications and the Manager

The managerial job is done in a network of individuals both inside and outside the organization who provide the manager with information. This information may be input into planning processes, feedback on how well subordinates are doing on assigned projects, notification of new problems, or for social or personal uses. So, communication takes an enormous amount of any manager's time. Managers, depending on the organizational level, spend anywhere from between 50 to 80 percent of their average workday in communication activities of some type. Top managers especially spend a high percentage of their time in mostly face-to-face communication (Mintzberg, 1973). However, communications from managers can be widely misunderstood in organizations. For example: managers believe they communicate more with their subordinates than subordinates report (Webber, 1970); there are frequent misunderstandings between superiors and subordinates, especially with respect to knowledge of job problems; and in many communication episodes between superiors and subordinates, superiors may believe they were giving their subordinates instructions, but the subordinates view the same communications just as helpful information.

A BASIC MODEL OF THE COMMUNICATION PROCESS

While communications is a complex process it can be represented in a very simple model. In Figure 7.1, we show that there is a message that emanates from a sender and is conveyed through some medium, or channel, to a receiver.

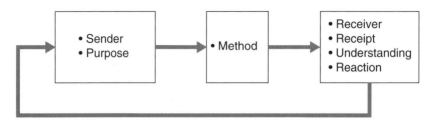

Figure 7.1   A communications model

> [The message is the] verbal and nonverbal form of the idea, a thought, or feeling that one person (the sender) wishes to communicate to another person or group (the receivers) . . . [The message travels through a] channel . . . to the receiver of the message. [the receiver may provide] a verbal or nonverbal response to the . . . message. [The message will be coded, or sent in the form of a verbal and/or nonverbal code.] Verbal code consists of symbols and a grammatical arrangement . . . Nonverbal codes consist of all symbols that are not words, including all bodily movements, use of space and time, clothing, and sounds other than words. [The receiver decodes the message, or] assigns meaning to the idea or thought. [There is often some noise] or interference in the encoding and decoding processes that reduces the clarity of and message. (Pearson et al., 2007)

Communication effectiveness is the degree to which a message is received and understood, and whether the receiver's reactions to the message correspond to the sender's purposes in sending it. What makes communications so problematical is that getting the sender's idea to the receiver involves translating the idea into language, then transmitting it. The language can be verbal or non-verbal, and neither of these is straightforward. Take verbal language as an example. We think of it as composed of words with meaning and grammar, which defines the language structure. Yet the words may be used as jargon, clichés and metaphors that have particular meanings to a specific group (for example plumbers, physicians, lawyers and information technology specialists) but may mean nothing to someone outside the group. It is the same with non-verbal language, where a specific gesture may have different meanings, depending upon the context and the culture in which it is used.

Our model of communications below shows this process. It illustrates a number of factors that can inhibit or facilitate the effectiveness of communications (see Figure 7.2). Some are individual characteristics of senders or receivers, such as emotional and perceptual limitations. Others include the forms of communication used, the characteristics of the organization, and the unique or episodic characteristics surrounding the communication interaction itself.

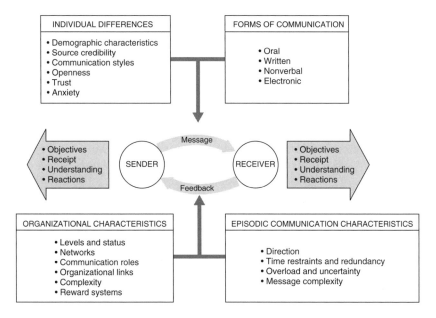

*Figure 7.2   Specific inhibiting or facilitating factors affecting
communication outcomes*

COMMUNICATION FORMS

Different forms of communication have advantages and disadvantages, and the appropriate form depends on the situation. The two most obvious communication forms are oral and written. Both may be one-way or interactive. For example, in one large university certain classes are televised in a large lecture hall, clearly a one-way oral communication process. Other classes use a discussion mode, with much interaction between the instructor and the students. Examples of one-way written communications are company letters, memos, employee handbooks or company newspapers. Interactive written communications are letters or memos that invite a response, and electronic media that organization members use to communicate via email networks. Some forms provide for visual and audio communication, as when the sender of a message can be seen as well as heard. When this is the case, nonverbal communication, such as body language, occurs. Sometimes it is unintentional. Two-way communication is more satisfying than one-way communication and leads to greater accuracy and receptivity of messages (Roberts, 1984). It is a much richer medium (Daft and Lengel, 1986). But it can be time-consuming, inefficient and unnecessary when the message is simple and easily understood, or acceptance of the message is not required. Two-way communication may be more critical when tasks are variable and complex, or when there might be resistance to the message.

Oral vs Written Communication

Most of us generally prefer two-way communication because meanings can be more easily transmitted, whether they are tentative or certain. Pauses and voice inflections give emphasis to different words, stress different parts of the message, and communicate the sender's feelings about the subject. Oral communication, however, generates more pressure to please the other party but at the same time gives the parties an opportunity to strengthen their personal relationship, which may lead to greater interpersonal attraction (Roberts, 1984).

There are also advantages to written communications. For example, comprehension may be greater because ideas and information can be expressed with more care and clarity and the message can be reread any number of times. In addition, written communications may include more supporting information to strengthen a particular viewpoint.

Non-Verbal Communication

Meaning goes beyond the language used in communication. The volume, rate and rhythm, pitch, pauses, sounds such as 'ahs' and 'ers', laughing and sighing may convey meaning. Gestures, posture and facial expressions all transmit information. Posture and gestures may imply status and social class. For example, upper social classes often attempt to maintain an image of dignity which requires some control of emotion or, at least, control of gestures signifying an emotional state (Bremmer and Roodenburg, 1992). Facial expressions such as smiles, frowns, amount of eye contact and other factors communicate feelings. For example, smiling during a negative statement increases the positivity of the statement, or sometimes the source of information may be perceived as less genuine (Krumhuber and Manstead, 2009). Maintaining a normal level of eye contact in a job interview is more likely to result in your being hired than averting eye contact (Burgoon et al., 1985), and raising your eyebrows is more likely when you are communicating important information (Flecha-Garcia, 2010).

Communication congruence is when non-verbal and oral communications carry the same meaning. When they are not congruent, non-verbal communication carries more meaning than verbal communication. For example, the use of gestures is highly correlated with language (Gentilucci and Volta, 2008), and hand gestures especially are more pronounced when presenting new information (Gerwing and Bavelas, 2004). And, like the conventional wisdom about knowing a liar, research shows not only that lies are more easily detected from the observation of body language while listening to the words (Manstead et al., 1984), but also that women appeared to be more likely to detect emotions than men (Ayron, 2008). The non-verbal messages are the more meaningful indicator of the sender's emotional state and feelings. A consistent discrepancy between a verbal and non-verbal language will lead to ambiguity, higher tension and anxiety on the part of others. However, interpretation of body language may be difficult, since some individuals often seem to communicate a different emotional state with their body than they are actually experiencing (Roberts, 1984).

Actions are another form of non-verbal communication that speaks louder than words. What one does reflects intentions and feelings better than what one says. When what a manager says and does are inconsistent, individuals pay more attention to what is actually done. This happened in a plant in which the manager was, ostensibly, trying to institute a total quality management (TQM) culture. Without exception, these are introduced with enthusiasm by top management. There are development programs and systems put in place. However the real key to success is if quality is demanded by the decisions and actions of managers, not the rhetoric. Thus, for credibility, a policy must be followed by appropriate actions.

Non-verbal behavior can create difficulties in cross-cultural communications. Some gestures are specific to a particular culture, while certain facial expressions such as laughing, weeping, yawning and blushing seem to be universal across many cultures and languages (Bremmer and Roodenberg, 1992). An inappropriate gesture could undermine a whole speech. For example, the gesture of raising your arm and joining your thumb and forefinger to communicate the positive meaning to a waiter in a restaurant in the United States that your dinner was very good, or OK, has a very different, negative and insulting meaning in other cultures.

Electronic Communication

Electronic communication is not a new phenomenon. It began in 1969 with a network between UCLA and Stanford University, but its public use accelerated in the 1990s (Akyac, 2008). Today there are an incredibly large number of ways to communicate electronically, such as Skype, Facebook, Flicker and what is now conventional teleconferencing. These new media can make communication more efficient.

New technologies lead to somewhat different behavioral outcomes than more traditional forms of communication. For example, communicating electronically rather than face to face produces more polarization, making it more difficult to obtain consensus on an issue (Sproull and Kiesler, 1986). This results, perhaps, because individuals feel psychologically closer to those in physical proximity and work harder to reach agreement with them. Electronic media also produces more uninhibited communication, such as swearing, probably because status differences among the parties are less obvious (Sproull and Kiesler, 1986). In addition, the new communication technologies, compared to face-to-face meetings, may result in a greater participation rate among those communicating but, maybe because of this, more difficulty in making a decision (Siegel et al., 1986).

Informal Communication and the Grapevine

One of these informal channels is the 'grapevine'. The grapevine is the channel of communication for the informal organization. Part of the grapevine's appeal is its usefulness for organizational sense-making; that is, stories and gossip help members understand something they may believe to have a great deal of ambiguity. Some of the anxiety experienced from this ambiguity can be resolved during organizational socialization as one learns about people in the organization and what happens to them when they behave in different ways.

Grapevine information, generally about 75 percent accurate, may be in the form of gossip, rumors and 'catching up', about both the workplace and the personal lives of organizational members (Kurland and Pelled, 2000; Langan-Fox, 2002); the sort of information that is not transmitted through the formal communication mechanisms. Gossip is 'informative and evaluative talk . . . among no more than a few individuals, about another member of that organization who is not present' (Kurland and Pelled, 2000). Gossip about another person may be positive or negative and its credibility may be high or low. Negative gossip is often a result of a sense of powerlessness, injustice, envy and resentment (Wert and Salovey, 2004). A rumor is information of interest to people, but there may not be clear evidence or support for it, leaving doubts about its truth. However, rumors usually have a relatively high degree of accuracy: around 80 percent to 90 percent are true (Pearson et al., 2007). The grapevine also helps a person to 'catch up', or learn more about what is going on in the organization. For example, one company announced that it was opening a manufacturing plant in a foreign country and that there would be no force reductions in the local operation. Some rumors validated this, but others refuted it. Eventually, word got out on the grapevine that there would indeed be no lay-offs. The source came from a conversation that a mid-level manager had with the CEO, who told her that the plan was expansion, not simply outsourcing jobs.

INDIVIDUAL DIFFERENCES AND COMMUNICATION

In organizations, personality differences and demographic characteristics such as gender, race, ethnicity and age affect communication behavior. Communications will also be affected by amount and type of education, occupational experience and organization experience.

Demographic Characteristics

There is evidence that communication can be affected by demographic characteristics. For example, the idea that men and women communicate differently in their relationships with others was the basis of the popular book *Men Are from Mars, Women Are from Venus* (Gray, 1992), though such differences may be exaggerated. There is some research evidence that supports the idea of different gender-based communication patterns. Women are more sensitive than men to interpersonal communication skills and, as we have noted above, are better able to detect lying from verbal and body language (Byron, 2008), and they are more attracted to articulate people (Carroll et al., 1988). They talk differently than men to bosses, and peers believed that women may be more concerned about impressing bosses and peers (Steckler and Rosenthal, 1985). Both women and minorities differ from white men in non-verbal behavior modes, which can cause misunderstandings in communication (Roberts, 1984).

Sex-related stereotypes may cause people to brand an action as appropriate or inappropriate depending on whether it is exhibited by a man or a woman (Heilman, 1984; Heilman and Haynes, 2005). For example, in one study it was found that women who were apparently successful in male-dominated jobs were not liked, were seen to have undesirable personal attributes and were less desirable as bosses (Heilman and Okimoto, 2007). Such stereotypes frequently cause communication problems between men and women. Male managers may have stereotypes about women that influence their opinion of female credibility, particularly when the male managers have limited information about women's qualifications (Fuchs et al., 2004; Heilman and Haynes, 2005). This bias appeared to be diminished when the evaluators have more information about the woman's role (Heilman and Okimoto, 2007).

Although communications may be intended to elicit particular reactions, other responses may occur simply because different groups put different meanings on identical words. Particular terms may evoke positive reactions, whereas others generate negative or neutral reactions. For example, managers and labor leaders may react quite differently to such terms as 'grievance',

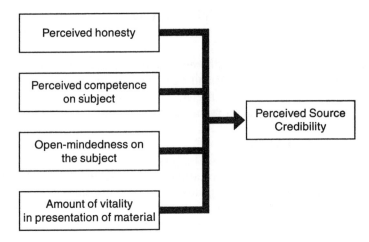

Figure 7.3   Factors related to source credibility

'arbitration' and 'seniority'. In one organization studied by one of the co-authors, different management levels had quite different reactions to and perceptions of such terms as 'incentives', 'budgets', 'conferences' and 'cooperation'. For example, a grievance may be viewed as a right and a protection by a union member, but as disloyal or an ungrateful act by a manager.

Source Credibility

Source credibility is the belief that information is truthful and unbiased. The source is perceived by the receiver to be honest and impartial (see Figure 7.3). Credibility is enhanced by: (1) vitality and dynamism of the presentation, such as when the message is articulated in a dynamic, energetic manner; (2) the perceived competence of the source, such as when your physician prescribes medication for your cold; (3) trustworthiness, such as when you have confidence that the source of the message is one which you believe to be honest and fair; (4) believing that your values are the same as those of the source of the message; (5) being open-minded; and (6) personally identifying with the source of the message (Pearson et al., 2007). This can be seen in the classic study of the effects of personal dynamism or vitality on source credibility that were shown in the famous Dr Fox studies (Ware, 1975). In these studies, an actor, Michael Fox, was hired to present lectures to students. The content and the delivery style of the lectures varied. In some, factual information was presented in a very dry manner; in others, the lecturer presented nonsense material to the students but in a very energetic and interesting manner. When the lecturer presented material in a dynamic and entertaining manner, he was rated quite highly by the students, even though the actual content of his lecture was nonsense.

Factors related to source credibility

Credibility is especially important in the superior–subordinate relationship; it affects how they judge each other and relates to trust at work. Higher credibility ratings of supervisors are associated with higher worker satisfaction with supervisors, perhaps because the personal characteristics contributing to high credibility ratings are generally admired (Hysong, 2008).

Managers tend to not have high credibility with their employees, especially on matters unrelated to technical expertise, especially when these managers are seen as being strongly committed to the organization (McCroskey et al., 2005). Further, credibility can be increased by providing adequate and high-quality information to subordinates (Thomas et al., 2009).

Openness   Openness is the willingness to listen, to accept bad news and to be tolerant of views divergent from one's own. Not dealing candidly with information can result in overlooking problems, inhibiting creativity and stifling innovation. Perceptions of openness are related to the actual behaviors of one person toward another. Openness about work-related problems affects motivation, performance and satisfaction (Kay and Christophel, 1995). Quite a number of studies have shown the relationship of openness in communication to the job satisfaction of workers and especially to satisfaction with their immediate supervisor (Judge et al., 2009; Judge and Ilies, 2002; Dansereau and Markham, 1987).

Trust in others   Trust can refer either to one's feelings about the competence of another, or to whether one thinks another person intends to pursue his or her best interests at your expense. Trust is related to some aspects of a manager's behavior toward subordinates. A superior who trusts subordinates' competence allows them to have more influence in decision making (Dirks and Ferrin, 2002; Korsgaard et al., 2002). A superior will not monitor the performance of a subordinate in whom he has trust as closely as that of one he doesn't trust (Lowin and Craig, 1968). A boss is likely to communicate more information to subordinates who are highly trusted.

A supervisor's personality affects the level of trust. High authoritarians have less trust in others than those who are less authoritarian (see Chapter 2). Trust in others is probably also influenced by their actual behavior: their past performance, demonstrated competence, and whether they have harmed others' interests given an opportunity to do so. Organizations that lay off employees frequently find it difficult to create much trust between workers and management.

Anxiety   Interpersonal anxiety is uneasiness or apprehension experienced subjectively when interacting with others. It affects the individual's feelings and beliefs that he or she may not be able to meet the interpersonal demands of others. For example, a person may feel anxious because of fear that others will think that he or she is stupid, dull or inarticulate. Communication anxiety is higher for introverts (Loffredo et al., 2008). Anxiety is a form of stress and can lead to such speech difficulties as repetition and tongue slips. When these occur, they may increase interpersonal anxiety. If anxiety increases sufficiently, it may affect the person's ability to comprehend and objectively evaluate information. People make more mistakes when they are highly anxious. In addition, the person's tense state may be very obvious to others, possibly raising their own tension levels which, in turn, will further inhibit communication.

ORGANIZATION CHARACTERISTICS AND COMMUNICATIONS

Organization design factors have an effect on the nature and flow of information. Here we discuss some effects of the following organization characteristics on communication:

1.   Organizational level and status differences.
2.   Organization complexity.
3.   Organizational reward systems.
4.   Communication networks.
5.   Communication roles.
6.   Communication links.

Organizational Level and Status Differences

Level and status differences may significantly affect the quality of communications among organization members. When individuals are socialized to defer to others of higher status and position, this takes the form of respect, submission and compliance. Those with higher status expect to control communication. The person in control of a communication event does not necessarily do most of the talking, and may control the situation by facial expressions, nods, body gestures and other tactics (Flecha-Garcia, 2010).

Symbols may also communicate an individual's status. Symbols are guides about how to act with those who possess them. They are often deliberately manipulated to influence others. Office location, desks, furnishings and organizational privileges may be status symbols. They create certain behavioral expectations about the appropriate amount of deference that should be shown to others.

There is good evidence that bosses are not aware of their subordinates' problems (Schnake et al., 1990). Managers believed that subordinates get sufficient information from them about goals and, at the same time, are able to influence the work situation. They also believed that in performance reviews, they adequately communicated how well subordinates performed, though the subordinates thought otherwise. Generally, subordinates believed that this disagreement contributed to a negative organizational climate.

Because organization level reflects status and power differences, some communication distortion is inevitable (Hall et al., 2006). Communication distortion occurs, in general, because individuals communicate what they perceive to be in their best interests (Monge and Eisenberg, 1987). For instance, when managers communicate with lower-level personnel, the subordinates are more accurate in decoding messages and, at the same time, the subordinates tend to send less clear messages upward (Hall et al. 2006). The greater the status differential, the more restricted the channels of communication, the more the tendency for information to flow from low- to high-status people, and the more distorted the content of the message. Upward communication is especially distorted when there is a large status differential between a superior and a subordinate, and the superior has the power over promotions for the subordinate. Higher-level individuals want better performance from lower-level personnel, and lower-level personnel are trying to obtain as many rewards as possible. These different objectives make individuals selective in what they bring to the attention of others.

Adler points out that women may have special problems in communication because of perceived status differences (Adler, 1997). She summarizes research which indicates that high-status individuals tend to speak louder and more rapidly, point with their fingers and maintain relatively frequent eye contact. At the same time, studies show that women tend to speak in a more tentative way in mixed-sex groups than they do in an all-female group. These communication behaviors may cause women to be attributed lower status and receive lower ratings of their competence, since this is not how high-status competent individuals communicate (Fuchs et al., 2004). When women do speak in an assertive way, their ratings of competence from males go up, but their likeability goes down. When their communications are seen as more warm and friendly, they are not rated as high in competence but are more likable.

Organizational Complexity

Organizations differ in structural complexity. Some consist of many different, specialized subunits, whereas others are smaller and simpler. When there are a large number of specialized subunits, coordination is more difficult and both formal and informal communication increases. Higher organizational complexity also leads to more formal, prescribed communications instead of the informal mutual adjustment processes used in simpler organization structures. When there are more specialized units, there are more committees established to facilitate communication among these units. This creates even more organizational linkages that exacerbate communication problems even more, because the different subunits often have contradictory objectives, differences in perspectives and educational backgrounds, and their own specialized languages.

Organizational Reward Systems

Ample evidence indicates that individuals respond to the organization's reward systems (see Chapter 3). Given this, we could expect that organizational reward systems influence what information is transmitted. When a superior controls promotion or other potential rewards for subordinates, the subordinates will communicate the information to the superior that will enhance their own careers (O'Reilly et al., 1987). They may also distort information for the same reasons. Competition for rewards among individuals or groups causes information flow among such competitors to be reduced.

Communication Networks

Communication networks are the channels through which information regularly flows between persons. Networks can take different forms that can affect how persons perform and their level of satisfaction. The earliest research focused on the effects of different network structures on individuals. In the earliest of these experiments, individuals were placed in cubicles and allowed to pass each other messages through slots in the cubicle walls. The slots among the cubicles were opened and closed by the experimenter to create the various types of networks (Siegel et al., 1986). Your location in different communication networks (see Figure 7.4) affects access to information.

These studies show that network effectiveness varies with the nature of the task (Bavelas et al., 2007; Leavitt, 1951). For example, a wheel-structured communication network is efficient for simple tasks, but the individuals at the end of the spokes, who simply take orders, are

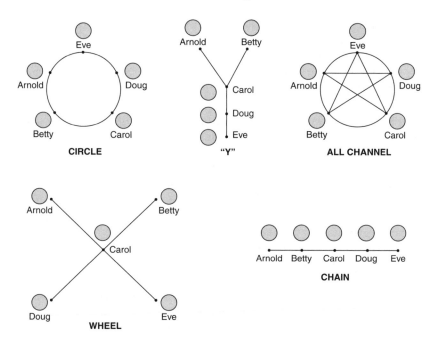

Figure 7.4   Communication networks

dissatisfied with their position. Performance on simple tasks is greatest in the Y structure, less in a chain, and least effective in a circle. However, the circle network, where each can communicate with all, seems to produce high performance and satisfaction for complex tasks, and it appears to be most effective when there are sudden and confusing changes in the task requirements. While the networks shown in Figure 7.4 are much less complicated than those in actual organizations, these studies provide some guides to solving real communication problems. For example, the all-channel would be appropriate where a task is very complex, since that pattern requires every individual to talk to all others. The wheel or the chains are probably sufficient when the task is simple and it is therefore unnecessary to obtain everyone's ideas (Langan-Fox et al., 2002).

The more recent research recognizes that the formal organization structure affects both formal and informal communication networks. In both types of networks, those who are in a central, key position will have formal authority, power or expertise and will dominate the network (Brass, 1984). For instance, in mechanistic organizations there is a dominant hierarchical and vertical structure of control and communication, but in organic structures there is a network structure, more flexible and horizontal, that responds to the nature of the tasks to be accomplished (Burns and Stalker, 1961). However, in both types of organizations, informal networks exist that are different from the formal structure (Soda and Zaheer, 2010). The overlap of these formal and informal networks may or may not contribute to performance, depending on the nature of coordination required. When coordination needs are relatively simple, high consistency between the formal and informal network contributes to effectiveness. However, when there is a task requirement for more extensive coordination, a moderate level of network overlap is more effective.

Networks are not rigid. They change to fit the task. For example, in one study of the effects of a change in technology it was found that those employees who adopted the new technology increased their power and gained a more central location in the communication network (Burkhardt and Brass, 1990). Also, becoming more central in the network preceded the person's level of power. It also appears that one's performance in the network is more than a matter of simple location, but is also affected by personality (Mehra et al., 2001). Persons who were high self-monitors did better than low self-monitors. Two things are clear from this research. One is that networks change to fit the task that is to be done, and the other is that those persons in it will affect the structure of the network.

Communication Roles

Individuals perform different communication roles in networks. Two important communication roles are the opinion leader and the liaison. Opinion leaders have high credibility with other members, especially in a particular subject area. Opinion leadership tends to be specific to certain topics or issues: the same person is not the opinion leader for several subjects, and anyone in a work group may be an opinion leader, depending on the nature of the problem or situation.

Persons in liaison roles pass on information to others. Liaisons connect two or more groups and may not be a member of any of them (Eisenberg, 1993). In the usual transmittal pattern one liaison passes information to several other managers. One of these may be another liaison person, who in turn passes it on. In a study of rank-and-file employees, 10 percent acted as liaisons, 57 percent were dead-enders who failed to pass on a message, and 33 percent were isolates who did not even receive a message (Eisenberg, 1993). Liaisons in organization boundary-spanning positions may secure information from outside the organization and pass it to the inside, often obtaining information about the technological or market environment. Having access to this information for use by the organization gives these boundary-spanners a great deal of influence and power (Hickson et al., 1971; Manev and Stevenson, 2001).

Communication Links

Changes, omissions, or distortions occur when a message is transmitted from one person to another (Monge et al., 1987). As the number of communication links through which the message passes increases, so do these problems. Individuals change messages in various ways and for various reasons. Sometimes it is deliberate, as when a subordinate tries to simplify information to avoid communication overload for the supervisor. However, omissions and distortions occur for other reasons. The omission or distortion may correspond to the receiver's attitudes, may have been done to please the next person in the communication chain, or may have resulted from oversimplification.

EPISODIC COMMUNICATION CHARACTERISTICS

Episodic communication characteristics are associated with a particular communication event, and they affect understanding. So do the contextual factors in which it occurs, such as time constraints and noise. The amount of information that is being transmitted may also affect communication effectiveness and, finally information complexity may make comprehension difficult.

Direction of Communication

One-way communication occurs when information is transmitted from one source to another without feedback. Much organizational communication is one way, from higher levels to lower. For example, instructions, goals and orders are often given without any feedback. One-way communication is especially likely when written communications are used and in situations where one individual must communicate to a large group.

Two-way communication is clearly more effective in problem solving as well as being more satisfying to participants, especially for complex problems. Where understanding is difficult, two-way communication may be necessary. Two-way communication has a cost: it takes time. When communicators are skilled, it is possible that one-way communication can save time. In highly structured organizations, where problems are routine and fairly simple, one-way communication may be more than adequate to achieve required task performance.

Time Constraints and Redundancy

When little time is spent in communicating or when noise interferes with receipt of the message, the communication may be missed entirely. Redundancy can reduce interference and noise and reduce the likelihood of missing the meaning of a message. Redundancy may mean different things. To some people, it means repeating an idea several times in different ways in order to increase understanding. To others, redundancy is excessive explanation, using too many words to express an idea. The former feel that redundancy is useful; the latter believe it is best to avoid it. Benign redundancy – repetition with variation to increase understanding – can be helpful. For example, redundant multi-source feedback tends to lead to higher leadership ratings of the boss (Smither et al., 2005).

Communication Overload and Uncertainty

Uncertainty is increasing for most organizations, and this trend is expected to continue. This is because of increasingly unstable outside environments, the adoption of non-routine technologies, organic organization structures and increased task interdependence. As uncertainty increases, the amount of information to be processed by the organization increases as well. This leads to information overload, which is one reason why superiors try to limit communications from subordinates. Although increased communication between subordinates and superiors improves the subordinates' satisfaction, it can also lead to overwork, more errors, neglect of important duties, increased frustration for the superior, and so on (Galbraith, 1995).

Communication overload occurs when the amount of information exceeds the capacity of individuals to absorb and process it. This is especially likely at higher organizational levels, where the amount of time spent in communication is greatest. When a unit starts approaching communication overload, it simply cancels the lowest-priority messages, which are not sent at all. When individuals deal with more than seven alternatives, the overload resulted in slowness in evaluating them (Baddeley, 1994).

Message Complexity

Messages can be too complex. The sender of a message may use words or concepts that are beyond the comprehension of receivers. Sometimes this is a matter of educational level and experience. For example, a financial analyst in an investment firm can easily understand a page of numbers that would bewilder a first-year accounting student.

Spotlight 7.2   Communications and culture

Effective communication between people from different cultures is universally difficult because people have different values and, therefore, different perceptions. As a result, they do not always agree on the meaning of words and could easily have dissimilar styles of expressing themselves. For example:

> Eastern cultures have so many nonverbal ways of saying 'no' without directly or unambiguously uttering the word. Needless to say, this practice has caused considerable misunderstanding when North Americans try to communicate with the Japanese. To illustrate, the Japanese in everyday conversation frequently use the word *hai* ('yes') to convey not agreement necessarily, but rather that they understand what is being said (Ferraro, 1998).

You should not expect, either, that communications will not be a problem even within a country cluster where the same language is spoken. For example, English is widely spoken around the world. This makes many Americans feel that they can cope quite well in other countries so long as they deal with individuals who can speak English. This is a mistake, for reasons beyond differences in values, perceptions, word meanings and styles of communicating. For instance, the German mode of communication is slow and ponderous compared to the French, resulting in slower decisions. The Japanese are less willing to make personal disclosures to others, while the French have the greatest willingness to express conflict (Ting-Toomey et al., 1991). Studies have shown that Americans are among the most ethnocentric in their attitudes (Hall and Hall, 1990). They tend more to discount what those from other countries say. For example, when a large US communication firm wanted to internalize the production of computers, it acquired an Italian computer company. This joint venture failed because the American managers working in Italy tended to think that they were right and the Italians usually wrong.

SUMMARY

Communication is a way for those in organizations to make sense of their work environment. Communication skills are also critical for managerial success. Communication is effective when it results in the action intended by the sender. This means that the receivers must have access to the message, be receptive to it, have the ability to comprehend it, and be motivated to react in the desired way. A number of factors affect the success of communication. These include the form of communication used, individual differences of receivers, characteristics of the organization and episodic characteristics of a particular message such as complexity and the use of feedback.

Dealing with such matters before a communication takes place might itself have a positive impact on communication effectiveness. There are several things that can be done to ensure that access, receptivity, comprehension and motivation to react are improved.

GUIDELINES FOR MANAGERS: COMMUNICATING WITH OTHERS

Communicating effectively isn't just a matter of thinking about and improving your own communication style; it is recognizing that the situation and condition of the other party or parties involved. For example, rereading the chapter on stress (Chapter 4), you see how situations, conditions and personality might affect one or both parties involved in a communication episode. Chapter 3 on attitudes discusses factors that affect perception and, obviously, what we perceive determines the meanings that we associate with information. There are, however, some general things to remember as we try to communicate with others and they try to communicate with us.

You Communicate More than You Think

Most of us believe that our communication acts are intentional, that is, when we intend to send a message in verbal or written form. However, as others observe us, they are often getting a message from how we are acting, whether we are alone or with others. For example, if we are observed laughing while having a conversation with someone, a third party might perceive that we are talking and laughing about him or her, or they might believe that they are 'outsiders' to some important information. While we can't control these perceptions and attributions of others, we should be aware that they occur.

Take Responsibility for Creating and Facilitating Understanding

Make sure that you know what you want to communicate. Gather and organize your thoughts and then think through how you want to say or write what you wish. This can be especially important when dealing with others about critical issues such as performance feedback, explaining things to clients and/or customers, or simply dealing with a spouse and your children. If they aren't clear about your message, they will interpret it their own way, and that may be different from what you really mean.

Be Clear and Articulate

Choose your words so that others can easily understand them. Don't use technical language when communicating with non-technical others. Don't use specialist jargon unless you are with specialists. And avoid using 'in-house' jargon when not communicating in-house. You should also avoid rambling from one idea to another. Complete your thoughts on one thing before moving to another. That will help others to avoid confusion, and make your task easier.

It's Not Only What You Say, It's the Way That You Say It

Tone of voice and your gestures convey a lot of information. As they say, 'Actions speak louder than words', so make sure that your actions are conveying the same meanings as the words you've chosen to use. For example, persons of high social, and often organizational, status want to create a perception of importance and dignity to others through their tone of voice, facial expressions and gestures. In many instances, the other person might feel a greater sense of distance, coldness and resentment toward them, which hinders understanding.

Maintain Consistency between Your Words and Your Body Language

As we said above, 'Actions speak louder than words'. A good example of this is provided in a study of charismatic leadership (Howell and Frost, 1989) in which there were language and verbal scripts for charismatic, considerate and structuring leader behaviors. Charismatic leaders spoke about tasks in overarching terms, communicating high expectations and confidence in subordinates. Their faces were animated and they were active, pacing or sitting. They leaned toward the group, in a relaxed way, and maintained direct eye contact. Structuring leader behavior was more reserved and neutral. These leaders sat upright behind a desk and maintained irregular eye contact. The considerate leader acted in a relaxed way, sitting on the edge of a desk, leaning toward the group, smiling and nodding. She spoke in friendly language that exhibited concern for the personal welfare of the group. The overall result of the study, which we discuss in more detail in Chapter 9, was that the charismatic leader had much stronger and positive effects that either of the other two types

Keep in Mind that Language can be a 'Help' or 'Hurt'

A simple Internet search will reveal that there are some well-known 'killer' phrases, or phrases which will suppress ideas and/or further communication. For example, when a new idea is proposed you can kill it by responding, 'That's a good idea, but . . .'. Or, 'It's too expensive', or, 'There are better ways than that.' On the other hand, you can support ideas by comments such as, 'That's worth a try', or 'A great idea!'

Maintain Connections with the Other Persons

It's easy for your listener to believe that you aren't interested in what is being communicated if you are doing something that misdirects attention. For example, it's appropriate to take notes about a conversation, particularly an important one, but not so appropriate to appear to be writing something else, or to allow your conversation to be interrupted by a telephone call.

Something else which helps you to connect is maintaining direct eye contact. This doesn't mean maintaining a cold, staring gaze, but rather look them in the eyes.

When You Ask a Question Give Others Time to Respond

We are sometimes impatient when we ask a question and don't get an immediate response. Others may be timid, intimidated or just thinking about an appropriate response before they are ready to answer. So, give them time to respond. It usually takes less than ten seconds to close the silence gap.

Be a Good Listener

The other side of sending messages is receiving them, so when involved in verbal communications, be a good listener. For one thing, silence is golden. Behave as if you are paying attention. Let your actions demonstrate that you are listening. Don't interrupt the other party. Let them get their ideas out as completely as possible. If you don't clearly understand the message, ask good questions, which means questions related to the other's agenda, not yours. You can also make use of reflective comments, such as: 'I'm not sure what you said', or, 'Would you please repeat that for me.' The one thing that you want to avoid are the killer phrases of the sort that we discussed above.

CASE: SO, WE'RE NOT FRIENDS ANY MORE?

Juan and Isabella are professors of banking in the same college business. During a meeting of the department, Juan expressed his opinion about the possibility of converting his undergraduate course to an 'online' course. This would contribute to the development of a teaching platform, and much of what he would do might also be useful in the Masters-level courses.

Isabella, as soon as he was finished, said in a calm but certain way, 'I am sorry, but I totally disagree. Some time ago, we evaluated the effectiveness of these courses and . . .'.

Juan interrupted her immediately, impetuous and touchy. He said, 'I can't believe it. We always agree on everything – and were also friends!'

Immediately, Isabella felt she was in a difficult situation: something had happened in the communications process or in the perceptions about it. In any case she felt she had to get out of this impasse.

Discussion

- How can Isabella get out of this situation?
- What do you think really happened in terms of the communications content and processes?

REFERENCES

Adler, L.L. (1997), *International Handbook on Gender Roles*. Westport, CT: Greenwood Press.

Akyac, M. (2008), When did Email Start Changing Our Lives. Ezine Articles, 1, 30 September, http://ezinearticles.com/?expert=Musa_Aykac.

Baddeley, A. (1994), The Magical Number Seven: Still Magic After All These Years? *Psychological Review*, **101**(2): 353–6.

Bavelas, J., J. Gerwing and K. Fiedler (2007), Conversational Hand Gestures and Facial Displays in Face-to-Face Dialogue. In *Social Communication*. K. Fiedler (ed.). New York: Psychology Press, pp. 283–308.

Brass, D.J. (1984), Being in the Right Place: A Structural Analysis of Individual Influence in an Organization. *Administrative Science Quarterly*, **29**(4): 518–39.

Bremmer, J. and H. Roodenburg (1992), *A Cultural History of Gestures*. Ithaca, NY: Cornell University Press.

Burgoon, J.K., V. Manusov, P. Mineo and J.L. Hale (1985), Effects of Gaze on Hiring, Credibility, Attraction and Relational Message Interpretation. *Journal of Nonverbal Behavior*, **9**(3): 133–46.

Burkhardt, M.E. and D.J. Brass (1990), Changing Patterns or Patterns of Change: The Effects of a Change in Technology on Social Network Structure and Power. *Administrative Science Quarterly*, **35**(1): 104–27.

Burns, T.G. and G.M. Stalker (1961), *The Management of Innovation*. London: Tavistock Institute.

Byron, K. (2008), Differential Effects of Male and Female Managers' Non-verbal Emotional Skills on Employees' Ratings. *Journal of Managerial Psychology*, **23**(2): 118–34.

Carroll, S.J., J.D. Olian and C. Giannantonio (1993), Mentor Reactions to Proteges: An Experiment with Managers. *Journal of Vocational Behavior*, **43**(3): 266–78.

Daft, R.L. and R.H. Lengel (1986), Organizational Information Requirements, Media Richness and Structural Design. *Management Science*, **32**(5): 554–71.

Dansereau, F. and S.E. Markham (1987), Superior–Subordinate Communication: Multiple Levels of Analysis. In *Handbook of Organizational Communication: An Interdisciplinary Perspective*. F.M. Jablin, L.L. Putnam, K.H. Roberts and L.W. Porter (eds). Thousand Oaks, CA: Sage Publications, pp. 343–88.

Dirks, K.T. and D.L. Ferrin (2002), Trust in Leadership: Meta-analytic Findings and Implications for Research and Practice. *Journal of Applied Psychology*, **87**(4): 611–28.

Eco, U. (1990), *The Limits of Interpetation*. Bloomington, IN: Indiana University Press.

Eisenberg, E.M. (1993), *Organizational Communication*. New York: St Martin's Press.

Ferraro, G. (1998), *The Cultural Dimension of International Business*. Englewood Cliffs, NJ: Prentice Hall.

Flecha-Garcia, M.L. (2010), Eyebrow Raises in Dialogue and their Relation to Discourse Structure, Utterance Function and Pitch Accents in English. *Speech Communication*, **52**(6): 542–54.

Fuchs, D., M.M. Tamkins, M.E. Heilman and A.S. Wallen (2004), Penalties for Success: Reactions to Women Who Succeed at Male Gender-Typed Tasks. *Journal of Applied Psychology*, **89**(3): 416–27.

Galbraith, J. (1995), *Designing Organizations: An Executive Briefing on Strategy, Structure, and Process.* San Francisco, CA: Jossey Bass.

Gentilucci, M. and R.D. Volta (2008), Spoken Language and Arm Gestures are Controlled by the Same Motor Control System. *Quarterly Journal of Experimental Psychology*, **61**(6): 944–57.

Gerwing, J. and J. Bavelas (2004), Linguistic Influences on Gesture's Form. *Gesture*, **4**(2): 157–95.

Gray, J. (1992), *Men are from Mars, Women are from Venus: a Practical Guide for Improving Communication and Getting what You Want in Your Relationships.* New York: Harper Collins.

Hall, E.T. and M.R. Hall (1990), *Understanding Cultural Differences: Germans, French, and Americans.* Yarmouth, ME: Intercultural Press.

Hall, J.A., J.C. Rosip, L.S. LeBeau, T.E. Horgan and J.D. Carter (2006), Attributing the Sources of Accuracy in Unequal-power Dyadic Communication: Who is Better and Why? *Journal of Experimental Social Psychology*, **42**(1): 18–27.

Heilman, M.E. (1984), Information as a Deterrent against Sex Discrimination: The Effects of Applicant Sex and Information Type on Preliminary Employment Decisions. *Organizational Behavior and Human Performance*, **33**(2): 174–86.

Heilman, M.E. and M.C. Haynes (2005), No Credit where Credit is Due: Attributional Rationalization of Women's Success in Male–Female Teams. *Journal of Applied Psychology*, **90**(5): 905–16.

Heilman, M.E. and T.G. Okimoto (2007), Why Are Women Penalized for Success at Male Tasks? The Implied Communality Deficit. *Journal of Applied Psychology*, **92**(1): 81–92.

Hickson, D.J., C.R. Hinings, C.A. Lee, R.E. Schneck and J.M. Pennings (1971), A Strategic Contingencies' Theory of Intraorganizational Power. *Administrative Science Quarterly*, **16**: 216–29.

Howell, J.M. and P.J. Frost (1989), A Laboratory Study of Charismatic Leadership. *Organizational Behavior and Human Decision Processes*, **43**: 243–69.

Hysong, S.J. (2008), The Role of Technical Skill in Perceptions of Managerial Performance. *Journal of Management Development*, **27**(3): 275–90.

Judge, T.A. and R. Ilies (2002), Relationship of Personality to Performance Motivation: A Meta-analytic Review. *Journal of Applied Psychology*, **87**(4): 797–807.

Judge, T.A., R.F. Piccolo and T. Kosalka (2009), The Bright and Dark Sides of Leader Traits: A Review and Theoretical Extension of the Leader Trait Paradigm. *Leadership Quarterly*, **20**(6): 855–75.

Kay, B. and D.M. Christophel (1995), The Relationships Among Manager Communication Openness, Nonverbal Immediacy, and Subordinate Motivation. *Communication Research Reports*, **12**(2): 200–205.

Korsgaard, M.A., S.E. Brodt and E.M. Whitener (2002), Trust in the Face of Conflict: The Role of Managerial Trustworthy Behavior and Organizational Context. *Journal of Applied Psychology*, **87**(2): 312–19.

Krumhuber, E. and A.S.R. Manstead (2009), Are You Joking? The Moderating Role of Smiles in the Perception of Verbal Statements. *Cognition and Emotion*, **23**(8): 1504–15.

Kurland, N.B. and L.H. Pelled (2000), Passing the Word: Toward a Model of

Gossip and Power in the Workplace. *Academy of Management Review*, **25**(2): 428–38.

Langan-Fox, J. (2002), Communication in Organizations: Speed, Diversity, Networks, and Influence on Organizational Effectiveness, Human Health, and Relationships. In *Handbook of Industrial, Work and Organizational Psychology, Volume 2: Organizational Psychology*, N. Anderson, D.S. Ones, H.K. Sinangil and C.Viswesvaran (eds). Thousand Oaks, CA: Sage Publications, pp. 188–205.

Leavitt, H. (1951), Some Effects of Certain Communication Patterns on Group Performance. *Journal of Abnormal and Social Psychology*, **46**: 38–50.

Loffredo, D.A., S.K. Opt and R. Harrington (2008), Communicator Style and MBTI® Extraversion–Introversion Domains. *Journal of Psychological Type*, **68**(4): 29–36.

Lowin, A. and J. Craig (1968), The Influence of Level of Performance on Managerial Style: An Experimental Object Lesson on the Ambiguity of Correlational Data. *Organizational Behavior and Human Performance*, **3**: 440–58.

Manev, I.M. and W.B. Stevenson (2001), Balancing Ties: Boundary Spanning and Influence in the Organization's Extended Network of Communication. *Journal of Business Communication*, **38**(2): 183–205.

Manstead, A.S.R., H.L. Wagner and C.J. MacDonald (1984), Face, Body, and Speech as Channels of Communication in the Detection of Deception. *Basic and Applied Social Psychology*, **5**(4): 317–32.

McCroskey, L., J. McCroskey and V. Richmond (2005), Applying Organizational Orientations Theory to Employees of Profit and Non-profit Organizations. *Communication Quarterly*, **53**(1): 21–40.

Mehra, A., M. Kilduff and D.J. Brass (2001), The Social Networks of High and Low Self-Monitors: Implications for Workplace Performance. *Administrative Science Quarterly*, **46**(1): 121–46.

Mintzberg, H. (1973), *The Nature of Managerial Work*. New York: Harper & Row.

Monge, P.R. and E.M. Eisenberg (1987), Emergent Communication Networks. In *Handbook of Organizational Communication: An Interdisciplinary Perspective*. F.M. Jablin, L.L. Putnam, K.H. Roberts and L.W. Porter (eds). Thousand Oaks, CA: Sage Publications, pp. 304–42.

O'Reilly, C.A., J. Chatman and J. Anderson (1987), Message Flow and Decision Making. In *Handbook of Organizational Communication: An Interdisciplinary Perspective*. F.M. Jablin, L.L. Putnam, K.H. Roberts and L.W. Porter (eds). Thousand Oaks, CA: Sage Publications, pp. 600–623.

Pearson, J.C., P.E. Nelson, S. Titsworth and L. Harter (2007), *Human Communication*, 3rd edn. New York: McGraw Hill.

Roberts, K.H. (1984), *Communicating in Organizations*. Chicago, IL: Science Research Associates.

Rogers Commission Report. (1986), U.S.C.S.S.h. 99-967, Editor. U.S. G. P. O: Washington D.C. p. 216. http://history.nasu.gov/rogersrep.

Schnake, M.E., M.P. Dumler, D.S. Cochran and T.R. Barnett (1990), Effects of Differences in Superior and Subordinate Perceptions of Superiors' Communication Practices. *Journal of Business Communication*, **27**(1): 37–50.

Siegel, J., V. Dubrovsky, S. Kiesler and T.W. McGuire (1986), Group Processes in Computer-Mediated Communication. *Organizational Behavior and Human Decision Processes*, **37**(2): 157–88.

Smither, J.W., M. London and R.R. Reilly (2005), Does Performance Improve Following Multisource Feedback? A Theoretical Model, Meta-Analysis, and Review of Empirical Findings. *Personnel Psychology*, **58**(1): 33–66.

Soda, G. and A. Zaheer (2010), The Interplay of Formal and Informal Organizational Architecture: Implications for Performance. Unpublished paper. Bocconi University: Milan, Italy.

Sproull, L. and S. Kiesler (1986), Reducing Social Context Cues: Electronic Mail in Organizational Communication. *Management Science*, **32**(11): 1492–512.

Steckler, N.A. and R. Rosenthal (1985), Sex Differences in Nonverbal and Verbal Communication with Bosses, Peers and Subordinates. *Journal of Applied Psychology*, **70**(1): 157–63.

Thomas, G.F., R. Zolin and J.L. Hartman (2009), The Central Role of Communication in Developing Trust and Its Effect on Employee Involvement. *Journal of Business Communication*, **46**(3): 287–310.

Ting-Toomey, S., G. Geo, P. Trubisky et al. (1991), Culture, Face Maintenance and Styles of Handling Interpersonal Conflict: A Study in Five Cultures. *International Journal of Conflict Management*, **2**: 275–96.

Ware, J. (1975), Seduction in the Classroom: the Doctor Fox Effect. *Midwest Academy of Management Proceedings*, pp. 20–23.

Webber, R.A. (1970), Perceptions of Interactions Between Superiors and Subordinates. *Human Relations*, **23**(3): 235–48.

Wert, S.R. and P. Salovey (2004), A Social Comparison Account Of Gossip. *Review of General Psychology*, **8**(2): 122–37.

8. Conflict

PREPARING FOR CLASS

Review the newspaper from the last few days and count the number of conflicts that are discussed. Classify each situation as political, organizational and business, or personal conflict. Be prepared to discuss these questions:

1. How many instances of conflict did you find?
2. What factors are involved in each conflict?
3. Using Figure 8.5 in this chapter, determine whether these conflict situations should be easy or difficult to resolve. Prepare to defend your diagnosis.

*   *

Consider these three examples. Firstly, the Kosovo and Bosnian peace agreement provides an all too familiar resolution to the years of conflict that divided the former Yugoslavia. The agreement partitions the country into sections where different ethnic factions can live. This has been a political strategy to resolve conflict that has saved many lives in several countries where there was serious conflict: India, Palestine and Ireland are examples of other countries where conflict was so intense that separating the groups was viewed as the only effective resolution (Kumar, 1997).

In the second example, Maria was born with music in her blood and she wanted to become a singer, maybe even a jazz singer. 'No way!' said her father, a bank manager with an economics degree and a Masters in banking from Esade. He was completely opposed to her on the matter. 'Darling, what's the problem? You can sing any time you want, with friends, in the shower, at the bars. But a profession is a profession and a hobby is a hobby. Do you understand?'

So choosing a college was very difficult for Maria. Her father told her, 'If you want to continue to study you must apply to a prestigious university here in Spain, or in Europe or the United States and study Law, Management, Economics, whatever: this will allow you to find a job, a real job, well paid, and then you can continue to sing, as a hobby. Otherwise,

269

you must find a job now. I don't want any more to talk about the Music Conservatory or studying jazz. Understood?'

But something changed when her sister brought home a brochure of a three-year course of Arts Management in her Department of Economics: the program included courses in art, music and painting, as well as courses in management of public goods, museums and broadcasting. Maria was pleasantly surprised when she found her father reading the brochure: he looked very interested.

In the third example: as her meeting approached with Johann and Michael, Marta felt the energy drain from her body. This had become a common feeling for her in her job as a mediator of disputes in her organization when she was facing a hard negotiation. When she entered the meeting, she saw the look of determination on the faces of Johann, the supervisor, and Michael, his subordinate. Marta had come to know this as a sign that both parties were going to take a hard line in the negotiations and that the resolution would be very difficult. She felt that the initial dispute, which was over Michael's poor performance appraisal rating, was a minor issue now. Both Johann and Michael were at a stage where each one wanted to prove that he was 'right'. It had become a matter of principle.

These three examples highlight the pervasiveness of conflict in our everyday life, which is most visible when it is between major parties: consider the Vietnam War, the Catholic–Protestant conflict in Northern Ireland, the Bosnian–Croatian conflict, the conflict in Rwanda, and the conflict in Afghanistan. Conflict between classes form an important topic in Marxist thought. Another type of conflict exists between governments and guerrilla groups, or groups engaged in asymmetric warfare.

In this chapter, we discuss the conflict process and how conflicts arise. We explore various styles of reacting to conflict and ways to manage and resolve conflict more effectively. We define conflict to include disagreements, the presence of tension or some other difficulty between two or more parties. It may occur between individuals or between groups. Conflict is caused when individuals or groups of individuals perceive that their goals are blocked. It can be public or private, formal or informal, or be approached rationally or irrationally. Conflict is an underlying theme in many areas of organizational behavior. For example, role conflicts of different types contribute to stress (see Chapter 4); exercising power and being involved in organization politics can be a source or a result of conflict; conflict can surface over differences in work tasks; and, obviously, there can be problems between people (interpersonal conflict), between groups (intergroup conflict), as well as within groups themselves (intragroup conflict).

While some level of conflict is healthy – even necessary – in organizations, it can also increase stress and have dysfunctional consequences as people take sides on issues such as budget allocation or goal priorities, or over how fairly they are being treated. Labor unions and management conflict over compensation and work conditions. Sometimes, the problems are minor and settled easily. Others go unresolved, or conflicts of varying intensity break out, from minor arguments to 'organizational warfare'. However, not all of the effects of conflict are bad. The key lies in how we view conflict and what we do to deal with it.

CONFLICT AS A PROCESS

Conflict is not a static condition; it is a dynamic process that involves several stages. Parties can go through the process in many different ways, and do so more than once. Figure 8.1 presents a model integrating different approaches to conflict that is the basis of our discussion of conflict in this chapter (Pondy, 1967; Thomas, 1990).

- Antecedent conditions.
- Perceived conflict.
- Manifest conflict.
- Conflict resolution or suppression.
- Aftermath.

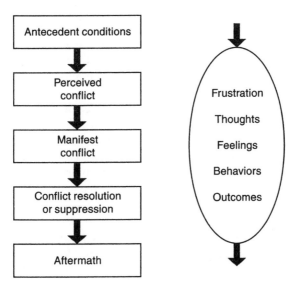

Figure 8.1   Conflict process

Antecedent conditions of conflict are the conditions that cause or precede a conflict episode. At this stage, conflict may remain below the surface because neither party presses its position. Sometimes an aggressive act can start the conflict process. For instance, one of your employees might deliberately hide tools that others need to do a job, or one department may have more resources than another department believes they should. Antecedents of conflict can also be subtle. Pressures on a production department to keep costs down may frustrate your marketing manager who wants to fill rush orders at short notice.

Perceived conflict is necessary for the conflict to progress. The parties must become aware of a threat. Any person might act to the disadvantage of another, but without awareness of the act, little else will happen. Even without an action, people might perceive a threat when none is there. When conflict, real or imaginary, is perceived it may trigger frustration, anger, fear or anxiety. Those involved start to question how much they can trust each other, and worry about their ability to cope with the difficulty. This stage of conflict is critical because this is when the parties tend to define the issues and start looking for ways to resolve their differences.

Perceived conflict develops into manifest conflict when people react to the perception. One of your employees might threaten to file a grievance, prompting you to take defensive steps. Other behaviors that signal manifest conflict include arguments, aggressive acts, appeal to goodwill, or constructive problem solving.

Conflict resolution can come about in several ways. Parties may agree about how to solve their difficulties and even take steps to prevent it in the future. Conflict can also be resolved when one party defeats another. Sometimes conflict is suppressed rather than resolved. This happens when the parties avoid strong reactions or try to ignore each other when they disagree.

Whether conflict is resolved or suppressed, feelings remain. Behaviors during the conflict aftermath can be just as varied as the ways in which conflict is manifested or resolved. Sometimes good feelings and harmony result; a new procedure may be developed that clarifies the relationships between the parties. For example, one of your employees might decide not to file a grievance because you are willing to agree with the union on a new rule that solves the original problem.

Unfortunately, the conflict aftermath can also result in poorer working relationships. If hard feelings and resentment persist, these can trigger the next conflict episode. For example, poor solutions or losses by one party may reduce communication or prepare each party for bigger battles to come. The key question is whether the resolution draws parties into cooperation or drives them further apart.

THE ROLE OF HISTORY IN CONFLICTS

Linkages between people and units of an organization persist over long periods of time. As a consequence, the parties develop a history of percep-tions, attitudes and behaviors toward each other. If one party has histori-cally been cooperative in its relationships toward others, a single incident of non-cooperation is likely to have no significant effect. On the other hand, a history of conflict can cause the parties to mistrust each other con-tinually, making opportunities for cooperation very difficult. In evaluating past behaviors, the parties are likely to put greatest weight on the most recent behaviors of the other.

For example, we have already noted the international political conflict in the former Yugoslavia. Conflict in that region, as well as many other regions, has long roots in history, sometimes dating back several hundreds of years. This is complicated when there are unresolved disputes where one or both sides feel that they have lost something in the past. These histori-cal traditions of conflict create difficulties for current-day negotiators who attempt to make opposing groups focus on modern issues.

VIEWPOINTS ON CONFLICT

There are different ways that you can think about conflict:

1. It is preventable.
2. It is inevitable.
3. It is healthy.

It is assumed, for example, that conflict can be avoided simply by making employees change their attitudes and behavior so that cooperation can prosper. It is also assumed that conflict is preventable if managers can create positive working relationships through good planning, and with policies and procedures that ensure mutual efforts toward common goals. This perspective has merit, of course, and is part of how managers should view their role. Some conflict in organizations is preventable, and some of it is a sign that something is wrong and can be corrected.

The second point of view – that conflict is inevitable and so there is no way to eliminate it entirely – may be true for many reasons; we have cited some throughout this book. For example, not all organizational goals are compatible. The goal of reducing costs is often in conflict with goals that call for innovation. Organizational design also leads to conflict. Employees are grouped into departments of specialists, each with its own point of view. Conflicts may arise between managers and auditors because the required work for each group actually creates problems for the other. Conflict also arises because plans and policies are rarely perfect enough to cover all situations that might arise.

If some conflict is inevitable, then trying to prevent it may be more frustrating (and time-consuming) than the conflict itself. The best strategy for you is to accept the inevitability of certain kinds of conflict. Your employees can be trained to anticipate where disagreements are bound to arise, and to resolve them before they become unmanageable. That way, we can keep conflict within tolerable limits and manage it effectively.

The third point of view is that some degree of conflict is healthy for an organization (Cosier and Dalton, 1990). When would this be the case? Suppose that the marketing, research and production departments never experienced tensions or disagreements with each other. The relative peace between the departments might mean that each department is not doing its job effectively. For example, marketing staff may not be responding to new product or market opportunities, so they rarely suggest changes that would create tensions with research and production.

Healthy benefits of conflict include creative approaches to resolving problems and making decisions. For example, Jehn (1995) reported that some level of conflict was productive in groups performing non-routine tasks but when tasks were routine, the presence of conflict reduced satisfaction and liking of members. In Chapter 6, we discussed some dysfunctional aspects of group dynamics such as groupthink. Groupthink occurs when groups attempt to achieve consensus and eliminate conflict. While this is useful so that groups can make progress, it has dysfunctional side-effects. Figure 8.2 suggests that there is probably some optimal level of conflict:

- Too little conflict in an organization can be a threat to effectiveness. Individuals may avoid each other instead of interacting to work on generating new ideas and developing creative approaches to solving problems.
- Too much conflict can also hamper effectiveness. With constant disagreement over too many issues, or through failures to appreciate the needs and problems of others, innovations may never come about, customers may be lost and key issues may go unresolved. The organization will suffer if members are consumed with defending themselves or with winning internal organizational battles.
- At the optimum level of conflict, quite different things happen. There are active attempts to improve quality and to introduce changes that might make the organization more competitive and more effective

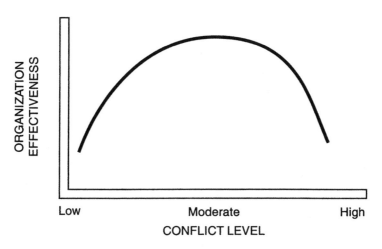

Figure 8.2   Optimum levels of organizational conflict

or efficient. Employees are stimulated; they are not bored and with-drawn. Individuals with different perspectives are willing to present their ideas and this may lead to improved performance. Tensions and frustrations are accepted and channeled into productive, rather than destructive, effort.

INTRAGROUP CONFLICT

Many managers have to be concerned with managing teams and groups. Often there is conflict between team members as well as between team members and the team leader. Much of what you should know about this appears in Chapter 6 on groups. Here, however, we focus on the more specific issue of managing conflict in project teams. The issues that could lead to conflict on these teams are (Thamhain and Wileman, 1975):

- deadlines;
- priorities between projects;
- managerial procedures for the project;
- technical compromises;
- who should be on the project team;
- cost control;
- scheduling;
- personality differences.

Different issues are important at different stages of a project (Jehn and Mannix, 2001). While deadlines are the most dominant issue over the life of a project, some appear to be related to the stage of the project (Lock, 2007). For example, in the initial stage more conflict is about deadlines, cost estimates, specific work assignments or allocation of resources (Graham, 1982). This is often because each project incorporates a degree of innovation and team members may be inexperienced in some aspects of the project.

What happens in this first stage is particularly important. Effective teams usually begin with low process conflict and low relationship conflict, both of which tend to increase over time (Jehn and Mannix, 2001). Interestingly, research shows that teams which begin with a high level of trust may experience lower trust among team members in later stages, as well as reduced individual autonomy and weaker task interdependence (Curseu and Schruijer, 2010; Langfred, 2007). When there is diversity of membership, teams in which members are interpersonally similar will be more creative, have greater social integration and have less task conflict in later stages, while teams with initially low interpersonal congruence are less effective overall (Polzer et al., 2002).

During the middle project stages conflict emerges over dates and management procedures that often leads to the first technical compromises (Archibald, 1992). Other sources of conflict in the middle stages are individual autonomy of project managers, issues of task interdependence, the management of the project, and mid-project assessment criteria.

In the final project stage, costs and deadlines cause team management problems. If the team members have a strong sense of ownership of the project, these types of conflicts can be resolved by increasing cooperation.

As teams deal with these conflicts over the life of the project, they tend to restructure themselves (Langfred, 2007). The team leader has a major effect on how well members resolve conflict and restructure themselves, and the project kick-off meeting is of great importance (Thoms, 1998). Team leaders with high levels of emotional intelligence and empathy are perceived to be more effective in managing teams (Clarke, 2010). They are likely to be better at managing the emotions of team members and, therefore, are more likely to lead more effective teams (Ayoko and Callan, 2010).

INTERGROUP CONFLICT

Organizations are made up of groups of groups, which are separated by 'faultlines'. A faultline exists when there is some factor that is clearly distinguishable between groups (Jehn and Bezrukova, 2010). Organizationally, for example, the process of organization design intentionally creates faultlines when departmental units are created on the basis of functional specialization or product specialization, or units are geographically dispersed (Polzer et al., 2006) . There can also be formal status faultlines between different levels of management (Jiatao and Hambrick, 2005). Organizational faultlines tend to be clear, and usually members are aware of them. However, when the faultlines are based on racial or demographic differences they may be dormant and activated generally when group membership differences become salient (Jehn and Bezrukova, 2010).

When one group is in conflict with another group, certain positive things similar to competition happen. Conflict can stimulate the group members to work harder to accomplish the task, especially if that helps them to protect their group or to look better than the other group. The group becomes more cohesive and coordinates its efforts to present a united front. Internal divisiveness may be avoided because it would weaken the group. In time, with intergroup conflict, members are also more likely to accept directive or autocratic leadership if it helps them in the conflict.

Groups in conflict will tend to view the other party negatively – perhaps even in threatening or hostile terms. Members will increase their alertness to the other group's actions and reduce the communication between groups. A win–lose mentality often develops. These intergroup behaviors can work against reaching a constructive outcome of the conflict. For example, demographic faultlines in joint venture management groups can lead to task and emotional conflict, behavioral disintegration and low performance (Jiatao and Hambrick, 2005). Faultlines between groups created by geographical dispersion have been related to increased conflict and low intergroup trust, especially when the groups are homogeneous in nationality (Polzer et al., 2006). Finally, when the faultlines are highly salient to group members, there may be lower member satisfaction, lower group performance and more coalitions formed (Jehn and Bezrukova, 2010).

WHAT TRIGGERS CONFLICT

To manage conflict situations effectively you have to understand the causes. Three major sources of conflict are shown in Figure 8.3:

1. Characteristics of individuals.
2. Situational conditions.
3. Organizational conditions.

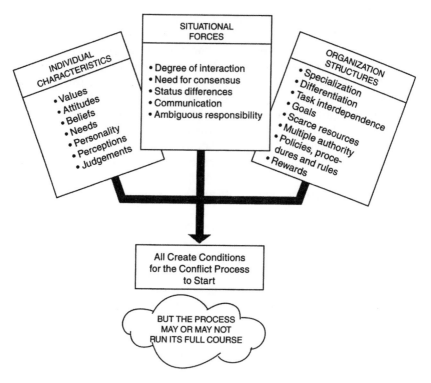

Figure 8.3   Antecedents and causes of conflict

Individual Characteristics

Individual differences make some people more likely to engage in conflict than others. While you have been introduced to these characteristics in earlier chapters, have we want to focus on how they influence conflict.

Values, attitudes and beliefs

Our feelings about what is right and wrong, and our predispositions to behave positively or negatively toward an event, can easily be a source of conflict. A worker who values autonomy and independence will probably react negatively when supervised too closely. Divergent values between groups can create tensions within the group as well as with other key groups in the organization; they may be a source of faultlines, and can lead to lower member satisfaction, reduced commitment to the group and increased desire to leave the group (Jehn et al., 1999).

Needs and personality

Another factor that is important in conflict and conflict resolution is personality. For instance, conflict can result when individuals differ in their needs and personality. For example, an energy company with five highly sequentially interdependent processing divisions attempted to improve performance by changing the criteria for promotion and salary increases to a divisional return on investment (ROI), from an overall corporate measure. The top management also sought to hire division heads who were entrepreneurial and high in achievement motivation. This strategy causes problems because the high-achievement-oriented division managers preferred to be evaluated by performance measures that did not depend on the work of others (see Chapter 3 on motivation). Personality is also a factor in how individuals resolve conflict. While all of the Big Five personality dimensions (see Chapter 1) are related to the style of conflict resolution (see discussion later in this chapter), the strongest predictors are agreeableness and extraversion (Wood and Bell, 2008). One study showed that persons with a strong tendency to focus on the involvement of others (similar to agreeableness) are more likely to make concessions so as to avoid straining relationships (Amanatullah et al., 2008). Agreeableness is also involved in preferences for conflict resolution. Persons low in agreeableness preferred the assertive use of power in resolving conflict (Graziano et al., 1996).

Demographic differences

Some important faultlines that separate groups are age, gender, racial and ethnic differences. Some, but not all, arise as organizations try to be more diverse, but diversity can shape conflict, which in turn affects performance (Pelled et al., 1999). While teams with diverse functional backgrounds are more likely to experience task conflict, race diversity and organization tenure differences lead to more emotional conflict, but age diversity appears to ameliorate emotional conflict. Teams in which members have very diverse values have lower satisfaction and commitment to the group (Jehn et al., 1999). What does seem to facilitate performance of diverse work teams is when the members: (1) have a strong team orientation; (2) focus on process; and (3) have a strong sense of similarity with others in the group (Polzer et al., 2002; Mohammed and Angell, 2004).

Perception and judgment

If we perceive another person as a threat, we may act toward them in a way that increases the potential for conflict. Conflict can also arise when people commit judgment errors such as the 'fundamental attribution error' (see

Chapter 2). One party might blame another for a problem and attribute its cause to the other person's motives. Conflict is more likely when situations are ambiguous, because ambiguity contributes to misperceptions and incorrect judgments.

Situational Conditions

A second set of factors that can contribute to conflicts considers the conditions found in different situations. In Chapter 1, our model shows that behavior is a function of individual characteristics and the environment. Conflict as a behavior also has environmental causes. In this subsection we focus on common situational causes; in the next subsection, we consider those found in common organizational environments.

Degree of interaction

Conflict is more likely when people are physically close, and when they need to interact. With frequent interactions such as occurs in complex projects, conflict potential increases even more. Interactions are the stuff of life in organizations, but they need not result in conflict. It has been shown that more productive work groups are ones that actively interact with each other by asking questions, working jointly on projects, and by sharing information and achievements (Ancona, 1990). One study demonstrated that in low-conflict organizations, ties between groups were strong and marked by frequent, productive interactions. In high-conflict organizations, ties were strong within the groups, but not between them (Nelson, 1989).

Need for consensus

Conflict may be a function of whether agreements are needed between the parties. For example, many organizational purchases are routine and require little interaction or agreement among departments, but consensus might be needed when many users may share purchasing items such as computers or office equipment. Conflicts over quality, cost or location could occur when pressure for consensus exists.

Status differences and incongruence

A classic analysis of status conflict in the restaurant industry was done by Whyte (1949). For a variety of reasons, cooks believed they had higher status than waitresses. When waitresses communicated their customer orders to cooks, the cooks often reacted as if people of lower status were personally ordering them around. They often responded to the waitresses by delaying meals.

Communication

Communication is a two-edged sword. Barriers to communication can cause conflict, but so can the opportunity to communicate. We have seen how the need to interact can stimulate conflict. When we communicate with others, we may discover unfair conditions or begin to see other people as threats. This can start conflict that would have been avoided with less communication.

Ambiguous responsibilities

When there is ambiguity about roles and responsibilities, conflict can arise when individuals or groups posture for position. In one organization, the advertising department took the initiative to locate and order various supplies on their own. The purchasing group accused them of overstepping their authority and violating procedures. This led to continuous conflict, and the distractions eventually affected the quality and success of advertising.

Organization Conditions

Organizational conditions naturally cause faultlines when large numbers of people come together. These are rooted in roles and responsibilities, interdependencies, goals, policies and reward systems.

Specialization and differentiation

Organizations also create expectations that make cooperation difficult. The classic relationships between production, marketing and research units provide a good case in point. Each unit has its own responsibilities and concerns. Marketing may concern itself with customers and competition. Production seeks cost reduction and efficiency. Research focuses on technical improvements with emphasis on scientific objectives. These factors can create a sharp faultline between these units and can be the basis for many disagreements. Nevertheless, it is very appropriate for these units to have different priorities. As we said, some conflict is inevitable and healthy, even though it may be difficult to resolve.

The distinction between line and staff departments is also a basis for conflict. Line departments are those that are directly part of the organization mission, such as production departments. Staff units, such as human resources or legal departments, are indirectly involved and exist primarily to support and assist the line units. They often evaluate other units in the organization and develop new programs and procedures for them. Staff units also impose policies and procedures that line units may not understand or cannot accept. The problem is made worse because staff personnel, compared to line personnel, are frequently younger, better educated and have fewer years of experience. Staff personnel may also use their own jargon, dress differently and have direct access to organizational leaders.

Goal setting

Clear goals can be an excellent source of direction and motivation in organizations, but they do not ensure that conflict is minimized or prevented. Even when goals are clear, the method for achieving those goals may be a source of conflict. Managers all pursuing the same goals can seriously disagree over new products or services, or whether to withdraw from certain markets.

Goals can also cause conflict within a single unit of an organization. For example, within a production department, efficiency goals can be incompatible with safety and maintenance goals. A production manager might run equipment at high speeds and reduce maintenance as a way of increasing productivity and reducing costs. This strategy can result in increased accidents and also increased long-run costs because poor equipment maintenance may cause it to break down sooner.

Scarce resources

Resources are almost always scarce in an organization, meaning that not enough exist to satisfy all the desires people might have. When resources are scarce, this may lead to conflict over the few resources that do exist. This engenders sharing of, and competition for, resources, either of which can create disagreements.

Multiple authority and influence

Many organizations are designed so that each employee has only one superior. In management theory, this is known as the principle of unity of command. It is intended to avoid putting employees in a position where they receive conflicting demands from higher-level managers. Unity of command is difficult to maintain, because every employee is subject to many influences besides their immediate superior. A request from any high-level manager in our organizations is difficult for most of us to ignore. In addition, peers can influence a fellow worker. These multiple sources of input can create conflict within the individual.

Policies and procedures

One purpose of an organization's policies and procedures is to reduce conflict by clarifying roles and responsibilities and smoothing the interaction between people. For example, a policy may state that computer maintenance is the sole responsibility of the technology assistance department.

Then, when computer problems or failures arise, disagreements about who is to fix it are then less likely to occur.

However, policies and procedures may contribute to conflict when they make people feel frustrated or insulted because they are overly controlled. Controls restrict our freedom and autonomy – something most of us value. We may feel a loss of trust and respect when controls are excessive.

Rewards

Disagreements commonly arise over how we are rewarded. Suppose you work as a medical claims adjuster for an insurance company and are told to provide good service and award claims appropriately without overpaying. When customers call with questions, you take the time to respond to them. When a claim is unclear, you contact the physician or hospital involved. At the end of each month, however, your supervisor tells you that you have not processed enough claims. You realize that to process more claims, you cannot continue to spend so much time talking to customers or clarifying information. You are experiencing tension over whether the quantity or the quality of your work is more important.

DIAGNOSING CONFLICT

Figure 8.4 shows a framework for diagnosing conflict situations (Greenhalgh, 1986). When we attempt to understand the issues involved in a particular conflict situation, there are many dimensions of conflict that we should consider:

- The issue in question.
- The size of the stakes.
- The interdependence of parties.
- The continuity of the interaction.
- The leadership.
- The involvement of third parties.
- The perceived progress of conflict.

The Issue in Question

Issues that participants view as matters of principle are the most difficult to resolve. In this case, they have made the issue one where a possible conflict of values and beliefs systems is involved. Occasionally participants in conflict situations make winning their focus, and saving face becomes

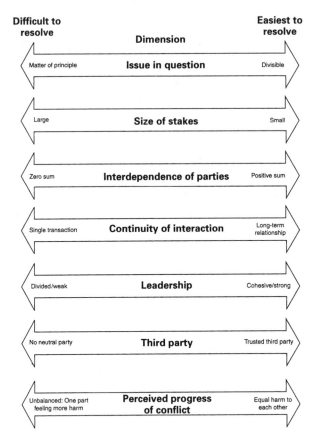

Difficult to resolve	**Dimension**	Easiest to resolve
Matter of principle	**Issue in question**	Divisible
Large	**Size of stakes**	Small
Zero sum	**Interdependence of parties**	Positive sum
Single transaction	**Continuity of interaction**	Long-term relationship
Divided/weak	**Leadership**	Cohesive/strong
No neutral party	**Third party**	Trusted third party
Unbalanced: One part feeling more harm	**Perceived progress of conflict**	Equal harm to each other

Source: Adapted from Greenlaugh (1986).

Figure 8.4   Conflict diagnostic model

more important than the original issue. This significantly complicates conflict resolution. The easiest conflicts to resolve are over issues or things that
are easily divided. This allows for compromises in positions so that both
parties can view the outcomes as a partial victory at least. For example, if
the issue is over a sum of money, compromise is possible because money
can be divided.

The Size of the Stakes

When the stakes in the outcome are large, conflict is more difficult to
resolve than when smaller stakes are involved. As discussed earlier,

---

Spotlight 8.1   Conflict resolution in the workplace: the role of arbitration panels in German employment relations

Germany is one country that has extensively formalized dispute resolution at work. Work councils are a widely used approach to deal with management hostility. When firm-level agreements are negotiated by unions without the direct involvement of work councils in German organizations, there is a greater tendency to use these arbitration panels.

One of the basic ideas underlying the use of arbitration panels and work councils is to institutionalize the process of conflict resolution in ways that focus on facts as opposed to the often emotion-laden processes that occur. These arbitration panels are an important mechanism for venting problems because they convert disputes into situations that allow them to be easily processed and resolved (Behrens, 2007).

---

organizations often experience conflict over budget allocations. The difficulty in resolving this type of conflict is often directly correlated with the proportion of budget that is being debated. If the proportion is considered by participants to be large, it is likely that a great deal of debate will occur because the parties are more likely to view the large sums of money involved as important for achievement of their individual unit's goals.

The Interdependence of Parties

The interdependence of the parties is also an important dimension for diagnosing conflict. In zero-sum interdependence, a gain by one side means a loss by the other side. These situations are more difficult than positive-sum interdependence, which is where compromise settlements can lead to gains for both sides of the conflict. Continuing the example of budget negotiations, when finite budget amounts are available and subunits are conflicting over their share of the budget, it would be a zero-sum negotiation. An increase given to one unit would be at the expense of another. An illustrative example of interdependence is the 'Ugli Orange' bargaining simulation in which two persons haggle over how to distribute a single orange. The negotiators are in interesting positions. One wants only the pulp of the orange, while the other wants only the skin. The case is a distributing game that could become cooperative through communication. Indeed, clarifying the specific needs of both parties would have reduced the information asymmetry – the potential cause of the conflict – in order to arrive at an optimal solution: one getting the pulp, the other the skin (Fischer et al., 1991).

The Continuity of the Interaction

A fourth dimension in diagnosing conflict is the continuity of the interaction among the parties in conflict. This considers the relationship among the parties. If we are talking about a conflict that has arisen between a firm and one of its long-term customers, it is likely that the conflict will be easier to resolve because both parties have an interest in protecting the long-term relationship. As a result, they may be more willing to seek compromise and may be interested in protecting the other side. When negotiations are between parties that have no previous relationship and have no plans for a future relationship, negotiation is likely to be more difficult.

The Leadership

The leadership of conflicting parties is another dimension to consider. When there is a clear leader who has the authority to negotiate and make decisions, conflict should be easier to resolve than when there is a lack of a clear leader. This issue is often evident in labor negotiations. If the chief management negotiator is not viewed as a party who can make decisions independently, and that may be second-guessed by the board of directors or other senior members of the organization, it complicates negotiations. The same can be said for the labor side. When both sides in a conflict have strong leadership who can decisively negotiate an agreement, it increases the confidence of all parties that promises made will be kept and supported, and thus makes the conflict easier to resolve.

The Involvement of Third Parties

Using third parties such as mediators or arbitrators increases the ease of negotiating a resolution to the conflict. The role of third parties is discussed in more detail in the next section, but their primary contribution is an objective view of the issues. Third parties may be able to see potential compromises that are not considered by parties who have a strong interest in the outcomes of the conflict negotiations.

The Perceived Progress of the Conflict

Finally, the perception of parties in conflict about the progress of the conflict is important in its resolution. When parties believe that both sides are compromising and giving up something of value, conflict is easier to resolve. When the perceptions of one party are that they have suffered more harm than the other party, they are likely to resist additional compromises until they feel things are more in balance.

CONFLICT RESOLUTION STYLES

Each of us deals with conflict in different ways. Some of us have an initial tendency to escape, and others of us are more prone to become involved. Once involved, people also vary in how they behave. There are five different styles of reacting to conflict, drawn from several important conflict theories (Blake and Mouton, 1969; Thomas and Kilmann, 1974) and there is some research which supports the validity of this approach (Van de Vliert and Kabanoff, 1990):

1. Avoiding.
2. Accommodating.
3. Competing.
4. Compromising.
5. Collaborating.

These five styles are set in a two-dimensional model, shown in Figure 8.5. Each style is a combination of these two dimensions and each style has different characteristics and different uses (Thomas and Kilmann, 1974). The horizontal dimension reflects the degree to which one party has concern for the other party's needs, interests and goals. High concern reflects itself in cooperation and a desire to maintain the relationship. The vertical dimension refers to how concerned a party is for its own needs and goals. If you are high on this dimension, you are assertive, and your main desire is to achieve your own goals, with little or no degree of sacrificing them.

Avoiding

Some of us become emotionally upset by conflict. Painful memories of past conflicts may make us want to withdraw from disagreement. Avoiding conflict can be based on a belief that conflict is evil,

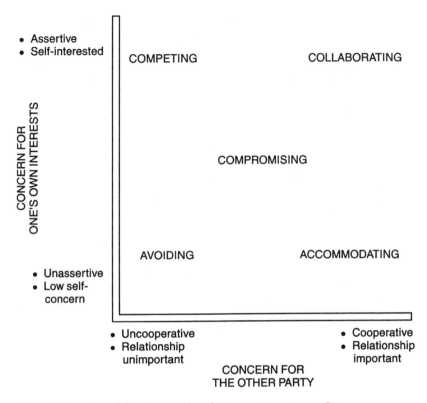

Figure 8.5   A model of personal stylistic reactions to conflict

unnecessary or undignified. If you are high in emotional intelligence you may also have a tendency to avoid conflict to protect yourself from potential stress situations, not to be involved in issues that have little meaning, or issues that have a low probability of success (Godse and Thingujam, 2010). You can withdraw by simply leaving the scene of a conflict. You can refuse to become involved by using silence or changing the topic of conversation. Psychologically, avoiders can also deny the existence of conflict or ignore it when it arises. Teams that had complex, non-routine projects functioned better when an avoiding strategy was used. It permitted them to focus more on task performance (De Dreu and Van Vianen, 2001).

Avoiding conflict can be wise when issues are insignificant or when the costs of challenging someone outweigh the benefits. It may also be useful when there is little chance of success. Why pursue a lost cause? Avoiding also buys time. It gives others a chance to cool down or to seek more information. Finally, it might be better to avoid conflict when others can resolve it more effectively or when it concerns the wrong issue.

Accommodating

Accommodating means you give in to the wishes of another person. Accommodators feel it is better to give up their own goals rather than risk alienating or upsetting others. Like avoiders, the value system of accommodators focuses on the desired involvement of others and they are high in agreeableness (Amanatullah et al., 2008). They have a perspective that conflict is bad, but rather than avoid it they give in so as to maintain or strengthen a relationship. This style can reflect generosity, humility or obedience. An accommodator may also feel that selfishness, an undesirable trait, is what causes most conflict.

Accommodation may be a very good strategy when you are on the wrong side of an issue; it permits the correct position to win and is a sign of reasonableness. It can be taken as a gesture of goodwill and helps to maintain a relationship. Giving in may be a good thing when the issue is much more important to the other party. Fighting is not very productive when the other party has much to lose and you have little to gain.

Competing

If your style is to compete, you pursue your own wishes at the expense of the other party (win–lose approach). The competitor defines conflict as a game to be won; that he or she is not about to become the loser. Competitors are both assertive and uncooperative. Winning means success and accomplishment; losing means failure, weakness and a loss of status. Competitors will use many different tactics such as threats, arguments, persuasion or direct orders. A competing approach appears to work well for design teams for which innovation is a key outcome (Badke-Schaub et al., 2010). However you should use this approach with some caution since a competitive approach to conflict resolution can result in lower team performance (Somech et al., 2009).

A forceful position may be the best style in crises, when there is no time for disagreement and discussion. If the issue is simply not debatable, the manager may have to deal with opposition in a directive manner. As a manager, you may wish to use this style when unpopular but necessary decisions must be made, such as ordering that overtime work is necessary to meet a deadline for an important customer. Competition may also be a style to use when the other party has a tendency to take advantage of you. Competing serves as a way to protect yourself.

Compromising

If you use a compromising style, you give and take based on the belief that people cannot always have their way; you think you should try to find a middle ground that you can live with. Compromise as way to resolve conflict is used by effective design teams which worked well together and are more innovative (Badke-Schaub et al., 2010). As a compromiser, you would look for feasible solutions and will use techniques such as trading, bargaining, smoothing over differences or voting. You value willingness to set personal wishes and sensitivity to the other person's position. Through compromise, relationships can endure if people hear each other's point of view and if they try to arrive at a fair agreement.

Compromise is a common way of dealing with conflict. It may be a particularly useful technique when two parties have relatively equal power and mutually exclusive goals. Situations like this are zero-sum: what one party gains, the other loses. Compromise can also be useful when there are time constraints. Time may not be available for problems that require a great deal of effort to resolve all the issues. Compromise can allow for a temporary solution until more time can be devoted to unravel and analyze the complexities. Finally, compromise may be useful when collaboration or competition fails to lead to a solution between the parties.

Spotlight 8.2 Conflict management styles of Turkish managers

Studies of the way managers in Turkey resolve conflict show that they are more likely to use a collaborating style instead of compromising or avoiding. This could be attributed to the fact that Turkey is a country high in collectivist values. There are some different strategies as a function of other factors. For instance, if competitive success is important these managers are more likely to prefer a competing style. If they value working alone, there is less collaboration. Finally, if one is able to subordinate personal needs to group interests, collaborating and accommodating are more likely to be used as methods of conflict resolution (Tabak, 2010).

Collaborating

Collaborating is a willingness to accept the other party's needs, while asserting your own (win–win). If you collaborate, you believe that there is some reasonable chance that a solution can be found to satisfy both parties in the conflict. Such a solution might not be possible, but a collaborator believes that it is worth trying to find one. For example, an organization planning to install a new computer system can use a collaborative approach. Different departments can join together to purchase the equipment or to design the system that meets various needs. Collaboration requires that both the parties express their needs and goals, and work diligently and creatively to generate all kinds of solutions.

Collaboration, therefore, requires openness and trust, as well as hard work. It follows the principles of good problem solving and decision making. Collaboration is useful when each party is strongly committed to different goals and when compromise is potentially very costly. It is also useful when people agree on goals, but disagree on means to achieve them. Collaboration can lead to an appreciation of other people's point of view. Therefore, it can strengthen relationships if mutual respect is maintained. When collaboration is successful, the commitment to the solution is high.

Style Flexibility: Overuse and Underuse

There can be harmful implications if any style is overused or underused (see Table 8.1). For example, a collaborating approach to resolving conflict was found not to be effective for design teams (Badke-Schaub et al., 2010). Managers should be flexible enough to use a particular style when it best suits the situation. This would require a diagnosis of the conflict conditions, the selection of an appropriate style, and the ability and willingness to use different styles. Managers should be trained to diagnose and practice each style.

IMPROVING YOUR CONFLICT MANAGEMENT STYLE

By conflict management, we mean that a manager takes an active role in addressing conflict situations and intervenes if needed. There are a number of ways to deal with conflict, ranging from preventing conflict to resolving it. Although avoiding conflict is a useful alternative, too much avoidance can be very damaging to an organization because problems will not be solved. Figure 8.6 shows three classes of ways to manage conflict:

1. Selecting and using one of the five styles discussed above.
2. Confrontation techniques.
3. Improving organization practices.

Table 8.1   Style flexibility, overuse and underuse of conflict reaction styles

Style	Overuse: using the style too much	Underuse: using the style too little
Avoiding	Subordinates deprived of help Disagreements persist Coordination suffers Subordinates decide Issues are not raised	Stirs unnecessary hostility Subordinates lose independence Nonavoider is overburdened Failure to set priorities
Accommodating	Lose self-respect/recognition Deprive others of ideas Seen as indecisive, weak Burdens others excessively Others feel manipulated into reciprocating later	Seen as rigid, unreasonable Prevents goodwill Ignores exceptions to rules False sense of losing face when opposite may be true
Competing	Others avoid competitor Makes others repeated losers Cuts off information from others Subordinate reluctance to fight Subordinates give in easily	Lose self-esteem Feel powerless, controlled by others Relinquish decision making Avoid/accommodate too much
Compromising	Others tire of 'deals' Gamesmanship atmosphere Game becomes more important than the issues Merits of issues can be lost	Seen as rigid, unreasonable Trapped into dealing and power struggles Lose opportunities to ease tensions
Collaborating	Some problems not worth it Unnecessary when stakes are low Can block accommodating Vulnerability to manipulation by others	Lose mutual-gain solutions Unduly pessimistic Lose chances for creativity Lose subordinate commitment Lose team cohesiveness

Source: Thomas and Kilmann (1974).

Many people have a dominant style of dealing with conflict and rarely or never use more than one or two other styles. A manager would benefit by appreciating and learning to use all styles. This would broaden the manager's repertoire in coping with disagreements, and help to prevent the costs of overuse and underuse of styles.

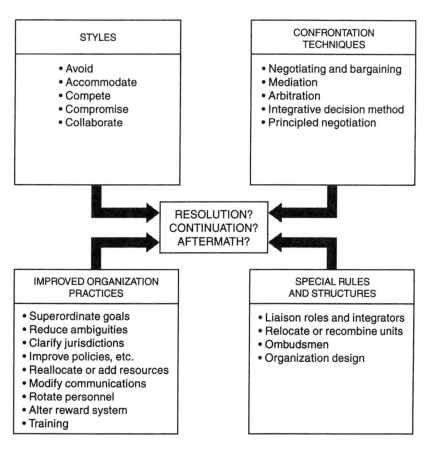

Figure 8.6   Conflict management strategies

Confrontation Techniques

We are not naturally disposed toward cooperating in the face of disagreement. It takes a special effort on our part to overcome past habits and attempt collaborative approaches. These are often referred to as confrontation techniques, and require that parties in conflict decide to face each other on the issues, and to do so constructively. The parties must be willing to work together to arrive at a consensus decision, one that both parties can accept. They do not avoid or give in. They may compete or compromise somewhat, but the major emphasis of confrontation techniques is to collaborate to find mutually acceptable and longer-lasting solutions. The aim is for both parties to satisfy their needs and goals to the greatest extent possible. Effective confrontation requires skill and experience and, above all, a positive and constructive attitude in which the parties are open to ideas and information.

In confrontation methods, third parties such as outside consultants or mediators from government agencies that offer such services are frequently used. Sometimes they come from within an organization, usually from the human resources department. Sometimes a specially trained manager can act as a third party in conflict resolution. As discussed earlier, the presence of a third party increases the chances of resolution. A third party can see to it that certain steps are followed, be a source of help and advice, make sure that all opinions are heard, and assist in many process decisions, such as when to have the parties work separately. In some instances, the third party may even make critical decisions that are binding on the parties.

Bargaining

Bargaining is primarily a compromising style, but effective bargainers use a variety of techniques. They will occasionally act competitively and use force or threats. They will use accommodation, hoping that a concession on their part will stimulate the other party to concede a point in return. It is also possible for two parties to collaborate on some issues, jointly searching for a solution that is useful to both.

In many bargaining situations, the goal of each party is to obtain the most it can, often at the expense of the other party. As discussed earlier, one factor that influences this behavior is the continuity of interaction. If the relationship is not a long-term one, people may drive a very hard bargain. You may bargain hard when buying a car, assuming you can buy elsewhere if the bargaining falls. In a labor–management negotiation, though, bargaining is tempered by the fact that the parties must work together when it is over.

Mediation

Mediation is often used in labor–management negotiations, as well as in many other social settings, such as an alternative to going to court. The parties can use third-party assistance to arrive at a solution. If both parties agree, a mediator is called in. Mediators are not empowered to make decisions or impose a solution, but they use many techniques to resolve differences. They may make suggestions and monitor the interaction of the parties. They can ease tensions with their methods and add objectivity to the process.

Arbitration

Arbitration is another third-party approach to conflict resolution. Arbitrators actually make decisions that bind both parties. Arbitrators are used predominantly in labor–management situations, such as when contract negotiations have reached an impasse. Another use is for grievances. The arbitrator hears both sides and may even follow a courtroom model. The points of view of both parties are presented. When the arbitrator has heard enough, he or she takes ample time to study the issues, then makes a decision, which is binding on both parties.

Principled Negotiation

Principled negotiation is based on a collaborative approach to problem solving (Fischer et al., 1991). Table 8.2 outlines the elements of the technique, and its four major requirements are highlighted in bold. Principled negotiation is compared to 'soft' and 'hard' approaches to conflict resolution:

- The soft approach is similar to accommodating and emphasizes giving in as a way to maintain a good relationship.
- The hard approach is similar to competing and emphasizes one party winning over the other and could lead to poor team performance (Somech et al., 2009).

Principled negotiation emphasizes the problem and tries to make the parties in conflict collaborate toward mutual gain. There are four steps in principled negotiation:

1. Separate the people from the problem. Instead of blaming each other, the parties must share their perceptions and needs, and put themselves in each other's shoes. This reduces the effects of harmful emotions. They must allow each other to let off steam in an accepting way. Active listening is essential. The problem must be stated in a way that contains no accusations and does not deny the goals and values of the parties. It is better to say, 'The problem is that we cannot agree on how to test the product', than, 'Your idea of a test is nonsense. We can't afford to do it.'
2. Focus on interests, not positions. Each party needs to state its interests and make its position explicit. For example, one party might say, 'What I want is a product test that is thorough and realistic'. The other party might say, 'What I want is a product test that is

Table 8.2   The principled negotiation technique compared to soft and hard methods of conflict resolution

Soft (relationship-oriented)	Hard (goal-oriented)	Principled negotiation (problem-oriented)
Participants are friends	Participants are adversaries	Participants are problem-solvers
The goal is agreement	The goal is victory	The goal is a wise agreement
Make concessions to cultivate the relationship	Demand concessions as a condition of the relationship	**SEPARATE THE PEOPLE FROM THE PROBLEM**
Be soft on the people and the problem	Be hard on the people and the problem	Be soft on people, hard on the problem
Trust others	Distrust others	Proceed independently of trust
Change your position easily	Dig in to your position	**FOCUS ON INTERESTS, NOT POSITIONS**
Make offers	Make threats	Explore interests
Disclose your bottom line	Mislead as to your bottom line	Avoid having a bottom line
Accept one-sided losses to reach agreement	Demand one-sided gains as the price of agreement	**INVENT OPTIONS FOR MUTUAL GAINS**
Search for the single answer: the one they will accept	Search for the single answer: the one you will accept	Develop multiple options to choose from; decide later
Insist on agreement	Insist on your position	**INSIST ON OBJECTIVE CRITERIA**
Try to avoid a contest of will	Try to win a contest of will	Try to reach a result based on standards independent of will
Yield of pressure	Apply pressure	Be reasonable; yield to principle, not pressure

Source: Fisher and Ury (1991).

feasible and done in a month.' Focusing on interests legitimizes the expression of needs without demeaning the other party. In a subtle way, the expression of interests also focuses the parties on the problem and on the future, rather than on each other and the troubled past. Together, the parties are hard on the problem, but soft on each other.

3. Invent options for mutual gain. The parties jointly generate a number of possible solutions, avoiding premature evaluation that might resolve their disagreement. During this process, they may uncover additional interests. They can examine how much cost and risk they are willing to accept. Common interests can be identified as well. In this manner, options can be generated that are more sensitive to both parties' needs.

4. Insist on objective criteria. Eventually, the parties should evaluate the options. Objective criteria consistent with principled negotiation include fairness, workability and the durability of the solution. The parties should openly ask, 'Which solutions do you consider to be fair?' or, 'Let's identify those solutions that will work and that will be lasting'. Solutions should also satisfy each party's interests as much as is possible.

IMPROVING ORGANIZATIONAL RESPONSES TO CONFLICT

Earlier in this chapter we discussed why the organizational context itself might be the cause of conflict in the organization. You should know and understand these causes so that you can take steps to try to change them.

Setting Superordinate Goals

Goals should be set that draw units into collaborative efforts. The dean of a college of business can unite the accounting, finance, management and marketing departments to work together in a fundraising campaign. If administrators, faculty, alumni and students meet together to plan the campaign, they can decide on how to approach different donors. Goals can also be set concerning how the funds raised will be used. The needs of the college can be integrated with the needs of each department to try to prevent conflict from erupting in the future.

Reducing Ambiguities and Jurisdictional Disputes

There are many ways to decrease ambiguities. The goal-setting process is one of these. Clear and non-conflicting goals clarify responsibilities so that each employee and unit does not interfere or compete with the work of the others. Good job descriptions can also clarify duties and expectations so that there is little dispute about who is responsible for what. Reporting relationships can be clarified by preparing organization charts and discussing who has the authority to make certain decisions.

Improving Policies, Procedures and Rules

Policies, procedures and rules can often be improved to reduce conflict potential. One such case arose in the research division of a large equipment manufacturer. The scientists and engineers in this division often attended conventions and professional meetings to keep up to date, to present papers and to work on problems with other scientists. Conflict repeatedly arose over attendance at these meetings. Some employees attended as many as five meetings, others only one. Complaints about fairness put many departments at odds with each other. A committee was established that prepared a fair policy to cover this situation. Costs were contained and conflict over the issues reduced.

Reallocating or Adding Resources

When conflict stems from resource sharing, you can look for creative solutions by reviewing personnel assignments, inventory flow and schedules. In one factory, there was constant conflict between the maintenance department and the production supervisors over maintenance priorities. Favoritism and personalities dominated, and complaints were frequent. The production manager solved the problem by reassigning some maintenance employees to production units. Each production supervisor was given maintenance responsibility and now had the personnel resources to achieve this. Conflict was virtually eliminated and responsibility and production delays were drastically reduced.

Modifying Communication

One way to improve communication is to eliminate some of it. Recall the study of the restaurant industry cited earlier (Whyte, 1949). Cooks were resistant to taking orders from 'lower-status' waitresses. The problem was greatly reduced by requiring the waitresses to submit written customer orders and requests. Their orders were clipped to a rotating spindle from which cooks could select. The face-to-face interaction with the cooks was reduced, and so was conflict between them. In many of today's restaurants, orders are transmitted electronically to the kitchen.

Rotating Personnel

Rotating personnel through different departments helps them to develop a fuller understanding of each unit's responsibilities and problems. Then, when the employee returns to his or her original unit, a basis for cooperation exists. Rotation is often used with new employees.

Changing Reward Systems

The way that rewards are administered may decrease the chances of conflict erupting. Managers can be reinforced with positive feedback and good performance appraisals when they promote harmony. Even financial rewards such as bonuses can be consistent with conflict reduction. In one factory, where heavy industrial equipment is assembled, employees used to work independently on various tasks such as welding, bolting parts together and wiring electrical circuits. They argued over assignments, space and tools. Many saw no benefit in helping each other. Management decided to create work teams and supplied each with enough tools and workspace to eliminate the competition. To prevent further conflict between the teams, productivity and cost-savings bonuses were introduced. In a short time, teams began to help their own team members and offer assistance to other teams.

Providing Training

Many organizations have training programs in which employees learn to prevent, anticipate and cope with conflict. They can assess their own conflict reaction style and learn how to use different styles. They are given the chance to practice techniques of conflict resolution, especially the demanding confrontation techniques discussed above.

Spotlight 8.3   Negotiating with the French

Managers from different countries tend to have different approaches to negotiations. Anglo-Saxon managers tend to come into any international negotiation with well-defined projects, a clear timetable and clearly developed cost estimates. Essentially, they are well prepared for negotiations before they start. French managers, on the other hand, tend to approach negotiations a little differently. For them, the beginning of the negotiation is less well defined. They prefer beginning negotiations by discussing what is to be accomplished, where it might be accomplished, and how the parties will be involved. This usually happens before discussions get serious. You can imagine how frustrating this would be to you if you showed up with your project plans well defined, but then were faced with a negotiation partner who wants to 'start at the beginning' (Newsom-Ballé, 1996).

SUMMARY

Since organizations involve so much interdependence between individuals and groups, conflict can easily arise and become a serious threat to organizational effectiveness. However, conflict – when managed properly – can be healthy for an organization. It can add to creativity, be a sign of health and bring different points of view to the attention of decision makers.

Conflict behavior, like any other behavior, often has multiple causes. Certain individual characteristics may lead some of us to become involved in more conflicts than others. Occasionally, characteristics of the situation may make conflict more likely. In organizations, conflict can arise as a result of many issues that just naturally occur in the workplace. When many diverse individuals work side by side in complex organizational structures with numerous goals and agendas, conflict is a natural outcome.

Resolving conflict is an important managerial role. While different managers may choose different styles of dealing with conflict, one thing is certain. Just as there are often multiple causes of individual conflict, so managers should consider multiple methods to resolve that conflict. Focusing on organizational goals and structural aspects of the organization are effective means of understanding and eliminating conflict.

GUIDE FOR MANAGERS: MANAGING CONFLICT CONSTRUCTIVELY

In addition to the approaches discussed above, here are a number of practical approaches for managing conflict in way that will maintain the healthy conflict that allows organizations to maintain creative and innovative energy (Eisenhardt et al., 1997).

Focus on the Facts

Many organizations have access to timely data from objective sources. However, it is common to allow discussions about opinions rather than facts to dominate discussions. Attempt to control discussion by challenging ideas and conclusions. Encourage managers to state up-front if their comments are based on anecdotal evidence or based on factual information.

Consider Multiple Alternatives

Rather than narrowing the focus to a small set of alternatives, it appears that teams with less conflict consider more alternatives. Individuals often suggest an alternative that they may not agree with, in an attempt to increase the options available to the group and to induce new ways of looking at existing alternatives. Multiple alternatives may also reduce polarization influences given that there are more than two positions to consider.

Create Common Goals

When parties have conflicting goals, other types of conflict are sure to follow. If common goals can be introduced this will more likely cause collaboration rather than competition. In the chapters on groups and teams we discussed the importance of goal clarity on team effectiveness. One reason that teams which don't have clear and common goals do not perform as well is because of the conflict that occurs.

Use Humor

Tension and stress are common by-products of groups involved in decision making under pressure. It was found that teams which had higher conflict lacked humor in their process. Humor is also an important element in combating the effects of stress.

Balance the Power Structure

As with many issues, fairness is a key to the acceptance of decisions. When there is a mismatch of power, higher tension is felt by individuals. Creating balance prevents one party from dominating the discussion and the decision process. When members feel that their input has equal value and possibility for acceptance, they are more willing to present their ideas. The openness of the process that ensues leads to higher willingness to accept the final decision and less conflict in the long run.

CASE: DESIGN SECTION E

Stork Aircraft Supplies has an excellent reputation for providing precision parts to the aircraft industry. They design and manufacture a variety of pumps, hydraulic devices, and mechanical controls for jet planes. Their devices are known for their reliability and durability throughout the industry. They have a large Research and Development Division (R & D) that designs and tests prototypes before sale and manufacture of them.

R & D usually has thirty or forty project teams working on new devices and modifications. One support group in R & D is the Design Division. It consists of twenty or so design engineers and draftsmen who serve each of the ongoing projects. On many occasions, demands by project leaders created chaos in the Design Division. To handle special requests and emergency or overflow work, Design Section E was set up. Six employees and a supervisor, Dan Reed, were assigned to the section.

After about a month of operation, Section E was in chaos itself. There were some arguments among his six designers, and dissatisfaction had set in. Three of the designers were upset because Dan kept trying to establish a schedule of assignments. They thought this was foolish, because they perceived the task of the group as not subject to a particular schedule. They felt that Section E was created to respond quickly to special work that was assigned to their unit.

The other three designers were upset and dissatisfied for other reasons. They were angry with Dan because he couldn't seem to stick to the schedule, or he would change it before it had expired. They also disliked having to set an incomplete project aside whenever a supposedly higher priority design was needed by a project manager. The other three designers exasperated them, too. These other three would often ignore the schedule and suggest various reassignments to meet what they felt were emergency requests.

The tension between Dan and his designers was growing by the day. His group was split down the middle on some key issues. Cooperation between the two subgroups was poor. The teamwork and cohesiveness he wanted was not happening.

- Would Section E benefit more from cooperation or competition given their task? What factors helped or hindered cooperation?
- Is helping important to Section E? Explain.
- What can Dan, the supervisor, do to enhance Section E's cohesiveness? How will cohesiveness help?

REFERENCES

Amanatullah, E.T., M.W. Morris and J.R. Curhan (2008), Negotiators Who Give Too Much: Unmitigated Communion, Relational Anxieties, and Economic Costs in Distributive and Integrative Bargaining. *Journal of Personality and Social Psychology*, **95**(3): 723–38.

Ancona, D.G. (1990), Outward Bound Strategies for Team Survival in an Organization. *Academy of Management Journal*, **33**(2): 334–65.

Archibald, R.D. (1992), *Managing High-Technology Programs and Projects*. New York: Wiley.

Ayoko, O.B. and V.J. Callan (2010), Teams' Reactions to Conflict and Teams' Task and Social Outcomes: The Moderating Role of Transformational and Emotional Leadership. *European Management Journal*, **28**(3): 220–35.

Badke-Schaub, P., G. Goldschmidt and M. Meijer (2010), How Does Cognitive Conflict in Design Teams Support the Development of Creative Ideas? *Creativity and Innovation Management*, **19**(2): 119–33.

Behrens, M. (2007), Conflict, Arbitration, and Dispute Resolution in the German Workplace. *International Journal of Conflict Management*, **18**(2): 175–92.

Blake, R.R. and J.S. Mouton (1969), *Building a Dynamic Corporation Through Grid Organization Development*. Reading, MA: Addison-Wesley.

Clarke, N. (2010), Emotional Intelligence and its Relationship to Transformational Leadership and Key Project Manager Competences. *Project Management Journal*, **41**(2): 5–20.

Cosier, R.A. and D.R. Dalton (1990), Positive Effects of Conflict: A Field Assessment. *International Journal of Conflict Management*, **1**: 81–92.

Curseu, P.L. and S.G.L. Schruijer (2010), Does Conflict Shatter Trust or does Trust Obliterate Conflict? Revisiting the Relationships between Team Diversity, Conflict, and Trust. *Group Dynamics: Theory, Research, and Practice*, **14**(1): 66–79.

De Dreu, C.K.W. and A.E.M. Van Vianen (2001), Managing Relationship Conflict and the Effectiveness of Organizational Teams. *Journal of Organizational Behavior*, **22**(3): 309–28.

Eisenhardt, K., J. Kahwajy and L.J. Burgeois III (1997), How Management Teams Can Have a Good Fight. *Harvard Business Review*, **75**(4): 111–21.

Fischer, R., W.L. Ury and B. Patton (1991), *Getting to Yes: Negotiating without Giving In*. New York: Penguin Books.

Godse, A.S. and N.S. Thingujam (2010), Perceived Emotional Intelligence and Conflict Resolution Styles among Information Technology Professionals: Testing the Mediating Role of Personality. *Singapore Management Review*, **32**(1): 69–83.

Graham, R.J. (1982), *Project Management*. New York: Van Nostrand.

Graziano, W.G., L.A. Jensen-Campbell and E.C. Hair (1996), Perceiving Interpersonal Conflict and Reacting to It: The Case for Agreeableness. *Journal of Personality and Social Psychology*, **70**(4): 820–35.

Greenhalgh, L. (1986), SMR Forum: Managing Conflict. *Sloan Mangement Review*, **27**: 45–51.

Jehn, K.A. (1995), A Multimethod Examination of the Benefits and Detriments of Intragroup Conflict. *Administrative Science Quarterly*, **40**(2): 256–82.

Jehn, K.A. and K. Bezrukova (2010), The Faultline Activation Process and the Effects of Activated Faultlines on Coalition Formation, Conflict, and Group

Outcomes. *Organizational Behavior and Human Decision Processes*, **112**(1): 24–42.

Jehn, K.A. and E.A. Mannix (2001), The Dynamic Nature of Conflict: A Longitudinal Study of Intragroup Conflict and Group Performance. *Academy of Management Journal*, **44**(2): 238–51.

Jehn, K.A., G.B. Northcraft and M.A. Neale (1999), Why Differences Make a Difference: A Field Study of Diversity, Conflict, and Performance in Workgroups. *Administrative Science Quarterly*, **44**(4): 741–63.

Jiatao, L.I. and D.C. Hambrick (2005), Factional Groups: A New Vantage on Demographic Faultlines, Conflict, and Disintegration in Work Teams. *Academy of Management Journal*, **48**(5): 794–813.

Kumar, R. (1997), The Troubled History of Partition. *Foreign Affairs*, **1**: 22–34.

Langfred, C.W. (2007), The Downside of Self-Management: A Longitudinal Study of the Effects of Conflict on Trust, Autonomy, and Task Interdependence in Self-Managing Teams. *Academy of Management Journal*, **50**(4): 885–900.

Lock, D. (2007), *The Essentials of Project Management*. Aldershot: Gower.

Mohammed, S. and L.C. Angell (2004), Surface- and Deep-Level Diversity in Workgroups: Examining the Moderating Effects of Team Orientation and Team Process on Relationship Conflict. *Journal of Organizational Behavior*, **25**(8): 1015–39.

Nelson, R.E. (1989), The Strength of Strong Ties: Social Networks and Intergroup Conflict in Organizations. *Academy of Management Journal*, **32**: 377–401.

Newsom-Ballé, L.G. (1996), Negotiating with the French. *Career Development Journal*, **5**(1): 15–20.

Pelled, L.H., K.M. Eisenhardt and K.R. Xin (1999), Exploring the Black Box: An Analysis of Work Group Diversity, Conflict, and Performance. *Administrative Science Quarterly*, **44**(1): 1–28.

Polzer, J.T., C.B. Crisp, S.L. Jarvenpaa and W. Kim (2006), Extending the Faultline Model to Geographically Dispersed Teams: How Colocated Subgroups can Impair Group Functioning. *Academy of Management Journal*, **49**(4): 679–92.

Polzer, J.T., L.P. Milton and W.B. Swann Jr. (2002), Capitalizing on Diversity: Interpersonal Congruence in Small Work Groups. *Administrative Science Quarterly*, **47**(2): 296–324.

Pondy, L.R. (1967), Organizational Conflict: Concepts and Models. *Administrative Science Quarterly*, **12**: 296–320.

Somech, A., H.S. Desivilya and H. Lidogoster (2009), Team Conflict Management and Team Effectiveness: The Effects of Task Interdependence and Team Identification. *Journal of Organizational Behavior*, **30**(3): 359–78.

Tabak, Z.M.A.E.A. (2010), Exploring the Impact of Collectivism on Conflict Management Styles: A Turkish Study. *International Journal of Conflict Management*, **21**(2): 169–85.

Thamhain, H.J. and D.L. Wileman (1975), Conflict Management in Project Life Cycles. *Sloan Management Review*, **16**(3): 31–50.

Thomas, K.W. (1990), Conflict and Negotiation Processes in Organizations. In *Handbook of Industrial and Organizational Psychology*, M.D. Dunnette (ed.). Palo Alto, CA: Consulting Psychologists Press.

Thomas, K.W. and R.H. Kilmann (1974), *Conflict Mode Instrument*. Tuxedo, NY: Xicom.

Thoms, P. (1998), Project Team Motivation. In *The Project Management Handbook*, J. Pinto (ed.). San Francisco, CA: Jossey-Bass.

Van de Vliert, E. and B. Kabanoff (1990), Toward Theory-Based Measures of Conflict Management. *Academy of Management Journal*, **33**(1): 199–209.

Whyte, W.F. (1949), The Social Structure of the Restaurant. *American Journal of Sociology*, **54**: 302–10.

Wood, V.F. and P.A. Bell (2008), Predicting Interpersonal Conflict Resolution Styles from Personality Characteristics. *Personality and Individual Differences*, **45**(2): 126–31.

9. Power in organizations

PREPARING FOR CLASS

Power in organizations is often evident in many aspects of the organizational environment. Individuals who are powerful in an organization often use that power to make their environment more pleasant. We have learned to expect that more senior supervisors and managers will have bigger offices and better furnishings. In many organizations, to draw many conclusions about organizational power all you have to do is walk through the building.

To prepare for this class, choose an organization that you can walk through fairly freely. It could be a business or even your university or college. As you walk through the facilities, take note of aspects such as the office size, furnishings and equipment, location of parking spaces, availability and proximity of administrative support, and so on.

1. What do you notice about the relationship between power and environment?
2. Besides comfort, are there any trappings of power that you notice that are useful in an individual maintaining his or her organizational power?

* *

A very clear example of what this chapter is about – power and politics in organizations – is the selection of the chief executive officer (CEO) to replace Alan Roberts at ORBCOMM. It shows how power and politics can be used in a major way – and how you can lose in a big way if your strategy does not work. Roberts had been CEO for several years after the splitting off of several subsidiaries after the deregulation of the communication industry. The company had been through some hard times because it had to compete in the long-distance business with new long-distance suppliers such as cable companies, Sprint and MCI. The reputation of ORBCOMM changed for investors during this period from that of a safe, dependable stock which was a sound buy for retirement, to that of a more risky, volatile equity.

As Roberts's tenure neared his retirement date, he and the ORBCOMM board of directors began to search for a successor. Normally this search would be done by an independent consultant in conjunction with the board, and with some inputs, perhaps significant, from Roberts. It was very different in this case: the process was almost completely controlled by Roberts. One unusual thing in the way CEOs were selected was to use two executive search consulting firms to find candidates. It was very clear to outsiders that the board's influence in the process would be minimal. In addition, Roberts appeared to have a very specific personal agenda: that the new CEO would come in, at first, as a sort of 'CEO understudy' to Roberts. Then, after Roberts stepped down, he would remain on the board of directors. In fact this was the implied, if not explicit, price for Roberts's support for the candidate.

The control that he had over the process had the effect of eliminating what executive recruiters call the 'A List' of candidates. This happened because Roberts's influence forced the discussion between the board and the consultants about candidates in a particular direction (Levina and Orlikowski, 2009). A candidate wasn't considered who did not meet Roberts's conditions. Why would top-notch CEO candidates want to come in as an understudy to an incumbent CEO and be tied to a commitment that he be appointed to the board, when they would, for sure, be on other important CEO candidate lists and be able to negotiate more latitude for themselves?

The two consulting firms, Roberts, and the board of directors finally found a candidate and appointed John Mark to the position of president and 'future CEO'. Mark had no experience in the communication industry or in any area of electronics. He had been the top executive of Carroll Industries, a company in a related industry.

Nine months after he had been appointed, Mark resigned from ORBCOMM. It was reported that the board of directors did not think he had the capacity to be CEO. Many thought, however, that the real reason was that he could not work with Roberts. Of course, Mark thought otherwise, but he had no choice. The board of ORBCOMM made it easier for him to swallow the resignation, giving Mark a golden parachute worth several million dollars.

Now the search process began again, but this time the board took control of the process away from Roberts. This time the nature of the conversations between the board and the consultants about potential successors changed (Levina and Orlikowski, 2009). No longer was it necessary that Roberts remain on the board, and no longer would the new CEO be an understudy. There were much stronger candidates this time, both from inside and outside the firm. In the end, the board appointed J. Michael Horn, chairman of Micronic Electronics. Horn had been a candidate in the first selection process but was eliminated early. One rumor was that he would not agree with Roberts's demand that he come in as 'understudy CEO' and appoint Roberts to the board. After Horn took over the job, it was announced that Roberts would not be on the board: he would retire.

Spotlight 9.1   Lord Acton on power

John Emerich Edward Dalberg-Acton, commonly known as Lord Acton, was a British historian in the late nineteenth century who did not believe in the unlimited power of the Pope to proclaim dogma. He made his famous statement about a particular Papal action:

> I cannot accept your canon that we are to judge Pope and King unlike other men with a favourable presumption that they did no wrong. If there is any presumption, it is the other way, against the holders of power, increasing as the power increases. Historic responsibility has to make up for the want of legal responsibility. Power tends to corrupt, and absolute power corrupts absolutely. Great men are almost always bad men, even when they exercise influence and not authority: still more [because of] the tendency or certainty of corruption by full authority. There is no worse heresy than the fact that the office sanctifies the holder of it. (Dalberg-Acton, 1949)

In this chapter, and in Chapter 10, we examine why and how these things happen, why people comply and particularly why important and sophisticated people like those on the board of directors of ORBCOMM might agree to the sort of scheme that Roberts had, to protect himself in ORBCOMM when he stepped down as CEO. In particular, in this chapter, we discuss the issues of influence, power and politics, which arise in every organization. We also discuss different types of power, how it is acquired, how it is used, how it is maintained and how it is related to different types of organizations.

A MODEL OF INFLUENCE PROCESSES IN ORGANIZATIONS

Roberts had successfully engaged in an influence attempt, and the board of directors engaged in an act of compliance. Influence attempts occur

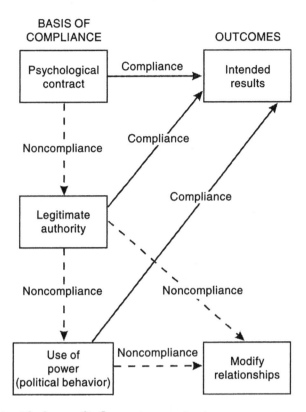

Figure 9.1   The bases of influence in organizations

when legitimate authority or power is used. These relationships are shown in Figure 9.1. It shows that the bases for influence in organizations are the psychological contract, legitimate authority and power. It also shows that influence attempts lead to results intended by the influence agent, or to a modification of the relationship between the influence agent and the target.

Influence is a process through which you attempt to extract compliance with your intentions from others. For influence to exist, two parties (A and B) must be in an interactive and dependent relationship. This means that the actions of A can affect the actions of B, and vice versa. Influence occurs when one of the parties (A) induces the other (B) to respond in an intended way. Consider the case of Roberts and the ORBCOMM board. Why did the members take a less active role in the selection of a new CEO? Perhaps they believed that their role should not be so active. Or, they might not have wanted to spend the necessary time. Perhaps Roberts had demonstrated a great deal of competence in the past, and for this reason the board trusted him. What is clear is that there was a strong dependence relationship between Roberts and the members of the board.

In an organization, there may be different motivational bases for dependence (Etzioni, 1961). In some cases, you might want to join an organization or interact with other persons because they share important values. This is usually the case for those who join political parties or religious organizations or become involved with ideological causes. The basis of these relationships is commitment, a strong, positive involvement in the dependence relationship. There is something very important that managers must remember about commitment: do not mistake compliance for commitment. Compliance can occur for other reasons, as you will see.

In other cases, a dependence relationship may be forced, as when a person is put in a jail or a mental institution. Then the person experiences alienation and wants to escape from the relationship. These dependence relationships must usually be maintained by force.

The third type of dependence relationship is calculative involvement, in which both parties assess the economic costs and benefits of maintaining the relationship. This is the type of dependence relationship that most often occurs in most work organizations (Etzioni, 1961). However, it is obvious that some levels of both commitment and alienation also occur frequently in work organizations.

The strength of influence one party has over another is a function of two factors. One is the need to maintain the relationship. When a person has a choice about whether to remain in a relationship, less influence can be exerted than when the relationship is necessary. A person with strong political beliefs who is a member of a party which espouses similar strong beliefs will be influenced much more by party leaders than by others with weaker beliefs. The second factor, power asymmetry, is related to the first, but is not necessarily the same thing. Power asymmetry means that one party (B) is more dependent upon the other, giving the other (A) more capacity to influence.

The Bases of Influence

The psychological contract is the basis for the distinction between legitimate authority and power which we use in this chapter; see also Chapter 3. The psychological contract is the mutual set of expectations that exist between you and an organization. These expectations cover what pay you will receive, as well as 'the whole pattern of rights and privileges' (Schein, 1970; Montes and Zweig, 2009). In return, you are expected to contribute both work and some commitment. As long as requests, commands and

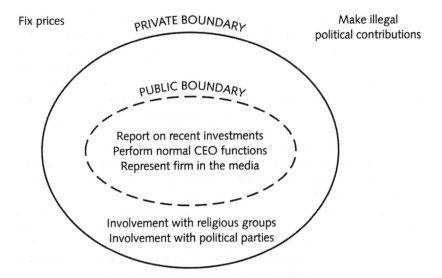

Fix prices

PRIVATE BOUNDARY

Make illegal
political contributions

PUBLIC BOUNDARY

Report on recent investments
Perform normal CEO functions
Represent firm in the media

Involvement with religious groups
Involvement with political parties

Figure 9.2   The hypothetical psychological contract of a CEO

directives fall within the boundaries of the psychological contract, you
will comply. Take the case of Roberts, whose hypothetical psychological contract with the board is shown in Figure 9.2. In general, he will do
anything that falls within the boundary of the psychological contract. As
you can see in Figure 9.2, Roberts would not fix prices or make illegal
political contributions. They are not only illegal, they also fall outside his
psychological contract.

However, there are two types of boundaries: public and real. The public
boundary includes those activities that you want others, especially your
superior, to believe are the elements of the psychological contract. In
this example, the board wants Roberts to make regular reports about the
return on investment of recent projects, to perform conventional CEO
functions and to represent ORBCOMM in the media.

In some instances, he may be asked to do something that falls outside
the public boundary, but inside the real boundary. The real boundary
represents the 'true' limits of the psychological contract. In our example,
we show two activities that fall in this zone: being involved with political
parties, and taking an active role in the leadership of some religious organizations. For obvious reasons, he will want the board to believe that the
psychological contract is constrained by the public boundaries, because
compliance with requests that fall between the real and public boundaries
will make it appear that he is 'doing a favor' for which there might be

some quid pro quo – a favor in return for exceeding the requirements of the job. For example, in the first CEO search, the board of ORBCOMM could have decided that Roberts should not be so extensively involved with the process, and that they could have managed it without his help. To do so would have required that they make it clear to him that this was what was going to happen. The fact that the corporate charter permitted this might have led Roberts to be less active, had the point been pushed. The board could have taken the position that his psychological contract really included the expectation that he yield to the board in such matters.

These boundaries are not static; they change. Sometimes they change by mutual consent, as when a person's job changes by promotion. Sometimes they change through the use of power exercised by another person.

We define all those requests from a superior, that fall within the real boundary of the psychological contract and are accepted by the subordinate, as legitimate authority. Power is used to extract compliance to requests that fall outside the real boundary, and sometimes it is used for directives which fall between the real and public boundaries.

Legitimate authority

Legitimate authority is the right of decision and command that a person has over others. It is sanctioned, or approved, by those in the organization. Legitimate authority is embedded in the psychological contract and, through it, a superior can expect a subordinate to comply with organizationally sanctioned requests.

Authority is seen as legitimate when the person who is the subject of influence believes that it is right and proper for another to exert influence or attempt to exert it. The board would be exercising legitimate authority by requesting Roberts to report regularly on company activities. It might fire him if he refuses, and could do so because the legitimate authority structure may contain those decision rights for the board's use in the case of non-compliance.

Legitimate authority is reflected in the organization's structure, which defines the general distribution of legitimate authority by position location. Higher-level positions have more legitimate authority than those at lower levels. Further, because legitimate authority accrues to a person as a function of his or her organization position, it is transferable from one person to another. This means that when you leave a position, you no longer have the authority associated with it. These are now the rights of your replacement.

There are different patterns of the distribution of legitimate authority depending upon whether it is in a mechanistic or organic organization (Tosi, 1992):

- In mechanistic organizations there will be relatively highly central-ized authority, policy and decision-making mechanisms. In addi-tion, the distribution of legitimate authority will be somewhat stable over long periods of time because there are fewer external pressures to change it.
- In organic organizations, the legitimate authority structure is less stable and will change as the environment of the organization changes and the firm adapts to it. Authority will be less centralized and exist closer to the projects that are being undertaken in the firm. There may also be instances of dual authority as personnel are assigned to different projects, or have both technical and functional supervisors, as would be the case in the matrix organization.

The organizational culture will also reflect the legitimate authority structure. When large differences in authority exist between levels of managers, there will most likely be very significant differences in status symbols. Managers at the top level may have spacious, well-decorated offices set in very desirable locations in the headquarters building, while those at the next lower level may have smaller, less attractive offices.

The acceptance of legitimate authority stems from several sources. First, every culture has a concept of legitimate authority in which it is generally accepted that some forms of authority, as well as relationships between superiors and subordinates, are appropriate while other forms and relationships are not. For example, highly centralized authority is cul-turally acceptable in some Latin countries (for example, Italy and Spain), but a more even distribution of authority across different organizational levels is preferred in Anglo-Saxon countries (the UK, Canada and the USA) (Hofstede, 1980).

Second, when you join an organization, its culture is transmitted through organizational socialization. An important theme in socialization is to rationalize the authority structure of the organization so that you accept it as legitimate. Third, your organizational orientation, initially developed by general socialization, affects legitimacy:

- An organizationalist usually has little trouble with most directives from higher levels.
- If you have professional orientation you may see many directives as less legitimate and respond more readily to influence attempts from colleagues.
- The indifferent responds primarily to reasonable job demands made during working hours and probably views everything else as non-legitimate.

Power

Power is a force that can be used to extract compliance, but it differs from legitimate authority. Power is not sanctioned by the psychological contract, whereas legitimate authority is (Pfeffer, 1992). The use of power, in fact, distorts the boundaries of the psychological contract. This is possible because the boundaries of the psychological contract are flexible and can be modified, even though it may take considerable pressure. The use of power in an organization is called organizational politics.

Power can be used to achieve organizationally sanctioned ends, or the ends desired by the political actor. A person pressured to act by someone with power in an organizationally unacceptable way may comply to avoid undesirable consequences. Suppose that an organization's culture supports ethical behavior in its practice, and the CEO is approached by a competitor to fix prices illegally and, at the same time, some important board members suggest that this is a good idea. The CEO might act unethically, at great personal and psychological cost, if the pressure were extreme. If the result is that the firm engaged in price fixing, the board members would have exercised power, not legitimate authority.

People often respond to power even when they are not threatened with physical harm or with economic loss. People often comply when power is exercised by someone with legitimate authority who exerts influence beyond legitimate bounds. People often respond to power even when they are not threatened with physical harm or with economic loss, even though their actions could harm others. This was dramatically shown in research in which subjects were asked to assist the experimenter in a study of the effects of punishment on learning (Milgram, 1974). The subject was asked to be the 'teacher'. The experimenter's confederate acted as the 'learner'. The confederate was taken to a separate room where he could be heard but not seen. The experimenter then showed the subject how to operate an alleged shock generator. Shock switches ranged from 15 to 450 volts and were labeled from 'slight shock' through 'danger: severe shock', to the highest two levels, which were simply marked 'XXX'. The subject was instructed to apply shock whenever the 'learner' gave a wrong answer, and to increase it when more wrong answers were given. Although no shock was actually administered, the subject was led to believe that it was. When mildly shocked, the confederate groaned. As the shock levels increased, the confederate's reaction accelerated to shouts, screams and cries to quit the experiment. After 330 volts, the confederate became silent. The experimenter prodded the subject to administer stronger shocks when the subject resisted. In one experiment, 63 percent of 40 male subjects, 20–50 years old, applied the maximum 450 volts.

A person may possess different types of power (French and Raven, 1959; Zimbardo, 2007). 'Reward power' exists when you have control over rewards desired by another. The more highly valued the rewards, the greater the power. Individuals in positions with high levels of legitimate authority have the right to make decisions about the allocation of rewards and promotions based on organizationally rationalized criteria. When they use organizationally sanctioned criteria, it is the use of legitimate authority, not reward power. However, reward power can be enacted through politics as a result of a person having legitimate authority. It could happen this way. Based on the 'Good-enough theory of promotion' (see Chapter 5), a candidate for promotion need not be the most qualified person for a job but must be good enough to enter the selection pool. Usually the criteria to be in the pool are clearly specified and organizationally sanctioned. From that pool, a person is selected who, usually, has the 'right' perspective as assessed by the judges. This is especially true when criteria and the judgments may reflect the use of power, not legitimate authority. In this sense, we can say that promotions in organizations are 'political' decisions.

'Coercive power' in an organization exists for the same reason as reward power. The difference is that, instead of rewarding another person, punishment is threatened or applied. An example of this is the Stanford Prison Experiment (Zimbardo, 2007). In this study, Stanford students were solicited to participate in a study that simulated a prison (with cells, bars, and so on) in the Psychology Building at Stanford University. These students were psychologically screened to ensure that there were no deviant personalities among the participants. They were then randomly assigned to the role of guard or prisoner. Prisoners were captured and assigned to a cell, and guards received no particular training but were told to act as guards. Essentially subjects relied on the broad social norms and expectations about how prisoners and guards would behave in a prison and, as a result, the subjects assigned to be prisoners adopted a 'prisoners' mentality' and acted as prisoners, and the subjects assigned to be guards did the same, adopting the 'guard mentality' and acting as guards. The behaviors of the guards became particularly coercive and, in the judgment of the researchers, dangerous enough that the experiment, intended to last two weeks, was concluded before the end of the first week.

Coercive power can easily be used in work organizations when someone pushes the limits of their legitimate authority. For example, in one large retail organization, a vendor, Louisa Datillo, lost her position as a supplier because her buyer, Susan Low, maintained that she was not performing well, was late with reports and had caused some problems because Louisa's own suppliers had trouble getting products shipped from China and Turkey. When the complete set of facts was analyzed, however, it was found that Louisa's small firm was among the most dependable, and actually had lower costs than the vendor to whom the new contract was to be awarded. In addition, other buyers in the firm were satisfied with her service levels. However, Louisa had openly disagreed with Susan in meetings, and frequently she was right. Another vendor, Earl Carole, who was almost as effective although his prices were slightly higher, replaced Louisa. The decision to remove Louisa was justified on the basis that the buyer's team would be able to work better with Earl. The short-run effect on the organization was not significantly bad, but Susan's actions made it very clear to the other vendors who sold to her that more than competence was necessary to succeed with her. They had to be able to work with her – in her way. What happened to Susan, a buyer who played organization politics? A short time after her decision, she was removed from her position as a buyer and was moved to a job in operations, in which she had no external contacts.

We rely on and accept recommendations from accountants, lawyers and physicians because we believe they have the knowledge to make correct decisions in their specific area of competence. The same thing happens in organizations: having 'expert power' means that you are able to influence others because you possess some particular skill or knowledge that they do not, and that skill or knowledge is necessary for them to do their job. For instance, in designing a management information system, systems experts will design the system, specify equipment and dictate how it should be used. Expert power usually takes time to develop; a person normally spends much time in formal training or developing skills on the job before this type of influence is acquired. Expert power is very task- and person-specific. For example, the systems expert may have a lot of influence in implementing computer information systems but no influence in the design of compensation plans for managers.

Because of its specificity, expert power cannot easily be transferred from one person to another in the way that legitimate authority can. For instance, if you become a plant manager, you will have the same legitimate authority as the previous manager. You may even be able to extend it so as to develop reward and coercive power, as discussed above, but expert power develops from your demonstrating competence or having it 'given' by others because you have the appropriate education, certification, experience and appearance. If you only have expert power and leave the organization, your replacement may not have the same amount of influence as you had until it is earned.

'Charismatic power' occurs when individuals are susceptible to influence because they identify with another person (French and Raven, 1959).

It is based on the feeling of oneness that a person has with another, the desire for that feeling, or the personal attraction to be like the other. The stronger the attraction, the stronger the power.

The charismatic leader, a person with charismatic power, is set apart from 'ordinary [persons] and treated as endowed with supernatural or superhuman or, at least, specifically exceptional powers or qualities not accessible to the normal person . . . What is important is how the individual is actually regarded by followers' (Weber, 1947). Some political and business leaders who have been called charismatic include Martin Luther King, John F. Kennedy, Fidel Castro, Charles DeGaulle, Mikhail Gorbachev, Enzo Ferrari, Gianni Agnelli, Bill Gates and Ted Turner. The attractiveness of many of these leaders may have been magnified to the extent that many of them were seen as making sacrifices for the group. In that case, a charismatic and sacrificing leader appears to have greater influence on group members (Yorges et al., 1999).

What differentiates someone with charismatic power from those with other types of power is the reaction of the followers:

> Followers of charismatic leaders do not feel pressed or oppressed. Charismatic leaders have the ability to engender unusually high trust in the correctness of their beliefs, affection for the leader, willing obedience to the leader, identification with the leader, emotional involvement of the follower in the mission, heightened goals of the follower, and the feeling on the part of the follower that he or she will be able to accomplish the mission or contribute to its accomplishment. (House, 1984)

This capacity of charismatic leaders may be even stronger for followers who do not have a strong group identification, or sense of belonging (Den Hartog et al., 2007). Perceived leader charisma is related to the level of compliance of group members, but it is more strongly related for those who felt a weaker identification with the group. This suggests an important effect of charisma: it can increase the degree to which persons identify with the leader and with the group and, in turn, result in greater compliance.

Like expert power, charismatic power cannot be transferred to another person. However, it can become institutionalized power when charismatic power is transformed into legitimate authority. It happens this way. In the beginning, a charismatic leader will attract followers and, as the number of followers increases, the beginnings of a hierarchy emerge. The charismatic leader appoints others to assist and delegates decision-making power to them. Others in the organization comply because they know that the leader chose these persons. Eventually rules, policies and procedures develop in which the philosophy and practices of the leader are embedded.

When the leader dies or leaves, the system of authority stays and becomes the structure of legitimate authority in the organization (Etzioni, 1963). As time goes on, the members comply with influence attempts that, by now, have become reasonable and proper. When new members join the organization, they are socialized to accept this system of legitimate authority.

Outcomes of Influence

The use of legitimate authority or power leads either to intended results or to some modification of the relationship between the influence agent and the target; see Figure 9.1.

Intended results

Intended results are the outcomes of influence attempts that are desired by the party that exerted the influence. From an organization's perspective, compliance should lead to organizationally valued results, such as high productivity and profitability. However, intended results may also occur because they are the wishes of a particular person, but are not necessarily part of the organizational requirements. For example, Roberts wanted the new president to appoint him to the board of directors when he, Roberts, stepped down as CEO. This was not the organizationally desired outcome; it was Roberts's intended result, and you can see that he achieved it with Walter, but not with Horn.

Usually when legitimate authority, charismatic power or expert power is used, the target person will react in a way intended by the power agent. The psychological response of the target is called 'acceptance', or compliance. He or she will engage in the desired behavior, as well as rationalizing and justifying the compliance as being the right way to behave. In fact, that is exactly the response to legitimate authority by the personality type we have called the organizationalist; see Chapter 3.

Charismatic power and expert power also lead to acceptance. When charismatic power is used, the target's justification is ideological and normative. For expert power, the acceptance is rationalized by the belief that the competence of the expert is necessary to satisfy the target's needs.

There can also be acceptance when reward or coercive power is used. This is particularly true when these types of power are the extension of legitimate authority. An example of this is when Roberts, the CEO with legitimate authority, exercised power in a political way to try to obtain a later board appointment. For acceptance under these conditions, the power agent must seek organizationally approved outcomes. When Roberts used his position to force Mark to accept his board appointment, the attempt was accepted and ultimately rationalized by the board.

Modification of relationships

When a target of influence resists or fails to comply with the influence attempt, there is usually some modification in the relationship between the actors. The idea is usually that the influence agent, particularly when he or she is a manager, can take some action such as firing or disciplining the target, usually a subordinate. For instance, when Mark eventually had problems working with Roberts, Roberts and the board forced a resignation. There are other ways in which a superior could modify relationships with those subordinates who do not comply, such as assigning them to less desirable projects, not supporting them for promotion and pay increases, or changing their personal relationship at work.

There are also ways that the target of the influence can modify the relationship, which is most likely to occur when reward or coercive power are used. One way is by resistance, which could take several forms:

- Appeal to reason is one form of resistance.
- Minimal compliance is another effective resistance strategy. This can be done by following the letter of the law, but not the spirit. When air traffic controllers in the USA want to protest, they often do it by slowing down landings at large airports such as Chicago and Atlanta, by following the exact formal requirements to maintain the necessary distance between landing planes, which creates delays.
- Outright sabotage is another way to resist. This may be done by a range of tactics, from delaying the implementation of decisions to actually destroying information or damaging equipment.
- Development of a counter force is another way to resist power. The person may try to develop their own power base, using approaches to acquiring power discussed in this chapter. They may develop coalitions, increase expertise, influence the environment or acquire a sponsor. Success with any of these strategies will modify the balance of power.
- Leaving the organization is perhaps the ultimate act of resistance. If you cannot accommodate to the power structure or modify it, you may simply quit and find another, better situation in which to live and work.

Organizational and Personal Bases of Influence

You can have influence for different reasons. One is because you are in an organizational position with legitimate authority; while in other instances, influence is strictly due to some attribute of the influence agent.

Organizationally-based influence

Obviously a person in a higher-level position has more legitimate authority than another lower in the hierarchy, making legitimate authority a type of organizationally-based influence. Further, studies have shown that a person may have organizationally-based power, which is the capacity to influence others beyond the range of legitimate authority, as discussed earlier (Milgram, 1974; Zimbardo, 2007). There are other types of position effects. Often a job description will give a person control over information desired by others. This is a source of power. Similarly, if you can control access to key people, power accrues. Executive secretaries and high-level staff assistants are likely to have influence because of this. Also, some people are in jobs where they seem to have some perceived influence over the futures of others, such as the personnel executive who handles transfers, assignments and personnel reductions.

Personal-based influence

You acquire personal-based influence when you possess attributes or skills desired by others. These attributes are usually independent of the organization's control. There are two types of personal-based influence:

- Expert power exists when a person has competence required by others.
- Charismatic power exists when one person becomes psychologically dependent upon another.

ACQUIRING AND MAINTAINING ORGANIZATIONALLY-BASED INFLUENCE

The pattern of power and influence relationships among units in an organization is called the 'power structure'. For example, the marketing department may be more powerful than the human resources (HR) department, and the finance group more powerful than both of them. However, the distribution of organizational power and influence is never what it appears to be on organization charts and in job descriptions. It is affected by a combination of situational factors and individual characteristics. For example, deans in a university do not have equal influence and power in the budgeting process. If they did, then budgets would be allocated to colleges on the basis of the number of students served and the cost of instruction. While these factors do count, a department's or college's power and importance also affect how much money it receives (Pfeffer and Salancik,

1974). Some colleges are more important than others, and some deans have stronger predispositions to use influence and power than others.

Spotlight 9.2 Nietzsche and the will to power

Nietzsche believed that anything that increases the feeling of power is good, and that man is happy when he possesses power and is able to overcome resistance. In his view, everyone strives to become a master of his own space and makes efforts in that direction. What becomes an obstacle is pressed back at. This will to power results in and justifies, in his view, the exploitation of others.

In this section, we first consider situational factors that affect the power structure of an organization, accounting for some key differences in legitimate authority between subunits. Then we examine individual characteristics related to the acquisition of legitimate authority, and the propensity to extend it to become reward and punishment power. Finally, we suggest how organizationally-based influence may be maintained.

Situational Determinants of Organizationally-based Influence: The Strategic Contingency Theory of Power

Just saying that more important organization units have more power than those that are less important is not enough. The question is: 'What is it about a subunit that makes it more important?' The strategic contingency theory of organizational power explains some of these power differences; see Figure 9.3 (Hickson et al., 1971). A subunit's power depends on whether, and by how much, it controls strategic contingencies, or a requirement of a subunit that is affected by the activities of some other subunit or some external agency. There are three conditions that make a subunit strategic:

1. Coping with volatility.
2. Substitutability of activities.
3. Workflow centrality.

Organization subunits that interact and cope with more volatile, threatening and uncertain environments have more power than those that interact with stable ones. If the subunit can successfully interpret an unclear environment and help the organization to cope effectively, it will be able

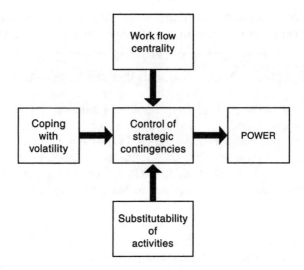

Figure 9.3   Factors affecting power from strategic contingency theory

to influence policy and strategy. This is one reason why physicians have so much power in hospitals. They control three of the critical variables that affect what happens in the hospital: the admissions, the length of stay and the demand for auxiliary services.

When there is no substitutability of the activities of a subunit, that subunit will be very powerful. For example, physicians in hospitals are also, for the most part, not substitutable, particularly when they are specialists. Because the physician has the technical competence to solve patients' problems, and other groups either do not have it or are restricted from using it, they have substantial power.

Workflow centrality has two aspects. Units with high workflow central-ity are interconnected with many others. Most accounting departments have high workflow centrality because they obtain information from many units and provide it to other organization units. A unit with low workflow centrality would be a legal department, which may provide services to only a few other subunits.

The second aspect of centrality is workflow immediacy. This is the 'speed and severity with which work flows of a subunit affect the final outputs of the organization' (Hickson et al., 1971). The higher the work-flow immediacy, the greater the power. Suppose a firm has a policy of maintaining very small finished goods inventories. The production unit has a high workflow immediacy because if production stops, then goods do not flow on to the customer.

Strategic contingency theory explains subunit power relationships very well. One classic study showed that the power of the maintenance department in a tobacco factory existed because it controlled the primary uncertainty that affected production machine breakdown (Crozier, 1964). In the different channels of distribution, the power of a supplier was related to three things:

1. Whether there were alternate suppliers.
2. Whether the resources controlled by the supplier were critical.
3. The level of transactions between the supplier and the customer (Bagozzi and Phillips, 1982).

In another study, a subunit's influence in semiconductor firms was related to the characteristics of the market at the time that a firm was founded (Boeker, 1990). In the early stage of the industry, when the primary market was the US military and the defense industry, the research and development (R&D) units were most dominant in semiconductor firms which began in that stage. Later, the industry faced price competition and, in firms founded during this stage, manufacturing units were the most influential. When the industry moved into a 'custom application' stage, the marketing departments dominated the new firms. There is also evidence about the influence of team members with groups that have high workflow centrality. Team members with similar functional experiences were significantly more central in decision making in the workflow networks. In addition, when team members were also able to provide support by drawing on their knowledge of other functional areas, they were more influential in decentralized teams (teams in which there are many opportunities to contribute and exert influence), rather than in centralized teams (Bunderson, 2003).

Environmental Changes and Power

The power structure of organizations tends to be relatively stable because those who hold power are reluctant to let it change. For example, in semiconductor firms, we know that the longer the founding entrepreneur stayed in the firm, the less likely it was that there was a shift in departmental power (Boeker, 1990). The initially dominant departments were able to institutionalize their initial, strong power position.

Power structures are more likely to change when markets or technologies change in ways that require different skills and competence (Tushman and Romanelli, 1985). For example, Rick Waggoner of General Motors (GM) was forced from the CEO position due to the dramatic, rapid decline of the firm in the late 1990s. For several decades, beginning in the late 1970s, the market share of GM was declining, as was its profitability. This was due in large part to the firm's inability to compete effectively with foreign automobile manufacturers. Then, in the financial crisis of the first decade of the 2000s, General Motors needed a significant bailout from the US government. As a result, the Obama administration pressured Waggoner to step down. He was replaced initially by Fritz Henderson, the chief operating officer (COO) of GM, who stepped down shortly thereafter and was succeeded by Ed Whitacre. This was a dramatic change for General Motors because it had the tradition of promoting 'car people', particularly GM car people, to the top spot. By the end of 2010, it appeared that these changes had led General Motors back to profitability.

Personal Attributes of Those Who Acquire Organizationally-based Power

Some people have very strong predispositions to seek, acquire and use power and authority, and they compete with others who have similar pre-dispositions (House, 1988). In this section, we discuss the personal characteristics of those who seek and acquire organizationally-based power, specifically legitimate authority and reward and punishment power.

Because legitimate authority depends on the position a person holds in the organization, it follows that to increase it, a person must advance in the hierarchy, increase the amount of discretion in the current position, or move into subunits that are more powerful. Those who seek to do this are likely to have these four characteristics:

- Competence.
- Self-confidence.
- An organizational orientation.
- Power needs.

Competence is necessary: a person must be good enough at his or her job to be judged capable of performing at higher-level positions. Competence is usually demonstrated by past performance and achievement. Self-confidence is your belief that you will be successful. People with high generalized self-confidence have stronger beliefs that their influence attempts will be successful (Mowday, 1980). An organizational orientation is also likely to be characteristic of someone seeking legitimate authority (see Chapter 2). The organizationalist finds organizational achievement and advancement reinforcing, making high position a sought-after goal for them. This orientation will also facilitate advancement, because an organizationalist with an adequate level of competence usually has the right combination of factors to be successful, according to the 'good-enough theory of promotion' (see Chapter 5). Power needs must be very strong. Power needs are a person's desire to have an impact on others, to establish, maintain or restore the prestige of power; see Chapter 3. Power needs are one dimension of the leader motive pattern discussed in Chapter 10, shown to be related to managerial success (McClelland and Boyatzis, 1982).

Spotlight 9.3 Power and emotions in conflict and negotiation

The manner in which emotions affect behavior of negotiators was examined in a study of a negotiation simulation in which MBA students participated. It was found that negotiators with high power needs were more likely to seek to dominate then negotiators with low power needs. Those negotiators with low power needs tended to yield to demands made by high-power negotiators, while high-power negotiators did not yield to demands easily. Also, those negotiators who had low power needs were more sensitive and responded to the emotions of their high-power-need counterparts more often. Overall, these results show that power and power needs of the negotiator are very important determinants of the outcome of negotiation (Butt et al., 2010).

In organizations, reward and punishment power stems from the extension of legitimate authority because the person has some discretion in how it can be used. Therefore, the personal attributes already listed above are necessary, because you have to be in a position with legitimate authority, but they are not sufficient to acquire reward and punishment power: the person must have a political orientation. A political orientation is the willingness or attempt to exert influence beyond the boundaries of legitimate authority. The stronger the political orientation, the more reward and punishment power will be sought and acquired. People with a political orientation have these tendencies (House, 1984):

- Machiavellianism.
- Strong personalized power motives.
- Cognitive complexity.
- Articulation skills.

Machiavellians have high self-confidence, high self-esteem and behave in their own self-interest. High Machs are cool, are not distracted by emotion, and can exert control in power vacuums. They use false or exaggerated praise to manipulate others and are able to detach themselves from a situation. Personalized power motives will be very strong for those who acquire reward and punishment power. People with a higher personalized power orientation have strong self-interest and exercise power in an interpersonal way with an adversary. A person with cognitive complexity is able to find what patterns and relations exist in a situation, even though they are embedded in noise and confusion. This is a necessary skill, because if you seek power you must be sensitive to subtle but complex situations in an organization so as to know when to exert influence. Accurate perceptions of the organization power structure are related to a person's power reputation (Krackhardt, 1990). Those who are attributed higher power by others tend to have more accurate perceptions of the power network. Being articulate is another important skill. The articulate person will be able to present arguments logically, which should facilitate persuasion. He or she may be able to form coalitions more easily and may be chosen by a group to represent them.

Maintaining Organizationally-based Influence

Legitimate authority and organizationally-based power can be perpetuated and strengthened by maintaining the current structure of organizational relationships and the organizational culture that support stable behavior patterns. In this way, the powerful subunit will maintain control over strategic contingencies, retain its centrality and protect its level of non-substitutability. By perpetuating the organizational culture, the norms and values that support the power structure will not change. Figure 9.4 shows some things that a subunit with institutionalized power can do to enhance it:

- Influence strategy.
- Affect behavioral control systems.
- Affect the redesign of the organization structure.

Influence over strategy
Managers in powerful subunits can affect organization strategy by influencing whether an organization takes an aggressive or a passive approach toward its environment. Stronger subunits can also influence strategic decisions about where the firm is located in the task environment. For example, a small electronics firm in California designed and manufactured advanced technological components for the defense department and NASA. Its technology had several consumer applications, so a group from the small marketing department prepared an excellent proposal to

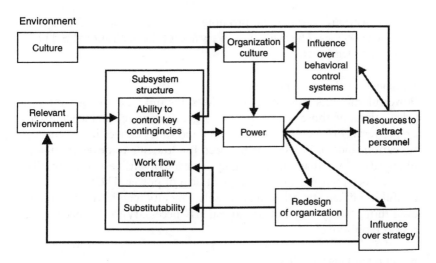

Figure 9.4   Maintenance of organizational-based power

develop a consumer products line. It was a well-conceived program that predicted substantial increases in revenue from the new product. The proposal was rejected by the top management group, which was composed mostly of engineers. They argued that the new product line would 'change the nature of the firm and cause too much disruption'. By remaining in the same market, the technically oriented top management retained its strong power position. It was not until recently, when there were substantial reductions in US defense budgets, that the proposal was resurrected. This, of course, has implications for the power of the engineers in the firm.

Attracting better personnel
An interesting analysis shows how a finance department in a firm perpetuated its power by attracting highly talented people (Pfeffer, 1992). The firm was experiencing financial control problems, and a large number of very highly talented people were hired in the finance department. Because this was a critical contingency for the firm and because good personnel were attracted, the subunit was able to cope more effectively with the environment. As the competence of the staff grew, so did the unit's power.

Influence over behavioral controls
Selection, promotion, compensation, training and socialization are types of behavior controls. If subunits can control and influence these activities, they will be able to perpetuate the power structure and their place within it. This occurs because the level of commitment and involvement

of those who are selected and promoted to key positions will be affected by these processes. They will most likely accept the institutionalized power structure as legitimate.

Defining selection criteria

Powerful subunits can affect both the skills mix and the general value orientations of those who enter the organizations, by influencing selection criteria. For example, one of the important changes in management education since the 1960s was the need for students to develop quantitative skills. Since that time, in many colleges of business, quantitatively oriented departments have had a great deal of power. They are often successful in influencing other areas to select faculty who have similar skills, even though they may not be particularly necessary to the teaching and research objectives.

Affecting promotion criteria

If an error is made in selection, it can be corrected by not promoting those who fail to meet expectations. We have already pointed out the necessity to have both competence and the 'right perspective' for advancement. By defining both the required competence and the right perspective, those who are in powerful positions can strengthen the existing culture, which reinforces the present power structure. This is exactly what was happening with Alan Roberts, in the example that opened this chapter. He wanted to maintain the organization culture that had developed under this leadership so that he might remain in a powerful position.

Influencing compensation

Because pay is important to status, the ability to influence pay criteria and decisions can perpetuate power. In one plant, the plant manager had a very strong interest in safety. When he took charge of the plant, he gave a great deal of legitimate authority to the safety engineering department. This group's power grew, and soon it became influential in most matters of plant engineering and design. It also had a significant effect on a very important compensation decision. The plant manager intended to implement an employee bonus based on achievement of production, quality and safety goals. Because he wanted to emphasize the interdependence of all activities, it was to be a plant-wide bonus system. The safety group, however, believed that the bonus would have a greater impact on safety if the safety component of the bonus was based on departmental performance. This meant that safety goals would be set for each department, not the whole plant. In the end, the bonus system had a plant-wide component and a departmental safety component.

Influencing training

Because of their strategic position in organizations, powerful units are better able to define the subject of training. This is an important type of influence because in training much information is transmitted about the culture of the organization. For example, when key executives in one firm decided that it should have a management-by-objectives (MBO) approach, they introduced it with a company-wide training program. Before the program was introduced, they were very careful to define what they meant by MBO. They developed very specific definitions of 'goal', 'tactic', 'objective' and 'action plan', which were made a basic part of the instructional program.

Influencing organizational socialization

The norms and values transmitted through organizational socialization reflect those of the dominant coalition. The effects of controlling sociali-zation on an organization's culture are shown in a study of a new plant start-up (Zahrly, 1985). The socialization of the workforce was carried out by training that stressed teamwork, group projects that required team-work, and discussions showing how teamwork was to be a foundation of the plant's management philosophy. Teams were formed and given a great deal of autonomy when they began working. Within 18 months, the teamwork norm was firmly embedded in the plant and transmitted to new employees.

Influencing organizational redesign

Through organization design decisions, it is possible to retain control over key contingencies, to maintain workflow centrality, or to protect the non-substitutability of activities. The example of departments of economics in colleges of business administration illustrates how this can occur. Because economics groups are often relatively large as well as very powerful, they are able to influence requirements, so students in most areas must take economics courses. This makes the work of the economics groups very central to the instructional program. It results in very large enrollments for these courses, justifying the addition of new faculty members in that area and, of course, with increased numbers there is usually increased power.

ACQUIRING AND MAINTAINING PERSONAL-BASED INFLUENCE

In some instances, influence is entirely a function of personal attributes. The expert attracts a following because of the skills possessed.

Entrepreneurs attract loyal subordinates because they believe in the entrepreneur's message. These are examples of expert and charismatic power, both personal-based and requiring a fit between the attributes of the power actor and the follower. Personal-based power is also important to managers. If they can develop it, it can supplement legitimate power and be helpful in 'motivating commitment to the tasks that require high effort, initiative, and persistence' (Yukl, 2007) However, it is more difficult to perpetuate personal-based power than organizationally-based influence.

Acquiring and Maintaining Charismatic Power

Charismatic power results from the identification of one person with another. It is based on personal attraction that develops in certain contextual settings that interact with the personal attributes of those involved. In itself, this personal attraction probably has the effect of increasing member identification. Charismatic leaders make followers 'feel good'. Leader charisma and the behavior which it arouses is strongly associated with positive affect (good feelings) and negatively associated with negative affect (bad feelings) (Erez et al., 2008). Followers who have lower core self-evaluations also appear to be less stressed with charismatic leaders, even though there may be significant pressures on them (De Hoogh and Den Hartog, 2009). Followers who are more emotionally stable are not so strongly affected.

Charismatic power develops in a crisis situation, when there are high levels of uncertainty and a group needs inspiration and direction. For example, the existence of crises is related to charismatic behaviors of US presidents (House et al., 1991). As long as the crisis continues, the charismatic leader will continue to have power. Martin Luther King became very influential during the turbulent period of the civil rights movement in the USA. Organization start-ups are another situation in which charismatic influence can develop. In start-ups, members are usually seeking direction and support for their involvement in the new organization.

One explanation for the emergence of charisma in both crisis and start-ups is that the situational context is 'weak'. There are few cues from the environment, and the situation does not generate uniform expectancies for those in it (Mischel, 1977). When the situation is unstructured, those in it may not know how to respond. In this weak context, the charismatic person can provide psychological boundaries and direction by creating new meanings and beliefs for the followers.

Some of the characteristics that we have already discussed as personal attributes of people with the capacity to acquire legitimate authority are attributes of charismatic leaders (McClelland and Boyatzis, 1982):

- Need for power.
- Self-confidence.
- Articulation skills.

In addition, two other attributes are present when charismatic power exists:

- Non-verbal communication skills. The charismatic person has the ability to convey meaning to followers easily with body language, gestures and symbols. Manipulating symbols is very important (Kirkpatrick and Locke, 1996). Revolutions all have slogans, symbols of unity or other signs that identify the struggle and convey meaning to those involved in them.
- Strong convictions about beliefs. This belief is transmitted to the followers both verbally and non-verbally.

As long as the crisis or uncertainty exists, the charismatic person will also retain power. When the crisis ends or the problems are solved, charismatic power can be perpetuated only if it has become institutionalized. Then the charismatic leader can remain, at least as a figurehead, because of the symbolic meaning that he or she conveys to the group. You can learn a lot about how this happens from the example of Fidel Castro. In the late 1950s, he led a revolution in Cuba as a young, charismatic rebel. He remained head of the government and had charismatic power for many years. Here is how he did it.

Perpetuating the charismatic image

By maintaining images of the leader during the period when charismatic power was the dominant model of influence and control, the perception of charisma can be retained. The way that the group sees the charismatic leader, after institutionalization, is usually very controlled so that the charismatic image is not destroyed. Charismatic leaders may also strengthen their image if they are seen as 'self-sacrificing' (van Knippenberg and van Knippenberg, 2005). Think about Fidel Castro as the years of his power in Cuba passed. Though much older, Castro maintained a similar appearance to that which he had during the Cuban revolution, one which is not particularly formal, reflecting his position as the leader of Cuba. He kept his beard and generally appeared in public in a fatigues-like uniform. Pictures of him are still everywhere in Cuba. Years after the Revolution, Castro still appeared to be 'of the people'.

Controlling interaction with groups

When the charismatic leader interacts with large groups, it is usually in controlled settings such as speeches, rites or ceremonies. These can reinforce the organization culture as well as present the charismatic leader in a very positive light. When there is a small group with more interpersonal interaction between the leader and the members, these situations are very controlled. Usually the meetings are of short duration. Normally, those who are in the meeting are carefully selected because they are loyal to the leader or to the organization. In most cases, they also appear to be representative of the larger group of followers.

Evoking specific negative images of the past

The effective use of imagery in language is important for a charismatic leader. In a study, subjects listened to a version of the inauguration speech of Franklin Roosevelt that was either 'high-imagery' or 'low-imagery' (Naidoo and Lord, 2008). Those who heard the 'high-imagery' speech rated the speaker much higher in charisma that those who heard the other version. This effect was stronger for those subjects who were higher in positive affect (see Chapter 1 on personality). Imagery lets the charismatic leader call to mind specific crises or times of uncertainty for group members. This reminds the group of 'how bad it was' (Conger and Kanungo, 1987). Revolutionary political leaders, like Castro, usually refer to very specific cases of tyranny and poverty under previous regimes. The charismatic business leader can evoke the difficult times when he or she was leading the firm through the crisis. The charismatic union leader can bring to union members' minds the low wages, poor safety practices and unfair working conditions of the past that gave rise to the need for a union.

Speaking in general, but positive, terms about the future (Conger and Kanungo, 1987)

This is the counterpart of the previous point. The charismatic leader can evoke images of 'how good it will be' in the future. This is most effectively accomplished when the leader speaks in general terms. Avoiding specifics allows followers to project their own meaning onto the leader's words. Because of the psychological connection between the group and the leader, this will result in a strengthened bond between them.

Acquiring and Maintaining Expert Power

Expert power results from the possession of the ability to do things valued and needed by others. It exists in situations in which specific skills are necessary in an organization, and when the individuals who possess these skills are in short supply. This often happens when the organization's environment is volatile. Then firms must import the newly required skills, and often there is little incentive to try to institutionalize them. Thus, the power remains with the individual.

To acquire expert power, you must possess the necessary physical, mental or interpersonal skills that can help others. There is no way, however, to specify what personality factors might characterize people with expert power because there are so many potential types of expert power. Expert power, however, can be facilitated by the organization or by other external institutions. Both of these can provide legitimacy by giving the expert the appropriate titles, licenses or certification.

Three conditions are necessary to perpetuate expert power:

1. If you have expert power, you must be able to maintain your competence. In one large law firm, for example, only one partner is the environmental law 'expert'. He is important to the firm because he accounts for a large share of the firm's revenue. To maintain his competence, he regularly reads, studies and attends seminars on the topic. Frequently, he teaches a class in environmental law at a nearby university.
2. It is important to ensure that the dependence relationship between the individual and the organization does not change in such a way as to weaken the expert's position. The law firm needs 'environmental expertise' because it is a growing area of practice and an important share of the firm's revenue.
3. The expert must maintain personal control of the expertise. This ensures that others cannot be substituted for him. If environmental law becomes a larger part of the firm's business, it may wish to add other experts in this area, threatening the expert's power. He does this by a careful selection of clients so that new attorneys are not needed, or by managing new experts who join the firm.

USING POWER IN ORGANIZATIONS

We have a very good idea of how managers use some of the influence strategies discussed above (Kipnis et al., 1984; Kipnis, 1987; Cable and Judge, 2003). Managers from the USA, the UK and Australia were asked to indicate their preferred ways to influence both subordinates and superiors. This is how these managers ranked the influence strategies they used in dealing with their subordinates:

1. Reason.
2. Assertive behavior.
3. Coalition formation.
4. Bargaining.
5. Appeals to higher authority.
6. Use of sanctions.

Reason is most frequently used as an influence tactic with superiors, as well as subordinates. It is an attempt to persuade someone else by providing him or her with information. The information is usually straightforward and presented in such a way that it results in the evaluation desired.

Assertive behavior, direct and forceful approaches toward another, especially subordinates, is also often successful. The 'iron law of power' states that the greater the discrepancy in power between the influencer and target, the higher the probability of assertive behavior (Kipnis, 1984). This is usually a strong, aggressive effort to obtain compliance from others. For managers with subordinates, this normally takes the form of giving them direct orders. Initially, however, managers prefer not to use assertive behavior. They prefer to start with reason and simple requests and appeals to legitimate authority. If they meet with resistance, then they are likely to become assertive.

Coalition formation is when two or more parties merge interests. Power can be increased because the alliance has greater control over strategic contingencies or more resources. A manager might form a coalition with a group of subordinates to support a particular project. Then when the time comes to bring others on board, they might be more susceptible to the group pressures; see Chapters 6 and 8.

One approach to coalition formation is co-optation. You co-opt individuals from groups with which you might have problems, into the power structure. When this happens, they are likely to adopt attitudes and values similar to those already in power. A striking example of this was illustrated in a classic study that showed how the attitudes of employees changed after they became managers (Lieberman, 1956). The study was done in a large public utility in which there was a very strong union. An attitude survey of the work force was conducted with a follow-up study to be done one year later. Between surveys, several workers had been promoted to supervisory positions and some were elected union stewards. The follow-up study showed that the attitudes of both groups had changed from the previous year. Those who became supervisors now had attitudes like those of the management group. The union stewards shifted their attitudes to become more strongly oriented toward union values. Becoming a member of the different groups changed their values. One year later, several of those who had been promoted or elected had gone back to the workforce. Their attitudes reverted back to those held by the rest of the workforce, of which they became a part again.

In bargaining, one person seeks to influence another through the exchange of benefits or favors. Whether bargaining is possible depends on three things:

1. Whether each has something, a 'good', desired by the other.
2. Whether either is able and willing to withhold their goods at a cost to the other.
3. Whether either is willing to negotiate.

When a subordinate is unwilling to act in the way that a manager wishes, one possibility always available for that manager is to appeal to the boss. This has the effect of demonstrating to the subordinate that the directive has more organizational legitimacy, as demonstrated by support from higher management levels.

Managers may also threaten subordinates with sanctions, or allocating rewards in punitive ways. They can do this through the legitimate authority of their position. For example, a common practice in some US government agencies is to solicit contributions for political campaigns from employees, even though such demands are illegal in most states. The incumbent politician makes it clear to workers that a 'voluntary' campaign contribution is expected. The politician usually receives these contributions, because the workers know that negative performance evaluations or undesirable work assignments might result if they are not on the list of contributors.

Managers try to influence their superiors, using more or less these same strategies. The main difference in the way that they approach their superiors is that assertive behavior is a much less frequently used strategy and, as you might expect, there is no indication of the use of sanctions. This is their order of preference when trying to influence superiors:

1. Reason.
2. Coalition formation.
3. Bargaining.
4. Assertive behavior.
5. Appeals to higher authority.

Managers use different patterns of these strategies (Kipnis et al., 1984; Kipnis, 1984). 'Shotgun managers' tended to use all the tactics with above-average frequency, apparently because they had many different problems to solve. They were also the least-experienced managers in the study. 'Tactician managers' attempted to influence others through the use of reason and logic and were about average in their use of other tactics. Tacticians tended to manage technically complex work groups, with skilled employees and work that required much planning. 'Bystander managers' reported below-average use of all the influence tactics studied and seemed to exert relatively little influence on others. In general, they managed relatively routine work and supervised a large number of employees. They were also the least satisfied with the effectiveness of their work.

A study by Cable and Judge shows that which influence strategy a manager uses appears to depend upon three things: personality, the leadership approach of the target of influence, and the type of work of the influencing manager (Cable and Judge, 2003). For example, extroverts tended to use inspirational appeals and ingratiation, and agreeable managers tended to avoid the use of confrontational and pressure influence tactics. When the target of influence was a transformational leader, their subordinates tended to use participative, consultative strategies, while laissez-faire managers were approached in more transactional ways. When managerial targets were seem as inspirational leaders, their subordinates resorted to a broad range of influence tactics such as ingratiation, seeking coalitions and legitimization approaches. An interesting finding was how functional work assignment was related to upward influence. Soft approaches were the preference of those in marketing positions, while harder approaches were used by managers in finance and accounting, a finding that is not surprising given the stereotypes usually associated with those types of positions (Cable and Judge, 2003).

Organizations, Power and Women

Notwithstanding substantial evidence that women have similar power motivation to that of men, many still hold stubbornly to the belief that women are less able to manage effectively with power (Winter, 1988; Heilman and Haynes, 2005; Vecchio, 2007). To some extent this may be traced to how women are viewed. For example, men are usually described using words that have a socially positive connotation: they are strong, large, assertive, analytical and they act on the world. Terms describing women have a largely 'negative' connotation; they are thought of as 'not men', small, weak and light (McClelland, 1975). This gender-based worldview finds itself reflected in differences in the way men and women are treated in the work setting.

We see, for example, that for many years, on average for the whole working population, women's earnings have fluctuated between 70 percent and 80 percent of what men earn. This is somewhat misleading in one sense because the large proportion of women in the workforce are in much lower-paying jobs than men, jobs such as secretaries and retail clerks. However, even when women work in jobs similar in level, author- ity and skill requirements to men, there is still a substantial wage gap. For example, female accountants earn about $10000 a year less than men, and male teachers average about $4000 per year more than women teachers. In a recent study of 2000 of the world's most profitable companies there were 29 (1.5 percent) women CEOs, and 2.6 percent in the Fortune 500 Global list. Yet the authors of the study say that this is 'some progress' (Hansen et al., 2010; Ibarra and Hansen, 2010). There seems to be no good basis for such differences. There is enough evidence that women can deal with power and be as effective as men in leadership situations. An analysis of studies that compared leadership effectiveness of men and women shows that, on average, women are evaluated as being as effective as men (Eagly et al., 1995), though there are some important differences. For example, men are seen as more effective when the work context and work roles tend to be defined in more 'masculine' terms, or the group is numerically dominated by men, as for example in military situations. Women, on the other hand, are more effective when the leadership role is more female- congenial, meaning that interpersonal skills are dominant requirements. This suggests that, overall, there are no meaningful differences in ability between men and women and that women can manage as well as men, but that there are some situations that facilitate male or female leaders in different ways (Eagly et al., 2010; Dobbins and Platz, 1986).

Spotlight 9.4   Culture and power

'Power distance' is the degree to which differences in power and status are accepted in a culture. Some nations accept high differ- ences in power and authority between members of different social classes or occupational levels; other nations do not. For example, the French are relatively high in power distance while Israel and Sweden score very low. In Israel and Sweden, worker groups demand and have a great deal of power over work assignments and conditions of work (Cole, 1989; Adler, 1991). French man- agers tend not to interact socially with subordinates and do not expect to negotiate work assignments with them. The experience of a French MBA student in a US firm illustrates the French sense of power distance. She was surprised to find on the first day of her internship in a US company that some workers called the manager by his first name and talked with him about their weekend activi- ties. She felt that this would rarely happen in a French factory.

There are some other consequences of power distance differences. For example, in low-power-distance countries such as
the USA, powerful individuals can be forced out of their position
or can be successfully challenged by less powerful individuals or
groups (Brislin, 1993). This is not likely to happen in a high-power-
distance country. In the low-power-distance country, individuals
feel less discomfort and stress when disagreeing with the boss.
For example, in Hong Kong (a high-power-distance culture),
individuals are less upset when they are insulted by high-status
individuals than people are in a low-power-distance culture, such
as the USA.

SUMMARY

This chapter deals with some of the most important and fascinating topics
in organizational behavior: influence, power, politics and compliance.
They are at the heart of what managers do to achieve things with and
through others. A model of compliance processes shows that compliance –
the degree to which a person acts in accordance with the wishes of another
– can occur for several reasons. In some cases, individuals comply because
of the psychological contract; in others it is because of legitimate authority; and in other instances the use of power may lead to compliance.

There is a distinction between legitimate authority and power.
Legitimate authority is the right of decision and command over others
that is accepted as appropriate. Power is the use of force outside legitimate
authority. Four types of power were discussed: reward power, coercive
(punishment) power, expert power and charismatic power.

The characteristics of the situation and the individuals are related to the
different types of influence that are acquired and exerted. The organizational context for power is related to the extent to which subunits interact
with volatile environments, perform non-substitutable activities, or are
central to organizational functioning.

We have also shown how power can be maintained in organizations.
Often maintaining power depends on a person's ability to perpetuate
the settings in which power was originally developed. This can be done
in different ways. In many instances, legitimate authority, reward power
and punishment power can be maintained because the power holders
have control of organization processes, such as the choice of strategies,
selection of personnel, and promotions.

GUIDE FOR MANAGERS: USING POWER IN ORGANIZATIONS

You must know that if you are going to manage anything, you can't escape using legitimate authority and power. As we pointed out earlier, power is not based on the psychological contract – legitimate authority is. This means that you should have little trouble using legitimate authority. The most important thing that you need to know about it is the boundaries of the psychological contract.

Power is different because you are going outside those boundaries. For that reason, it is best, in organizations, not to use brute force and coercion, but rather to use power in much more subtle ways. If force and coercion are used, those in opposition will probably try to use counter force. This will result in force against force, open conflict that organizations try to avoid because harmony is so highly valued. The subtle use of power allows the appearance of logic and rationality to be maintained.

You can have your way without overt pressure and force by using some of the approaches discussed here. But you must remember two old proverbs when you become involved in the use of power, the game of organizational politics. One is: 'What goes around, comes around.' The second, maybe a little more precise, is: 'Those who live by the sword, die by the sword.' This means that even if you are successful in getting others to do what you want them to do, if they have lost something there may come a time when you will have to pay for your success. Before you start, however, you should ask yourself if you have the stomach for the game. The way to know this is to review the sections of this chapter that discuss the personal attributes of those who acquire organizational and personal power. Without these, you might not fare well in this contest. Here is a list of things that you can do, mostly suggested by Pfeffer (1992).

Control the Context

If you have the legitimate authority to do so, you can structure the context so that the intended behaviors are likely to occur. Your legitimate authority can be extended in political ways because a position in an organization gives you some degree of control over the allocation of resources, the distribution of rewards and the implementation of sanctions. As a manager, you can exert influence in many ways by careful contextual control of others' behavior and decisions. Suppose that you are a vice-president of marketing and have been asked by the CEO to make a recommendation about which one of five new products a firm should develop. A non-political evaluation process would subject each product to a rigorous assessment of costs and benefits. Suppose, however, that you prefer one of the products over the others. You could influence the choice process by appointing a committee composed of people who are likely to favor the product.

Define the Problem Your Way

As a manager, especially with subordinates, you can often select or define the problem that is to be solved. This limits the range of solutions that can be considered. If the academic vice-president of the university asks a committee to develop a program to 'enhance the reputation of the university', the committee will attack the issue differently than they would if the problem is, 'How can the university enhance its reputation as a graduate institution?' People will have an opportunity to exercise some influence over the different ways that the problem is solved, but not over the selection of the problem, which by definition was confined to graduate emphasis.

Make Subjective Use of Objective Criteria

An effective way to use political power is to influence the criteria used in decision making. For example, as the marketing vice-president involved in the product choice decision above, you could define the criteria that will be used in the product evaluation process. In other words, you can 'structure' them in a way that will lead to a favorable evaluation of the preferred alternative.

A second, related, political strategy is to discount objective criteria so that although one of the alternatives appears better than others, the rating of this alternative is lowered for political reasons. Suppose the board of directors has two candidates for the CEO position: one is from inside the firm and the second from outside. Suppose that the outside candidate is now the president of a small but very profitable firm. Those who favor the inside candidate might argue that the success of the smaller firm is not due to the president but to other factors such as luck, lack of competition or a special competitive advantage such as a patent. If they are successful in discounting the outside candidate's performance, then the insider will be selected. Though a little different in specifics, this is what Alan Roberts did in the example that opened the chapter.

Use Outside Experts

You can get support for your position by using outside experts to justify and rationalize decisions. This combines legitimate power and expert power. At one extreme, expert opinion can be brought in through research reports and published articles to support a position. At the other extreme, consultants or members of the board of directors can be used to make recommendations, to introduce changes and to reinforce decisions. You can see how this worked in the Alan Roberts succession case. Robert was able to use the two consulting firms in ways that furthered his agenda. By letting candidates know that the position would be 'CEO-in-training', neither consulting firm could come up with the 'Class A' list of candidates, leaving those on the list who were more likely to agree to his agenda.

Control the Flow and Quantity of Information

A person can control when information is released, how much is released, and what others get. Suppose the board of directors, in the example above, favors an inside candidate for president. The number of outside candidates can be limited in several ways. One is by delaying the announcement of the position and setting an early date for the appointment. The board could also affect the selection through limited release of information. When prospective candidates inquire about the job, the board may provide general, not specific, information about salaries and benefits.

Controlling the agenda of meetings is another way to manage the flow and type of information. Both the content of the agenda and the order in which items are considered can influence decisions. This is a common occurrence at stockholder meetings. The board of directors usually determines the agenda, with little time for shareholders interested in other matters to raise them. If such issues are raised, then the board can usually influence the decision because it controls the proxies.

Acquire a Sponsor

A sponsor is a person at a higher organizational level or in a powerful position who represents and advances the interests of another. Sponsorship provides influence in two ways:

1. The sponsor may be an advocate for a person in a promotion decision. This could result in advancement for the person while at the same time creating a loyal subordinate for the sponsor.
2. The sponsor may advance ideas and projects that are developed by the person. If the projects and ideas are good, the sponsor may even be given some credit for bringing them to the attention of decision makers.

The two things that you have to do to acquire a sponsor are to demonstrate competence and to engage in ingratiation. If you do well on important tasks, you will usually come to the attention of someone at a higher-level position, who may be a willing sponsor. Then, by ingratiation, you can increase your attractiveness to others. It is usually accomplished through flattery and a display of commitment or potential commitment. Flattery positively reinforces the target. In one organization, a young engineer with high power needs successfully used ingratiation to acquire the sponsorship of a senior project engineer. The senior engineer had been assigned the task of improving the productivity of a plant that was having serious performance difficulties. He had very little support from the plant's staff because they feared that his changes would reduce their status. The young engineer, in a quiet and discreet way, began to let the senior engineer know that he believed the project could work. He gave the senior engineer a good deal of positive feedback about the plans that were being developed. He also made certain that the senior engineer believed that he too thought the resistance from the old staff was unwarranted. While he supported the change project, there was only one problem: because he was new to the organization, he told the senior engineer, it did not seem wise to support the proposals publicly. Because there were no other supporters, the senior engineer began to confide in the younger person. He also started to sponsor him, recommending him for special assignments and early promotion.

Use Impression Management

One way to develop power is by impression management to create the illusion that one has it. This is done by the control of information, or cues, imparted to others to manage their impressions. Specialists practice impression management when they use jargon unique to their profession. The doctor's white coat and use of medical terms does nothing to increase technical competence, but it conveys important meanings to patients. A top executive may try to create the impression of power by high activity levels and demonstrations of organizational loyalty. This may be done by using symbols such as large offices, deep carpets and special furniture. The executive may also remain aloof and apart from lower-level members to maintain status distinctions.

Those at lower levels can also try to manage impressions of them by superiors. They may seek to give the impression that they are loyal and to create the belief that they are competent in their job and always busy. Being a 'good' subordinate may be a way to gain power because superiors may place trust in him or her. Then the subordinate may be able to expand the power from the current legitimate authority base.

CASE: THE FACULTY OF ECONOMICS

When Rosario Romano was appointed Rector of the San Gregorio University in 2007 he was given the charge, by the Administrative Council, to improve the quality of student performance. His strategy for achieving this was to implement his philosophy of 'competence and delegation'. First, he would find very strong and very competent deans for each of the faculties. Second, he would give each of them a great deal of autonomy. He allowed deans to make hiring decisions, to evaluate professors, to make salary decisions and to decide how to spend the budget allocated to each faculty.

From 2007 to 2010, San Gregorio University made significant gains in student achievement. However, there was one faculty, Economics, which was a problem for Romano. The Dean of Economics was David Scalise. Scalise was one of the first deans that Romano hired, but now Romano believed that he had made a mistake.

In Economics, the professors did not seem to care about the students. They were, by any measure, mediocre. However they were very loyal to Scalise. He was well liked by them and they supported him. The reason was that Scalise never put any pressure on them for performance and did not really hold them accountable.

When Romano became aware of this, he discussed it with Scalise. Scalise became angry and threatened to quit. He told Romano that the reason Economics wasn't a good faculty was because Romano didn't give them enough resources to do the job properly. Romano pointed out the opposite. In fact, by every budget measure, Scalise and the Faculty of Economics were well treated.

By 2010, Scalise and Romano were on very bad terms. They argued often and all the other deans saw Scalise as an uncooperative prima donna. In one of their arguments, Scalise threatened to resign. Romano told him, 'Bring me the letter, now!' Scalise left the office and returned 20 minutes later with a letter of resignation. Romano didn't hesitate: 'I'll take it,' he said.

Romano searched for a replacement and found Giuseppe Verona, a bright young professor in a nearby university. When he hired Verona, Romano told him: 'I want you to get Economics straightened out and I'll help you. The professors are well paid, and you've got good resources there, but the job does not get done.

'One of the main problems you will have is that most of the professors are very loyal to Scalise. They won't help you much, but I'll give you whatever help and support you need.'

Verona's approach was straightforward. He would let everyone know what was expected of them, make pay as contingent on performance as possible, and hire good new professors. He thought that in three or four years there would be enough turnover that, with subsequent replacement, he could make Economics into a high-performing faculty.

Romano watched Verona's progress and he was pleased. Three new young professors were hired. Verona instituted a different evaluation approach to that under Scalise: he started to give substantial recognition to the good professors and less to those who weren't so good. This was a major departure from the way Scalise had managed the faculty, and many of the Scalise loyalists were angry. Some complained to Romano and some filed official complaints. When Romano and the Administrative Council investigated, they found that the charges were without foundation. It is true that things had changed, but now the school was not managed in the style of Scalise, but in a performance-oriented style by Verona.

This was exactly what Romano thought had to be done. Between 2007 and 2010, student performance improved considerably. However, many of the professors who were old Scalise supporters were dissatisfied. They continued to complain and grumble. Each time they came to Romano, however, he supported Verona.

In late 2010, Romano left San Giorgio University for a high position in the Ministry of Education. Andrea Bergamini replaced him. Bergamini had been an assistant to Romano for several years. There were two things about Bergamini that were of concern to Verona. First, Bergamini had been a professor in Economics during the first years of Scalise's time as dean. They had, in fact, become close friends. Secondly, Bergamini announced that he was going to centralize many activities that had been performed previously by the deans. No longer would the deans make budgeting decisions, evaluate personnel or hire faculty. Giuseppe Verona was very worried.

1. What was the basis of Giuseppe Verona's power during his tenure? How does it differ from that of Scalise?
2. What are the potential effects of the change to centralization on Verona?
3. How do you think the supporters of Scalise will react to the change? To Verona?

REFERENCES

Adler, N.J. (1991), *International Dimensions of Organizational Behavior*. Boston, MA: PWS-KENT Publishing Company.

Bagozzi, R. and L. Phillips (1982), Representing and Testing Organizational Theories: A Holistic View. *Administrative Science Quarterly*, **77**: 459–88.

Boeker, W. (1990), The Development and Institutionalization of Subunit Power in Organizations. *Administrative Science Quarterly*, **34**: 388–410.

Brislin, R. (1993), *Understanding Culture's Influence on Behavior*. Fort Worth, TX: Harcourt Brace Jovanovich.

Bunderson, J.S. (2003), Team Member Functional Background and Involvement in Management Teams: Direct Effects and the Moderating Role of Power Centralization. *Academy of Management Journal*, **46**(4): 458–74.

Butt, A.N., J.N. Choi and A.M. Jaeger (2010), Does Power Matter?: Negotiator Status as a Moderator of the Relationship between Negotiator Emotion and Behavior. *Journal of Organizational Behavior*, **21**(2): 124–46.

Cable, D.M. and T.A. Judge (2003), Managers' Upward Influence Tactic Strategies: The Role of Manager Personality and Supervisor Leadership Style. *Journal of Organizational Behavior*, **24**(2): 197–214.

Cole, R.E. (1989), *Strategies for Learning: Small Group Activities in American, Japanese, and Swedish Industry*. Berkeley, CA: University of California Press.

Conger, J.A. and R. Kanungo (1987), Toward a Behavioral Theory of Charismatic Leadership in Organizational Settings. *Academy of Management Review*, **12**(4): 637–47.

Crozier, M. (1964), *The Bureaucratic Phenomenon*. Chicago, IL: University of Chicago Press.

Dalberg-Acton, J. (1949), *Essays on Freedom and Power*. Boston, MA: Beacon Press.

De Hoogh, A.H.B. and D.N. Den Hartog (2009), Neuroticism and Locus of Control as Moderators of the Relationships of Charismatic and Autocratic Leadership With Burnout. *Journal of Applied Psychology*, **94**(4): 1058–67.

Den Hartog, D.N., A.H.B. De Hoogh and A.E. Keegan (2007), The Interactive Effects of Belongingness and Charisma on Helping and Compliance. *Journal of Applied Psychology*, **92**(4): 1131–39.

Dobbins, G.H. and S.J. Platz (1986), Sex Differences in Leadership: How Real are They? *Academy of Management Review*, **11**(1): 118–27.

Eagly, A.H., S.J. Karau and M.G. Mikhijani (1995), Gender and the Effectiveness of Leaders: A Meta-Analysis. *Journal of Applied Psychology*, **117**(1): 121–45.

Erez, A., V.F. Misangyi, D.E. Johnson, M.A. LePine and K.C. Halverson (2008), Stirring the Hearts of Followers: Charismatic Leadership as the Transferal of Affect. *Journal of Applied Psychology*, **93**(3): 602–16.

Etzioni, A. (1961), *A Comparative Analysis of Complex Organizations*. New York: Free Press.

Etzioni, A. (1963), *Modern Organizations*. New York: Prentice-Hall.

French, J.R.P., Jr. and B. Raven (1959), The Bases of Social Power. In *Studies in Social Power*, D. Cartwright (ed.). Ann Arbor, MI: University of Michigan Institute for Social Research;. pp. 150–67.

Hansen, M.T., H. Ibarra and U. Peyer (2010), The Best-Performing CEOs in the World. *Harvard Business Review*, **88**(1–2): 104–13.

Heilman, M.E. and M.C. Haynes (2005), No Credit Where Credit Is Due: Attributional Rationalization of Women's Success in Male–Female Teams. *Journal of Applied Psychology*, **90**(5): 905–16.

Hickson, D.J., C.R. Hinings, C.A. Lee, R.E. Schneck and J.M. Pennings (1971), A Strategic Contingencies' Theory of Intraorganizational Power. *Administrative Science Quarterly*, **16**.

Hofstede, G. (1980), *Culture's Consequences: International Differences in Work-Related Values*. Beverly Hills, CA: Sage Publications.

House, R.J. (1984), Power in Organizations: A Social Psychological Perspective. Working paper. University of Toronto.

House, R.J. (1988), Power and Personality in Complex Organizations. In *Research in Organizational Behavior*, B.J. Staw and L.L. Cummings (eds). Greenwich, CT: JAI Press, pp. 305–57.

House, R.J., W.D. Spangler and J. Woycke (1991), Personality and Charisma in the US Presidency: A Psychological Theory of Leader Effectiveness. *Administrative Science Quarterly*, **36**(3): 364–96.

Ibarra, H. and M.T. Hansen (2010), Women CEOs: Why So Few? Interaction. *Harvard Business Review*, **88**(3): 14–15.

Kipnis, D. (1984), The Use of Power in Organizations and in Interpersonal Settings. In *Applied Social Psychology Annual*, S. Oscamp (ed.). Beverly Hills, CA: Sage Publications, pp. 179–210.

Kipnis, D. (1987), Psychology and Behavioral Technology. *American Psychologist*, **42**(1): 30–36.

Kipnis, D., S.M. Schmidt, C. Swaffin-Smith and I. Wilkinson (1984), Patterns of Managerial Influence: Shotgun Managers, Tacticians, and Bystanders. *Organizational Dynamics*, **12**: 58–67.

Kirkpatrick, S. and E.A. Locke (1996), Direct and Indirect Effects of Three Core Leadership Components on Performance and Attitudes. *Journal of Applied Psychology*, **81**(1): 36–51.

Krackhardt, D. (1990), Assessing the Political Landscape: Structure, Cognition, and Power in Organizations. *Administrative Science Quarterly*, **35**: 342–69.

Levina, N. and W.J. Orlikowski (2009), Understanding Shifting Power Relations Within and Across Organizations: A Critical Genre Analysis. *Academy of Management Journal*, **52**(4): 672–703.

Lieberman, S. (1956), The Effects of Changes in Roles on the Attitudes of Role Occupants. *Human Relations*, **9**: 385–402.

McClelland, D.A. (1975), *Power: The Inner Experience*. New York: Irvington.

McClelland, D.A. and R.E. Boyatzis (1982), Leadership Motive Pattern and Long-Term Success in Management. *Journal of Applied Psychology*, **67**: 737–43.

Milgram, S. (1974), *Obedience to Authority*. New York: Harper & Row.

Mischel, W. (1977), The Interaction of Person and Situation. In *Personality at the Crossroads: Current Issues in Interactional Psychology*, D. Magnusson and N.S. Enders (eds). Hillsdale, NJ: Erlbaum.

Montes, S.D. and D. Zweig (2009), Do Promises Matter? An Exploration of the Role of Promises in Psychological Contract Breach. *Journal of Applied Psychology*, **94**(5): 1243–60.

Mowday, R.T. (1980), Leader Characteristics, Self-Confidence and Methods of Upward Influence in Organization Decision Situations. *Academy of Management Journal*, **44**: 709–24.

Naidoo, L.J. and R.G. Lord (2008), Speech Imagery and Perceptions of Charisma: The Mediating Role of Positive Affect. *Leadership Quarterly*, **19**(3): 283–96.

Pfeffer, J. (1992), *Managing With Power*. Boston, MA: Harvard Business School Press.

Pfeffer, J. and G. Salancik (1974), Organizational Decision Making as a Political Process: The Case of the University Budget. *Administrative Science Quarterly*, **19**: 135–51.

Schein, E.A. (1970), *Organizational Psychology*. New York: Prentice-Hall.

Tosi, H.L. (1992), *The Environment/Organization/Person Contingency Model: A Meso Approach to the Study of Organizations*. Greenwich, CT: JAI Press, Inc.

Tushman, M.L. and E. Romanelli (1985), Organizational Evolution: A Metamorphosis Model of Convergence and Reorientation. In *Research in Organizational Behavior*, L.L. Cummings and B.M. Staw (eds). Greenwich, CT: JAI Press, 171–222.

van Knippenberg, B. and D. van Knippenberg (2005), Leader Self-Sacrifice and Leadership Effectiveness: The Moderating Role of Leader Prototypicality. *Journal of Applied Psychology*, **90**(1): 25–37.

Vecchio, R.P. (2002), Leadership and Gender Advantage. *Leadership Quarterly*, **13**(6): 643–71.

Weber, M. (1947), *The Theory of Social and Economic Organization*. New York: Free Press.

Winter, D.G. (1988), The Power Motive in Men and Women. *Journal of Personality and Social Psychology*, **54**(3): 510–19.

Yorges, S.L., H.M. Weiss and O.J. Strickland (1999), The effect of leader outcomes on influence, attributions, and perceptions of charisma. *Journal of Applied Psychology*, **84**(3): 428–36.

Yukl, G.A. (2007), *Leadership in Organizations*. Saddle River, NJ: Prentice Hall.

Zahrly, J.H. (1985), An Analysis of the Source of an Organization's Culture. In Midwest Business Administration Association Meetings. Chicago, IL: pp. 12–15.

Zimbardo, P. (2007), *The Lucifer Effect: Understanding how Good People Turn Evil*. New York: Random House.

10. Leadership in organizations

PREPARING FOR CLASS

When you think of a leader, who comes to your mind? Think of someone whom you consider to be an effective leader and someone who you view as an ineffective one. When you have two individuals firmly in mind, answer these questions:

1. Did you base your judgment of their leadership effectiveness on the behaviors they exhibit? Did you base it on who they were as a person (their traits)? Or did you base it on their success in leading others?
2. Did you use the same criteria for the ineffective leader as you did for the effective one?
3. Can you evaluate the reason for the differing effectiveness of the two leaders you considered? Would you attribute their differing effectiveness to behaviors, traits or measures of success?
4. What conclusions can you draw about leadership from this comparison?

* *

We are fascinated with leadership – whether it is in business, government or sports – and one of the interesting questions is why someone is thought to be a good leader. We know that boards of directors very often use a psychological selection model that seeks to find new chief executive officers (CEOs) who are experienced, who have performed well and, more importantly, are highly charismatic (Khurana, 2002). Typically, the compensation of these charismatic CEOs is extremely high, but they do not lead the firms to better performance (Khurana, 2002; Tosi et al., 2004). Yet, we know from the research, as we know from common sense, that leaders do have strong effects on organizations. For instance, changing CEOs can affect the price of the stock of a firm (Huson et al., 2001). We also know that when the new CEO uses charismatic language in conveying information to stockholders in the annual report, security analysts tend to rate the stock of the company more highly and provide a strong 'buy' recommendation (Fanelli et al., 2004). All this is well and good, but there is an important caveat. Simply replacing one poor manager with another is not the answer. A competent replacement is required. A study of the effects of coach replacements on team performance in the National Basketball Association (NBA) showed that replacing a coach, alone, had little effect on team success. What made the difference was the competence of the new coach, as measured by experience in the NBA and success in turning other teams around (Pfeffer and Davis-Blake, 1987).

Those who select managers and coaches are faced with the difficult problem of predicting success, a problem so difficult that millions of dollars and much time are spent thinking, talking and writing about leadership. This theorizing, speculation and research on leadership has persisted for a long time, always with the same objectives: to understand leadership in ways that make it possible to select persons who are likely to be effective leaders, and to improve training and development in leadership skills.

Leadership is the process 'of influencing others to understand and agree about what needs to be done and how it can be done effectively, and the process of facilitating individual and collective efforts to accomplish shared objectives' (Yukl, 2002; House and Mitchell, 1974). This definition places leadership in the broad domain of influence, power, authority and politics discussed in Chapter 9, but there is an important difference. In this chapter, we discuss leadership theory that, almost without exception, focuses on individuals in organizational positions with legitimate authority to make decisions about others. The reason is that, with the exception of some research on charisma, most empirical tests of leadership have been done in organizations.

We have made another important choice in this chapter. We think that the best way to learn about leadership is to focus on the most well-developed leadership theories about which there has been some substantial empirical support for the theories. For that reason you won't find two types of approaches in this chapter. First, there are two approaches discussed in many organizational behavior books that are not included here. One is 'path–goal theory' (House, 1971) and the other is the maturity approach of Hersey and Blanchard (1988). In the case of path–goal theory there is a substantial body of research (Schreisheim and DeNisi, 1981) that fails to support the model. And while the Hersey–Blanchard model has apparent face validity and widespread popularity, there has been no substantial effort to test it. Second, you will not find leadership ideas from popular leadership books by consultants. So you won't learn how to be a *One Minute Manager* (Blanchard, 1985) or what are *The 7 Habits of Highly Effective People* (Covey, 2004). And if you like the Mafia, you can read *Tony Soprano on Management* (Schneider, 2004), but if you want to stay on the good side,

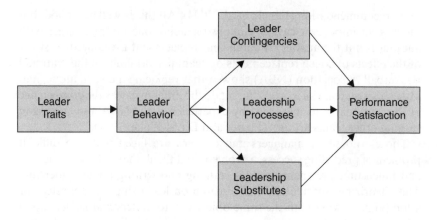

Figure 10.1   A leadership model

there is the *Leadership Wisdom of Jesus* (Manz, 2005). While these sorts of books may be interesting, inspirational and even motivational, they don't meet our test of theoretical development or empirical assessment.

Figure 10.1 shows our general approach to leadership and leadership theory. You will remember that in Chapter 1 we said that personality traits are predispositions to act in a particular way. This fits nicely with the ideas that were the bases of the early research on leadership, when leadership was studied as a collection of personal traits of persons identified as leaders. Then the focus shifted, and emphasized leadership as behaviors, or a behavioral repertoire, designed to help a group to achieve its objectives. Then, beginning in the mid-1960s, attention shifted again and was directed toward contingency theories of leadership that are built on the notion that effective leadership behavior depends on the situation in which leader and followers interact. Then some writers began to suggest that leadership wasn't the only way to achieve results, that there could be some factors that could 'substitute' for leadership. More recently, the focus is on the leadership process, an approach that examines not just the traits or behavior of the leader, but also the critical dimensions of the relationship between the leader and the followers that lead to leader influence. These themes are the main ideas about leadership theory and research discussed in this chapter.

TRAIT APPROACHES

We often hear that leaders are forceful, tend to be very outgoing, and are persuasive. These commonsense observations form the basis of the belief that the personalities of effective leaders are different from those of non-leaders. Trait theories of leadership are based on this idea and are the basis for much of the early research on leadership. Studies have examined factors such as age, height, intelligence, academic achievement, judgmental ability and insight, all of which have been associated with successful leadership (Judge et al., 2004; Judge and Cable, 2004). These studies were done in a wide variety of settings such as military units, business firms, student organizations, elementary schools and universities.

The results of this research initially led to a rather disappointing conclusion. No specific traits seem to be consistently correlated with leadership in all situations (Judge et al., 2009). However, there are several explanations for such a result. First, just because a person has a particular single trait, this is not a sufficient condition to be in a leadership position or a management job and to be successful at it. Recall that a trait is a particular, relatively stable and enduring individual tendency to react emotionally or behaviorally in a specific way. So, just because you have a particular trait, or set of traits, associated with leadership, it is entirely possible that you may not be an effective leader. You must want the job, seek it and want to be effective. Also, traits do not operate alone, but in consonance with other factors. In addition, your behavior must be 'leadership behavior' (as we discuss below), and while you may have such a grouping of leadership traits, you will have an advantage over those who do not, and over those who have a similar constellation; but if you do not want to be in a leadership or management position or simply don't act in leader-like ways, then you won't be a leader (Bass, 2009). The second reason why these research studies produce very divergent results is that the studies have been done in too many different situations. Traits may be related to effectiveness in some situations, but not in others. Third, there is also the possibility that the trait research tended to focus on very specific traits instead of more general factors.

More recently, however, the trait approach has been shown to be useful in understanding leadership (Bass, 2009; Judge et al., 2009). Bass and Stogdill (Bass, 1990) two of the most prominent and important leadership theorists, argue that like the Big Five personality dimensions, if the many specific leadership traits studied were grouped into general classes of factors, there would be differences between effective and ineffective leaders. Bass and Stogdill (Bass, 1990, 2009) grouped these many factors into the following general characteristics that they associated with leadership:

1. Capacity refers to an individual's ability to solve problems, make judgments and generally work harder. Specific traits are intelligence, alertness, verbal facility, originality and judgment.
2. Achievement: effective leaders tend to do better in academic work,

have more knowledge and accomplish more in athletics than ineffective leaders.

3. The specific traits that reflect responsibility – another general characteristic of effective leaders – are dependability, initiative, persistence, aggressiveness, self-confidence and a desire to excel.

4. Participation and involvement are higher for effective leaders than for ineffective ones. Effective leaders tend to be more active and more sociable, have greater capacity to adapt to different situations, and show higher levels of cooperation than less effective leaders.

The Big Five Personality (and Other) Dimensions and Leadership

An ambitious, and interesting, approach to trait theories of leadership has been developed by Judge et al. (2009). They conducted an extensive review of the relationship between leadership and the Big Five personality dimensions, core self-evaluations, intelligence, charisma, narcissism, hubris, dominance and Machiavellianism. A focus on the Big Five dimensions of personality shows that they are not only an important predictor of performance motivation, as we have noted in Chapter 1 on personality, but they are also related to leadership. Specifically, Judge et al. (2002) showed that four of the Big Five traits (extraversion, conscientiousness, emotional stability and openness to experience) were strongly related to leadership emergence and effectiveness.

A unique, and creative, wrinkle in the analysis by Judge et al. (2009) is how they differentiated between positive and negative effects of 'bright side' (or socially desirable) personality traits and 'dark side' (or socially undesirable) personality traits. This is an obvious point that seems to have been generally overlooked until recently: the bright side traits (conscientiousness, extraversion, agreeableness, openness to experience, core self-evaluations, intelligence and charisma) that we know that are related to leadership may also have negative effects in some situations (Van Iddekinge et al., 2009). For example, conscientious leaders might not react well in very uncertain conditions because they may feel that they don't have the necessary time to analyze the situation and arrive at the best decision, or highly intelligent leaders may overanalyze a situation and delay action. Similarly, the dark side traits (narcissism, hubris, social dominance and Machiavellianism), which appear generally to be linked to negative leader effects, may in some instances have a positive impact. For example, a manager high in Machiavellianism may tend, typically, to act in unethical ways and be very politically oriented, but may also think very strategically and influence choices in ways that might have significant effects on firm performance. One study which did test how these dark traits affected subordinates through the characteristics of their jobs found that subordinates with hostile leaders had lower job commitment, lower job satisfaction and higher anxiety than those who worked for less hostile leaders (Schaubroeck et al., 2007).

Spotlight 10.1 Machiavelli's suggested leadership style

Everyone believes that it is laudable for a prince to rule with honesty and not with guile and cunning. However Machiavelli's experience was that princes who were successful 'have held good faith of little account' and have known how to use craft and cunning to go back on their word, and win in the end. According to Machiavelli, there are two ways of dealing with others: one is to rely on the law, and the other is to use force. Relying on the law is typical of men, but beasts use force. Because depending on the law is often ineffective, a prince must often elect for the use of force. This means that the Prince must be able to operate both as a man, relying on the law, and also as a beast, relying on force. The beasts that the Prince should use as models are the fox and the lion. A lion cannot defend himself against snares and traps, while the fox is vulnerable to wolves. Being a fox permits the Prince to find the traps, and as a lion he can fend off the wolves. So, Machiavelli says, the wise prince cannot rule simply with honesty, when this may be turned against him. It is not enough to be simply a lion; a Prince who knows how to act as the fox will be more likely to succeed.

McClelland's Leader Motive Pattern

Another important trait-like leadership approach is the 'leader motive pattern' (McClelland and Boyatzis, 1982). This configuration of personality dimensions has been related to managerial effectiveness (McClelland, 1975, 1985):

1. Power needs that are higher than achievement needs and affiliation needs.
2. High power inhibition.

Power needs refer to the person's desire to have an emotional or behavioral impact on others. Low affiliation means that the person does not require interaction with, or positive acceptance by, others. Power inhibition means that the person has discipline and self-control in the use of power. A study of senior managers found that a pattern existed among those who succeeded (McClelland and Boyatzis, 1982):

1. Managers who are concerned about influencing others.
2. Managers who are less concerned about being liked.
3. Managers who have a moderate degree of self-control.

These managers are more likely to succeed than those without this pattern. These results are impressive because the personality evaluation of the managers in the study was done 8 and 16 years before the measure of success was assessed. Other studies show that the leader motive pattern of branch managers appears to be important at higher managerial levels (Cornelius and Lane, 1984; Thomas et al., 2001).

BEHAVIORAL APPROACHES TO LEADERSHIP

While trait approaches are useful in describing leadership, they do present a particular problem that is apparent when you think about training or developing leaders. Imagine a firm or the military, thinking about how to train managers or officers. How do you train a trait? You don't, since traits are, stable psychological (internal) characteristics that are significantly a result of your genetic make-up, and they are manifested by behaviors and actions. If that is so, then why not try to understand how leaders behave, or act (see Figure 10.1, showing that traits lead to behavior)? That is the theme of the behavioral approaches to leadership that examine how what a leader does is related to leader effectiveness. How many times does the leader discipline an employee? How often does the leader communicate with employees?

There are two classes of behavior that have received much attention in the leadership literature:

1. Decision influence behaviors.
2. Task and social behaviors.

The Distribution of Decision Influence

Many studies have been conducted on how the distribution of decision-making influence between superiors and subordinates is related to the performance and satisfaction of individuals and work groups. One of the important works in this area was done over 70 years ago (Lewin et al.,

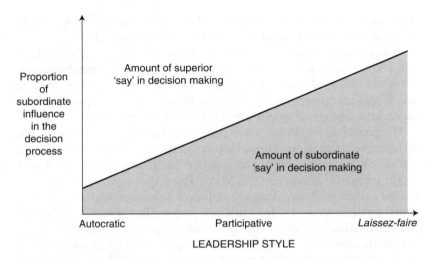

Figure 10.2   Subordinate influence in decision making

1939). From this study, a classification of leader behavior emerged that was based on the sharing of decision making between a leader and a follower that has continued to be reflected in much of today's work. Leaders were described in three ways:

1. Autocratic.
2. Participative.
3. Laissez-faire.

These leadership styles can be represented on a continuum that shows different levels of subordinate influence in the decision process, as shown in Figure 10.2. In autocratic leadership, the leader makes all decisions and allows the subordinates no influence in the decision-making process. These leaders are often indifferent to the personal needs of subordinates. For example, an autocratic manager would assign a worker a task or a goal without any discussion with the subordinate. The manager simply meets with subordinates and gives them a set of goals that he has prepared.

Participative leaders consult with subordinates on appropriate matters and allow them some influence in the decision-making process. Participative leadership is not punitive and treats subordinates with dignity. The participative leader might set goals with subordinates after talking with them to determine their preferences. For instance, a manager might communicate departmental goals to subordinates in a meeting. Using this information, subordinates would then develop their goals, or the superior might develop goals for the subordinate and later meet to arrive at some mutual agreement about the subordinate's goals.

In laissez-faire leadership, the leader allows the group to have complete autonomy. They rarely supervise directly, so that group members make many on-the-job decisions themselves, such as what jobs they want to do. With such an approach, subordinates set their own goals with no managerial inputs and work toward them with no direction.

The problem is to know when to use each different leader style. For instance, effective groups have had autocratic leaders and participative leaders (Bass, 1990, 2009). Participative leadership is associated with higher levels of subordinate satisfaction. Those who work for participative leaders are less resistant to change and show more organization identification than those who work for autocratic leaders. The laissez-faire style has not been studied as much as the autocratic and participative styles, but the results are consistent, showing that subordinate satisfaction and performance under laissez-faire are lower than under the participative approach, but higher than under the autocratic approach (Bass, 1990, 2009).

How to choose a leadership style: the Vroom–Yetton model
A useful way to decide when and which of these leadership styles should be used has been developed by Vroom and Yetton (1973). As you have seen in Chapter 6 on groups, they propose five different types of decision making, ranging at one extreme from a unilateral or autocratic style (a quick and efficient way to get things done), to the other extreme of a participative, almost laissez-faire style of leadership. Their important contribution is to specify a sequence of questions about the decision to be made in a decision tree format that results in a path that leads to the 'best' approach or approaches for making the decision.

Task and Social Behaviors

Two very important programs of research on leader behavior were conducted at Ohio State University and the University of Michigan. They centered on whether effective leaders emphasize task activities and assignments or tend to concentrate on trying to keep good relationships and cohesion among group members, or do both of these things. You will recall that in groups, task functions and socio-emotional functions are the two key sets of activities; see Chapter 6.

The Ohio State studies
From the late 1940s through the 1960s, a group of researchers at Ohio State University conducted extensive studies of leadership and effectiveness in

industrial, military and educational institutions. They developed instruments to measure leadership and evaluated factors that might determine group effectiveness. Two leadership behavior dimensions consistently emerged from these studies:

1. 'Consideration' is the extent to which the leader is likely to have job relationships characterized by mutual trust, respect for subordinates' ideas and consideration of their feelings. Considerate leaders tend to have good rapport and two-way communication with subordinates.
2. 'Initiating structure' is the extent to which the leader is likely to define and structure his or her role and those of subordinates toward goal achievement. High-initiating-structure leaders play an active role in directing group activities, communicating task information, scheduling and trying out new ideas.

The Ohio State studies had a profound impact on leadership thinking and research. Perhaps their major effect is the wide use of the Leader Behavior Description Questionnaire (LBDQ) for measuring consideration and initiating structure. The concepts of initiating structure and consideration have become part of the current theoretical and conventional wisdom about leadership, and are the basis of many programs to train managers in all fields – business, military and educational. And, though they are over 50 years old, a recent meta-analysis demonstrates that they are related to effective leadership:

> Consideration . . . and Initiating Structure . . . have moderately strong . . . relations with leadership outcomes. Consideration was more strongly related to follower satisfaction (leader satisfaction, job satisfaction), motivation, and leader effectiveness, and Initiating Structure was slightly more strongly related to leader job performance and group-organization performance . . . Overall, the results provide important support for the validity of Initiating Structure and Consideration in leadership research. (Judge et al., 2004)

The Michigan studies
At about the same time, the Institute of Social Research at the University of Michigan conducted a number of studies in offices, railroad settings and service industries. From early studies, the researchers concluded that leadership behavior could be described in terms of two styles: a supervisor may be production-centered or employee-centered.

1. In production-centered leadership, the supervisor was primarily concerned with high levels of production and generally used high pressure

to achieve it. He or she viewed subordinates merely as instruments for achieving the desired level of production.
2. In employee-centered leadership, the supervisor was concerned about subordinates' feelings and attempted to create an atmosphere of mutual trust and respect.

The group at Michigan at first concluded that employee-centered supervisors are more likely to have highly productive work groups than production-centered supervisors. This is an important difference between the Ohio State and Michigan studies. In the early stages of the Michigan studies, leaders were described as engaging in behavior that was either production-centered or employee-centered, while the Ohio State studies characterized an individual on both dimensions (Bass, 1990, 2009).

A later Michigan study by Bowers and Seashore (1966) refined the concept of leader behavior. Four supervisory behaviors, reflecting task and social dimensions, associated with satisfaction and performance were found in a study of 40 agencies of an insurance company:

1. Support: behavior that enhances someone else's feelings of personal worth and importance.
2. Interaction facilitation: behavior that encourages members of the group to develop close, mutually satisfying relationships.
3. Goal emphasis: behavior that stimulates an enthusiasm for meeting the group's goals or achieving excellent performance.
4. Work facilitation: activities that help toward achieving goal attainment by doing things such as scheduling, coordinating, planning and providing resources such as tools, materials and technical knowledge.

A closer look at these four dimensions, as you will see later in this chapter, reveals their relationship to the early Michigan studies and the Ohio State studies. Support and interaction facilitation have characteristics similar to consideration behavior, and goal emphasis and work facilitation can be thought of as components of initiating structure.

CONTINGENCY THEORIES OF LEADERSHIP

The interest in contingency theories of leadership emerged in the 1960s and grew out of the fact that there were some inconsistencies in the research results. For example, initiating structure might be related to performance and satisfaction in some studies, but not in others. Similar inconsistencies were found for the effects of consideration. The idea developed among contingency theorists that there might be different situations in which different leadership styles would be effective. They developed contingency theories of leadership that systematically account for how situational factors might result in different relationships between what leaders do and their effectiveness. Contingency theories tell you how a leader's behavior is related to effectiveness in different circumstances. This kind of work on leadership provides us with more specific prescriptions about how a manager should function in different types of situations. In this chapter we discuss the two most prominent contingency theories: Fiedler's contingency theory of leadership (Fiedler, 1967), and the Vroom and Yetton (1973) model, briefly discussed above but explained in more detail in Chapter 6 on groups.

Fiedler's Contingency Model

Fiedler's contingency model describes how leadership orientation, the group setting and task characteristics interact to affect group performance. Much research has been done on this theory since it was introduced, and the evidence shows fairly strong support for it (Strube and Gorcia, 1981; Peters et al., 1985).

There are three important things about this theory. First, it was the first theory to account systematically for situational factors. Fiedler integrated situational factors such as relationships between the leader and the group, task structure and leader power into a theory of leadership.

Second, Fielder's concept of leadership considers the leader's orientation, not leader behavior. This orientation is a function of leader personality. Although this may affect a leader's behavior, it is the leader's orientation toward those with whom he or she works that determines how effective the group is.

Third, because leadership orientation is relatively stable, it is not likely that a leader will change orientations when confronted with different situations, though the leader can change his or her behavior when it is necessary and when the leader wants to. There is evidence that a manager can change behavior from directive to supportive, and vice versa, in different situations (Fielder and Chemers, 1974; Fodor, 1976). For example, when a critical, stressful situation exists at work, the supervisor is likely to act in a directive way with subordinates. In a low-stress situation, the same supervisor may be much more considerate. This was demonstrated in a study of supervisors' behavior under both stressful and non-stressful conditions (Fodor, 1976). When stress was low, the supervisors were less directive and tended to reward subordinates more. When situations became threatening, the supervisors became more directive and were less likely to reward subordinates.

Situational variables

There are three important situational factors that determine leader effectiveness in this theory:

1. Leader–member relations.
2. Task structure.
3. Position power.

These determine the amount of situational control that a leader has (Fielder, 1978). The more these are present, the more control the leader has over the situation. The level of situational control determines whether a particular leader orientation will be effective.

Leader–member relations refer to the trust a group has in the leader and how well the leader is liked. When leader–member relations are good, there is usually high satisfaction with work, individual values are consistent with organizational values, and there is mutual trust between the leader and the group. When relations are bad, mutual trust is lacking. Group cohesiveness is low, making it difficult to make members work together. If group cohesiveness is high but leader relations are bad, the group works together to sabotage the organization and the leader.

A job with high task structure is spelled out in detail: you know what the goals are and how to achieve them. You have little leeway in doing the job and must follow the instructions. For example, the telephone salesperson who works at a computer terminal has very high task structure. For the whole workday, the person sits at a terminal, answers the phone, enters the order, enters the customer's name and other relevant information, and then completes the sale.

Low task structure is present when the objectives of the task or the way it is to be done are somewhat ambiguous. With low task structure, you must decide how to perform a task each time it is to be done. For example, a machinist may work in the tool room of a factory and be responsible for making a wide range of different parts needed to keep equipment operating. The work of managers and many professionals is unstructured.

Position power is a critical factor. High position power exists when you have much legitimate authority, which means that you can make important decisions without having them cleared by someone at higher organization levels. Low position power means that you have only limited authority.

Leader orientation: the LPC scale

Leader orientation is one aspect of your motivational hierarchy. It is not leader behavior, but does reflect a behavioral preference (Fielder and Chemers, 1974). Your leader orientation is determined by how you view the person that you least like to work with, whether you see him or her in a positive or a negative way. If you have positive views of least-preferred co-workers, you are more likely to act in more considerate ways. If you have negative views, you are more likely to focus on tasks, not people.

Leader orientation is measured by the least-preferred co-worker (LPC) scale. You are asked to think about someone that you worked least well with, then indicate if you have positive or negative feelings about the least-preferred co-worker. Suppose, for example, that there are three persons in your group and John is the one who has been the biggest problem for you and who you dislike more than anyone else you have worked with. If you are a high LPC leader, you have relatively favorable views of your least-preferred co-worker, John. High LPC leaders are people-centered and more positively oriented toward the feelings and the relationships of people in the work group. These leaders are able to see some positive things in the people they least like to work with. The high LPC leader wants to be accepted by others, has strong emotional ties to people in the workplace, has higher status and self-esteem, and is more likely to act in a considerate way (Fielder, 1992). If you are a low LPC leader, you have more negative views of your least-preferred co-worker, John. Low LPC leaders are more oriented toward the task, and personal relationships tend to have secondary importance for them. They tend to be directive and controlling and to make subjective, rather than reasoned, judgments about those who work with them.

Leader effectiveness
Either high or low LPC leadership orientations can be effective, depending on the situational control that the leader has. This leader has high situational control:

1. Leader–member relations are good.
2. There is high task structure.
3. The leader has high position power.

This leader has low situational control:

1. Leader–member relations are poor.
2. There is a low task structure.
3. The leader has little position power.

In this case, obviously, the leadership situation is not a favorable one. Moderate situation control means that the situational characteristics are mixed. Some work to the advantage of the leader (for instance, high position power) whereas others do not (poor leader–member relations).

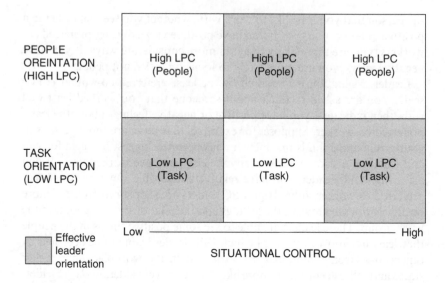

Figure 10.3   Relationships between leader orientation, leader effectiveness and situational control in Fiedler's theory

These levels of situational control require leaders with different LPC orientations, as shown in Figure 10.3. The low LPC leader, with a strong task orientation, is most effective when situational control is either very low or very high. Weak situational control is good for the low LPC leader. The group may fall apart or it may not attend to the task requirements unless the leader exerts a good deal of direction. When situational control is strong and the conditions are favorable, the low LPC leader is also more effective. The group may be willing to accept the task-oriented leader since success is assured because of their own performance and the vigilance of the leader.

The high LPC leader is most effective when there is moderate situational control. In this case, the high LPC may be more effective in motivating group members to perform better and to be cooperative toward goal achievement. The low LPC leader does not have tendencies to do those sorts of things, and would probably exert pressures to work harder to produce more, which may counteract good performance,

Cognitive resource theory
A serious weakness of leadership theory, in general, is that leader ability is not considered. With the exception of intelligence, a proxy for problem-solving ability, leadership theory has focused on traits, behaviors and situational properties. Cognitive resource theory is a modification of Fiedler's

contingency theory that integrates cognitive resources into the original model (Murphy et al., 1992). Cognitive resources are the person's intelligence, job competence and technical knowledge and skill that can be used in the task of managing.

Cognitive resource theory is based on two assumptions:

1. Managers communicate their plans and strategies to subordinates through directive behavior.
2. Smarter and more experienced leaders can make better decisions than those who are less intelligent and less experienced.

However, intelligent and experienced leaders will not be effective across all situations. For example, leader experience contributes to performance only in stressful conditions, while leader intelligence contributes only under stress-free conditions (Murphy et al., 1992). In the stress-free condition, the leader can resort to normal problem-solving behavior, based on intelligence. However, under stress, the experienced leader can:

> fall back on a wide range of previously learned automatic behaviors and . . . will perform better than a less experienced leader who lacks a large repertoire . . . When someone starts shooting at you, it is safer to obey the primitive impulse to run rather than to stop and consider alternative options. (Murphy et al., 1992)

The research support for cognitive resource theory, beyond the original research from which it was derived, has not been extensive. One study did show that leader intelligence was more strongly related to group performance for directive leaders than for non-directive leaders (Vecchio, 1990). Another found that group performance was higher when leaders who had technical training were more directive, but that technically trained groups performed better when the leaders were non-directive (Murphy et al., 1992). Perhaps the strongest support for cognitive resource theory is a meta-analysis which showed that intelligence and leadership were more strongly related when leader stress was low and when leaders exhibited directive behaviors (Judge et al., 2004).

PROCESS THEORIES OF LEADERSHIP

Trait approaches, behavioral approaches and contingency approaches focus mainly on the leader, what the leader is or what the leader does. Some recent theories, called process theories of leadership, explain the processes by which a relationship develops between leaders and subordinates. There are two prominent process theories:

1.   Leader–member exchange (LMX) theory.
2.   Transformational leadership theory.

Leader–Member Exchange Theory

The leader–member exchange (LMX) theory focuses on the relationship between the leader and the subordinate in a different way from other models (Dansereau et al., 1975). In trait approaches, the leader is measured by his or her responses to some form of psychological measurement instrument. For example, achievement motivation and power motivation are assessed by the responses to the Thematic Apperception Test (McClelland, 1975). In behavioral approaches, leader style is measured by descriptions of the leader by subordinates. For example, initiating structure and consideration behaviors are measured in this manner.

LMX theory is different. In LMX theory, responses from both the leader and the subordinate about their relationship are considered. The assumption is that leadership can be understood best in terms of role relationships between managers and subordinates – members of a vertical dyadic relationship – in an organization. Managers must ensure that the superior–subordinate relationships are well defined, since managerial success depends on subordinate performance. Therefore, managers and subordinates negotiate these role relationships through a range of formal and informal processes that occur primarily in the early stages of their relationship

This negotiation results in different relationships with different subordinates. In LMX theory, the agreement between leaders and subordinates about the degree of trust in the relationship, subordinate competence, loyalty and similar factors is measured. Leader–member relationships are classified into in-group and out-group categories depending on the level of agreement:

1.   In-group relationships between leaders and subordinates are close, the leader spends more time and energy in them, role participants have more positive attitudes toward the job and there are fewer problems than in out-group relationships (Dienesch and Liden, 1986). The quality of the linkage affects some subordinate behaviors and perceptions, but has not been related to subordinate performance.
2.   Out-group subordinates spend less time on decision making, do not volunteer for extra assignments, and are rated lower by subordinates (Liden and Graen, 1980).

The nature of the LMX is related to supervisory performance ratings. This means that in-group members' performance is more highly rated than that of out-group members, even after controlling for rating bias and different ways of measuring LMX (Gerstner and Day, 1997), though it is not clear that LMX is related to subordinate performance (Dienesch and Liden, 1986). However, the quality of supervisor–subordinate relations affects subordinates' perception of the organization's climate (Kozlowski and Doherty, 1989). Subordinates who had high-quality relationships with supervisors had more positive perceptions about the climate. Also, their climate perceptions were similar to those of the supervisors, and there was greater consensus about the climate than was the case for out-group subordinates. It has also been shown that high-quality leader–member relationships lead to more positive perceptions of organizational justice (Piccolo et al., 2008).

LMX theory is a very useful way to study the relational aspect of leadership because it may be linked to several other important aspects of life in organizations. It could be, for example, that the nature of the relationship is an important predictor of subordinate advancement. Further, it may better define the critical dimensions of the leader–subordinate relationship. It also emphasizes the evolution of that relationship, which has received little attention in the other leader literature.

Transformational Leadership Theory

Transformational leadership theory explains how leaders develop and enhance the commitment of followers. In this approach, transformational leaders are contrasted with transactional leaders (Downton, 1973). In transactional leadership, the leader and subordinate are bargaining agents, negotiating to maximize their own position. The subordinate's motivation to comply with the leader is self-interest, because the leader can provide pay-offs, perhaps both economic and psychological, that are valued by the follower. The transactional view of leadership makes three assumptions:

1. Human behavior is goal-directed and individuals will act rationally to achieve those goals.
2. Behaviors that pay off will persist over time, while those that do not pay off will not persist.
3. Norms of reciprocity govern the exchange relationship.

This is the style of the transactional leader (Bass, 1990, 2009):

1. Use contingent rewards: rewards are associated with good performance and accomplishment.

2.	Manage by exception: the leader acts when he or she anticipates that performance is likely to deviate from standards, or takes action when standards are not met.
3.	Take a hands-off approach: the leader acts in a laissez-faire manner, abdicating and avoiding responsibility,

Transformational leadership is based on the leader's effects on the followers' values, self-esteem and trust, and their confidence in the leader and motivation to perform above and beyond the call of duty (House and Singh, 1987). The transactional leader's influence is derived from the exchange process, but it is different in an important way from transformational leadership. Transactional leadership works within the context of the followers' self-interests, while transformational leadership seeks to change that context (Bass 2009; Bass 1990).

The transformational leader's influence is based on the leader's ability to inspire and raise the consciousness of the followers by appealing to their higher ideals and values. This may be because transformational leaders tend to engage in high levels of moral reasoning (Turner et al., 2007). Further, transformational leaders are also more extroverted (Bono and Judge, 2004). The result is that the charisma and other transformational behaviors lead to an increased dependence of the followers on the leader as well as an increased sense of follower empowerment (Kark et al., 2003). Specifically, this is the style of a transformational leader (Buss 1990):

1.	To use his or her charisma: the charismatic leader creates a special bond with the followers and is able to articulate a vision with which the followers identify and for which they are willing to work.
2.	To be inspirational: the leader creates high expectations and effectively communicates crucial ideas with symbols and simple language. A recent study showed that high-imagery speeches resulted in higher ratings of charisma than low-imagery speeches (Naidoo and Lord, 2008).
3.	To practice individual consideration: the leader coaches, advises and delegates to the followers, treating them individually.
4.	To stimulate followers intellectually: the leader arouses them to develop new ways to think about problems:

Figure 10.4 shows some task behaviors, social behaviors, influence techniques of transformational leaders, and corresponding subordinate behaviors and feelings:

●	The task behaviors of the leader are the heightening of task goals, articulating paths to achievement and proposing innovative

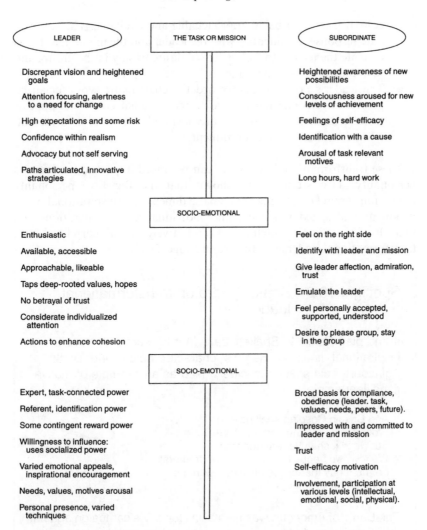

Figure 10.4   Transformational leader and subordinate behavior and attitudes

strategies. Subordinates become aware of new possibilities, have increased feelings of self-efficacy, are willing to work longer and harder, have higher task identification and stronger achievement motives, and more emotional involvement with the work.

- The socio-emotional behaviors of the leader involve showing enthusiasm and trustworthiness, acting in ways to increase group cohesiveness, and being approachable and available. The subordinate response is to identify with the leader and the mission, to try to emulate the leader, to feel increased desire to stay in the group, and to admire and trust the leader.

- The leader's power tends toward the charismatic type, socialized power, unconventional behaviors and different emotional appeals to subordinates. The subordinates respond with more involvement, trust, compliance and commitment.

These transformational behaviors can be traced in part to the leader's personality. Two studies have shown that the Big Five personality dimensions are related to the charismatic dimensions (inspirational motivation and idealized influence) and individualized consideration, and that all of the Big Five factors are, collectively, highly correlated with transformational leadership (Bono and Judge, 2004).

Spotlight 10.2 Shakespeare on transformational leadership

In the play *Henry V*, Shakespeare (Act IV, scene iii) gave these inspirational lines to Henry's character before the Battle of Agincourt. This speech is widely used as an example of motivational leadership:

And Crispin Crispian shall ne'er go by,
From this day to the ending of the world,
But we in it shall be remembered –
We few, we happy few, we band of brothers;
For he today that sheds his blood with me
Shall be my brother

The Battle of Agincourt was pivotal in Henry V's campaign against the French in 1415. Although severely outnumbered by the French (with at least 30 000 troops, some think as many as 150 000), the English, with perhaps around 6000 troops, won the battle. The French lost as many as 10 000 soldiers while English losses may have been less than 500 (Taylor, 1982).

Overall, it appears that transformational leaders may have strong positive effects on performance, member satisfaction and commitment (Bass, 1985; Bass et al., 1987; Deluga, 1988; Judge and Piccolo, 2004). For example, transformational patterns of managers and naval officers are very strongly related to desirable organizational outcomes (Howell and Higgins, 1990; Seltzer and Bass, 1990; Bycio et al., 1995; Kirkpatrick and Locke, 1996). Successful champions, or advocates, of new technologies exhibit transformational leader behavior patterns (Howell and Higgins, 1990).

The concept of transformational leadership raises some interesting questions. For example, as we discussed earlier in this chapter, charismatic CEOs (read: transformational leaders) are more highly paid than those who are not (Fanelli et al., 2009). Their use of charismatic imagery also leads to higher ratings of the firm's stock than the language of less charismatic leaders does. Yet these highly charismatic CEOs do not appear to increase firm performance, except when the firm is operating in a very uncertain environment (Tosi et al., 2004). So while transformational CEOs may have effects on individuals and groups, as shown in the studies cited above, it is still open to question as to whether or not they manage a firm effectively from the stockholders' perspective.

Another question is whether it is possible to develop a transformational style. There is some research which suggests that it is possible to develop a charismatic style through training (Howell and Frost, 1989; Kirkpatrick and Locke, 1996). In a most important study, actresses learned scripts that portrayed charismatic leaders, structuring leaders and considerate leaders (Howell and Frost, 1989). Emotional state, body language, facial expressions and other symbolic cues were described and learned for the charismatic role. The charismatic leader was able to gain high productivity from the experimental group. Subjects generated more alternatives and were more satisfied with both the task and the leader.

The 'full range of leadership' model
A transformational leader does not always enact the transformational behaviors discussed above. They just do so more often than not. For example, they frequently act transactionally. The 'full range of leadership' model explains how transactional and transformational leadership are related (see Figure 10.5) (Avolio and Bass, 2001). The transformational behaviors of individualized consideration, intellectual stimulation, inspirational motivation and idealized influence are more active behaviors as well as being more effective. On the other hand, the transactional behaviors of laissez-faire and management-by-exception are more passive and less effective. Contingent reward, also a transactional dimension, can also have some positive effects, as some research has shown.

TRANSACTIONAL LEADERSHIP			TRANSFORMATIONAL LEADERSHIP			
Laissez-Faire	*Management By Exception*	*Contingent Reward*	*Individualized Consideration*	*Intellectual Stimulation*	*Inspirational Motivation*	*Idealized Influence*
Passive Ineffective			**Active Effective**			

Source:	Adapted from Avolio and Bass (2001).

*Figure 10.5	The full range leadership model*

SUBSTITUTES FOR LEADERSHIP

The very image of the leader in leadership theory is of a person who is able to influence others to act toward organization objectives. This image is reinforced by the popular press, television and films (Meindl et al., 1985). However, we know that other factors such as ability, intrinsic motivation, the nature of technology and the structure of the organization also affect the performance and satisfaction of organization members. In fact, sometimes these factors may be even more crucial to performance than leadership. They can serve as leadership substitutes because they, not the action of the leader, contribute to success or failure (Kerr and Jermier, 1978).

Suppose that the effectiveness of a group depends on two things: performing the task, and good working relationships among members. From a leadership behavior perspective, by initiating structure behavior you could provide the members with knowledge about how to perform the task. Good working relationships can also develop because as a leader you use a considerate style of behavior. However, there are other ways that task knowledge and good relations can be present, and they are substitutes for the behavior of the leader. Task knowledge may be present because those who work for you know how to do the job, or because there are specific procedures that are well known by them. These work in place of initiating structure. There may be good working relationships because of work group norms, because all the workers are friends, or for many other reasons. These are substitutes for consideration.

There are three classes of leadership substitutes: the subordinate characteristics, the task factors and the organizational dimensions. Specific substitutes are shown in Table 10.1. This table shows that, for example, if you receive feedback because the task itself allows you to make a judgment about how well things are going, there is no need to have a manager give you feedback.

Table 10.1   Some substitutes for leadership

Subordinate Characteristics	Task Factors	Organization Dimensions
Ability	Repetitiveness	Formalization
Experience	Clarity	Availability of special staff
Background and training	Task-provided	Work group cohesiveness
Professional orientation	feedback	Spatial distance between the
Indifference toward		leader and the group
organization rewards		

Source: Kerr and Jermier (1978).

The concept of substitutes for leadership is important for two reasons. First, it suggests that contextual control is an alternative to active leadership to obtain good results. The many studies that have been done show that these substitutes can have effects in the predicted direction on employee attitudes, role perceptions, and both task and contextual performance. In fact, the effects of substitutes for leadership on subordinate attitudes and role perception are stronger than the direct effects of leadership alone, though together leader behaviors and the substitutes have very strong positive effects on these variables (Podsakoff et al., 1996). This means that for managers, performance improvements can result from strategies such as selecting competent and motivated people or using job enrichment. In fact, team management and other management approaches to organizational design are often meant to be a substitute for leadership, trying to improve performance with intrinsically motivating work, supportive working conditions and a pay structure which provides incentives to learn new skills. Of course, it takes leadership and the use of power to create leadership substitutes and the conditions for them to operate effectively in organizations.

Second, there are implications about the interaction of leadership, leadership substitutes and the nature of the organization. The various factors that may act as substitutes will differ, depending upon the type of organization. For example, in mechanistic organizations, the task itself will provide clarity, formalization will provide direction, and lower-level workers will be indifferent toward organization rewards. In organic organizations, however, task competence, high intrinsic task motivation and cohesive work groups will be more powerful substitutes.

The effects of leadership substitutes will also vary by organization level. At higher levels in mechanistic organizations, socialization and experience are likely to be more powerful factors that affect performance than at lower levels. At lower levels, formalization and technology may be stronger substitutes.

Spotlight 10.3   Managerial leadership and culture

The effects of cultural differences among managers in selected countries were studied (Child, 1981; Laurent, 1986). The results show the following.

German managers, more than others, believe that creativity is essential for career success. In their mind, the successful manager is the one who has the right individual characteristics. Their outlook is rational: they view the organization as a coordinated network of individuals who make appropriate decisions based on their professional competence and knowledge. German managers want to be informed about everything that is going on, and they show less interest in their subordinates

British managers hold a more interpersonal and subjective view of the organizational world. According to them, the ability to create the right image and get noticed for what they do is essential for career success. They view the organization primarily as a network of relationships between individuals who get things done through influencing each other through communicating and negotiating. In the UK, managers delegate and decentralize more, they have a greater interest in their subordinates and, unlike the Germans, they only want to be informed about exceptional events.

French managers look at the organization as an authority network where the power to organize and control the actors stems from their positioning in the hierarchy. They focus on the organization as a pyramid of differentiated levels of power to be acquired or dealt with. French managers perceive the ability to manage power relationships effectively and to work the system as particularly critical to their success. French managers see their job as an intellectual activity that requires intensely analytical work (Beyer, 1981). They value and excel in quantitative analysis and strategic planning. Above all, those who head large firms must be clever. This emphasis on cleverness is manifested in their recruiting materials, which almost never mention motivation and drive as requisites for a managerial position. The French seem to prefer managers with an analytical mind, independence and intellectual rigor. They have a strong bias for intellect, rather than action.

Unlike the Anglo-Saxon view of management, they do not place high emphasis on the interpersonal skills and communication that are important managerial attributes in other countries.

US managers tend to be hard driving and solution-oriented. They take different approaches to problem solving. American managers are more direct – they will give you action plans; Europeans will take a more strategic, theoretical look at problems.

SUMMARY

There are some other points to consider. One is that, as you can see, though the theories are different, there is much conceptual overlap. You can see in Figure 10.6 the similarities in the way that some of the important leadership approaches use the concepts of initiation of structure and consideration. This conceptual overlap is also a reason why many of the different theories show relationships with performance and satisfaction. These different theoretical concepts are tapping similar leader traits and behaviors.

Another important question that arises in this research is the direction of causality. That is, is it the behavior of the leader that causes higher

The Ohio State Studies	*Initiating Structure*		*Consideration*	
Early Michigan Studies	*Production-centred*		*Employee-centred*	
Bowers and Seashore	*Goal Emphasis* *Work Facilitation*		*Support* *Interaction Facilitation*	
Transformational Leadership Theory	*Intellectual Stimulation* *Inspirational Motivation*		*Individualized Influence* *Charisma*	
Fiedler's Contingency Theory	*Production-centred* *(Low LPC)*	**Situational Factors** Position Power Task Structure Leader-Member Relations	*People-centred* *(High LPC)*	
Vroom-Yetton Decision Styles (See Chapter 6)	*Autocratic Style*	Acceptance Quality Information Conflict Goal Congruence	*Consultative Group*	

Figure 10.6   Overlap of leadership concepts

performance, or is it possible that follower performance causes the leader to act in certain ways? Much of the leader behavior research consists of field studies that use correlation methodology, which does not prove causality. Some research, on the other hand, supports the idea that leader behavior may be a result of the group's performance as well as affecting it. One very convincing study is an experiment in which managers were hired for part-time student work groups (Lowin and Craig, 1968). Prior to employment, the applicants were introduced to one of the workers and asked to supervise him for a period of time. In some cases, the worker was said to be very competent, but in other instances the applicants were told that the worker was less competent. Those who managed the competent worker did not supervise him closely and engaged in more consideration and less initiating structure behaviors. Those who managed the less competent worker were more directive. Studies like this show that leader consideration both increases the satisfaction of subordinates and is increased by it. The initiation of structure by the leader (if structure is low) improves the subordinates' performance, which in turn increases the leader's subsequent consideration and reduces the leader's initiation of structure.

In the end, we can say that organizations are concerned with leadership because of the need to select and promote individuals into management positions. The manager's role is to make sure the work of the organization is done through the effective use of physical and human resources. Therefore, we believe that an effective manager should be a good leader.

GUIDE FOR MANAGERS: CHOOSING A LEADERSHIP STYLE

These theories can help you do a better job as a leader if you follow their implications in your work as a manager. Perhaps the main idea that you can come away with is to recognize the importance of having a clear understanding about the situation itself – and then to do your best to adapt your style to it. First we will outline some of specific actions that are part of the different behavioral repertoires. Then we will suggest some ways to think about the context in which they will occur.

How to Act Like a Leader

The research on which leadership theories in this chapter are based provides some useful guides for specific actions that are elements of the broader behavioral repertoires. In addition, you should read again the guides for motivation (Chapter 3). Much of what was said there applies here also.

One thing that you must know is your own behavioral tendencies and your own personality. The reason is, as we note in several places in the book, that these behavioral tendencies will be your most likely, and probably most comfortable, response when faced with any situation. To be an effective manager, you will sometimes cognitively have to modify your actions to be more appropriate for the situation. Can you do this? The research, and common sense, says that you can – but within reason. You should obviously avoid engaging in any ways that appear to be feigned and forced; then you would be seen as untrustworthy, something that is a problem for any manager. Here are some actions that fall within each leader behavior repertoire.

Directive behaviors
There are times when it is critical to provide direction and guidance to subordinates. A subordinate will generally perceive your actions to be directive if you engage in work-oriented interactions – and you take the initiative in these interactions. We emphasize, though, that providing guidance is not the same thing as dominating and demeaning someone. Instead, it is giving direction and clarification as to how to do something, or what is expected. This means that you have to be careful here and not create the perception that you are overly rigid or dominating. Some ways to be directive are:

- Clearly define responsibilities.
- Provide the necessary information to do the job.
- Emphasize the policies and procedures that should be followed.

- Make regular checks of the subordinate's progress.
- Behave in ways that reinforce status differences between you and your subordinate.
- Provide constructive feedback on a regular basis.

Considerate, supportive behaviors

Like the dangers of appearing too directive and dominating, the dangerous side of acting in considerate, supportive ways towards subordinates is that some might view this as a sign of weakness and lack of concern for performance. However, if you know when to act in this way and can, you will get better performance. Here are some ways that you can be considerate or supportive:

- Show concern for the personal well-being of subordinates.
- Be an active listener. Let the subordinate do most of the talking.
- Personalize the way you deal with subordinates, minimizing organizational status differences.
- Encourage individualism, creativity and initiative.

Transformational Leader Behaviors

In this chapter we have discussed the fact that managers have been successfully trained to behave in transformational ways. When you examine the content of that training, here are some of the behaviors that they learn:

- Articulate a vision that subordinates can understand and accept. Do this by providing an optimistic and attainable view of the future.
- Show self-confidence.
- Challenge subordinates, but be sure that they are capable of stretching to achieve the goals.
- Find ways to use non-verbal cues and symbols that are consistent with your message.
- Be dramatic and outgoing, but in ways that are consistent with your personality. This means that you sometimes have to take personal risks that others know about and believe are important to the success of your organization.
- Empower subordinates. This means two things. First, you must be willing to delegate important responsibilities to them to demonstrate your confidence in their ability. Second, you have to use language that lets them know that you believe they can succeed and that you will help them to succeed.

Knowing When to Use a Particular Behavioral Repertoire

The one thing that is clear from the research on leadership is that one style does not fit all cases. Below are some things that you should consider:

Look first at results, then at the person

Before acting in any situation, you want to ensure that you avoid the fundamental attribution error; see Chapter 3. Otherwise your biases, assumptions and likes for that manager will color your evaluation. That means if you have a performance problem with a manager with whom you have a good relationship, you will tend to be considerate and supportive even though a directive approach might be more effective. Likewise, a performance problem with a manager that you do not like as well might lead to more directive actions when a considerate, supportive approach is called for.

When performance of a lower-level manager is not up to par, then replace the leader or change the situation

This is one way to attain some congruence between leader behavior and the situation. For example, if it is called for, task structure can be increased or decreased. Jobs can be made more routine and simple or be enlarged and the task structure reduced. The position power of a manager can be increased by delegating more authority and responsibility, or it can be reduced by taking them away. Leader–member relationships may be improved through any number of different training and group development methods.

Identify and remove barriers to performance

Remember that it is not your job as a manager to make someone's job more difficult. You want to make it easier, because your success depends upon their success. One of the more important things that you can do, and often one of the easiest, is to make the job of subordinates easier by eliminating difficulties that are in their performance path. Another way to make a subordinate's job easier is to make sure that they have the necessary competence to do the work, which might entail that they have some training.

Know what those in your group are capable of doing

There are two facets to this: their ability and their motivation. If those who work for you are very capable, then you should avoid, when possible, directive leader styles and emphasize the considerate, supportive style. When subordinates don't have the requisite competence, information or resources, a directive style is probably more effective.

From the motivational side of the issue, it is helpful to know how intrinsically motivated your subordinates are. For those who are highly motivated with high ability, you will want to be considerate and supportive and get out of their way. For those who have high ability but lower motivation, a more directive style will be effective.

The level of stress that a subordinate is experiencing should also affect your choice of style. The stress could be from organizational sources or external sources. For your subordinates it probably makes no difference; for you, a manager, it does – but not in the way that you might like. Consider stress from external sources first. You might prefer that employees do not bring it to the workplace, but they will. And if they do, the effects of the stressors on their work will be the same as if they are job stressors. So you will have to deal with them. Your leader behavior style in this situation should be, at least at first, considerate and supportive so that you do not make the situation even worse. At some point, if there are still performance problems, you might have to take a more directive approach. You want to be careful, though, and not switch to that style prematurely.

Finally, as a manager you should experiment some and try to find behavior that works for you with your group. What could be the biggest enemy to your effectiveness is your own rigidity and unwillingness to be flexible.

CASE: BANK OF SOMERSET

Some years ago, Alex Spooner was appointed president of the Bank of Somerset in the United Kingdom. At the time, Bank of Somerset was a small, marginally profitable bank controlled by an old Somerset family, the Oliver family. The bank was having some managerial and financial problems and Bill Oliver, the chairman of the board, thought that Alex was the person to bring the bank back to profitability. Alex Spooner had the qualifications for the job. He had graduated from university in 1970 with an MBA. For ten years he worked with an accounting firm. Eventually he became a partner and was well known in financial circles in the region.

When Alex took charge of the bank, he made some significant changes. First, he was successful in attracting several of Somerset's largest business firms to use the bank's services. He also made some very sound loans and, more importantly, was able to work out a solution to some of the problem investments that the Bank of Somerset had made. Second, he was able to improve the internal operating efficiency of the bank through a careful study of the bank's operating systems.

Over the years, Alex Spooner became the dominating force in the Bank of Somerset. This is because he is an excellent businessman, he keeps almost complete control of all the bank's operations, and he has personally picked all the current managers.

Now Spooner is near retirement. The board of directors, still heavily influenced by the Oliver family, has asked a consultant to help them select a new chief executive. The consultant proposed, first, that an analysis of the management structure of the bank would be useful because this would help him understand what kind of person would best meet the bank's needs.

Here is what the consultant found:

1. Spooner selected executives who were loyal and committed to him. They were expected to know all the different phases of the bank's operations.
2. There were ambiguous job descriptions and policies governing the work of those bank executives who reported to Spooner. Spooner was unwilling to formalize policies and procedures for them.
3. Spooner was often vague in making assignments to these managers. Often the goals and the activities assigned to them were not clear. Sometimes he would assign the same project to more than one person. Very rarely did he give anyone enough authority to get the job done. Usually, the manager would have to come to Spooner for approval for some aspects of a project.

4. Often Spooner went directly to lower-level managers to find out about problems. It was not unusual for him to short-circuit his direct subordinates.

1. Analyze the leadership style of Spooner.
2. What is the basis of his power in this organization?
3. What kind of replacement would you recommend if you were the consultant?
4. What changes would you suggest for the Bank of Somerset? What would have to be done to make them work?

REFERENCES

Avolio, B.J. and B.M. Bass (2001), *Developing Potential Across a Full Range of Leadership TM: Cases on Transactional and Transformational Leadership.* London: Psychology Press.

Bass, B.M. (1985), *Leadership Beyond Expectations.* New York: Free Press.

Bass, B.M. (1990), *Bass and Stogdill's Handbook of Leadership: Theory, Research, and Managerial Applications.* New York: Free Press.

Bass, B. with R. Bass (2009), *The Bass Handbook of Leadership Theory, Research, and Managerial Applications.* New York: Simon & Schuster.

Bass, B.M., B.J. Avolio and L. Goodheim (1987), Biography and Assessment of Transformational Leadership at the World Class Level. *Journal of Management,* **13**(1): 7–19.

Blanchard, K.H. (1985), *Leadership and the One Minute Manager: Increasing Effectiveness Through Situational Leadership.* New York: Morrow.

Bono, J.E. and T.A. Judge (2004), Personality and Transformational and Transactional Leadership: A Meta-analysis. *Journal of Applied Psychology,* **89**(5): 901–10.

Bowers, D.G. and S.E. Seashore (1966), Predicting Organizational Effectiveness with a Four-Factor Theory of Leadership. *Administrative Science Quarterly,* **11**: 238–63.

Bycio, P., R.D. Hackett and J.S. Allen (1995), Further Assessments of Bass's Conceptualization of Transactional and Transformational Leadership. *Journal of Applied Psychology,* **80**(4): 468–99.

Child, J.C. (1981), Culture Contingency and Capitalism in the Cross-National Study of Organizations. In *Research in Organizational Behavior,* L.L. Cummings and B.M. Staw (eds). Greenwich, CT: JAI Press, pp. 303–56.

Cornelius, E.T. and F.B. Lane (1984), The Power Motive and Managerial Success in a Professionally Oriented Service Industry Organization. *Journal of Applied Psychology,* **69**(1): 32–9.

Covey, S.R. (2004), *The 7 Habits of Highly Effective People: Powerful Lessons in Personal Change.* New York: Free Press.

Dansereau, F., G. Graen and W.J. Haga (1975), A Vertical Dyad Linkage Approach to Leadership Within Formal Organizations: A Longitudinal Investigation of the Role Making Process. *Organizational Behavior and Human Performance,* **13**: 46–78.

Deluga, R.J. (1988), Relationship of Transformational and Transactional Leadership with Employee Influencing Strategies. *Group and Organization Studies,* **13**: 456–67.

Dienesch, R.M. and R.C. Liden (1986), Leader–Member Exchange Model of Leadership: A Critique and Further Development. *Academy of Management Review,* **11**(3): 618–34.

Downton, J.V. (1973), *Rebel Leadership: Commitment and Charisma in the Revolutionary Process.* New York: Free Press.

Fanelli, A.M., F. Vilmos and Henry L. Tosi (2009), In Charisma We Trust: The Effects of CEO Charismatic Visions on Securities Analysts. *Organization Science,* **20**(6).

Fiedler, F.E. (1967), *A Theory of Leadership Effectiveness.* New York: McGraw-Hill.

Fiedler, F.E. (1978), The Contingency Model and the Dynamics of the Leadership Process. In *Advances in Experimental Social Psychology*, L. Berkowitz (ed.). Academic Press: New York, pp. 59–111.

Fiedler, F.E. (1992), Time Based Measures of Leadership Experience and Organizational Performance: A Review of Research and a Preliminary Model. *Leadership Quarterly*, **3**: 5–21.

Fiedler, F.E. and M. Chemers (1974), *Leadership and Effective Management*. Glenview, IL: Scott, Foresman.

Fodor, E.M. (1976), Group Stress, Authoritarian Style of Control, and the Use of Power. *Journal of Applied Psychology*, **61**: 313–18.

Gerstner, C.R. and D.V. Day (1997), Meta-analytic Review of Leader–Member Exchange Theory: Correlates and Construct Issues. *Journal of Applied Psychology*, **82**(6): 827–44.

Hersey, P. and K. Blanchard (1988), *Management of Organizational Behavior*. New York: Prentice-Hall.

House, R.J. (1971), A Path-Goal Theory of Leader Effectiveness. *Administrative Science Quarterly*, **16**: 334–8.

House, R.J. and T.R. Mitchell (1974), Path-Goal Theory of Leadership. *Journal of Contemporary Business*, **4**: 81–97.

House, R.J. and J.V. Singh (1987), Organization Behavior: Some New Directions for I/O Psychology. *Annual Review of Psychology*, **38**: 669–718.

Howell, J.M. and P.J. Frost (1989), A Laboratory Study of Charismatic Leadership. *Organizational Behavior and Human Decision Processes*, **43**: 243–69.

Howell, J.M. and C.A. Higgins (1990), Champions of Technological Innovation. *Administrative Science Quarterly*, **35**: 317–41.

Huson, M.R., R. Parrino and L.T. Starks (2001), Internal Monitoring Mechanisms and CEO Turnover: A Long-Term Perspective. *Journal of Finance*, **56**(6): 2265–97.

Judge, T.A. and D.M. Cable (2004), The Effect of Physical Height on Workplace Success and Income: Preliminary Test of a Theoretical Model. *Journal of Applied Psychology*, **89**(3): 428–41.

Judge, T.A. and R.F. Piccolo (2004), Transformational and Transactional Leadership: A Meta-analytic Test of their Relative Validity. *Journal of Applied Psychology*, **89**(5): 755–68.

Judge, T.A., et al. (2002), Personality and Leadership: A Qualitative and Quantitative Review. *Journal of Applied Psychology*, **87**(4): 765–80.

Judge, T.A., A.E. Colbert and R. Ilies (2004), Intelligence and Leadership: A Quantitative Review and Test of Theoretical Propositions. *Journal of Applied Psychology*, **89**(3): 542–52.

Judge, T.A., R.F. Piccolo and R. Ilies (2004), The Forgotten Ones? The Validity of Consideration and Initiating Structure in Leadership Research. *Journal of Applied Psychology*, **89**(1): 36–51.

Judge, T.A., R.F. Piccolo and T. Kosalka (2009), The Bright and Dark Sides of Leader Traits: A Review and Theoretical Extension of the Leader Trait Paradigm. *Leadership Quarterly*, **20**(6): 855–75.

Kark, R., B. Shamir and G. Chen (2003), The Two Faces of Transformational Leadership: Empowerment and Dependency. *Journal of Applied Psychology*, **88**(2): 246–55.

Kerr, S. and J. Jermier (1978), Substitutes for Leadership: Their Meaning and Measurement. *Organizational Behavior and Human Performance*, **22**: 375–403.

Khurana, R. (2002), *Searching for a Corporate Savior: The Irrational Quest for Charismatic CEOs*. Princeton, NJ: Princeton University Press.

Kirkpatrick, S. and E.A. Locke (1996), Direct and Indirect Effects of Three Core Leadership Components on Performance and Attitudes. *Journal of Applied Psychology*, **81**(1): 36–51.

Kozlowski, S.W.J. and M.L. Doherty (1989), Integration of Climate and Leadership: Examination of a Neglected Issue. *Journal of Applied Psychology*, **74**: 546–54.

Laurent, A. (1986), The Cross-Cultural Puzzle of International Human Resource Management. *Human Resource Management*, **25**(1): 91–102.

Lewin, K., R. Lippitt and R.K. White (1939), Patterns of Aggressive Behavior in Experimentally Created Social Climates. *Journal of Social Psychology*, **10**: 271–99.

Liden, R.C. and G. Graen (1980), Generalizability of the Vertical Dyad Linkage Model. *Academy of Management Journal*, **23**: 451–65.

Lowin, A. and J. Craig (1968), The Influence of Level of Performance on Managerial Style: An Experimental Object Lesson on the Ambiguity of Correlational Data. *Organizational Behavior and Human Performance*, **3**: 440–58.

Manz, C.C. (2005), *Leadership Wisdom of Jesus: Practical Lessons for Today*. San Francisco, CA: Berret-Koedhler Publishers.

McClelland, D.A. (1975), *Power: The Inner Experience*. New York: Irvington.

McClelland, D.A. (1985), *Human Motivation*. Glenview, IL: Scott, Foresman.

McClelland, D.A. and R.E. Boyatzis (1982), Leadership Motive Pattern and Long-Term Success in Management. *Journal of Applied Psychology*, **67**: 737–43.

Meindl, J.R., S.B. Ehrlich and J.M. Dukerich (1985), The Romance of Leadership. *Administrative Science Quarterly*, **30**: 78–102.

Murphy, S.E., D. Blyth and F.E. Fiedler (1992), Cognitive Resources Theory and the Utilization of the Leader's and Group Member's Technical Competence. *Leadership Quarterly*, **3**: 237–54.

Naidoo, L.J. and R.G. Lord (2008), Speech Imagery and Perceptions of Charisma: The Mediating Role of Positive Affect. *Leadership Quarterly*, **19**(3): 283–96.

Peters, L.H., D.D. Harke and J.T. Pohlman (1985), Fiedler's Contingency Theory of Leadership: An Application of the Meta-Analysis Procedures of Schmidt and Hunter. *Psychological Bulletin*, **97**(2): 274–85.

Pfeffer, J. and A. Davis-Blake (1987), Administrative Succession and Organizational Performance: How Administrator Experience Mediates the Succession Effect. *Academy of Management Journal*, **29**: 72–83.

Piccolo, R.F., M. Bardes, D.M. Mayer and T.A. Judge (2008), Does High Quality Leader–Member Exchange Accentuate the Effects of Organizational Justice? *European Journal of Work and Organizational Psychology*, **17**(2): 273–98.

Podsakoff, P., S. McKenzie and W. Bommer (1996), Meta-Analysis of the Relationship Between Kerr and Jermier's Substitutes for Leadership and Employee Job Attitudes, Role Perceptions, and Performance. *Journal of Applied Psychology*, **81**(4): 380–400.

Schaubroeck, J., F.O. Walumba, D.C. Ganster and S. Kepes (2007), Destructive Leader Traits and the Neutralizing Influence of an 'Enriched' Job. *Leadership Quarterly*, **18**(3): 236–51.

Schneider, A. (2004), *Tony Soprano on Management: Leadership Lessons Inspired by America's Favorite Mobster*. New York: Berkley Books.

Schreisheim, C. and A.S. DeNisi (1981), Task Dimensions as Moderators of the Effects of Instrumental Leadership: A Two-Sample Replicated Test of Path–Goal Leadership Theory. *Journal of Applied Psychology*, **66**: 589–97.

Seltzer, J. and B.M. Bass (1990), Transformational Leadership: Beyond Initiation and Consideration. *Journal of Management*, **16**: 693–703.

Strube, M.J. and J.E. Garcia (1981), A Meta-Analytic Investigation of Fiedler's Contingency Model of Leadership Effectiveness. *Psychological Bulletin*, **90**: 307–21.

Taylor, G. (ed.) 1982, *William Shakespeare*. Oxford: Oxford University Press.

Thomas, J.L., M.W. Dickson and P.D. Bliese (2001), Values Predicting Leader Performance in the US Army Reserve Officer Training Corps Assessment Center: Evidence for a Personality-Mediated Model. *Leadership Quarterly*, **12**(2): 181–96.

Tosi, H.L.M., F. Vilmos, Angelo Fanelli, David A. Waldman and Francis J. Yammarino (2004), CEO Charisma, Compensation, and Firm Performance. *Leadership Quarterly*, **15**(3): 405–20.

Turner, N., J. Barling, O. Epitropaki, V. Butcher and C. Milner (2002), Transformational Leadership and Moral Reasoning. *Journal of Applied Psychology*, **87**(2): 304–11.

Van Iddekinge, C.H., G.R. Ferris and T.S. Heffner (2009), Test of a Multistage Model of Distal and Proximal Antecedents of Leader Performance. *Personnel Psychology*, **62**(3): 463–95.

Vecchio, R.P. (1990), Theoretical and Empirical Examination of Cognitive Resource Theory. *Journal of Applied Psychology*, **75**: 141–7.

Vroom, V.H. and P.W. Yetton (1973), *Leadership and Decision Making*. Pittsburgh, PA: University of Pittsburgh Press.

Yukl, G.A. (2002), *Leadership in Organizations*. Saddle River, NJ: Prentice Hall.

Name index

Subject index